T5-DGX-535

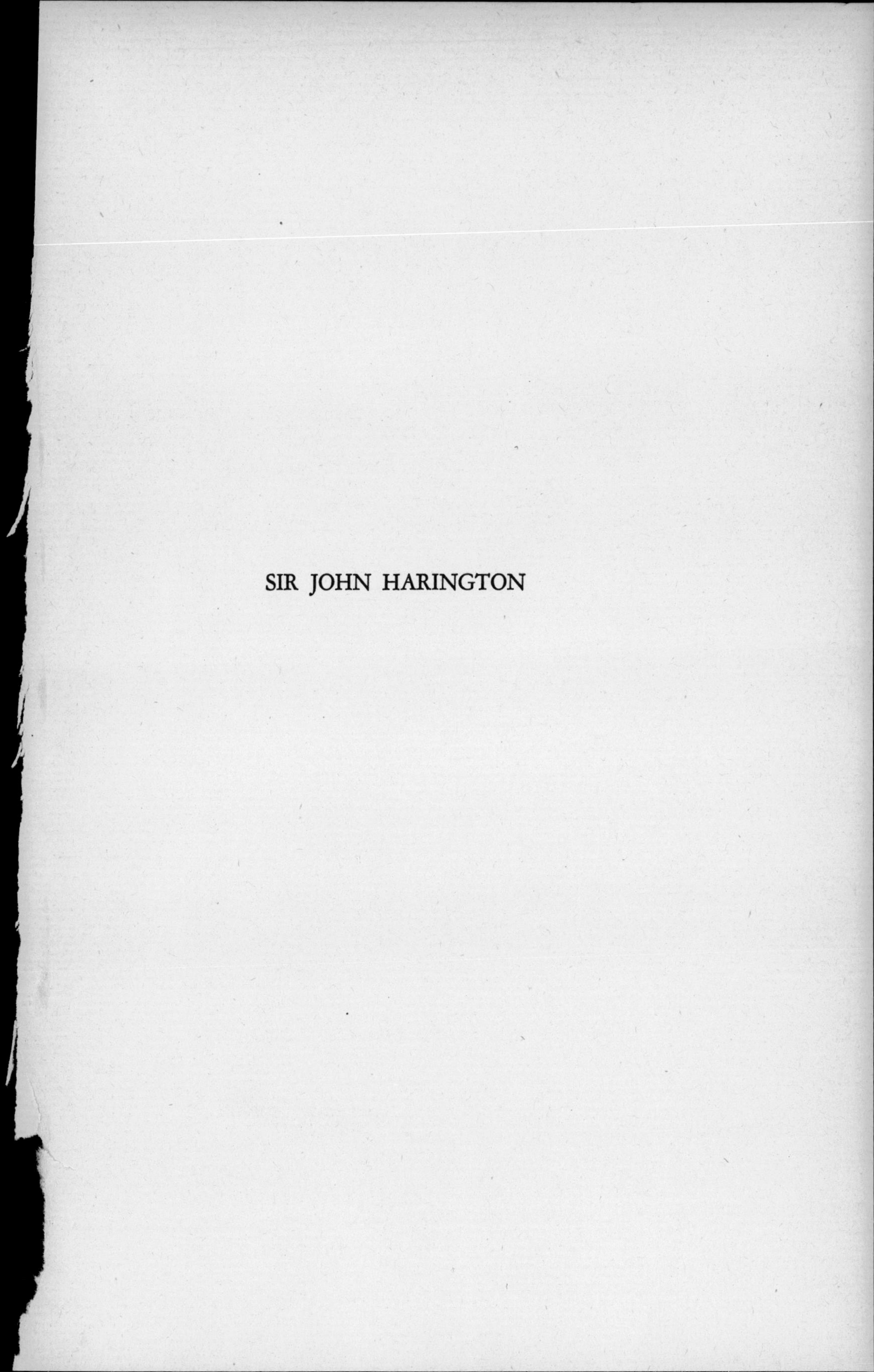

SIR JOHN HARINGTON

SIR JOHN HARINGTON

THE LETTERS AND EPIGRAMS OF SIR JOHN HARINGTON

TOGETHER WITH

THE PRAYSE OF PRIVATE LIFE

Edited with an Introduction by

NORMAN EGBERT McCLURE

Professor of English, Ursinus College

Foreword by

FELIX E. SCHELLING

PHILADELPHIA

University of Pennsylvania Press

London, Humphrey Milford, Oxford University Press

MCMXXX

Printed in the United States of America

FOREWORD

SIR JOHN HARINGTON is remembered in the books for his translation of Ariosto's *Orlando Furioso,* for his fine "defence of poetry" in the introduction to that work, for his many witty epigrams, for his gossipy letters, and for the scandal, even in his own time, attending a book of his with an atrocious punning title in which he honestly advocated the introduction of a simple mechanical device, since universally adopted, but in which he set forth his argument in terms so ingeniously gross, if at times perversely learned, that he has deserved the consequent neglect, if not altogether the obloquy, into which his name has fallen. With *The Metamorphosis of Ajax* we have happily nothing to do. In 1926 the *Epigrams* were edited in a scholarly and definitive edition by Professor McClure, and it is gratifying here to record that the demand for that edition justifies the inclusion of the *Epigrams* in the present volume.

In both these works of Harington an incurably robust Rabelaisianism has obscured only too often their veritable wit. Indeed, we owe even the translation of the *Orlando* to the same recurrent perversity. According to an often-told tale, Queen Elizabeth, observing tittering and, let us hope, some confusion and blushing in a bevy of her maids of honor who were gathered about the gay young courtier, John Harington, inquired into the matter to find that the rascal was reading to the girls certain improprieties which he had translated into ready verse out of Ariosto. Suiting the penalty perfectly to the offence, the Queen ordered John into retirement, not to show his face in Court until he had completed the translation of Ariosto's *Orlando.* Harington was soon back in attendance, his task completed, and shortly after, in 1591, the work was handsomely published with a dedication to Elizabeth. Let us hope that the Queen remembered that there are better things in Ariosto.

Harington was by birth a courtier with a flair for society, a critical eye, and a jocular mood towards it. His father, a man of good family and a courtier before him, had obtained a certain advancement at Court by marrying a natural daughter of his king, Henry VIII; and among the political vicissitudes that followed that monarch's death, had remained a devoted servant to his wife's half-sister, the then Princess Elizabeth. After his wife's death he married one of Elizabeth's maids of honor, and the Queen stood godmother to their son. For young Harington she showed an indulgent liking and often permitted him liberties of speech in the royal presence which more important personages would not dare. Harington was well educated in the orthodox succession of Eton, King's College, Cambridge, and Lincoln's Inn; and entered *con amore* into the petty intriguing for favor and emolument, reaching his height of station as High Sheriff of Somerset and the expensive honor, on one occasion, of entertaining his august godmother at Kelston, his seat in that county. Harington followed the fortunes of the Earl of Essex, as did so many of the younger set towards the latter part of Elizabeth's reign. But he followed them circumspectly, and succeeded, despite his participation in the disastrous Irish campaign, in avoiding consequences that ruined several of his fellows. Harington was among the sixty knights somewhat incontinently dubbed by Essex in Ireland before fortune turned against him; and Harington suffered, therefore, a brief eclipse at Court in the royal displeasure. It was upon the occasion of his coming to Court soon after Essex that her majesty exclaimed, "What! did the fool bring you too? Go back to your business." ". . . And I went home," concludes Harington, "as though all the Irish rebels were at my heels." Despite all his levity, however, Harington contrived to leave behind him both sound and sagacious observations on the conduct of disordered Ireland, published in 1879 under the title *View of the State of Ireland in 1605*. But Harington's day was over; for try as he would, he made little way in the favor of King James; and, born in 1561, Harington died in 1612, remembered perhaps chiefly by his ageing fellow-"servants," as the old word went, in the vanished Court of Queen Elizabeth.

In the ensuing volume Professor McClure has collected sixty-two letters of Sir John Harington. Nineteen of these appeared in Harington's *Nugae Antiquae* (1779, 1804); and a few others in the *Reports of the Historical Manuscripts Commission,* and elsewhere. The remainder are here printed for the first time from manuscripts, most of them in Harington's own handwriting. They range in point of date from 1571, when Harington was a child of ten writing from Eton, to the year 1612, when the writer had as yet but a few months to live. Their quality for wit, vivacity, and shrewd comment on the manners of his age has long been recognized; and the reputation of Harington as a letter-writer will lose nothing by these additions.

The other prose of the volume is a treatise entited *The Prayse of Private Life.* It is less a translation than a treatise inspired by Petrarch's *De Vita Solitaria,* of which there was apparently no Elizabethan translation. In his text Harington follows Petrarch's general plan and paraphrases the original in certain passages, discanting with much freedom elsewhere. This tract is printed from a transcript of the manuscript presented by Samuel Daniel, the well-known court poet, to the Countess of Cumberland. It is nowhere so much as mentioned by historians of literature.

As to the *Epigrams,* the writer of these introductory words feels that the alert and ready scholarship of the present editor leaves little for him to say. In the extensive and often illuminating literature of epigram, Sir John Harington will always find his place for his directness, his sagacious observation, his caustic outspokenness, and the flash of his ready wit.

FELIX E. SCHELLING.

CONTENTS

ILLUSTRATIONS

PREFACE

ALTHOUGH Sir John Harington was one of the most interesting men in Elizabethan England, he has been given scant attention by students of our literature. That this neglect has been due in part to the inaccessibility of the best of Harington's work is the present writer's warrant for preparing this edition.

The first account of Harington's life was written by Thomas Fuller for his *History of the Worthies of England.* This fragmentary sketch was improved only slightly by subsequent writers until Creighton prepared his article on Harington for the *Dictionary of National Biography.* Creighton's biography is incomplete and, in many details, inaccurate. The best account of Harington is the late Professor Raleigh's article, "Sir John Harington," which appeared in *The New Review,* XV (September, 1896), and which was reprinted in *Some Authors* (Oxford, 1923). Raleigh's article, though undocumented, is generally accurate. The following study of Harington, which makes use of some evidence unknown to previous writers, considers his life and work in greater detail than any earlier account.

Harington's letters are here for the first time collected and edited. Of the sixty-two letters in this volume, nineteen were printed in Henry Harington's *Nugae Antiquae* (1779, 1804), and a few others have appeared elsewhere.

The Prayse of Private Life, hitherto unknown to students of Elizabethan literature, is printed from a transcript of the copy presented by Samuel Daniel to Margaret Clifford, Countess of Cumberland (British Museum Addit. MS. 30161). In this discourse and in the letters the abbreviations and contractions common in Elizabethan manuscripts are expanded; the letters *i, j, u,* and *v* are brought into accord with modern usage; initial *ff* is printed *F;* the first word of a sentence is capitalized; and in a few places meaningless vagaries in punctuation have been corrected.

No edition of Harington's epigrams has appeared since 1633 except the present writer's edition of 1926, which included eighty epigrams previously unpublished. The epigrams appear in four editions and two manuscripts. The first edition (1615) contains 116 epigrams, all of which are included in the first complete edition (1618) of 346 epigrams. All of these, with the exception of the last epigram, are included in the third edition (1625), which is a careless page-for-page and line-for-line reprint of the 1618 edition. The fourth edition (1633), which is a reprint of the 1625 edition, corrects a few of the more obvious errors. The two manuscripts are in Harington's autograph. British Museum Addit. MS. 12049 (herein designated A), which was written about 1603 and later revised, contains 414 epigrams; Cambridge University Library Addit. MS. 337 (herein designated B), which was written in 1600, contains fifty-two epigrams. MS. A contains all but one of the epigrams in B, 329 of the 346 epigrams in 1618, and eighty-five epigrams not included in 1618. The text of both A and B is so different from that of 1615 and 1618 as to preclude the supposition that either manuscript was used in the preparation of either edition.

The present text is based upon that of 1618. Since the manuscripts exhibit variant readings, and since A is apparently a careless transcript of various shorter manuscripts, one may assume that the 1618 edition presents a text which is as trustworthy as that of A and B. The text of 1618 has been collated with the manuscripts, and variant readings of importance are indicated in the footnotes. The spelling and punctuation of the 1618 edition are retained except when the manuscripts offer necessary corrections. To change the arrangement of the epigrams, which in the editions and the manuscripts is haphazard, would invalidate the many references to specific epigrams made in such works as Warton's *History of English Poetry.* Accordingly, the arrangement and numbering of the epigrams are unchanged, and, for convenience of reference, independent numbers (1–428) have been added.

It is a pleasure to acknowledge here the many obligations incurred in preparing this edition. To the Marquis of Salisbury I am indebted for permission to use the Hatfield manuscripts, and to his librarian, the Reverend W. Stanhope-Lovell, for his generous help. To the Master and Fellows of Gonville and Caius College, Cambridge, to the Treasurer and Masters of the Bench of the Honourable Society of the Inner Temple, and to the Master and Wardens of the Company of Merchant Taylors, I am grateful for the privilege of examining manuscripts in their keeping. I have been under special obligation to Mr. John E. M. Harington, whose interest and help have been constant, and who has permitted the reproduction of previously unpublished portraits of his ancestor, Sir John Harington. I gratefully acknowledge my debt to Professor Jacob Zeitlin, of whose translation of Petrarch's *De Vita Solitaria* (University of Illinois Press, 1924) I have made frequent use. Finally, I wish to record my gratitude to Dean W. A. Kline, of Ursinus College, to Professor Felix E. Schelling, and to Professor Albert C. Baugh, of the University of Pennsylvania, for their kind encouragement and helpful advice.

N. E. McClure.

Collegeville, Pennsylvania,
November 19, 1929.

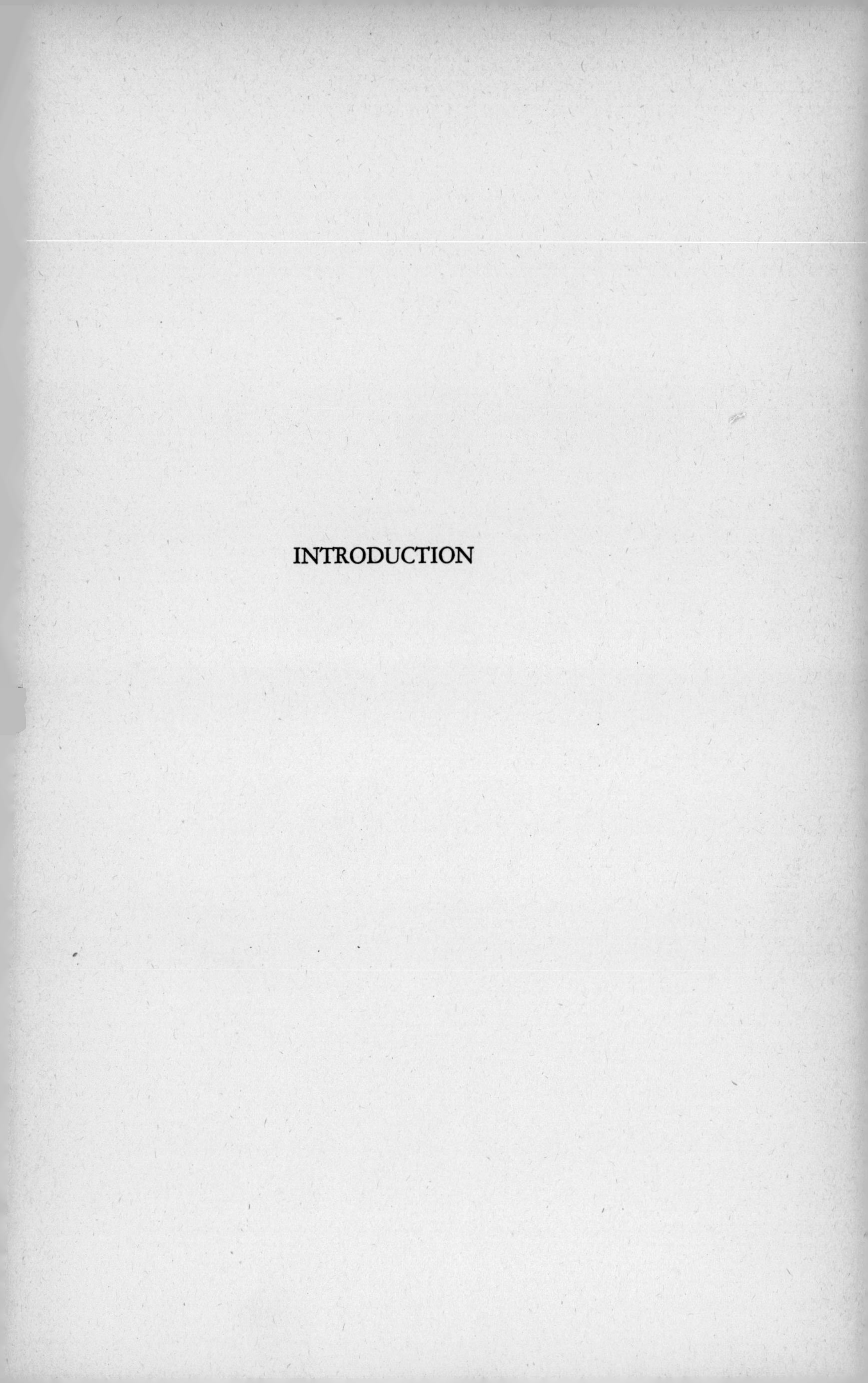

INTRODUCTION

INTRODUCTION

I

THE name John Harington[1] was well known in Elizabethan and Jacobean England. During the period five men of that name attained prominence: (1) John Harington (1520?–1582) of Cheshunt and Stepney was the friend of both King Henry VIII and Queen Elizabeth; (2) his son was Sir John Harington (1561?–1612) of Kelston, the epigrammatist and translator of Ariosto; (3) the latter's son was John Harington (1589–1654), known as "The Parliamentarian"; (4) Sir John Harington, first Lord Harington of Exton (d.1613), the son of Sir James Harington of Exton, and a cousin of Sir John Harington of Kelston, was guardian and tutor of the Princess Elizabeth, daughter of King James; (5) his son, Sir John Harington, second Lord Harington of Exton (1592–1614), was a friend and correspondent of Henry, Prince of Wales. The inevitable confusion of names that has resulted has been increased by the fact that several of these men had similar interests. Both John Harington of Stepney and his son, Sir John Harington of Kelston, were poets. Both Sir John Harington of Kelston and his cousin, the first Lord Harington of Exton, were familiar figures at the Court of Elizabeth and of James. Both Sir John Harington of Kelston and the second Lord Harington of Exton were friends and correspondents of Henry, Prince of Wales. Not only do the five John Haringtons perplex posterity; two other members of the family are still remembered. Lucy Harington, Countess of Bedford, who lives in the verses of many poets, was the daughter of the first Lord Harington of Exton. James Harington, author of *Oceana,* was the grandson of a younger brother of the first Lord Harington of Exton. The annoying similarity of names had led many writers into error.[2]

1. It is less frequently spelled Harrington, Haryngton, Harryngton.

2. Space permits the mention of only a few instances of such confusion. In the index to *The Cambridge History of English Literature,* IV, the works of John

Sir John Harington—scholar, poet, translator, courtier, soldier, letter-writer, and epigrammatist—came of an old and distinguished family. The name is derived from Haverington, in Cumberland, where the Haringtons were barons from the earliest days. Their chief seat was at Aldingham, in Lancashire, where they resided from Edward I's time. The last Baron Harington fell at the battle of Wakefield (1460).[1] Two representatives of the family, Sir Robert and Sir James Harington, for bearing arms at the battle of Towton (1461) and for taking Henry VI prisoner, were attainted by Henry VII, and twenty-five large manors were forfeited to the crown.[2] Sir James Harington, of Brierley, in Felkirk, Yorkshire, subsequently entered the Church, and died Dean of York. John Harington, father of the epigrammatist, was the son of Alexander Harington, and grandson of Sir James Harington, of Brierley.[3] Large estates in Rutland and Lincolnshire were owned by another branch of the family, from which was descended John Lord Harington of Exton.[4]

John Harington, father of our writer, restored the fortunes of his branch of the family. He held, under Henry VIII, several important offices. In 1542, he was referred to as "treasurer of

Harington of Stepney and of Sir John Harington of Kelston are attributed to Sir John Harington, second baron of Exton. In *Reports of the Historical Manuscripts Commission, Salisbury Manuscripts* (1910), 187–188, 199, letters from Sir John Harington of Kelston to Sir Robert Cecil are attributed to Sir John Harington of Exton. Even so careful a writer as J. B. Mullinger, in a detailed account of the founding of Sidney Sussex College, assigns to Sir John Harington of Kelston the important services to Cambridge rendered by Sir John Harington of Exton. *The University of Cambridge from the Royal Injunctions of 1535 to the Accession of Charles I,* 1884, 357–360.

1. William Dugdale, *The Baronage of England,* 2 vols., 1675–1676, II, 99–100; 416. *Nugae Antiquae,* 1779, III, 306–312.

2. *Harleian MSS.* 1549; John Collinson, *The History of Somersetshire,* 3 vols., Bath, 1791, I, 128.

3. *Grants of Arms named in Docquets and Patents to the End of the Seventeenth Century,* ed. W. H. Rylands. Harleian Society, LXVI (London, 1915), 115. See also *Notes and Queries for Somerset and Dorset,* IV, 155. Sir James Harington is mentioned by the epigrammatist as his great-grandfather. *Nugae Antiquae,* 1779, II, 143–144. Cf. Letter 54, *infra.*

4. Collinson, *op. cit.,* I, 128.

the wars."[1] There is preserved, under date of June 5, 1544, a warrant issued to him, as "vice-treasurer of the vanguard of the army in France," for payment of troops.[2] In 1548, he was "Treasurer of the King's Camps and Buildings."[3] He was, for a time, one of the Lord Admiral Thomas Seymour's "men,"[4] and in 1549 at Seymour's trial he testified that "there was never conference of any love or marriage between the Lady Elizabeth and my Lord Admiral that ever he knew of or suspected."[5] About 1546 Harington married Ethelred Malte, King Henry VIII's illegitimate daughter. Her death left her husband in possession of several large estates that had been granted her by the king. Among these was the manor of Kelston, in Somersetshire, which became the chief residence of the family.[6]

Harington showed his gratitude to King Henry by devoting himself to the service of the Princess Elizabeth. He was a cultivated man and a poet.[7] In his visits to the Princess Elizabeth at Hatfield he wrote verses in praise of her six gentlewomen, but soon singled out among them Isabella Markham, daughter of Sir John Markham, of Cotham, Lieutenant of the Tower,[8] and

1. *Historical Manuscripts Commission, The MSS. of the Duke of Rutland,* IV (1905), 329–332; 334–335.

2. British Museum, Addit. MS. 27632, f. 3. This is a commonplace book used by several members of the family.

3. Strype, *Memorials,* III, Part 1, 366.

4. Harington's translation of *Orlando Furioso,* ed. 1634, p. 151.

5. *Historical Manuscripts Commission, Salisbury MSS.,* Part I (1883), pp. 63, 65, 66; *Salisbury MSS.,* Part XIII, Addenda (1915), p. 26. Seymour was executed March 20, 1549.

6. Collinson, *op. cit.,* I, 128. In 1591, his son, Sir John, mentions the generosity of Henry VIII, "whose bounty and magnificence can never be forgotten while this realme shall be peopled, or any histories read." *Orlando Furioso,* ed. 1634, 213.

7. He translated Cicero's *De Amicitia. The booke of freendeship of Marcus Tullie Cicero,* 1550; reprinted, London, Essex House Press, 1904. Several of his poems are included in *Nugae Antiquae,* and a stanza that he composed is inserted by his son in *Orlando Furioso,* Book XIX, stanza 1. See also notes following Book XIX.

8. "The prayse of six Gentle-Women attending of the Ladye Elizabeth her Grace at Hatfield," *Nugae Antiquae,* ed. 1804, II, 390. "Verses made on Isabella Markhame, when I firste thought her fayer, as she stood at the Princess's Windowe in goodlye attyre, and talkede to dyvers in the Courte-Yarde," *Nugae Antiquae,* ed. 1804, II, 324.

eventually John Harington and Isabella Markham were married. In 1554 he was imprisoned for eleven months in the Tower for "carrying a letter to the Princess Elizabeth," and Isabella Markham "was obliged to dwell with Master Topcliffe, as an heretic."[1] Their zealous attachment to her during this period established them so firmly in her favor that she retained them in her service when she became queen, and stood godmother to their eldest son, the epigrammatist.[2]

II

Neither the date nor the place of Sir John Harington's birth is known. It is difficult even to conjecture where his parents resided after the accession of Elizabeth. Collinson states that John Harington, the elder, took up his residence at Kelston about 1546,[3] but this is almost certainly too early a date. The children of Thomas Harington, who was rector at Kelston from 1565 to 1616, and who was presented to the living by John Harington, his brother or uncle, are the first Haringtons mentioned in the Kelston parish registers. None of the children of John Harington are entered there in the Baptismal Roll.[4] Although the grant of arms made to him in 1568 names Kelston as his residence,[5] he probably lived in Cheshunt, in Hertfordshire, in 1567, when he purchased the estate known as Cheshunt Park. In the indenture the property is described as "now or late in the tenure of Harington."[6] It is probable that he was tenant there as early as 1561, for one "Danyel, Horsekeeper with Mr. Harrington," was buried there September 15 of that year.[7] Sir

1. Letter 47.

2. *Nugae Antiquae,* 1804, I, 127.

3. John Collinson, *The History of Somersetshire,* 3 vols., Bath, 1791, I, 128. "Where born I know not," wrote Fuller, *Worthies of England,* 1840, III, 103.

4. *Miscellanea Genealogica et Heraldica,* II (1878), 361. The Kelston Registers have not been printed in full; A. M. Burke, *Key to the Ancient Parish Registers of England and Wales,* London, 1908.

5. *Grants of Arms named in Docquets and Patents to the End of the Seventeenth Century,* Harleian Society, LXVI, 115.

6. The indenture is in *Miscellanea Genealogica et Heraldica,* IV (1884), 191.

7. *Op. cit.,* IV (1884), 207. The Cheshunt Registers have not been printed; A. M. Burke, *Key to the Ancient Parish Registers of England and Wales,* Lon-

John's earliest memories, however, go back, not to Cheshunt, but to Stepney: "To speake of the furthest of my memorye, I remember how the Lo. Haistinges of Loughborrowe came to dynner to my father's, who lay then at Stepney, and while prayers were saieng he walked out into the garden, which my mother taking ill, for she was ever zealous in her faith, said to her brother Mr. Thomas Marckham (who brought the same Lord Haistings thither) that if he brought guestes thither that scorned to pray with her, she would scorne they should eate with her."[1] It seems probable, therefore, that he was born either at Cheshunt or at Stepney.

The date of his birth is equally uncertain, although biographers and historians name, without positive proof, the year 1561. It is certain that he was born after 1554. On this point we have his own testimony: "I may truly say this Prelate [Bishop Gardiner] did persecute me before I was born; for my father was by his command imprison'd in the Tower for eleven months, for only carrying a letter to the Princess Elizabeth."[2] In the inquisition following the death of his father in 1582, he is mentioned as aged "twenty-one and upwards."[3] A third bit of evidence is to be found on the title-page of his translation of *Orlando Furioso.* Here an engraved portrait of the translator bears the caption, "Primo Augusti anno Domini 1591 aetatis suae 30." In the lack of more positive evidence, it may be assumed that the traditional date, 1561, is approximately correct.

John Harington found distinguished godparents for his son. The Queen herself stood godmother,[4] and William, Earl of

don, 1908. The first entry in the Cheshunt Registers is dated 1559. The Rev. Charles B. Law, of Cheshunt Vicarage, writes me that the name of Harington does not occur in the Baptismal Register from 1559 to 1566.

1. Sir John Harington, *A Tract on the Succession to the Crown,* written 1602, Roxburghe Club, 1880, 102–103. Baron Hastings of Loughborough died in 1573. The Baptismal Register of St. Gregory's by St. Paul's, where Harington's parents were buried, contains no mention of Harington from 1559, the date of the first entry, to 1566. For this information I am indebted to the Rev. Lewis Gilbertson, Rector of St. Martin's, Ludgate, to which St. Gregory's is now conjoined.

2. Letter 46. This occurred in 1554.

3. *Miscellanea Genealogica et Heraldica,* IV (1884), 207.

4. When John was a student at Eton, Queen Elizabeth sent him a copy of her

Pembroke, was his godfather.[1] It appears that the family continued to live at the "Prebende howse neere the Bushops Pallace of London."[2] The father's later career was one of moderate prosperity, and there is a grant of arms to him in 1568.[3] He died at Lambeth in 1582, and was buried in the Parish Church of St. Gregory by St. Paul's.[4] The mother was of the Queen's privy chamber until her death in 1579.[5]

In the meantime, John Harington, the younger, was educated at Eton and Cambridge. Reminiscences of these years are found in many of his works. "About the yeare 1570, he [William Wickham, later Bishop of Winchester] was vice-provost of Eaton, and (as the manner was in the schoolemaisters absence) would teache the schoole himselfe, and dyrect the boyes for their exercises, (of which my self was one) of whom he shewed as fatherly a care, as if he had bene a second tutor to me."[6] He tells how William Day, the Provost, broke his leg by falling from a horse, "whereupon some waggish schollers, of which I thinke my selfe was in the *quorum,* would say it was a just punishment, because the horse was given hym by a gentleman to place his sonne in Eaton, which at that tyme we thought had bene a kinde of sacriledge, but I may say, *Cum eram parvulus, sapiebam ut parvulus.*"[7] He writes that one of his earliest tasks was to translate into Latin Foxe's account of Elizabeth's trials

address to Parliament, 1575, together with the following letter: "Boye Jacke, I have made a clerke wryte faire my poore wordes for thyne use, as it cannot be suche striplinges have entrance into parliamente assemblye as yet. Ponder theme in thy howres of leysure, and plaie wythe them e tyll they enter thyne understandinge; so shallt thou hereafter, perchance, fynde some goode frutes hereof when thy Godmother is oute of remembrance; and I do thys, because thy father was readye to sarve and love us in trouble and thrall." *Nugae Antiquae,* ed. 1804, I, 127–128.

1. *Nugae Antiquae,* ed. 1779, II, 194.

2. Harington, *A Tract on the Succession to the Crown,* 102–103.

3. *Grants of Arms,* etc., Harleian Society, LXVI, 115.

4. The funeral certificate is to be found in *Miscellanea Genealogica et Heraldica,* IV (1884), 195.

5. Harington, *A Tract on the Succession to the Crown,* 40–41. The funeral certificate is to be found in *Miscellanea Genealogica et Heraldica,* IV (1884), 195.

6. *Nugae Antiquae,* ed. 1804, II, 92. 7. *Ibid.,* p. 96.

during the reign of Mary, "as M. Thomas Arundell and Sir Edward Hobby can tell, who had their parts in the same taske, being then schollers in Eaton as I was."[1]

At Cambridge he matriculated as a fellow-commoner from King's College in 1576, and remained in residence until 1581.[2] He informs us that he was "a truantly scholar," and had "as good a conscience as other of my pew-fellows, to take but a little learning for my money."[3] He was perhaps not unlike "that old school-fellow of mine in Cambridge, that having lost five shillings abroad at cards, would boast he had saved two candles at home by being out of his chamber."[4] Years later he recalls plays that he saw presented at St. John's,[5] and he explains the methods of "our stage-keepers in Cambridge, that for fear lest they should want company to see their comedies, go up and down with vizors and lights, puffing and thrusting, and keeping out all men so precisely, till all the town is drawn by this revel to the place; and at last, tag and rag, fresh men and sub-sizers, and all be packed in together so thick, as now is scant left room for the prologue to come upon the stage."[6] His more serious interests, too, hold their place in his memory. In the preface to his translation of *Orlando Furioso* he recalls the teaching of Doctor Samuel Fleming, who, though a defender of classical learning against the attacks of the more bigoted Protestants, deprecated the influence of Italian literature. "I began to think, that my Tutor, a grave and learned man, and one of a very austere life, might say to me . . ., Was it for this, that I read *Aristotle* and *Plato* to you and instructed you so carefully both in Greeke and Latin? to have you now become a translator

1. *Orlando Furioso,* notes following Book XLV; ed. 1634, 393. He adds in a marginal note, "This little book was given to her Majestie."

2. Venn, *Alumni Cantabrigienses,* I, 310. Creighton, in *The Dictionary of National Biography,* repeats the usual error of supposing that Harington was of Christ's College.

3. *The Metamorphosis of Ajax,* 1596; ed. 1814, 23.

4. *Ajax,* ed. 1814, p. x. He later wrote "A Treatise on Play," which is included in *Nugae Antiquae,* ed. 1804, I, 186–232.

5. *Orlando Furioso,* ed. 1634, Sig. ¶ 6. See also G. Gregory Smith, *Elizabethan Critical Essays,* II, 424.

6. *An Apology,* ed. 1814, 21.

of Italian toyes."[1] Doctor William Chatterton, later Bishop of London, he remembers as "a learned and grave Doctor" at Cambridge, who "was beloved amonge the schollers, and the rather, for he did not affect any sowre and austere fashion, either in teaching or government, as some use to do; but well tempered both with courage and curtesie."[2] And of Doctor John Still, later Bishop of Bath and Wells, he writes with real affection and respect: "When my selfe came to him to sue for my grace as bachelor, [he] first examind me strictly, and after answerd me kyndly, that 'the grace he graunted me was not of grace, but of merit'; who was often content to grace my young exercises with his venerable presence; who, from that time to this [1607], hath given me some helpes, more hopes, all encouragements in my best studies; to whom I never came, but I grew more religious; from whom I never went, but I parted better instructed."[3]

His Cambridge career did not meet with the entire approval of his father and others interested in his welfare. The great Lord Burghley wrote him, in 1578, a charming letter of kindly admonition, urging him to apply himself to his studies, and to become "a fytte servaunte for the Queene and your countrey, for which you weare born, and to which, next God, you are moste bounde."[4] His conduct appears to have displeased his father, and in a letter addressed in 1580 to Sir Edward Dyer he seeks reconciliation. He has, he points out, been misunderstood, and he promises that he will obey his father, and that he will not marry against the will of his advisers.[5] On November 2 of the same year, he wrote Sir Francis Walsingham from King's College, saying that he had begun the study of law[6] under Doctor Thomas Byng, Regius Professor of Civil Law.[7]

1. *Orlando Furioso,* ed. 1634. Sig. ¶ 8v. A marginal note adds, "Samuel Flemming of King's Colledge in Cambridge."

2. *Nugae Antiquae,* ed. 1804, II, 113–114.

3. *Ibid.,* p. 157. Boswell, in eulogizing Johnson, quotes the latter part of this passage. *Boswell's Life of Johnson,* ed. G. B. Hill, IV, 484, note 4.

4. *Nugae Antiquae,* ed. 1804, I, 131–135.

5. Letter 2.

6. Letter 3.

7. MS. Rawlinson, B. 162, f. 9.

In the following year, 1581, Harington took his M.A. degree, and proceeded to the Inns of Court. He was admitted to Lincoln's Inn, November 27, 1581,[1] where Thomas Egerton, later Lord High Chancellor, was a Reader.[2] There he remained for a short time, and, as he wrote years after, "studied Littleton but to the title of discontinuance."[3]

Upon the death of his father in 1582,[4] he changed his plans. He was his father's heir,[5] and came into possession of his lands June 26, 1583.[6] Two months later he married Mary Rogers,[7] daughter of Lady Jane Rogers, of Cannington, Somersetshire, widow of Sir George Rogers,[8] who had died the year before.[9] Harington forthwith gave up the study of law, and sought preferment at Court. He was now a landed proprietor and rich in influential friends. The friendship of men like Burghley, Walsingham, Mildmay, and Egerton, the Queen's regard for his parents, and her interest in her promising godson, led him to expect a bright future at Court.

Immediately after his marriage he established his residence at

1. Venn, *Alumni Cantabrigienses,* I, 310.   2. MS. Rawlinson, B. 162, f. 9.

3. *Metamorphosis of Ajax,* ed. 1814, 62, 109. A manuscript volume written by Harington about this time, and preserved by Mr. John E. M. Harington, of London, contains several discourses that reveal the interests of the young student and prospective courtier. The longest discourse is Sir Thomas Smith's *Dialogue concerning the Queen's Marriage,* written in 1560 and first printed in John Strype's *Life of Sir Thomas Smith.* Other manuscript copies of the dialogue are British Museum Addit. MS. 4149, Ashmole 829, and Cambridge University MS. Gg. 3. Harington's "little dialogue of mariage" that in 1591 he said he had written in his "young daies" is apparently lost. In addition to less interesting matter, the volume contains the petition urging marriage which in 1566 the House of Lords through Nicholas Bacon presented to Elizabeth, and Sir Philip Sidney's spirited protest against her proposed marriage with Alençon. (*Orlando Furioso,* notes following Book XXIII; Camden, *History of Elizabeth,* 1635, 68–69; Albert Feuillerat, *The Works of Sir Philip Sidney,* III, 51–60. Professor Feuillerat does not mention Harington's copy in his list of the manuscript versions of Sidney's discourse.)

4. Funeral certificate, *Miscellanea Genealogica et Heraldica,* IV (1884), 195.

5. *Abstracts of Somersetshire Wills,* ed. Frederick Brown, V, 25.

6. *Miscellanea Genealogica et Heraldica,* IV (1884), 207.

7. September 6, 1583. *Somerset Parish Registers,* ed. W. P. W. Phillimore, VI (1905), 94.

8. *The Visitation of the County of Somerset in the Year 1623,* ed. F. T. Colby, Harleian Society, XI (London, 1876), 99.

9. *Miscellanea Genealogica et Heraldica,* III (1880), 219.

Kelston, Somersetshire, three miles from Bath. This estate, which his father had acquired about 1546, and which remained in the possession of his descendants until the latter part of the eighteenth century, was his home until his death in 1612. There in 1587 he erected a handsome manor-house after a plan of the celebrated architect, James Barozzi, of Vignola.[1] There he reared a large family,[2] and there in 1592 he entertained the Queen, and they "dined right royally under the fountains which played in the Court."[3] He accompanied her Majesty to Oxford in the same year.[4]

III

The years from 1583 to 1590 Harington spent on his Somersetshire estate. In 1586, however, he was a few months in Ireland,[5] as one of the "undertakers" for the repeopling of the province of Munster. During this visit he showed himself inquisitive of popular superstitions regarding St. Patrick,[6] witchcraft, and charms.[7] The expedition was a failure, and upon his return to England he settled down at Kelston. In 1584 he was named among those qualified to serve her Majesty as Justice of the Peace;[8] in 1588 he assisted in the defense against the ex-

1. Collinson, *History of Somersetshire,* I, xiii and 128.

2. There were eleven children. *Miscellanea Genealogica et Heraldica,* IV (1884), 191. The Kelston Registers are deficient in burials and marriages, 1575–1595; *Parish Registers Abstract,* 277; *Somersetshire Parishes. A Handbook of Historical Reference,* ed. A. L. Humphreys, London, 1905, 403. Records of his family at Kelston date from 1582.

3. John Nichols, *Progresses of Queen Elizabeth,* 1823, 250–251.

4. *Nugae Antiquae,* 1779, I, 156 ff., 173. See also Epigram 13.

5. MS. Rawlinson, B. 162, f. 3; see also note in *Orlando Furioso,* ed. 1634, 80; *Cambridge Modern History,* III, 599.

6. "At my being in Ireland, where I taried a few months, I was inquisitive of their opinion of this Saint, and I could learne nothing, other then a reverent conceit they had of him, as becomes all Christians to have of devout men and chiefly of those by whom they are first instructed in the Christian Faith: but for his Purgatory, I found neither any that affirmed it or beleeved it." Note in *Orlando Furioso,* ed. 1634, 80.

7. Note in *Orlando Furioso,* ed. 1634, 94.

8. Lansdowne MS. 737 contains a list of persons qualified to serve as Justice of the Peace in every county. The Somersetshire list, consisting of forty-four names, includes that of John Harington. See also *Notes and Queries for Somerset and Dorset,* II, 59.

pected Spanish invasion;[1] in the following year he and twelve other residents of Somersetshire contributed £50 each towards defraying the expense incurred in repulsing the Spanish Armada;[2] in 1592 he was Sheriff of Somersetshire.[3] Much of his time during these years he spent at Court, despite the complaints of his wife and his mother-in-law.[4] According to a doubtful tradition, his translation of Ariosto's *Orlando Furioso* was the result of one of these visits. To entertain the ladies of the Court he translated the twenty-eighth book of this poem. When the Queen discovered this, she thought it proper to affect indignation at some indelicate passages, and banished him from Court, until he should have finished the translation of the entire poem.[5] The task was eventually completed, and the book appeared in 1591 with a dedication to the Queen.[6]

Harington's translation preserved the *ottava rima* of the original and much of its spirit. It is, however, notable for fluency rather than for poetic power. The work is of most uneven merit. At times he attains to distinction of phrase:

1. The nature of his service is not clear. In a letter to Sir Robert Cecil, dated 1601, he writes, "In the yeer 88. my Cowntry can witnesse my forwardnes." Letter 21.

2. *Notes and Queries for Somerset and Dorset,* I, 38. See also Epigram 185.

3. Collinson, *History of Somersetshire,* I, xxxvii.

4. Epigrams 369, 382.

5. Thomas Park, in his edition of *Nugae Antiquae,* 1804, states (p. x) that this story was told him by "Mr. Walker," who heard it told by "the late Earl of Charlemont." It is recorded also in *Nugae Antiquae,* ed. 1779, III, iii. A casual remark made in a letter to his wife lends credence to this tradition. He mentions the Queen's admiration of his "little learninge and poesy," which he "did so much cultivate on her commande." Letter 27. Fuller, in his account of Harington, makes no mention of this tradition. *Worthies of England,* 1840, III, 103 ff. In the notes following the twenty-eighth book of *Orlando Furioso,* Harington writes, "History nor allegory, nor scant anything that is good, can be picked out of this bad booke." Ed. 1634, 232.

6. Not, as Fuller states, to "Lady Elizabeth, since queen of Bohemia," *Worthies of England,* 1840, III, 103.

The library of the late Sir George Holford contained a presentation copy of the first edition, now owned by Dr. A. S. W. Rosenbach, of Philadelphia. At the bottom of the title-page Harington wrote, "To Sir Thomas Coningsby by the frendly guift of the autor." Coningsby was knighted by the Earl of Essex in 1591.

Like to the rose I count the virgine pure,
That grow'th on native stem in garden faire,
Which while it stands with wals environ'd sure,
Where heardmen with their heards cannot repaire
To favor it, it seemeth to allure
The morning deaw, the heate, the earth, the aire.
Yong gallant men, and lovely dames delight
In their sweet sent, and in their pleasing sight.

But when at once tis gathered and gone,
From proper stalke, where late before it grew,
The love, the liking little is or none,
Both favour, grace and beautie all adew.
So when a virgin grants to one alone
The precious floure for which so many sew,
Well he that getteth it may love her best,
But she forgoes the love of all the rest.[1]

At other times the phrasing is less felicitous; even slang and proverbial expressions find their way into his verse:

If one death did unto my fault belong,
One hundred deaths were fit to thine to give,
And though my selfe am in this place so strong,
That if I list, thou shouldst no longer live,
Yet will I do to thee no further wrong,
But pardon thee, and thou shalt me forgive,
And quite each other, all old debts and driblets,
And set the hares head against the goose gyblets.[2]

Harington has altered the original by compressing or expanding some passages and by entirely omitting others. It was probably this fondness for paraphrase that evoked the condemnation of that staunch advocate of literal translation, Ben Jonson, who declared "that John Harrington's *Ariosto,* under all translations, was the worst."[3] This judgment, however, was not shared by Jonson's contemporaries, for Harington's work was hailed as a real achievement. A second edition appeared in 1607, and a third in 1634. His translation of *Orlando Furioso* is

1. Book I, stanzas 42, 43.
2. Book XLIII, stanza 136.
3. *Conversations with Drummond,* Shakespeare Society, 1842, 3.

preceded by *A Preface, or rather a Briefe Apologie of Poetrie, and of the author and Translator,* which is, like everything he has written, both witty and interesting. It owes much to Sidney's *Apology,* which Harington read in manuscript, and is notable chiefly for its defense of trisyllabic rime.

Orlando Furioso brought Harington fame, but no promotion at Court.[1] Accordingly, he returned to Kelston and spent several years as a country gentleman, improving his estate and waiting for an opportunity to serve the Queen. "I came home to Kelstone, and founde my Mall, my childrene, and my cattle, all well fedde, well taughte, and well belovede. 'Tis not so at Cowrte; ill breeding with ill feedinge and no love but that of the lustie god of gallantrie, Asmodeus."[2]

During this period one of his interests was printing. That he attempted to set up a private press is indicated by a letter from the Privy Council, May 31, 1592: "We are informed that by sinister and indirect meanes you have formerly withdrawn one Thomas Wels from his master, Augustine Rither, printer and graver of London, to serve you in that profession, being a matter contrary to your quallity and calling, and having at last with much adoe restored him to his master, you have of late gotten him again by like indirect meanes from his said master, deteining him still, to the utter impoverishing of the poore man whose living onely consisteth on his mestier and manual occupaccion, wherein with much travel and chardges he hath brought up and instructed his said apprentice, hoping to reape som benefit and releef thereby as were fit. We have thought good to let you know that we very much merveil at and mislike your uncharitable manner of dealing in this matter, not fitting a gentleman of your place and haviour, and do therefore strictly require you immediatly upon sight hereof to redeliver him back to his said master, or to make your personal apparance before us without delay to answear your default therein."[3] There is nothing to

1. He writes of his "thankelesse paines and fruitlesse cost." Epigram 74.
2. "Breefe Notes and Remembraunces," *Nugae Antiquae,* 1804, I, 166.
3. *Acts of the Privy Council,* XXII, 504.

show that Harington did not "redeliver him back to his master."

His many friends at Court remained active, and, in 1593, by Act of the Privy Council a letter was sent to the "Maiour and Aldermen of Bath to elect Mr. John Harington of —— in the countie of Sommerset, esquire, Steward of that towne, the place being presentlie void and in their guift."[1] His desire for a more active life led him again to Court, where his next attempt to advance himself brought him temporary disgrace and rustication. In 1596, under the pseudonym Misacmos, he wrote a pamphlet entitled *A New Discourse of a Stale Subject; called the Metamorphosis of Ajax.*[2] With the pamphlet appeared its supplement, *An Anatomy of the Metamorphosed Ajax. . . . By T. C.,* presumably Thomas Combe, Harington's confidential servant. *The Metamorphosis* is a Rabelaisian blend of farfetched erudition, volatile wit, and telling satire. It created a storm at Court, not because of the humble topic that it discussed, but because of its allusions, now obscure, to contemporary persons and events. Though the Queen may have been pleased by the humor of the work, she "did conceive much disquiet on being tolde" that the author "had aimed a shafte at Leicester."[3] An anonymous writer, probably of Brasenose College, Oxford, answered Harington with a scurrilous pamphlet entitled *Ulysses upon Ajax.*[4] Harington answered his critics in several epigrams[5] and in an *Apology* which did little to allay

1. *Acts of the Privy Council,* XXIV, 266. His place of residence was for some reason not mentioned.

2. Ajax is a meiosis for "a jakes."

3. *Nugae Antiquae,* 1804, I, 240.

4. This is included in S. W. Singer's edition of *The Metamorphosis of Ajax, The Anatomy,* and *An Apology,* Chiswick, 1814. Singer attributes this pamphlet to Harington, but a consideration of the style shows this ascription to be incorrect. The following passage suggests that it may have come from the pen of an Oxford man: "I could tell you more as he hath done (out of that most learned author, the book of Merry Tales, from whence his best jests are derived), but that as the old *Manciple* of *Brazen-nose College* in *Oxford* was wont to say; There are more fools to meet with." (Edition of 1814, 22.) Furthermore, John Davies of Hereford, in an epigram addressed to Harington, definitely assigns the pamphlet to another writer. (*Wit's Bedlem,* 1617, Epigram 233.) Davies' epigram was probably written about 1610.

5. Epigrams 44, 45, 46, 52, 53, 109, 227.

unfavorable comment. "For some that may seem secretly touched, and be not openly named, if they will say nothing, I will say nothing. But, as my good friend M. Davies said of his epigrams, that they were made like doublets in Birchin-lane, for every one whom they will serve: so if any man find in these my lines any raiment that suits him so fit, as if it were made for him, let him wear it and spare not: and for my part, I would he could wear it out."[1]

Harington's reason for writing *The Metamorphosis* is obvious: he hoped that it would attract favorable attention at Court. "Some," he wrote in his *Apology,* "surmised against me, that because the time is so toying, that wholesome meats cannot be digested without wanton sauce; and that even at wise men's tables, fools have most of the talk, therefore I came in with a bable [bauble] to have my tale heard: I must needs confess it."[2] In a letter to Lady Russell, asking her to intercede to avert the wrath that *The Metamorphosis* had stirred up at Court, he wrote, "I was the willinger to wryte such a toye as this, because I had layne me thought allmost buryed in the Contry these three or fowre yeere; and I thought this would give some occasion to have me thought of and talked of. . . . My Education hath bin suche, and I truste my Limmes and sperit both are suche as neither shalbe defectyve to the service of my Prince and Contry, whether it be with wryting or weapon; only my desyre is my service may be accepted, and I doubt not, but yt shalbe acceptable."[3]

The result of this ill-advised display of his talents was a threatened Star-Chamber suit and banishment to Kelston. A year later his cousin wrote him from Court: "Since your departure hence, you have been spoke of, and with no ill will, both by the nobles and the Queene herself. Your book is almoste forgiven, and I may say forgotten; but not for its lacke of wit or

1. *The Metamorphosis of Ajax,* ed. S. W. Singer, 1814, 133.
2. *An Apology,* ed. 1814, 9–10.
3. Letter 5. Lady Russell, daughter of Sir Anthony Cooke, was widow of Sir Thomas Hoby and later of Lord John Russell.

satyr. . . . Tho' her Highnesse signified displeasure in outwarde sorte, yet did she like the marrowe of your booke. Your great enemye, Sir James, did once mention the Star-Chamber, but your good esteeme in better mindes outdid his endeavors, and all is silente again. The Queen is minded to take you to her favour, but she sweareth that she believes you will make epigrams and write *misacmos* again on her and all the courte; she hath been heard to say, 'that merry poet, her godson, must not come to Greenwich, till he hath grown sober, and leaveth the ladies sportes and frolicks.' "[1] The translator of *Ariosto* and the disciple of Rabelais had earned little from his labors. "I have spente my time, my fortune, and almoste my honestie, to buy false hope, false friends, and shallow praise;—and be it rememberd, that he who castethe up this reckoning of a cowrtlie minion, will sette his summe like a foole at the ende, for not beinge a knave at the beginninge."[2] A courtier and a politician by birth and opportunity, he lacked those qualities essential to success in Elizabeth's Court. Of that "incorrigible and losing honesty" which Sir Thomas Hoby in his translation of Castiglione's *Il Cortegiano* mentions as befitting a true courtier, Harington had too abundant a store. "I doubte not your valor nor your labor," wrote his cousin, Robert Markham, "but that damnable uncoverd honestie will marr your fortunes."[3] Coupled with this was an equally incorrigible and losing gaiety. His candor, his loquacity, and his irrepressible spirits were impediments to one who aspired to hold positions of trust in the state. Having gained the reputation of a wit, the Queen's "saucy godson" was considered merely a "merry poet" and a privileged jester. He had elected to play the clown, and neither his friends nor his enemies could forget that he had worn the motley.

In 1599 Harington was called from Kelston to accompany the Essex expedition to Ireland to subdue the rebellious Tyrone. Essex informed him by letter of his appointment: "Her Majesties

1. *Nugae Antiquae,* 1804, I, 239–240.
2. "Breefe Notes and Remembraunces," *ibid.,* p. 168.
3. *Ibid.,* p. 240.

Grace appointethe me to go to Irelande, and hath speciallie commended yourselfe to my assistance and notyse; hence you are to lerne myne affections for hir commandes. You muste get forwarde and well accouterde in all haste for thys undertakynge. I shall provyde you to a commande of horsemen in consorte and commande of the Earl of Southamptone; youre sarvys shall not be ill reportede or unrewardede for the love the Queene bearethe you. I will confer soche honor and advantages as are in my breste and powere, forasmoche as hir Majestie makethe me to commaunde peace or warre, to truce, parley, or soche matter as seemethe beste for our enterpryse and goode of hir realme. Be nowe assurede of my love for hir sake who byds it, and accounte youre happynesse in hir favor, and hys whom she favorethe, even myselfe, who wyshethe youre advauncemente. I have beaten Knollys and Montjoye in the councele, and by God I will beat Tyr-Owen in the feilde; for nothynge worthye hir Majesties honor hathe yet beene atchievede."[1]

Harington's cousin, Robert Markham, wrote him from Court, urging caution: "I hear you are to go to Ireland with the Lieutenant, Essex; if so, mark my counsel in this matter. . . . Observe the man who commandeth, and yet is commanded himself; he goeth not forthe to serve the Queenes realme, but to humour his owne revenge. Be heedful of your bearinges; speake not your minde to all you meete. I tell you I have ground for my caution; Essex hath enemies; he hath friendes too: now there are two or three of Montjoys kindred sent oute in your armie; they are to report all your conduct to us at home. As you love yourself, the Queene, and me, discover not these matters; if I did not love you, they had never been tolde. High concerns deserve high attention; you are to take accounte of all that passes in your expedition, and keepe journal thereof, unknown to any in the company; this will be expected of you. I have reasons to give for this order:—If the Lord Deputy performs in the field what he hath promised in the council, all will be well;

1. *Ibid.*, p. 245.

but, tho' the Queene hathe graunted forgivenesse for his late demeanor, in her presence, we know not what to think hereof.[1] She hath, in all outwarde semblance, placed confidence in the man who so lately sought other treatment at her handes: we do sometime thinke one way, and sometime another; what betydeth the Lord Deputy is known to Him only who knowethe all; but when a man hath so manie shewing friendes, and so manie unshewing enemies, who learneth his end here below? I say, do you not meddle in any sorte, nor give your jesting too freely among those you know not: obey the Lord Deputy in all thinges, but give not your opinion; it may be heard in England. Tho' you obey, yet seem not to advise, in any one pointe; your obeysance may be, and must be, construed well; but your counsel may be ill thoughte of, if any bad businesse followe. You have now a secret from one that wishes you all welfare and honour; I know there are overlookers set on you all, so God direct your discretion. Sir William Knolles is not well pleased, the Queene is not well pleased, the Lord Deputy may be pleased nowe, but I sore fear what maye happen hereafter. The hart of man lieth close hid oft time; men do not carrye it in their hand, nor should they do so that wish to thrive in these times and in these places; I say this that your owne honestie may not shew itself too muche, and turn to your own ill favour. Stifle your understandinge as muche as may be; mind your bookes, and make your jestes, but take heed who they light on. My love hathe overcome almoste my confidence and truste which my truthe and place demandethe. I have said too much for one in my dependant occupation, and yet too little for a

1. "For whereas she thought Sir *William Knolles,* unckle to *Essex,* the fittest man of all others to be sent into *Ireland,* and *Essex* obstinately perswaded her that Sir *George Carew* was rather to be sent, that so he might ridde him from the Court, yet could not by perswasions draw her unto it: He forgetting himselfe, and neglecting his dutie, uncivilly turneth his backe, as it were in contempt, with a scornfull looke. She waxing impatient, gave him a cuffe on the eare, and bade him be gone with a vengeance. He layed his hand upon his sword, the Lord Admirall interposing himselfe, hee sware a great oath, that he neither could nor would swallow so great an indignitie, nor would have borne it at King *Henry* the 8. his hands; and in great discontentment hasted from the Court." (Camden, *Annales,* 1635, 493.)

friende and kinsman, who putteth himself to this hard tryal for your advantage. You have difficult matters to encounter, besyde Tirone and the rebels; there is little heed to be had to showe of affection in state businesse; I finde this by those I discourse with dailie, and those too of the wiser sorte. If my Lord Treasurer had livede longer,[1] matters would go on surer. He was our greate pilot, on whom all caste their eyes, and soughte their safetie. The Queenes Highnesse dothe often speake of him in teares, and turn asyde when he is discoursed of; nay, even forbiddeth any mention to be made of his name in the council. . . . My sister beareth thys to you, but dothe not knowe what it containethe; nor would I disclose to any woman my dealinges in this sorte; for danger goeth abroad, and silence is the safest armor. . . . God speed your jorneys, and keep you safelie to returne to us againe."[2]

The expedition left England in April, 1599, and Harington, as captain of horse under the Earl of Southampton, played an honorable, though inconspicuous, part in the campaign.[3] Essex, after desultory and indecisive fighting, made a premature and impermanent peace with Tyrone. During the course of his inglorious campaign he created some threescore knights, among them Harington.[4]

In the subsequent events, culminating in the disgrace and rebellion of Essex, Harington played an interesting rôle. The Lord Deputy's unsuccessful campaign, his early peace, his liberality in making knights, his return contrary to the Queen's orders, and his unannounced appearance at Court, displeased Elizabeth. He was tried, deprived of office, and sentenced to remain a prisoner in his house. Harington, having returned to England soon after Essex, incurred the temporary displeasure of the Queen.[5] "I enterd her chamber, but she frownede and

1. Burghley died August 8, 1598.
2. *Nugae Antiquae,* 1804, I, 240–245.
3. *Ibid.,* pp. 253–293.
4. July 30, 1599. Venn, *Alumni Cantabrigienses.*
5. He arrived at Richmond, November 6, 1599. Essex reached Nonesuch, September 28. (*Calendar State Papers, Ireland, 1599–1600,* 235–236.)

saiede, 'What, did the foole brynge *you* too? Go backe to your businesse.' "[1] In another letter he wrote, "She chaffed muche, walkede fastly to and fro, looked with discomposure in her visage; and, I remember she catched my girdle when I kneelede to hir, and swore, 'By God's Son I am no Queen; that man is above me;—Who gave him commande to come here so soon? I did sende hym on other busynesse.' It was longe before more gracious discourse did fall to my hearynge; but I was then put oute of my trouble, and bid 'Go home.' I did not stay to be bidden twise; if all the Iryshe rebels had been at my heels, I shoude not have had better speede, for I did now flee from one whom I both lovede and fearede too."[2] In a third letter Harington adds further details: "I came to court in the very heat and height of all displeasures: after I had been there but an hour, I was threatened with the Fleet; I answered poetically, 'that coming so late from the land-service, I hoped that I should not be prest to serve in her Majesty's fleet in Fleet-street.' After three days every man wondered to see me at liberty. . . . But I had this good fortune, that, after four or five days, the Queen had talked of me, and twice talked to me, though very briefly. At last she gave me a full and gracious audience in the withdrawing chamber at Whitehall, where herself being accuser, judge, and witness, I was cleared, and graciously dismissed."[3] The Queen's forgiveness was partly the result of her recognition of Harington's innocence in obeying Essex's orders, and partly the result of her examination of Harington's account of the Irish campaign, written at the suggestion of his cousin, Robert Markham, who, like many others, doubted the loyalty of Essex.[4] The "Queen did so aske, and I may saye, demande my accounte, that I coude not withholde shewing it; and I, even nowe, almost tremble to rehearse hir Highnesse displeasure hereat. She swore, by God's Son, we were all idle knaves, and the Lord Deputy worse, for wasting our time and hir commandes, in such

1. Letter 34.
2. Letter 45.
3. Letter 11.
4. *Nugae Antiquae,* 1804, I, 241, 268–293.

wyse as my Journale doth write of."[1] The journal served the double purpose of clearing Harington of all suspicion of disloyalty, and of inflaming the Queen's rage against Essex.

After a few weeks at Court, Harington returned to the quiet of his Somersetshire estate, where he had leisure to consider his experiences with Essex. "What perylls have I escaped! I was entrusted by Essex, whom I did adventure to visite, withe a message to the Queenes Majestie, settinge forthe his contrition and sore greivance for his manie offences. I was righte glade to heare suche contrition, and labourede to effecte this matter: but ere I coude beare these tydinges, (whiche I was well advysede to do,) the earle's petition reached her hand, and I fear her displeasure too, but herein I bore no parte. I was muche encouraged to go throughe this friendlye parte on manie sides, but I saide,—'Charitie did begin at home, and shoud alwaies sayle with a faire winde, or it was not likelie to be a prosperous voyage.' I had nearly been wracked on the *Essex coaste* in my laste venture, as I tolde the Queene, had it not been for the sweete calme of her specyal forgivenesse. I have hearde muche on bothe handes, but the wiser *he* who reportethe nothinge hereof. Did either knowe what I knowe either have saide, it woulde not worke muche to contentemente or goode lykinge.

"It restethe wyth me in opynion, that ambition thwarted in its career dothe speedilie leade on to madnesse; herein I am strengthened by what I learne in my lord of Essex, who shyftethe from sorrowe and repentaunce to rage and rebellion so suddenlie, as well provethe him devoide of goode reason or righte mynde. In my laste discourse, he uttered strange wordes borderinge on suche strange desygns, that made me hasten forthe and leave his presence. Thank heaven! I am safe at home, and if I go in suche troubles againe, I deserve the gallowes for a meddlynge foole."[2]

He was for a time quite willing to remain in obscurity at Kelston. To Sir Anthony Standen he wrote, "In December [1599]

1. Letter 45.
2. "Breefe Notes and Remembraunces," *Nugae Antiquae,* 1804, I, 178–179.

I came hither, but since, I hear little and do nothing but sit by a good fire, and feed my lean horses, and hearken for good news. . . . Let this suffice from a private country knight, that lives among clouted shoes, in his frize jacket and galloshes, and who envies not the great commanders of Ireland."[1]

He had been unfortunate in his efforts to serve the Queen; he had unwisely accepted a knighthood from Essex; his reward had been censure and neglect. "Essex tooke me to Ireland; I had scante tyme to putte on my bootes; I followede withe good wyll, and did returne wyth the Lorde Leiutenante to meet ill wyll; I did beare the frownes of hir that sente me; and, were it not for hir good lyking, rather than my good deservynges, I had been sore discountenancede indeede. I obeyede in goinge wythe the Earle to Irelande, and I obeyede in comynge wythe him to Englande. But what did I encounter thereon? Not his wrathe, but my gracious Soveraigns ill humour. What did I advantage? Why, trulie, a knighthood; whych had been better . . . sparede by him that gave it."[2] In the trial of Essex, June 5, 1600, "his making so many knights" was one of the "five special crimes charged on the earl."[3] In this matter Elizabeth herself was active. "The great number of knights made by the earl in Ireland having given great offence to the queen, she had an intention of degrading them from that dignity by a proclamation, and commanding that no antient gentleman of the kingdom should give them place. But secretary *Cecil,* by his interest stop'd the warrant sign'd for this proclamation."[4] Harington wrote Cecil, commending his action, and discussing the matter in characteristic fashion. He drew a parallel between knighthood and baptism, with illustrations from cases in which St. Ambrose and King Edward were concerned, concluding that the rite cannot be annulled. He pointed out further that such a proclamation would be at that time impolitic, and—"to omitte many more seriows consyderacions"—would be "accompanyed with the se-

1. Letter 11.
2. Letter 34.
3. Birch, *Memoirs of Queen Elizabeth,* II, 448.
4. *Ibid.,* pp. 455–456.

creat and most bitter curses of dyvers and some very fayr Ladyes, who are not yet so good philosophers as to neglect honor, and embrace paciens."[1]

During the troublesome and doubtful days that followed the rebellion and execution of Essex, Harington was seldom at Court. He was, however, in London at the time of Essex's outbreak, February 8, 1601, and was one of those who protected the Queen.[2] Again in the following summer Sir John made a short and unsatisfactory visit to Court. "I had," he wrote his friend, Sir Hugh Portman, "a sharp message from her [the Queen] brought by my Lord Buckhurst, namely thus, 'Go tell that witty fellow, my godson, to get home; it is no season now to foole it here.' I . . . will not leave my poor castle of Kelston, for fear of finding a worse elsewhere, as others have done. I will eat Aldborne rabbits, and get fish (as you recommend) from the man at Curry-Rival; and get partridge and hares when I can, and my venison where I can; and leave all great matters to those that like them better than myself."[3]

Sir John determined to employ his leisure in the building up of his dwindling patrimony. He made an unsuccessful attempt —begun before he left for Ireland—to recover by lawsuit the lands that had been in the possession of Sir James Harington of Brierley, Yorkshire, who had been attainted during the reign of Henry VII.[4] In this suit he sought and gained the help of Sir Robert Sidney and Sir Robert Cecil.[5] In 1601 he applied to Sir Robert Cecil for the commission of colonel in the County of Somerset.[6] Having failed in both these endeavors, he set out to secure, by persuasion and cajolery, the inheritance of his mother-in-law's property to his children. To Lady Rogers he addressed many epigrams, and in the copy of his *Orlando Furioso* that he sent her, December 19, 1600, he copied fifty-two epigrams from his "scattered papers" to remind her of "the kind and sometimes unkind occasions on which some of them were written."[7]

1. Letter 12.
2. Letter 21.
3. Letter 22.
4. Letters 14–17.
5. Letter 20.
6. Letter 21.
7. Letter 18.

Her personal peculiarities, her fondness for pet dogs, her dislike of the odor of garlic, her parsimony, her love of flattery, the proper hour for dinner, the management and the ultimate disposition of her property—all are recorded in these epigrams. In his legacy-hunting Sir John found a resolute rival in his brother-in-law, Edward Rogers. Their relations had for years been far from amicable. As early as 1594, Harington preferred charges against Rogers, alleging that he had used intemperate language, had attempted to stir up strife between Harington and his wife, and had made threats against his life. He further alleged that "coming out of Westminster Hall together in the Court of the Hall he offered to have stricken the said John Harington in the face with his hand, but he putting by his hand, and offering no other violence in regard of the place, the said Edward Rogers hath boasted since that he pulled out a handful of hair from the said John Harington's beard at the same time."[1] When Lady Rogers died in January, 1602, the family feud came to a head. Acting as the representative of his wife, who was one of the executors of the will, Sir John took possession of the Lady Rogers' house, and refused admittance to her son. Rogers forced an entrance, and locked up Sir John without light or food for several hours. Later Rogers brought an action in the Star Chamber without success.[2]

Despite his earlier disappointments Sir John continued to seek preferment at Court. He had influential friends and Elizabeth's regard, but the old Queen was now in no mood to enjoy the company of scholars and wits. To Sir Robert Cecil, who, in June, 1602, stood godfather at the baptism of Sir John's son, Robert,[3] he turned for help: "Yf yowr shall proceed to second mee with yowr good word when I shall get her highnes moved for soch a place, as nature, and breeding, and my earnest desyre make mee think my selfe fit for, . . . yowr honor shall see I

1. *Historical Manuscripts Commission, Salisbury MSS.*, Part IV (1892), 472.

2. *Miscellanea Genealogica et Heraldica,* IV (1884), 261; *Nugae Antiquae,* 1804, I, xv–xvi; Letter 37.

3. Letter 23 and Notes.

cownt no vyce more fowl then Ingratitude."[1] In December, 1602, when he was again at Court, he wrote Lady Harington of the Queen's failing health and of her kindness to him: "Her Majestie enquirede of some matters which I had written; and as she was pleasede to note my fancifulle braine, I was not unheedfull to feede her humoure, and reade some verses, whereat she smilede once, and was pleasede to saie;—'When thou doste feele creepinge tyme at thye gate, these fooleries will please thee lesse; I am paste my relishe for such matters.' "[2]

Sir John, even before the death of Elizabeth, sought to win the favor of her probable successor. That Harington loved the old Queen there can be not the slightest doubt: his affection shines through everything he writes about her. But he was a courtier, and with the others he had to prepare for the future. In a letter to his wife telling of the last days of Elizabeth he writes: "I cannot blote from my memorie's table the goodnesse of our Sovereigne Ladie to me, even (I will saie) before borne; her affectione to my mother who waited in privie chamber, her betterring the state of my father's fortune (which I have, alass! so much worsted), her watchings over my youthe, her likinge to my free speech, and admiration of my little learninge and poesy, which I did so muche cultivate on her commande, have rootede such love, suche dutyfull remembraunce of her princelie virtues, that to turne askante from her condition withe tearlesse eyes, woud staine and foule the springe and founte of gratitude."[3] Nor was he, after her death, less generous in his praise. In 1606 he wrote, "As I did bear so much love toward hir Majestie, I know not well how to stop my tales of hir virtues. . . . I never did fynde greater show of understandinge and lerninge, than she was bleste wyth . . . I write from wonder and affection."[4] With this genuine regard for the old Queen, he turned, as her death approached, to the North to welcome the "orient king."

1. Letter 20.
2. Letter 27.
3. Letter 27.
4. Letter 45.

IV

Before the accession of James, Harington set out to establish for himself the reputation of a sober politician. He had finally learned that he at least could not "wisely . . . mix serious things with jests."[1] In a letter to Richard Langley, "Schoolmaster of Eaton," where his son was a student, he wrote, "I find him apt enough to verses, and I desire not hee should bee much addicted to them least yt hinder him (as yt hath done mee) of better studies."[2] To James he sent a curiously wrought lantern, symbolic of the fading light of Elizabeth and the full splendor of her successor.[3] It was accompanied by explanatory verses in Latin and in English.[4] The right of James to the throne he defended by epigram[5] and by a prose tract, the publication of which the undisputed accession of James rendered unnecessary.[6] To King James and to Queen Anne he addressed lauda-

1. Cf. Epigram 419.
2. Letter 26.
3. This is described in *Nugae Antiquae,* 1804, I, 325–327 and in British Museum Addit. MS. 12049, f. 207.
4. *Ibid.*
5. Epigrams 349, 375, 399.
6. *The Tract on the Succession to the Crown,* ed. Clements Markham, Roxburghe Club, 1880. It is written in Harington's most pleasant style. His discussion of the civil and ecclesiastical policy of England is enlivened with anecdotes of all kinds. The right of James to succeed to the throne he maintains by appealing in turn to Protestants, Puritans, and Papists, and by quoting the view of an accepted authority of each group. For the Protestant he cites the letter of the Protector Somerset to the Scots, for the Puritans the writings of Peter Wentworth, and for the Papists a book by the Jesuit Dolman or Parsons. The undisputed accession of James having rendered publication unnecessary, Harington probably loaned the manuscript to his friend, Bishop Toby Matthew, of York (cf. *Nugae Antiquae,* 1804, II, 255–266), who added the tract to the chapter library. There it was found, in 1880, by Clements Markham, who edited it.

Although the manuscript is anonymous, internal evidence proves that it is Harington's. The author says his mother's brother is Thomas Markham, that he has a brother named Francis, that his father wrote some lines upon Bishop Gardner and translated Cicero's *De Amicitia* while he was a prisoner in the Tower, that he was a friend of Essex, that he served in Ireland, and that his mother was of the Queen's bedchamber. He speaks of being from the West, he tells stories of the Somersetshire justices, he reads cantos of Ariosto to several people, and he complains of the destruction of a Harington tomb. There is at the beginning a letter from King James, thanking him for a copy of the translation of Ariosto. Furthermore, the author quotes one of Harington's epigrams:

> My verses oft displease you, what's the matter?
> You love not to hear truth, nor I to flatter.

tory poems, which were presented to the new monarchs at Burleigh.[1] In Latin and in English verses, written in April, 1603, he bade farewell to his "wanton Muse." His soul aspires now to more serious thoughts; he will serve James as soldier, counsellor, scholar, architect, engineer; he awaits the King's commands.[2]

Sir John was doomed to disappointment; he had grown Scottish in vain.[3] Before King James reached London, Harington was imprisoned for debt, and remained a prisoner in the Gatehouse during the summer of 1603.[4] After his release, his attempts to obtain recognition at Court were unsuccessful. The new King rewarded the ambitious poet only with an interview, which Sir John, in a letter to Sir Amias Paulet, has described with inimitable wit.[5] Again he returned discouraged to Kelston. "Here now wyll I reste my troublede mynde," he wrote in his diary, "and tende my sheepe like an Arcadian swayne, that hathe loste his faire mistresse; for in soothe, I have loste the beste and faireste love that ever shepherde knew, even my gracious Queene; and sith my goode mistresse is gone, I shall not hastily put forthe for a new master. . . . I wyll keepe companie with none but my *oves* and *boves,* and go to Bathe and drinke sacke, and wash awaie remembraunces of paste times in the streams of Lethe."[6] And he adds in a letter to Dr. John Still, Bishop of Bath and Wells: "He that thryvethe in a courte muste put halfe of his honestie under his bonnet; and manie do we know that never parte that commoditie at all, and sleepe wyth it all in a bag."[7]

During the next year or two Harington's fortunes reached their lowest ebb. In 1604 he was compelled by the press of

External evidence, too, is not lacking. Some notes on the tract, included among the Salisbury manuscripts, attribute it to Harington. "Some notes for remembrance out of Sir Jo. Harington's book on the behalf of the K. of Sc. succession. The three sorts of Religion in England—Protestant, Papist, Puritan," in *Historical Manuscripts Commission, Salisbury MSS.,* Part XIV, Addenda (1923), 245.

1. Epigrams 425, 426.
2. Epigram 427.
3. Cf. Epigram 420.
4. Letters 29–33.
5. Letter 35.
6. *Nugae Antiquae,* I, 180.
7. Letter 34.

poverty to part with some of his lands at Lenton, and was at the same time involved in a suit against Sir John Skinner.[1] As early as 1603 he speaks of himself as "strycken in yeares and infirmyties,"[2] in 1605 he mentions his poverty and sickness,[3] and in 1606 his cousin, Lord Harington of Exton, alluded to his poor health.[4]

He remained undaunted by his misfortunes, and in 1605 he made a final and amazing effort to obtain honorable preferment. He addressed to Sir Robert Cecil, now Viscount Cranborne, and to Charles Blount, Earl of Devonshire, a highly characteristic letter, requesting that they urge the King to appoint him Archbishop of Dublin and Lord High Chancellor of Ireland.[5] He has learned that men that "obskure themselves shall not bee sought for with torchlyght, but rather this age ys aptest to thinke better of them that thinke best of themselves." He has twice visited Ireland, and has learned that the Irish "suspect all strawngers and specially a lawyer." He has studied law, and has "in nature a disposycion and some dexterytye to deal in soche cawses." He understands the Irish people: "I thinke my very *genius* doth in a sort lead me to that cowntry." He is, moreover, "somewhat more than ordinarily acquainted with all the Erls and great men thear." He wrote two years before "a kynde of farewell to all poetry and lyght studyes,"[6] which for the edification of their Lordships he includes in his letter. He has had, furthermore, "a kynde of purpose to studye wholly dyvinytye," and his many troubles "have not only quickned my understanding and encreased my experyence and knowledg in matters of the starchamber and chawncery, . . . but allso mortyfyed my vayn and ydle affections, and made mee apt for a more holly vocacion." The Holy Scripture teaches that if a man desire the office of a bishop, he desireth a good work,

1. Letters 29, 36.
2. Letter 34.
3. *View of the State of Ireland in 1605,* ed. W. D. Macray, Oxford, 1879, 13, 24.
4. Letter 44, Notes.
5. Printed as *View of the State of Ireland in 1605,* ed. W. D. Macray, Oxford, 1879.
6. Epigram 427.

and he points out that he can fulfil the conditions laid down by St. Paul in his epistle to Timothy: he is "unreproovable, husband of one wyfe, watching, sober, modest, harberows, apt to teach, not gevn to wyne, no quarrellor," and especially, "not gevn to fillthy lucre." He cites examples to prove that it is "not new or strawnge" for "a knight, a Layman, and one moche conversant in lyght studyes and poetry to bee made a Byshop," and points out that "a poet hathe one step unto a prophet," and that no one is a prophet in his own country. He adds that "his Majesties often and admirable discowrses in theology have stird and confyrmed this godly desyre." He has served as a captain in the late Queen's army; he now desires similar rank in the Church Militant. He concludes "that the world is a stage and we that lyve in yt are all stage players. . . . I playd my chyldes part happily, the schollar and students part to neglygently, the sowldyer and cowrtyer faythfully, the husband lovingly, the contryman not basely nor corruptly. . . . Now I desyre to act a Chawncellors part hollyly, that my last act may equall my fyrst, and that I may not *in extremo actu deficere*." There is no record of the reception given to this extraordinary request. Harington's letter is dated April 20, 1605; in the following October, Thomas Jones, Bishop of Meath, was appointed to the offices that Sir John had sought.

During the remaining seven years of his life, Harington lived at Kelston with his wife and his seven surviving children.[1] "I have nowe passed my storms," he writes in 1606, "and wishe for a quiet harbour to laye up my bark; for I growe olde and infirme."[2] His visits to Court, however, were not wholly discontinued. He was present during the visit of King Christian of Denmark, July, 1606, and wrote a most interesting account of the festivities.[3]

Lord Thomas Howard wrote him, about 1607, a letter that reveals not only Harington's reputation at Court but the peculiarities of King James as well:

1. *Miscellanea Genealogica et Heraldica,* IV (1884), 191.
2. Letter 45.
3. Letter 44.

"If you have good will and good health to perform what I shall commend, you may set forward for courte, whenever it suiteth your own conveniency: the King hath often enquired after you, and would readily see and converse again with the 'merry blade,' as he hath oft called you, since you was here. I will now premise certaine thinges to be observed by you, toward well gaining our Prince's good affection:—He doth wondrously covet learned discourse, of which you can furnish out ample means; he doth admire good fashion in cloaths, I pray you give good heed hereunto; strange devices oft come into man's conceit; some one regardeth the endowments of the inward sort, wit, valour, or virtue; another hath, perchance, special affection towardes outward thinges, cloaths, deportment, and good countenance. I woud wish you to be well trimmed; get a new jerkin well borderd, and not too short; the King saith, he liketh a flowing garment; be sure it be not all of one sort, but diversly colourd, the collar falling somewhat down, and your ruff well stiffend and bushy. We have lately had many gallants who failed in their suits, for want of due observance of these matters. The King is nicely heedfull of such points, and dwelleth on good looks and handsome accoutrements. Eighteen servants were lately discharged, and many more will be discarded, who are not to his liking in these matters. I wish you to follow my directions, as I wish you to gain all you desire. Robert Carr is now most likely to win the Prince's affection, and dothe it wonderously in a little time. The Prince leaneth on his arm, pinches his cheek, smoothes his ruffled garment, and, when he looketh at Carr, directeth discourse to divers others. This young man dothe much study all art and device; he hath changed his tailors and tiremen many times, and all to please the Prince, who laugheth at the long grown fashion of our young courtiers, and wisheth for change every day. You must see Carr before you go to the King, as he was with him a boy in Scotland, and knoweth his taste and what pleaseth. In your discourse you must not dwell too long on any one subject, and touch but lightly on religion. Do not of yourself say, 'This is good or bad'; but, 'If it were your Majesties good opinion, I myself should think so and so.' —Ask no more questions than what may serve to know the Prince's thought. In private discourse, the King seldome speaketh of any man's temper, discretion, or good virtues; so meddle not at all, but find out a clue to guide you to the heart and most delightful subject of his mind. I will advise one thing:—the roan jennet, whereon the King rideth every day, must not be forgotten to be praised; and the good furniture above all, what lost a great man much notice the day. A noble did come in suit of a place, and saw the King mounting the roan; deliverd his petition, which was heeded and read, but no answer was given. The noble departed, and came to courte the nexte day, and got no answer again. The Lord Treasurer was then pressed to move the King's pleasure touching the petition. When the King was asked for answer thereto, he said, in some wrath, 'Shall a King give heed to a dirty paper, when a beggar noteth not his gilt stirrops?'—Now it fell out, that the King had new furniture when the noble saw him in the courte-yard, but he was overcharged with confusion, and passed by admiring the dressing of the horse. Thus, good knight, our noble failed in his suit. I coud relate and offer some other remarks on these matters, but Silence and Discretion should be linked together like dog and bitch, for of them is gendred Security: I am certain it proveth so at this place. You have lived to see the trim of old times, and what passed in the Queen's days. These thinges are no more the same. Your Queen did talk of her subjects love and good affections, and in good truth she aimed well; our King talketh of his subjects fear and subjection, and herein I think he dothe well too, as long as it holdeth good. Carr hath all favours, as I told you before; the King teacheth him Latin every morning, and I think some one should teach him English too; for, as he is a Scottish lad, he hath much need of better language. The King doth much covet his presence; the ladies too are not behind hand in their admiration; for I tell you, good knight, this fellow is straight-limbed, well-favourede, strong shoulderd, and smooth-faced, with some sort of cunning and show of modesty;

tho' God wot, he well knoweth when to shew his impudence. You are not young, you are not handsome, you are not finely; and yet will you come to courte, and thinke to be well favoured? Why, I say again, good knight, that your learning may somewhat prove worthy hereunto; your Latin and your Greek, your Italian, your Spanish tongues, your wit and discretion, may be well looked unto for a while, as strangers at such a place; but these are not the thinges men live by now a days. Will you say the moon shineth all the summer? That the starrs are bright jewels fit for Carr's ears? That the roan jennet surpasseth Buchephalus, and is worthy to be bestridden by Alexander? That his eyes are fire, his tail is Berenice's locks, and a few more such fancies worthy your noticing? Your lady is virtuous, and somewhat of a good huswife; has lived in a courte in her time, and I believe you may venture her forthe again; but I know those would not quietly reste, were Carr to leer on their wives, as some do perceive, yea, and like it well too they shoud be so noticed. If any mischance be to be wished, 'tis breaking a leg in the King's presence, for this fellow owes all his favour to that bout; I think he hath better reason to speak well of his own horse, than the King's roan jennet. We are almost worn out in our endeavors to keep pace with this fellow in his duty and labour to gain favour, but all in vain; where it endeth I cannot guess, but honours are talked of speedily for him. I truste this by my own son, that no danger may happen from our freedoms. If you come here, God speed your ploughing at the courte: I know you do it rarely at home. So adieu, my good knyght, and I will always write me

"Your truly loving old freinde,

"T. HOWARD."[1]

Harington was in London in July, 1607. With many others he attended King James and Prince Henry when they dined at Merchant Taylors' Hall. After the King had been welcomed, "at the upper end of the Hall there was sett a chayer of state

1. *Nugae Antiquae,* 1804, I, 390–397.

where his Majesty sate and viewed the Hall, and a very proper child well spoken being clothed like an Angell of gladnes with a taper of fracinnsence burning in his hand delivered a short speech contayning xviii verses devised by Master Benjamin Johnson the Poet, which pleased his Majesty marvelously well. And upon either side of the Hall in the windowe neere the upper end were galleries or seates made for musique in either of which were seaven singuler choice musitions playing on their lutes. And in the shipp which did hang aloft in the Hall three rare men and very skilful who sang to his Majesty. And over the skreene cornettes and lowd musique, wherein it is to be remembred that the multitute and noyse was so greate that the lutes nor songes could hardly be heard or understood. And then his Majesty went up into the Kinges Chamber where he dyned alone at a table which was provided only for his Majesty and the Queene (but the Queene came not). In which chamber was plaied a very ritch paier of organs, whereupon Master John Bull, Doctor of Musique, and a brother of this Company, did play during all the dynner tyme. And Master Nathanyell Gyles, Master of the Children of the Kinges Chappell, together with divers singing men and children of the said Chappell did sing melodious songes at the said dynner. And be it also remembred that the Prince did dyne in the great Hall and that the long table at the upper end of the Hall was taken away and three tables distainct one from an other placed in the rome thereof, viz. one table in the middest where the Prince sate alone in state, and the tables on ether side were wholly furnished with Ambassadors and noble men. And the service to the King and Prince for the first course was carried up by the knightes, aldermen, maisters, assistauntes and Lyvery, having their hoods upon their shoulders, the service being ritch and bountifull as by the charge will appeare, unto which dynner the Prince sent three brace of bucks. And Sir Thomas Challoner did by letter written by his highnes commaundement signifie that his highnes with his owne hande plaied the woodman to kill them. And when the Kinges most excellent Majesty had dyned and withdrawne himself into his inner chamber, the Master and fower wardens and Master Baron Sotherton and the Aldermen of the Company resorted unto his Majesty, and Master Recorder of London, being there present, did in the name of the whole Company most humbly thanck his Majesty that it had pleased him to grace the Company with his presence that day. And the Maister of the Company did present his Majesty with a faier purse wherein was one hundreth poundes in gould. And Richard Langley, the common Clarck of the Company, did moast humbly deliver unto his Majesty a Rôle in vellam which he had collected out of the auncient bookes and recordes of the Company . . . wherein was entred the names of seaven Kinges, one Queene, seaventeene Princes or Dukes, two Dutchesses, one Archbisshop, thirty-one Earles, fyve Countesses, one viscount, twenty-fower bisshops, threescore and six barons or Lordes, two Ladies, seaven Abbotts, seaven Pryors and one Sub-Prior, omitting a number of Knights, esquiors, etc. who had bene free of the Company, which his Majesty most graciously accepted and said that he himself was free of another Company, yet he would so much grace the Company of Marchauntailors that the Prince, his eldest sonne, should be free thereof. And that he would see and be a witnes when the garland should be put upon his head. And then they in like manner resorted to the Prince and the said Master presented his highnes with an other ritch purse wherein was fyfty poundes in gould and the Clarcke delivered his highnes a like role which were alsoe graciously accepted, and his highnes said that not only himself would be free of the Company but commaunded one of his gentlemen and the Clarck of the Company to goe to all the Lordes present and require all of them that loved him and were not free of other companies, to be free of this company. Whereupon these Lords whose names ensue, with humble thancks to his highnes, accepted of the freedome. . . .[1] And then the Master and Wardens according to their usuall manner went with their Garlandes on

1. Seventy-eight names follow, including "Sir John Harrington."

their heades to publish theleccion, it pleased the Kinges moast excellent Majesty to resort into the little lobby out of whiche there was a faier windowe made of purpose for his Majesty to looke into the Hall, and there his Majesty observed the whole manner of the Ceremony. And it did moast graciously please the Prince to call for the Maisters garlande and to putt the same upon his owne heade whereat the Kinges Majesty did very hartely laugh. And so the old Master and Wardens proceeded to the publicacion of theleccion of the newe Master and Wardens who were all here present, to the good liking of the Company. After all which his Majesty came downe into the greate Hall and sitting in his chayre of state did heare a mellodious song of farwell song by the three men in the Shipp being apparelled in watchet silke like seamen, which song so pleased his Majesty that he caused the same to be sung three tymes over. And his Majesty and the noble Prince and honorable Lordes gave the Company harty thanckes and so departed."[1]

During these years Harington's attempts to win the favor of King James were continued. In 1607 he tried to induce the wealthy Thomas Sutton to make Charles, Duke of York, his heir.[2] For Prince Henry he wrote before 1605 "a comment on the sixt booke of Vergill."[3] About 1606 he copied out and presented to the young prince more than four hundred of his epigrams.[4] In 1608 he wrote for Henry a supplement to Bishop Godwin's *Catalogue of the Bishop*.[5] From Kelston he wrote the

1. The Records of the Merchant Taylors' Company, Court Minutes, Vol. V, Thursday, July 16, 1607.

2. Letters 49, 50, 51.

3. *View of the State of Ireland in 1605,* ed. W. D. Macray, Oxford, 1879, 20. Harington's commentary is lost.

4. Letter 46 and Notes.

5. Harington's supplement was printed in 1653 by his grandson, Doctor John Chetwind, under the title of *A Briefe View of the State of the Church of England as it stood in Q. Elizabeths and King James his Reigne to the yeere 1608.* Chetwind's text was reprinted in *Nugae Antiquae* (1779). Thomas Park, editor of *Nugae Antiquae* (1804), used Harington's manuscript to correct the errors in the earlier editions. He used Harington's title: *A Supplie or Addicion to the Catalogue of Bishops to the Year 1608.* The original manuscript is now in the British Museum (Royal MSS. 17 B xxii). Harington's avowed purpose is

Prince a charming letter about his dog, Bungay, and in the following year sent him a copy of his translation of *Orlando Furioso,* the second edition of which had appeared in 1607.[1]

It was probably for Prince Henry that Harington translated into verse the *Regimen Sanitatis Salernitanum.* The *Regimen* is a Latin poem written in the twelfth century as a domestic manual of health by physicians of Salerno. Throughout the Middle Ages and even in Tudor times it was highly esteemed. In 1607 Harington's translation appeared anonymously under the title *The Englishman's Doctor.* In a preface the publisher states: "It [the manuscript] came to me by chance, as a Jewell that is found, whereof notwithstanding I am not covetous, but part the Treasure amongst my Country-men. The author of the paines, is to be unknowne, and I put this Childe of his into the open world without his consent."[2] Harington's version, which is the first of the rimed translations, is fluent and spirited. The following excerpt illustrates his method:

> Si tibi deficiant Medici, medici tibi fiant
> Haec tria: mens laeta, requies, moderata diaeta.
>
> Use three physicians still, first doctor Quiet,
> Next fellow Mery-man, and doctor Diet.

Here, as in everything he wrote, he found material for jest:

> Canary and Modera, both are like
> To make one lean indeede (but wot you what)
> Who say they make one leane wold make one laffe.
> They meane, they make one leane upon a staffe.

The book went through seven editions between 1607 and 1624.

to instruct the young prince, but he includes in his account of the bishop his usual witty observations and anecdotes. His book is the most diverting of church histories.

1. Letters 52, 54.

2. *The School of Salernum, Regimen Sanitatis Salernitanum,* New York, P. B. Hoeber, 1920. This assertion may be entirely true. It is, however, more likely that Harington, a courtier, was unwilling to publish this work in the usual manner of "professional" writers, whom he so much despised. Cf. Epigram 424.

Harington's last years were uneventful. He interested himself and others in making certain repairs to the Church of SS. Peter and Paul, Bath.[1] His account books and memoranda show that he became frugal and increasingly fond of quiet.[2] His *Prayse of Private Life,* written at this time, reveals his mood. He busied himself with a translation of the Psalms. Earlier, in the bustle and stir of life at Court, he had written, "Each nighte do I spende, or muche better parte thereof, in counceil with the aunciente examples of lerninge; I con over their histories, their poetrie, their instructions, and thence glean my own proper conducte in matters bothe of merrimente or discretion";[3] and to his wife, "Nexte monthe I will see thie swete face, and kiss my boys and maids, which I praie thee not to omitte on my accounte. Send me up, by my manne Combe, my Petrarche."[4] With his books, with his wife and boys and maids, he spent his last few years in the peace and solitude of his pleasant country-house at Kelston.

On May 18, 1612, Harington, "sicke of a dead palsie," was brought to Bath to see his old friend, Robert Cecil, Earl of Salisbury, who died six days later.[5] Harington died in November, and was buried at Kelston, December 1, 1612.[6]

Harington was survived by his wife until 1634,[7] and by his brother, Francis, until 1639.[8] Of the latter little is known. He was a student at Christ Church, Oxford.[9] He translated the first fifty stanzas of Book XXXII of *Orlando Furioso.*[10] In 1599

1. Letters 49, 51, 53, 59.
2. Manuscripts in the possession of John E. M. Harington, Esq., Vol. IX, 129.
3. Letter 28. 4. Letter 27.
5. Francis Peck, *Desiderata Curiosa,* 1779, 209; *Historical Manuscripts Commission, Tenth Report, Part IV, Manuscripts of the Earl of Westmorland* (1885), 14–15.
6. Venn, *Alumni Cantabrigienses.* He apparently died intestate. (P. C. C., Administration Act Book, 1612, f. 82.)
7. Collinson, *History of Somersetshire,* I, 129.
8. *Miscellanea Genealogica et Heraldica,* III (1880), 219.
9. Sir John Harington's *Tract on the Succession to the Crown,* 1880, 113; "A Supply, or Addicion," *Nugae Antiquae,* 1804, II, 208.
10. *Orlando Furioso,* 1634, 265–266.

he married Mary Weeks,[1] and in 1606 he married Joane Baylie, of Kelston.[2] His son, Thomas, was baptized at Kelston in the following year.[3] In 1609 he borrowed from Sir John the sum of £15.[4] A son, Ralph, was buried at Kelston in 1622.[5] In 1637 he received a bequest, made by Lady Mary Harington, the widow of Sir John, of all her "interest in a Lease of Fieldgrove in the Parish of Bitten," in Gloucestershire.[6] There two years later he died.[7]

Of the eleven children of Sir John, seven were living at the time of his death.[8] His eldest son, John, an Eton boy,[9] matriculated from Trinity College, Oxford, in 1604, aged fifteen. He migrated to Cambridge and was incorporated there in 1607. In 1608 he was admitted to Lincoln's Inn, and in 1615 he became a barrister-at-law.[10] Contrary to the tenets of his father, he supported Puritan principles. He sat for Somerset in the Long Parliament, 1646–1648, and in 1654 he died.[11]

V

Among Elizabethan writers Harington holds an interesting place. By birth and training a courtier, he belonged always to the Court circle, and despised the professional men of letters like Nashe.[12] Master Samuel Daniel and Master Henry Constable he called his "very good friends."[13] In an age when the

1. *The Registers of the Abbey Church of SS. Peter and Paul, Bath,* 2 vols., Harleian Society, 1900, I, 204.
2. *Miscellanea Genealogica et Heraldica,* IV (1884), 191.
3. *Ibid.,* III (1880), 194.
4. British Museum Addit. MS. 27632, f. 41.
5. *Miscellanea Genealogica et Heraldica,* III (1880), 195.
6. *Ibid.,* p. 228.
7. *Ibid.,* p. 219.
8. *Ibid.,* IV (1884), 191; see also III (1880), 316.
9. British Museum Addit. MS. 12049, f. 194.
10. Venn, *Alumni Cantabrigienses,* l. 310.
11. This brief account is here introduced because he is so often confused with his father, Sir John. Venn states that he was probably M.P. for Somerset in 1656 (*Alumni Cantabrigienses,* I, 310). The same erroneous statement appears in Collinson, *History of Somersetshire,* I, xxxii, and in *Miscellanea Genealogica et Heraldica,* III (1880), 399. Cf. *Notes and Queries for Somerset and Dorset,* I, 42.
12. Cf. Epigram 132.
13. Epigram 126 and *Orlando Furioso,* notes following Book XXXIV; edition 1634, 288.

writing of verse was a gentleman's pastime, he employed his talents for the entertainment of himself and his friends.

I near desearvd that gloriows name of Poet;
No Maker I, nor do I care who know it.
Occasion oft my penn doth entertayn
With trew discourse. Let others Muses fayn;
Myne never sought to set to sale her wryting.
In part her frends, in all her selfe delighting,
She cannot beg applause of vulgar sort,
Free born and bred, more free for noble sport.
  My Muse hath one still bids her in her eare;
  Yf well disposd, to write; yf not, forbear.[1]

To the Queen, to Essex, to Bishop John Still, to his wife, to his mother-in-law, and to a score of others, he addressed epigrams. These were circulated in manuscript, and were not given to the public while he lived.

During his lifetime only three of his works were published: *Orlando Furioso, The Metamorphosis of Ajax,* and *The Englishman's Doctor.* His *Tract on the Succession, State of Ireland in 1605, Supply or Addition to the Catalogue of Bishops,* and a few of his letters were published long after his death. Two works mentioned in *Ulysses upon Ajax*—the *Succinct Collection of History* and the *Compendious Observations on the Emperors' Lives*—are lost. In addition to the works already considered, an interesting "Treatise on Playe," written about 1597, and a brief diary that contains scattered entries from 1594 to 1603 have been printed.[2] In the former he discusses forms of "playe" as varied as psalm-singing and dicing. The following defence of "dissimulation" illustrates the style and tone of the work: "Wee goe brave in apparell that wee may be taken for better men than wee bee; we use much bumbastings and quiltings to seeme better formed, better showlderd, smaller wasted, and fuller thyght, then wee are; wee barbe and shave ofte, to seeme yownger than wee are; we use perfumes both inward and outward to seeme sweeter then wee bee; corkt shooes to seeme

1. Epigram 424.
2. *Nugae Antiquae,* 1804, I, 186–232, 165–182.

taller then wee bee; wee use cowrtuows salutations to seem kinder then wee bee; lowly obaysances to seeme humbler then we bee; and somtyme grave and godly communication to seem wyser or devowter then wee bee. And infynit such thinges wee may observe in ourselves, which are some of them commendable in this respect, that, by good and trew endevour to seeme to bee, we may obtayne at last the habyt and grace to become to bee such indeed, according to the excellent cownsell, *Labour to bee as you would bee thought.*"[1]

From his diary, which he calls "Breefe Notes and Remembraunces," several passages have already been quoted. Many of his comments are illuminating. "The Queene loveth to see me in my last frize jerkin, and saith *'tis well enoughe cutte.* I will have another made liken to it. I do remember she spit on Sir Mathew's fringed clothe, and said *the fooles wit was gone to ragges.*"[2] Another entry follows: "Yesterday I was near drunkene, and to daye am neare sicke, and perchance to-morrowe may be bothe sicke and sorrie; my cosin did chide me, and saide, 'I bade my man lighte his taper at the moone.' It may be so, Horace saithe *Coelum ipsum petimus stultitia.*"[3] Of Essex in his disgrace he writes, "The Queene well knowethe how to humble the haughtie spirit; the haughtie spirit knoweth not how to yield, and the man's soule seemethe tossede to and fro, like the waves of a troubled sea."[4]

Throughout all of Harington's work are digressions and irrelevances which serve as commentary not so much on the context as on the man himself. "Prose," he points out, "is like a faire greene way, wherin a man may travel a great jorney and not be weary; but verse is a miry lane, in which a mans horse puls out one leg after another with much ado, and often drives his master to light to helpe him out."[5] Accordingly, he dismounts from his Pegasus at the end of each canto of *Orlando Furioso* and writes a page or more of notes, into which he introduces not

1. *Nugae Antiquae,* 1804, I, 209–210. 2. *Ibid.,* p. 167.
3. *Ibid.,* pp. 169–170. 4. *Ibid.,* pp. 179–180.
5. Notes following Book XXXII of *Orlando Furioso;* edition 1634, 266.

merely explanation of Ariosto's meaning but all manner of reminiscence and autobiographical data. His reasons for so doing he explains in his Preface: "Whereas I make mention here and there of some of mine owne friends and kin, I did it the rather, because *Plutarke* in one place speaking of *Homer,* partly lamenteth, and partly blameth him, that writing so much as he did, yet in none of his works there was any mention made, or so much as inkling to be gathered of what stock he was, of what kindred, of what towne, nor save for his language, of what country. Excuse me then, if in a worke that may perhaps last longer then a better thing, and being not ashamed of my kindred, name them here and there to no mans offence."[1] This solicitude for posterity, combined with his habitual predilection for the humorous, makes these comments more than ordinarily interesting. His parents, his brother, and his friends are remembered in his notes. Inkhorn annotation he avoids, and draws his comparisons from the life about him. "In *Pinabello* and his wife, that thought to revenge the scorne they received, with doing the like scorne to others, we may see, how base and dunghill dispositions follow not any course of value or true reputation, but onely to wreake their malice on some body, not caring whom: as they are wont to tell of *Will Sommer* (though otherwise a harmlesse foole) that would evermore if one had angerd him, strike him that was next him."[2] He can never forgo a jest. To his translation of Ariosto's criticism of the Amazons' laws, he adds in a marginal note: "There were too many speakers (belike) in their Parliament when they made such a law as they were driven to change so soone after."[3] All his works contain similar witticisms; he cannot long remain solemn. Even his *Tract on the Succession to the Crown* and *Supply or Addition to the Catalogue of Bishops* are crowded with anecdotes and reminiscence.

Harington's interests were scholarly. Varied as his activities

1. *Orlando Furioso,* ed. 1634, Sig. ¶ 8v.
2. Notes following Book XXII of *Orlando Furioso;* edition 1634, 175.
3. *Orlando Furioso,* 1634, 155.

were, he found much time for study and reading. The range of his reading was wide. In a single book, *The Metamorphosis of Ajax,* he quotes Rabelais, Ovid, Augustine, Lodovico Vives, Martial, Suetonius, Pliny, Homer, Aristotle, Plutarch, Cicero, Livy, Tertullian, and many others. Like all of the cultivated men of his day, he knew the classics. Seneca, Cicero, Vergil, Horace, Ovid, and Martial are his favorite writers among the ancients. With the Renaissance Latin writers he is less familiar. Among the French and Italian, Rabelais, Ariosto, and Petrarch he mentions most frequently. He and his father collected in manuscript a large number of poems by Wyatt, Surrey, Sir Thomas Chaloner, Thomas Phaer, Campion, and others.[1] English drama, too, he collected. About 1610 he compiled a list of the plays that he owned.[2] He had 129 distinct plays in eleven bound volumes. During the years 1600–1610 he obtained ninety out of 105 plays that were printed in London in that decade.[3] There were in the collection eighteen quartos of fifteen of Shakespeare's plays, three being duplicates of *Pericles, Lear,* and *The Merry Wives of Windsor.* Oddly enough, he makes no mention of Shakespeare or of the London theatre in any of his extant writings. In his account of a dramatic "entertainment and show" at the Court of James, he writes, "I have much marvalled at these strange pegeantries, and they do bring to my remembrance what passed of this sort in our Queens days; of which I was sometime an humble presenter and assistant."[4] His part in these plays was probably slight.[5]

Harington's hitherto unpublished treatise *The Prayse of Private Life* was written, there seems little doubt, after he had retired to Kelston to pursue the graver studies that had always

1. British Museum Addit. MS. 36529 and Egerton MS. 2711.

2. British Museum Addit. MS. 27632, f. 43. See also F. J. Furnivall in 7 *Notes and Queries,* IX (1890), 382.

3. E. K. Chambers, *The Elizabethan Stage,* III, 183.

4. Letter 44.

5. He is not mentioned, even as "an humble presenter and assistant," in Nichols' *Progresses of Queen Elizabeth* or in Robert Withington's *English Pageantry.*

interested him. His old friend, Samuel Daniel,[1] too, had sought in Somersetshire the leisure and quiet of country life, and it is probable that the two poets often met there as well as at Court. It is certain that Daniel read Harington's treatise, for at some time after 1605 he presented a manuscript copy to Margaret Clifford, Countess Dowager of Cumberland,[2] to whose daughter, Lady Anne, he had been tutor. The Cliffords had remained grateful to the old poet. A family picture at Appleby Castle includes Daniel's portrait next that of Lady Anne Clifford, and a detail of the painting shows a shelf on which Daniel's poems stand beside Spenser's. After Daniel's death, Anne Clifford, then Countess of Dorset, built a monument to him in Beckington Church, Somersetshire.[3] Daniel's gift was an appropriate one, for the discourse was probably to the taste of the pious Margaret Clifford,[4] and the author was a relative by marriage.[5] It was probably Harington's treatise that Lady Anne Clifford had read when she wrote, March 17, 1619, "This day I made an end of my Lady's Book of Praise of a solitary life."[6]

The Prayse of Private Life is derived from Petrarch's *De Vita Solitaria.* Although Harington follows Petrarch's plan and in many of his chapters paraphrases the original, there is much in his essay that is his own. Lacking the gaiety and sprightly wit that distinguish much of his earlier writing, *The Prayse of Private Life* reveals the author as an old man, grave and reasonable, who found in Petrarch's treatise much that his busy and

1. Epigram 126.

2. The present version is printed from a transcript (British Museum Addit. MS. 30161). The original, formerly preserved at Skipton Castle, has apparently been destroyed.

3. M. A. Scott, *Elizabethan Translations from the Italian,* 1916, lxxviii.

4. Daniel had previously addressed to her the dignified *Epistle to the Lady Margaret, Countess of Cumberland.* She was the widow of the dashing and wayward George Clifford, third Earl of Cumberland, who died in 1605. Her daughter writes that she preserved in her trunk "many papers of philosophy." (*The Diary of Lady Anne Clifford,* 1923, 84.)

5. Lucy Harington, Countess of Bedford, and first cousin once removed to Harington, was the wife of her nephew.

6. *The Diary of Lady Anne Clifford,* 90. "My Lady" is her mother, Margaret, Countess of Cumberland.

disappointing life had convinced him was memorable. It is a welcome addition to what is known of an unusually interesting and versatile Elizabethan.

Though Harington is known chiefly as an epigrammatist, as the author of *The Metamorphosis of Ajax,* and as the translator of Ariosto, he deserves consideration as one of the most interesting of letter-writers. The charm of Harington's personality, his witty and agreeable accounts of happenings at the Court of Elizabeth and of James, his penetrating characterizations of the men he knew, make these letters the best of their day. To his wife, to Lord Thomas Howard, to Bishop John Still, to Justice Barlow, to Robert Markham, to Sir Amias Pawlett, to Sir Robert Cecil, and to Prince Henry, he addressed letters that display his keen wit and his mastery of phrase. Of especial interest are his accounts of the last days of the old Queen, of festivities at the Court of James, and of his interview with that monarch,[1] but whether he writes of himself or his dog, of the Earl of Essex or Ireland, or of the fatuous King James, he is witty and entertaining.

Of all Harington's writings, his epigrams are perhaps the most interesting. The word "epigram" was used in Elizabethan England to designate almost any short poem. Ben Jonson, in dedicating his *Epigrams* to William, Earl of Pembroke, points out that epigrams "carry danger in the sound," and he adds in Epigram 2 that the reader will expect them to be

> bold, licentious, full of gall,
> Wormwood, and sulphur, sharp, and tooth'd withal.

Jonson, however, included in his *Epigrams* many kinds of poems: distichs translated from Martial, several satirical poems thirty or forty lines in length, poems of a lyric quality ("Epitaph on Salathiel Pavy," "Epitaph on Elizabeth," "Follow a shadow, it still flies you"),[2] and a burlesque narrative poem, "On the Famous Voyage," which is 196 lines in length. Few of his epi-

1. Letters 27, 44, 35.

2. This last Jonson terms an epigram in *Conversations,* Shakespeare Society, 1842, 25.

grams terminate in a point, and few are satirical. Despite the fact that Jonson employed the term somewhat loosely, he was quick to censure his rivals when they took similar liberties and widened the province of the epigram. John Owen, he told Drummond, "hath no thinge good in him, his Epigrammes being bare narrations,"[1] and "that when Sir John Harrington desyred him to tell the truth of his Epigrammes, he answered him, that he loved not the truth, for they were Narrations, and not Epigrames."[2] On the whole, Jonson's conception of the epigram approximates the Greek rather than the Roman, and in this respect he departs from the practice of his age.

It was Martial's influence—direct and indirect—that determined the form and matter of the Elizabethan epigram. "It is certain," writes Harington, "that of all poems the epigram is the wittiest; and of all that write epigrams, Martial is counted the pleasantest."[3] An examination of the extant collections, which certainly represent only a small part of the mass of epigrams that were circulated in manuscript, and a consideration of the many contemporary allusions to the epigram, reveal the fact that the Elizabethan epigram was essentially a satire in little. Harington points out that Thomas Bastard's epigrams are designed "to make in men's ill manners, good amendment."[4] "Epigrams," writes Robert Hayman, "are like Satyrs, rough without."[5] Edward Guilpin emphasizes the same point:

> The Satyre onely and Epigramatist
> (Concisde Epigrame, and sharpe Satyrist)
> Keep diet from this surfet of excesse,
> Tempring themselves from such licenciousness.
> The bitter censures of their critticke spleenes
> Are antidotes to pestilentiall sinnes;
> They heale with lashing, seare luxuriousness:
> They are philosophicke true Cantharides

1. *Conversations,* p. 17.
2. *Ibid.,* p. 3.
3. *The Metamorphosis of Ajax,* ed. S. W. Singer, 37. See also T. K. Whipple, "Martial and the English Epigram from Sir Thomas Wyatt to Ben Jonson," *University of California Publications in Modern Philology,* X (1925), 279–414.
4. Epigram 160.
5. *Quodlibets,* 1628, 61.

To vanities dead flesh. An Epigrame
Is papish displing rebell flesh to tame;
A plaine dealing lad that is not afraid
To speak the truth, but calls a jade a jade.
And Mounsieur Guulard was not much to blame,
When he for meat mistooke an Epigrame;
For though it be no cates, sharpe sauce it is
To lickerous vanitie, youths sweet amisse.
But oh! the Satyre hath a nobler vaine:
He's the stappado, rack, and some such paine
To base lewd vice: the Epigram's Bridewell,
Some whipping cheere; but this is follies hell.[1]

Nicholas Breton alludes to the satirical intent of epigrammatists in general, and of Guilpin in particular:

Tis strange to see the humors of these daies:
How first the Satyre bites at imperfections:
The Epigrammist in his quips displaies
A wicked course in shadowes of corrections:
The Humorist hee strictly makes collections
Of loth'd behauiours both in youthe and age:
And makes them plaie their parts vpon a stage.[2]

From 1590 to 1620 the epigram passed current among the wits in the universities, in the taverns, and at the Court. To this popularity, the many printed collections and the numerous references bear witness. Marston, in *The Scourge of Villanie,* writes of Tuscus, a retailer of wit:

But roome for Tuscus, that iest-moungering youth,
Who neer did ope his apish gerning mouth,
But to retaile and broke another's wit.
Discourse of what you will, he straight can fit
Your present talke, with, *Sir, I'll tell a iest,*—
Of some sweet ladie, or grand lord at least.
Then on he goes, and neer his tongue shall lie,
Till his ingrossed iests are all drawne dry:
But then as dumbe as Maurus, when at play,
Hath lost his crownes, and paun'd his trim array.

1. "Satyre Preludium," *Skialetheia. Or a shadowe of truth in certaine epigrams and satyres,* 1598; edited by A. B. Grosart, 1878.

2. *No Whipping, nor Tripping: but a kinde friendly Snipping,* 1601; Isham Reprints, 1895, stanza one.

He doth nought but retaile iests: breake but one,
Out flies his table-booke, let him alone,
He'll haue it i' faith: Lad, hast an Epigram,
Wil't haue it put into the chaps of Fame?
Giue Tuscus copies; sooth, as his own wit,
His proper issue, he will father it.[1]

The custom of employing epigrams for personal satire, and of circulating them in manuscript, is shown in *Satiromastix:*

Crispinus. They're bitter epigrams compos'd on you
By Horace.
Demetrius. And disperst amongst the gallants
In several coppies, by Asinius Bubo.[2]

And in the same play, the sentence pronounced on Horace, who is Jonson, is illuminating: "In brieflynes, when you sup in tavernes amongst your betters, you shall sweare not to dippe your manners in too much sawce, nor at table to fling epigrams, embleams, or play-speeches about you (lyke hayle-stones) to keepe you out of the terrible daunger of the shot."[3] Dekker, in *Guls Horn-Booke,* tells how to attract attention at a tavern: "After a turne or two in the roome, take occasion (pulling out youer gloues) to haue some *Epigrams,* or *Satyre,* or *Sonnet* fastned in one of them that may (as it were vnwittingly to you) offer itselfe to the Gentlemen: but without much coniuration from them, and a pretty kind of counterfet loathnes in yourselfe, do not read it; and though it be none of your owne, sweare you made it."[4] Harington's fame as a wit obviated the necessity of employing any such ruse to obtain an audience. Thomas Fuller tells the following story: "It happened that, while the said Sir John repaired often to an ordinary in Bath, a female attendress at the table, neglecting other gentlemen who sat higher, and were of great estates, applied herself wholly to him, accommodating him with all necessaries, and preventing his asking any

1. *The Scourge of Villanie, 1598.*
2. *"Poetaster" and "Satiromastix,"* ed. J. H. Penniman, Belles Lettres Series, 1913, III, ll. 329–331.
3. "The shot" was the tavern bill. *Ibid.,* V, ii, 381–386.
4. *Guls Horn-Booke,* 1609; *The Non-Dramatic Works of Thomas Dekker,* edited by A. B. Grosart, 5 vols., 1884–1886, II, 240.

thing with her officiousness. She being demanded by him the reason of her so careful waiting on him? 'I understand,' said she, 'you are a very witty man; and if I should displease you in any thing, I fear you would make an epigram of me.' "[1]

Harington was most at home, however, not in the tavern, or the university, but at the Court, where he was a privileged jester. The old Queen indulgently called him "that merry poet, my godson," and her successor alluded to him as "the merry blade."[2] Elizabeth liked his witty verses, and read them aloud to the Court.[3] Even when the Queen had but a few months to live, he read her "some verses, whereat she smilede once, and was pleasede to saie;—'When thou doste feele creepinge tyme at thye gate, these fooleries will please thee lesse.' "[4]

Harington's epigrams, unlike those of Ben Jonson, follow the Latin model rather than the Greek. Some of them are drawn directly from Martial; a few come from the Renaissance Latin epigrammatists; but most of them are suggested by his everyday experiences and conversations.[5] Although most of the epigrams are satires in little, Harington's attitude is not that of the professional satirist. He has none of Marston's misanthropy or of Hall's cynicism. Instead of savage indignation one finds urbanity:

> Treason doth neuer prosper, what's the reason?
> For if it prosper, none dare call it Treason.[6]

Often he borrows an idea from Martial and makes it completely his own.[7] Many of his epigrams are versified "merry tales." Very few of his epigrams are encomiastic, though he is capable of framing graceful compliments.[8] He is, for his age, surpris-

1. Thomas Fuller, *Worthies of England,* 3 vols., London, 1840, III, 103–104.
2. *Nugae Antiquae,* 1804, I, 240, 391.
3. He writes his wife of the Queen's "likinge to my free speech"; (Letter 26). See also Epigram 267 and note.
4. Letter 27.
5. His sources are indicated in the notes that follow the text.
6. Epigram 259.
7. Notable examples are Epigrams 12 and 76.
8. Epigram 43.

ingly temperate in his laudation of the mighty; he could not, like Jonson, address James as "best of kings" and "best of poets."[1] His dislike of flattery appears in his reproof of Thomas Bastard, who found it possible to "magnify Magistrates, yet taunt the times."[2] His satire is not infrequently personal, and many of his readers were doubtless able to identify those for whom his shafts were intended. Accordingly, it is not his custom to mention names:

My Lorde, though I by yow am often prest
To know the secret drift of my entent
In these my pleasent lynes, and who are meant
By Cinna, Lynus, Lesbia, and the rest,
Yet pardon though I graunte not your request;
Tis such as I thereto may not assent. . . .[3]

That each of the Latin names that Harington uses to mask the object of his satire represents always the same person is proved not only by his statement[4] but also by a careful reading of the epigrams and by an examination of his use of his sources. In twenty-eight of the many epigrams in which Harington gives a Latin name to the person he satirizes, he paraphrases Martial; but in twenty-four of these twenty-eight the only significant change he makes is in the name, apparently for the sole reason that he had in earlier epigrams given that name to a living person known to his readers. It is difficult for the modern reader to know "who are meant by Cinna, Lynus, Lesbia, and the rest." "Paulus" may be Raleigh, although there are objections to this identification. "Galla," the woman of fashion who married a "lofty prelate," may be the widowed sister of Sir George Gifford, whose marriage with Richard Fletcher, Bishop of London, "was talked of at least nine days," or she may be the wife of Thomas Godwin, Bishop of Bath and Wells, who married, "some thought for opinion of wealth, a widow of London."[5] "Peleus is perhaps Sir Matthew Arundell, the father of that

1. Jonson, *Epigrams,* 4.
2. Epigram 180.
3. Epigram 423.
4. *Ibid.*
5. *Nugae Antiquae,* 1804, II, 46, 151.

soldier of fortune, Thomas, first Lord Arundell of Wardour. "Lynus" may be Barnabe Barnes.[1] Although after more than three hundred years we may not always "know the secret drift" of Harington's intent, we may be sure that his satire was seldom misunderstood by those at whom it was directed.

No one will contend that Harington's epigrams have any great literary merit; that they are extremely interesting for the light that they throw upon the customs and manners of the time, no one can deny. Harington was well acquainted with the many-sided life of the age, he was witty, and he was skilful in the manipulation of phrase. He was, with the probable exception of Ben Jonson, the most important of Elizabethan epigrammatists. His epigrams are more thoroughly English and less classical in tone and matter than Jonson's. They were, furthermore, much earlier than Jonson's, and were more influential in establishing the vogue of the epigram in the Court circle.[2] They are, in every respect, superior to the feeble efforts of Bastard and Weever, and even to the better work of Sir John Davies and Guilpin. What they did to establish the English satirical epigram as a literary form, and what they did to popularize epigrammatic terseness and vigor of expression, are matters solely of conjecture. That Harington was considered one of the greatest wits of his day, and that his epigrams were widely read and admired both before and after publication, there is not the slightest doubt. That belated Elizabethan, Charles Lamb, searching for superlatives wherewith to praise some of Cole-

1. A detailed discussion of these conjectures may be found in the *Times Literary Supplement,* March 10, 1927 (G. C. Moore Smith), May 19, 1927 (N. E. McClure), July 14, 1927 (V. T. Harlow).

2. Harington's epigrams date from about 1585 to 1603. The dates are assigned, whenever possible, in the notes that follow the text. Several of his epigrams are included in the comments subjoined to each canto of his translation of *Orlando Furioso* (1591). The earliest mention of Harington's epigrams is made by Sir John Stradling, who addressed an epigram to him: "Ad D. *Io. Harington* Equ. doctiss. de quibusdam epigrammatis suis *Stradlingo* Equ. dono missis 1590." (*Epigrammatum Libri Quatuor,* 1607, p. 32.) Jonson's epigrams were entered S. R. in 1612 and published in 1616. Though he wrote of them as "the ripest" of his studies, it is evident that some of them were written several years earlier, but certainly not as early as Harington's.

ridge's epigrams, concluded triumphantly: "Take 'em all together, they are as good as Harington's."[1]

1. *The Letters of Charles and Mary Lamb,* ed. E. V. Lucas, 258.

Bibliography

I. A. Orlando | Fvrioso | in English | Heroical verse, By | *Iohn Harington,* [Richard Field, London, 1591].

Folio. Elaborate title-page engraved by Thomas Coxon. Forty-five full-page plates by an unknown engraver. As a preface Harington wrote his *Apologie of Poetrie,* which was reprinted in Joseph Haslewood's *Ancient Critical Essays,* London, 1811–1815, 2 vols., and in G. Gregory Smith's *Elizabethan Critical Essays,* Oxford, 1904, 2 vols.

B. Orlando | Furioso | in English | Heroical verse, By *Sir* | *Iohn Harington* | *of Bathe Knight.* Now | secondly imprinted the yeere. 1607. [Richard Field for John Norton and Simon Waterson.]

A line-for-line reprint of the edition of 1591.

C. Orlando | Furioso | in | English Heroical | verse. By | *Sir Iohn Harington* | of Bathe Knight. Now thirdly revised and | amended with the Addition | of the Authors Epigrams. | London printed by G. Miller | for J. Parker 1634.

A line-for-line reprint of the edition of 1607.

II. The Englishmans Doctor . . . 1607.

W. C. Hazlitt enumerates six editions: 1607, two in 1608, 1609, 1617, 1624. The Henry E. Huntington Library contains a copy of an edition printed in Edinburgh, 1613. The 1608 edition, printed for John Helme and John Busby, was reprinted by P. B. Hoeber, New York, 1920.

III. A. Epigrammes by Sir J. H. and others. . . .

Appended to "Alcilia, Philoparthens loving folly" by J. C., 1613. Printed by R. Hawkins.

B. Epigrams | Both | Pleasant and Seriovs, | Written by that All-worthy Knight, | Sir Iohn Harrington: | and neuer before Printed. | *Pro captu Lectoris habent sua fata libelli.* | [Device] | London | Imprinted for Iohn Budge, and are to be sold at his | shoppe at the South dore of Pauls, and | at Britaines Burse. | 1615.

4°. A-F4. Without pagination.

This edition contains 116 epigrams, all of which are included in the edition of 1618. All but seventeen of these (numbered, in the present edition, 16, 279, 284, 289, 301, 306, 308, 309, 310, 312, 315, 321, 322, 327, 342, 343, 346) are to be found in Harington's autograph in British Museum Addit. MS. 12049. One of these seventeen (Epigram 289), appears in Harington's autograph in Cambridge University Library Addit. MS. 337.

C. The | most elegant | and | witty epigrams | of Sir *Iohn Harrington, Knight,* | digested into fovre | Bookes: Three whereof neuer | *before published.* | Fama bonum quo non fœlicius vllum. | [Device] | London | Printed by G. P. for *Iohn Budge:* and are to be | sold at his shop in Paules Church-yard at the signe | of the *Greene Dragon.* 1618. |

8°. A3; B-M8; N1. Without pagination.
This edition contains 346 epigrams, of which 116 are included in the edition of 1615. The ninety-two epigrams that comprise Book Four of the edition of 1618 are included in the 1615 edition with the single exception of Epigram 92. Despite the different arrangement of the epigrams and various phraseological changes it is probable that the same manuscript or manuscripts were used by the printer. Of the 346 epigrams in the 1618 edition, 329 appear in Harington's autograph in British Museum Addit. MS. 12049, and two others in University Library Cambridge Addit. MS. 337.

D. The | Most Elegant | *and* | Witty Epigrams | of | Sir *Iohn Harrington, Knight.* | Digested into Fovre | *Bookes.* | Fama bonum quo non fœlicius vllum. | [Device] | London | Printed by *T. S.* for *Iohn Budge:* and are to be | sold at his shop in Paules Church-yard at the | *signe of the Greene Dragon,* | 1625.

8°. A-L8; M4. Without pagination. This edition is a hurried and careless resetting from the 1618 edition. It is page-for-page and line-for-line reprint, except (1) for variations in the title page and preliminary matter; (2) that the last line on M4 recto is printed as the first line on the corresponding page (N verso) of the 1618 edition; and (3) that the last epigram (Book IV, number 92) is omitted. There are ten mistakes in catchwords in the 1618 edition; six of these are corrected in the 1625 edition; four were left uncorrected in the 1625 edition; and three new errors were made. The 1618 edition made two errors in the numbering of the epigrams; in the 1625 edition these errors remain uncorrected and numerous others were made.

E. The | Most Elegant | and | Wittie Epigrams | of Sir Iohn Harington, Knight, | Digested into foure Bookes. | *Fama bonum quo non fœlicius ullum.* | [Device] | London, | Printed by George Miller. | MDCXXXIII.

Folio. Oo4—Ss2. In sixes.
This edition is appended to the 1634 edition of *Orlando Furioso* and the signatures are continued throughout. It is a careful reprint of the 1625 edition.

F. The Epigrams of Sir John Harington. Philadelphia, 1926. A reprint of the 1618 edition with eighty epigrams previously unpublished. Edited by N. E. McClure.

IV. A. A new discourse of a stale subject, called the Metamorphosis of Ajax written by Misacmos to his friend and cosin Philostilpnos. At London: Printed by Richard Field, dwelling in the Blackfriars 1596.

Edited by S. W. Singer, Chiswick Press, 1814, and Peter Warlock and Jack Lindsay, Fanfrolico Press, 1927.

B. The same with name of printer omitted.

C. The same with name of printer omitted.

V. An Anatomy of the Metamorphosed Ajax. Wherein by a tripartite method, is plainly, openly, and demonstratively declared, explained, and eliquidated, by pen, plot, and precept, how unsavory places can be made sweet, noisome places made wholesome, filthy places made cleanly. Published for the common benefit of builders, housekeepers, and house-owners. By T[homas] C[ombe] Traveller, apprentice in poetry, practiser in music, professor of painting; the mother, daughter, and handmaid of all the muses, arts, and sciences.

Printed with IV, B and C, with continuous signatures. Edited by S. W. Singer, Chiswick Press, 1814, and by Peter Warlock and Jack Lindsay, Fanfrolico Press, 1927.

VI. An Apologie; 1. Or rather a Retraction; 2. Or rather a Recantation; 3. Or rather a Recapitulation; 4. Or rather a Replication; 5. Or rather an Examination; 6. Or rather an Accusation; 7. Or rather an Explication; 8. Or rather an

Exhortation; 9. Or rather a Consideration; 10. Or rather a Confirmation; 11. Or rather all of them; 12. Or rather none of them.

Since it was published without title-page, and commences on signature A a, it was intended to be bound with IV and V. Edited by S. W. Singer, Chiswick Press, 1814.

VII. Ulysses upon Ajax. Written by Misodiaboles to his friend Philaretes. [Device]. At London: Printed for Thomas Gubbins. 1596.

There are two editions of the same date bearing the name of Thomas Gubbins as publisher, but differing in the number of pages, in the typographical arrangement, and a few other trifling particulars. This pamphlet is not by Harington, but often attributed to him. Edited by S. W. Singer, Chiswick Press, 1814.

VIII. A. A Briefe View of the State of the Church of England as it stood in Q. Elizabeth's and King James his Reigne to the yeere 1608; being a character and history of the bishops of those times, and may serve as an additional supply to Doctor Goodwin's Catalogue of Bishops, 1653.

Published by one of Harington's grandsons, John Chetwind.

B. Reprinted in *Nugae Antiquae,* edited by Henry Harington, Bath, 1779, 3 vols.

C. Reprinted, with corrections, in *Nugae Antiquae,* edited by Thomas Park, London, 1804, 2 vols. Harington's autograph copy (British Museum, Royal MSS. 17 B xxii) was used in preparing this edition.

IX. A. Nugae Antiquae: being a Miscellaneous Collection of Original papers in Prose and Verse: Written in the Reigns of Henry VIII. Queen Mary, Elizabeth, King James, &c. By Sir John Harington, the Translator of Ariosto, and others who lived in those Times. Selected from Authentic Remains. By the Rev. Hen. Harington. A.M. of Queen's College, Oxon. and Minor Canon of the Cathedral Church of Norwich. London and Bath, 1779, 3 vols.

A first volume appeared in 1769, without the editor's name; a second volume, issued in 1775, bore Henry Harington's name on the title-page.

B. Reprint of A, 1792.

C. Edited and revised by Thomas Park, London, 1804, 2 vols.

X. View of the State of Ireland in 1605.

Edited by W. D. Macray, Oxford, 1879. From MS. Rawlinson B. 162, part 1.

XI. A Tract on the Succession to the Crown (A.D. 1602). By Sir John Harington, Kt., of Kelston. Printed for the first time from a manuscript in the chapter library at York, and edited with notes and introduction by Clements R. Markham. Printed for the Roxburghe Club. London, 1880.

LETTERS

LETTERS

1

To Mistress Penn

[Eton, 1571]

Althoughe good Mistres Penn my longe silence maie make you suppose that I ame unmyndefull bothe of yow and also of your benefites yet trulye it is nothinge so. For I have often tymes since my commynge to Eaton purposed to wryte to you and now at the lengthe I have founde leysure to wryte theis letters whiche thoughe they be rude and unworthie of your sighte yet I truste you will accepte them as comminge from an humble and lovynge mynde. Many thinges you have at many tymes bestowed one me more I knowe then I can requyte but not more suerlye then I willingely beare in minde and entend alwaye hereafter to shew my selfe thankefull for. You promised that you woulde send me a letter when I was withe you laste: and I woulde gladly se it that I mighte have occasione to wryt to you agayne. I woulde verie gladlye here that Master Penn were in good heathe [*sic*]. Thus wishinge you with Master Penn great helthe and longe life I take my leave of you this 19 day of May anno 1571.

Youres to commaunde

Jhon Harringeton.

2

To Edward Dyer

[Cambridge, 1580]

There be two thinges, that if a man can attaine in his doinges he muste needes prosper: the one is that it be well mente; the other that it be well taken: the one a man maye provide for, the other he muste praye for, or else yf he want it, his good meaninge may have ill successe, and this plainly appeareth in my case, at this present, which if others would take as well as I mente, they should rather have cause to commend my discretion, then reason to rebuke my rashnes. As for my Tutors Lettres I knowe not what was in it, and it may be that he for the good affeccion, greate Love, and speciall care, he hath of me, would doubt the worste, feare the hardest, and write the moste. But if you knewe all the trewth, and nothinge but the trewth, and would bringe with you no prejudiciall opinion of the matter, I thincke you would not be in suche dyspaire of my well doinge as you seem to be. I doe assuredly promise that my dewtie, care, and obedience to him is and shalbe suche that whatsoever and howsoever I remaine, whether scholer in Cambridge, or student at the Inns of the Courte, whether marryed or unmarryed, whether in the Court or in the Countrye, whether in England, or beyonde the sea, his likinge shalbe my comfort, his will my warrant, his commandement my guide, and his displeasure my greatest greife and sorrowe. God never prosper me in any thinge I take in hand, yf I write not as I thincke, and doe not as I promyse. No no I have to many examples by which I may take heede of that which you mistruste. Since I went to Cambridge Sir John Byrons sonne and heire whose doinges I deteste, drawne by desire, ledd by luste, wone by wantonnes, undutifully, undiscreetly, unhonestly, without consente or counsell of Father or freind, to his owne shame, his freindes greife, the universities reproache, marryed or rather marred himselfe to a gentlewoman, unable eyther for wealth to maintaine him, or for freindes to defend him, or for bewtie to contente him: what becam of it? The deed was abomynable, the losse unrecoverable, the effecte lamentable, and the ende like to be myserable: for his father they saye hath quite caste him of and disherited him. Have I not a more nere and famyliar warninge then this was? I wishe I had not. But alas god forbidd that all that offend this way should be quite caste of. Youth is slippery, fleshe is fraile, Love is light, weddinge is destinye. But for my parte if I faulte . . . 1580

3

To Sir Francis Walsingham

[King's College, Cambridge, November 2, 1580]

Si magnitudini officii mei, par foret multitudo literarum mearum, credo, neque mihi facultas ac varietas ad scribendum, neque tibi aut voluntas ad legendum aut otium suppeteret. Verum existimo te, hominem omnium sapientissimum et amicissimum, non quoties scribam, sed quid proficiam cogitare, magisque a te meos progressus in literis, quam diligentiam in epistolis requiri. Quod cum ita esse sentiam (vir honoratissime) cum mihi gratulor, tum etiam tuo honori quantas possum maximas gratias habeo, quod me semper idoneum existimaveris, cujus vix mediocrem indolem, et approbatione, commendares, et consiliis augeres, et institutis conformares. Et quidem jus civile, tuis auspiciis magis quam meo privato consilio agressus sum, cujus studium ita jucundum, scientiam ita praestantem, usum vero ita necessarium esse perspicio, ut non minimum beneficium a te accipisse videar, cum mihi tam praeclari studii, tam illustris autor esses. Neque tamen hoc, etiamsi magnum est, solum est in quo mihi illuxit splendor benignitatis tuae. Nam et magister Goad, hujus Collegii, praepositus, vir magna gravitate ac pietate mihi, tuo maxime rogatu, in nullo humanitatis genere jamdiu defuit. Et adolescens summa nobilitate, egregia indole, eximia virtute Comes Essexius, me humanissime utitur, quod sane facit ille, partim suae naturae comitate, partim sedulitate officiorum meorum, sed multo maxime, quod intelligat me inter eos numerari, quorum tibi studia et salus curae sint. Quare res erit, ut mihi videtur, et honore tuo dignissima, et illi ornatissimo adolescenti acceptissima, et mihi tuo amantissimo supplici accommodatissima, si is intelligat, hanc ejus erga me humanitatem, tibi gratam esse. Vale Cantabrigia Regali Collegio. ii Novembris. 1580.

Honori tuo deditissimus

Joannes Harington.

4

To Lord Treasurer Burghley

[Kelston, 1595.]

My Worthie Lorde,

It affordethe me no small joye to hear by Master Bellot, whom good fortune did throw in my way at the Bathe, that your gouty disorder was growing to better humour. It is a plague, like the greedy parasite, the better fed the longer guest: but your lordship dothe not invite the stay of such friends by rich wines, or strong spices; yet, like many others, it will come to your door, which shutteth against none.

Your message to me for my budget of wit, is ill-timed. I am very busy, yet very idle; very well, yet very ill; very merry, yet very sad. Busy with my workmen, yet idle myself; I write nought but long bills: well in my body, but sick in my purse; merry to think my house well nigh done, and sad to say 'tis not well nigh paid for. In an old book of my father's I read a merrie verse, which, for lack of my own, I send by Master Bellot, to divert your lordshippe; when (as you say) weighty pain and weightier matters will yield to quips and merriment. This verse is called the *Blacke Sauntus,* or monkes hymne to *Saunte Satane,* made when Kynge Henry had spoylede their *synginge.* My father was wont to say, that Kynge Henry was used, in pleasante mood, to sing this verse; and my father (who had his good countenance, and a goodlie office in his courte, and also his goodlie Esther to wife) did sometyme receive the honour of hearing his own songe; for he made the tune which my man Combe hath sent herewith; having been much skilled in musicke, which was pleasing to the King, and which he learnt in the fellowship of good Maister Tallis, when a young man. Bishop Gardener woud not have liked him the better, had he known he was guilty of such jibes; which, perhaps, he had heard of too.

Our work at the Bathe dothe go on *haud passibus aequis:*— we sometime gallop with good presents, and then as soon stand still, for lack of good spurring: but it seemeth more like a church than it has aforetime, when a man could not pray without danger of having good St. Stephen's death, by the stones tumbling about our ears, and it were vain to pray for such enemies. But now, to pray for our friends may not be ill taken on earth, or in heaven. So may God give your lordship all comfort, ease, and health of body, till he shall (*O dies procul esto!*) receive your soul. If I every pray'd better for myself, I become a greater sinner by so much of a lie; for I never did, nor ever will. In all dutie, I reste

Your humble well-wisher,

John Harington.

Kelston, 1595.

5

To Lady Russell

[August 14, 1596].

Right Honorable and my speciall good Lady, having written not long since this fantasticall treatise, and putting yt to the print under a covert name. The first two leaves of yt (wherein is allmost nothing but all skurrill and toying matter) was show'd my Lord Treasorer, by my ill happ as I count yt, yf his goodnesse and honorable dispocition doe not the better interpret yt, which makes me now thus bould, to intreate your Honor, to send his Lordship the rest of it, which I have, before now, for the moste part of it read unto you. Humbly praying you, to delyver your favorable censure of it, at least so farr, that it is pleasaunt and harmeles.

And for the devyse yt selfe, I knowe my Lord would not leave yt, yf it weare at Tiballs, (as I say merely in the booke, the 118 page) for 1000^{li} and to doe his Lordship service, I will ryde thether, and enstruct his workemen to doe yt for lesse then a thowsand pence.

And that I may confesse trewly and franckly to you (my best Lady, that have even from my childehood ever so specially favord me) I was the willinger to wryte such a toye as this, because, I had layne me thought allmost buryed in the Contry these three or fowre yeere; and I thought this would give some occasion to have me thought of and talked of. Not as he that burned the Temple of Diana to make him famous; Nor as Absolon, that burned Joabs corne, to make him come to speech with him: But rather as Sophocles to save him self from a writt of dotage, showde the worke he was preasently in hand with.

I observe this, that in all common wealthes, the gowne and the sword rule all; and, that the Pen is above the sword, they that wear plumes above their hellmetts doe therein (though they know yt not) confesse according to the saying, *Caedant arma togae*. My Education hath bin suche, and I trust my Limmes and sperit both are suche as neither shalbe, defectyve to the service of my Prince and Contry, whether it be with wryting or weapon; only my desyre is my service may be accepted, and I doubt not, but yt shalbe acceptable; to the which, his Lordships good conceyt of me, I count would be a good stepp, and to that good conceyt your Honors commendacion, I perswade me would be a good meanes. So I humbly take my leave this xiiiith of August.

Yowr honors most bownde

John Haryngton.

6

To Sir William Dethick

[June 14, 1597]

Master Garter. I have dellt effectually with Master Clarencieux, who hathe taken some payns in serching the pedegrews and hath fownd in the ryght lyne from Nicholas Harington to James harington Dean of Yorke matches of Nevell of Egremont and others, whearby he thinketh that not only by the adoption of my Cosen Stephen (which he seemeth to make no great accownt of) and by the testemony of my fathers patent of Armes witnessing him of the howse of Bryerleghe, and owr last patent from her Majestie that geves us the right to the Haringtons land, I say Master Clarentieux thinketh that thear may with yowr consent some other coat bee added to this I now geve, and this with some lesse difference or none at all.

I pray yow conferre with him in frendly sort as yow may, and grow to some agreement between yow in the matter, and yf yow will delyver to this bearer a drawght in color of that yow shall agree uppon, with the forme of the new grawnt I showld bee very well satisfyed in my mynde and yow shold bee bothe I truste to your lykyngs presently recompensed and yf god make mee better able heerafter eyther by recovering some of this land or any other preferment I will not bee unmyndefull of yowr cowrtesyes and payns heerin and so I comit yow to god this xxiiii[th] of June 1597.

Your very loving Frend

John Haryngton.

7

To Sir Hugh Portman

[May or June, 1598.]

My good Friend,

I have been to visit at the house which my Lord Treasurer dothe occupy at the Bathe, and found him and another cripple together, my cosen Sir John Harington, of Exton; when it greeved me to see so much discretion, wisdom, and learning in peril of death. My lord doth seem dead on one side, and my cosen on the other, though both in their health were ever *on one side*. It gave me some comfort to hear their religious discourse, and how each did despise his own malady and hold death in derision, because both did not despair of life eternal. The Treasurer asked me if I had any ailment, and smiled to see me look gravely at their serious talk. I wished them all benefit, and that the waters might wash away all their deadness, save that to iniquity, which would still hold them both unto death. My cosen said, "you are not dead to good works, for even now this churche doth witness of your labour to restore it to its ancient beauty." In good sooth, we want good men who build unto the Lord to forward this work; and many indeed have passed assurance of such helpe. Her Highness doth much lament her good servants malady; my Lady Arundel came with earnest suit from court, touching the treasurer's state, and did bring an excellent cordial for his stomach, which the Queene did give her in charge; and said, "that she did intreat heav'n daily for his longer life:—else would her people, nay herself, stand in need of cordials too." If I may venture thus much, it seemeth as though this good man had little else to do on earth than die.

I have not got what you do so much covet from me, nor can I hitherto obtain an audience from the bishop on such account; but you shall hear further in good time, as my own business doth yet stand unmoved, and giveth me matter of disquiet. The Lord Treasurer's distemper doth marvelously trouble the Queen, who saith, "that her comfort hath been in her people's happiness, and their happiness in his discretion:" neither can we find, in ancient record, such wisdom in a Prince to discern a servant's ability, nor such integrity to reward and honour a Prince's choice—*Quando ullum inveniat parem?* I reste in good hope of seeing your lady, and such branches of olive as may adorn your table, before Christmas next; and may they bring you more peace than the branches which adorn your neighbour Hatton's brows; but—*levius sit patientia, et conjugem corrigere est nefas.*

John Harington.

What other news doth happen I will bear with me at my coming.

8

To Sir Anthony Standen

Athlone, in Ireland, 1599.

I dowt not but many pens and tongues utter, after many fashions, the report of our late unfortunate journey, but yet I thought it not amiss to write you this breif narration of it; which I may say, *quaeque ipse miserrima vidi, et quorum pars una fui.* On Sunday last the governor marched with one and twenty companies, or colours, (for indeed some of them were but mere colours of companies, having sixty for a hundred and fifty,) from Tulske, eight miles beyonde Roscommon, to the abbey of Boyly, some fourteen miles; and hearing belike that the enemy was but weak in the Curlews, and that they expected not his coming; (because captain Cosby the very day before came from Boyly towards Roscommon:) on this account the governor, God bless him, resolved to possess the Pare that nyght, being two miles from the abbey. This was against the minds of most of the captains: the soldiers being weary and fasting, insomuch that they spake for meat ere they went up, but the governor promist them that they should have beef enough at nyght, and so drew them on: but many, God wot, lost their stomachs before supper. The order was this:—captain Lister led the forlorn hope; Sir Alexander Ratcliff and his regiment had the vauntguard; my Lord of Dublin led the battle; Sir Arthur Savage, the rear; the horse were appointed to stand in a little pasture at the foot of the hill, to the intent that, when the Pare had been cleared, they might have come up. After our men had gone up the hill and entered part of the Pare, the rebels begun to play upon them from a barracado that they had made; but our men soon beat them from it, and Sir Alexander Radcliff very bravely beat them out of a thin wood into a bog on the left side of the Pare; and we who stood at the foot of the hill might see them, and all men thought the Pare had been ours. But after the skirmish had lasted an hour and half very hot, and our shot had expended all our powder; the vantguard wheeled about in such a fashion, that, what with that, and some strange and causless fear, that fell upon our men, the vant-guard fell into the battayle; and in conclusion all fell in rout, and no man could stay them. The governor himself, labouring to turne them, lost his breath, his voice, his strength, and last of all, his life; or, which is worse, in the rebels hands, and none could force him off. How it can be answered at home by such as it concerned most I know not, but so vile and base a part I think was never played among so many men, that have been thought of some desert. But now, the horse standing at the foot of the hill, and seeing through the woods and glades some disorder, though not suspecting so ill as it was, charged up the hill another way that lay on the left: if it may be called a way, that had stones in it six or seven feet broad, lying above ground, and plashes of bogs between them. But with this charge we made the enemy retire; whereby all the foot and colours came off; but we bought this small reputation (if so it will be taken) very dearly, for our own commander of the horse had his arm broken with a shot, and had another shot through his clothes, and some seven or eight horse more killed and several proper men. Captain Jephson was next to Sir Griffith Markham in the head of Lord Southampton's troops, and charged very gallantly. I would not for all the land I have, but I had been well hors'd. I verily think the idle faith which possesses the Irishry, concerning magic and witchcraft, seized our men and lost the victory. For when my cozen Sir H. Harington, in a treacherous parley with Rorie Ogie, a notable rebel, was taken and conveyed to his habitation a prisoner; his friends not complying with the terms offerd for his ransom, sent a large band to his rescue, which the rebel seeing to surround his house, rose in his shirt, and gave Sir Henry fourteen grievous wounds, then made his way through the whole band and escaped, notwithstanding his walls were only mud. Such was their panick, as verily thinking he effected all by dint of witchery, and had by magic compell'd them not to touch him. And this belief doth much daunt our soldiers when they come to deal with the Irishry, as I can well perceive from their discourse. You will hear more from other captains of further advances:

So I reste, to all commande,

John Harington.

9

To Master Thomas Combe

[Ireland, August 31, 1599].

Good Thomas, I have received sundry letters from you, and namely the last dated August 24th, which came not to my hands till the xxxth of September, whereby it seems the messenger made slow speed, and who it was I know not; and therefore, as I have directed others, so I wish you to name in your letters, if you may, by whom you send them, that they may receive thanks or blame, according to their care and speed. In sundry of your letters, I have received good advertisement and honest counsels, and great good wishes, all which I take in good part; to satisfy you in part of my being here, and what I have seen, and how I have sped (for I find you hear variable reports) you shall understand, that, since my Lord Lieutenant came into Ireland, the forces being divided as occasion required; some into Munster, some to Lesly, many into the North, and a few into Connoght; it was partly my hap, and partly my choice, for Sir Griffin Markhams sake, and three Markhams more, to go into Connoght; where I spent some weeks about Aloane, Ballinglow, Clanrickard, Galloway, and lastly, Roscommon, the place then appointed for garrison. This while I saw many things, and some well worth the observing, both for war and peace; and notwithstanding all the dangerous passages through paves, (as they call those woods, which are full of rebels), and through divers fordes, which are likewise places of great disadvantage, yet we passed through all with small losse; notwithstanding, I say, the attempts and ambushes of fiery Machue, of Connor Roe, of the Obrians, of some of the Bourks, and other the rebels, such as the Jaytes, and O'Maddins, and many mad knaves beside. And this while my Lord Lieutenant went through Munster as far as Asketon, and was sometimes fought with upon places of advantage, but without any great loss on either side. Neither in all that journey was any thing done greatly worth speaking of, but the taking of Cathyre, and one or two castles beside.

After this, the next journey was to O'phaley, where Sir Cunynes Clyfford, the Governor of Connought, met my Lord, and Sir Griffin Markham, and six of the best gentlemen of his troop came with him, and served bravely on foot; for no horse could passe the way they came: they burned and spoiled a country called Ferrallie, and won a castle of Terryllies, one of the shrewdest rebels of Ireland, and his companies did no lesse; so that all the countrey was on fire at once, and our comming was so unlook'd for, that in the towns where we came, the rebels had not leisure to carry away their young children, much lesse their corn and other stuff. In all this journey I was comerade to the Earl of Kildare, and slept both on one pillow every night for the most part; here, at the parting, my Lord gave Sir Griffin Markham great commendations, and made him colonel and commander of all the horse in Connoght; and gave me and some others the honour of knighthood in the field: and so, my honest Thomas, with honour, conquest, and content, we returned again into Connoght. But see the changes and chances of warr.—The Governor woud needs undertake a journey to Sligo, with twenty-one weak companies, that were not 1400 strong; and a less proportion of horse than had been requisite for such a purpose; and yet, out of his too much haste and courage, after two long days march, with small rest, and less repast, he would needs draws his men to set upon the enemy in a place of great disadvantage, called the Curlews; where, though the enemy was at first repulsed, yet at last their numbers encreasing, and our munition failing, or some secret cause, that we know not, dismaying the footmen, they fell all in rout: the Governor and Sir Alexander Radcliffe were slain 'ere they coud come to their rescue. Some of our horse gave a desperate charge upon the hill, among rocks and bogs, where never horse was seen to charge before; it is verily thought they had all been cut in peices, at least lost all their colours; so that, if reputation were to be challenged when so great loss accompanied it, we might take upon us to have won some honour; having, as Sir Henry Davers did pleasantly write to Sir Griffin Markham, "not Roman citizens, but rascal soldiers, who, so their commanders had been saved, had been worthy to have been half hanged for their rascal cowardliness." Neither was this good service of ours unpaid for:—beside the loss of two or three good horses, and better men, Sir Griffin Markham was shot through the arm with a musket; and though he bare the hurt admirable well, for a day or two, and especially at the instant, yet ever since he hath kept his bed of it; and hath been in danger of his arm by the hurt, and of his life by an ague: but now he is, I hope, out of danger of both, and safe at Dublin. Myself (after I had conducted him in a horse-litter safe beyond danger of the rebels, within eight miles of Dublin,) went to Trim, the place appointed for our garrison; and from thence have visited Navan and Arbrachan, where my Lord Lieutenant lay yesterday, and the day before, and meant to go from thence to the Brennys; but most men think, by means the weather falls out so monstrous wet as the like hath not been seen, that he will not go far north.

I lye here at Master Robert Hammon's house, who is this year port-reeve of Trim, as much in effect as mayor. He shows the greatest gratitude to me, and to all my friends for my sake; that to my remembrance I can say no man hath done more. Yet was he not beholden to my father for one foot of his living, but only for his breeding. I recommend this example the rather unto you, because I would have you follow it, as far as your ability and opportunity will give leave.

Now you see by the course of this letter, that I have reason to thank God very greatly, that among so many as have been hurt and slain, where I have been, and some shot even in the very same ranks I was of, I have escaped all this while without bodily hurt. I protest there is much rather great cause to thank God, who hath kept me so long in bodily health at Roscommon, where not so few as sixty died within the walls of the castle, in which we lay; and some as lusty men as any came out of England. In the camp, where drinking water, and milk, and vinegar, and aqua vitae, and eating raw beef at midnight, and lying upon wet green corn oftimes, and lying in boots, with heats and colds, made many sick; yet myself (in a good hour be it spoken and a better heard) was never sick; neither in the camp nor the castle, at sea or on land. Besides all this, to vaunt myself at large, to you; I have informed myself reasonably well of the whole state of the country, by observation and conference; so that I count the knowledge I have gotten here worth more than half the three hundred pounds this jorney hath cost me: and as to warr, joyning the practise to the theory, and reading the book you so prays'd, and other books of Sir Griffin Markham's, with his conference and instructions, I hope at my coming home to talk of counterscarpes, and cazamats, with any of our captains.

The Irish lords, gentry, yea, and citizens, where I come, I have found so apt to offer me kindness, so desirous of my acquaintance, that my friends think it a presage of a fortune I might rise to in this kingdom; though myself do little affect it, and much less hope to effect it. My "Ariosto" has been entertained into Gallway before I came. When I got thither, a great lady, a young lady, and a fair lady, read herself asleep, nay dead, with a tale of it; the verse, I think, so lively figured her fortune: for, as Olympia was forsaken by the ungrateful Byreno, so had this lady been left by her unkind Sir Calisthenes; whose hard dealing with her cannot be excused, no not by Demosthenes.

Lastly, (which perhaps will seem strange to you, and was very grateful to me,) three sons of my cousin Robert Markhams of Cottam, whom you know the world mistook to have been wronged by me, and consequently deeply offended at me, have in their several kinds and places offerd me such courtesies, kindnesses, nay, such services, as if they held me for one of their best friends in Ireland.

Thus, gentle Thomas, I have, in recompence of your long letters, enlarged the discourse of my Irish affairs; but I must not forget nor cease to tell her Majestie's good, wise, and gracious providings for us, her captains, and our soldiers, in summer heats and winter colds, in hunger and thirst, for our backs and our bellies: that is to say, every captain of an hundred footmen doth receive weekly, upon every Saturday, his full entertainment of twenty-eight shillings. In like case, every lieutenant fourteen shillings; an ensign, seven shillings; our sergeant, surgeon, drum, and fife, five shillings pay, by way of imprest; and every common soldier, three shillings; deliverd to all by the pole weekly. To the four last lower officers, two shillings weekly; and for every common soldier, twenty pence weekly, is to be answerd to the full value thereof, in good apparel of different kinds, part for winter, and part for summer, which is orderd of good quality and stuff for the prices; patterns whereof must be sent to the Lord Deputy to be compared and prepared as followeth.

Apparel for an officer in winter.

A cassock of broad cloth with bays, and trimmed with silk lace, 27 shillings and 7 pence.

A doublet of canvass with silk buttons, and lined with white linnen, 14 shillings and 5 pence.

Two shirts and two bands, 9 shillings and 6 pence.

Three pair of kersey stockings, at 2 shillings and 4 pence a pair, 7 shillings.

Three pair of shoes of neats leather, at 2 shillings and 4 pence per pair, 7 shillings.

One pair of Venetians, of broad Kentish cloth, with silver lace, 15 shillings and 4 pence.

In Summer.

Two shirts and bands, 9 shillings 6 pence.

Two pair of shoes, 4 shillings 8 pence.

One pair of stockings, 2 shillings 8 pence.

A felt hat and band, 5 shillings 5 pence.

Apparel for a common soldier in winter.

A cassock of Kentish broad cloth, lined with cotton, and trimmed with buttons and loops, 17 shillings 6 pence.

A doublet of canvass with white linnen lining, 12 shillings 6 pence.

A hat cap coloured, seven shillings.
Two shirts of Osnabridge holland and bands, 8 shillings.
Three pair of neats leather shoes, 2 shillings, 4 pence each, 7 shillings.
Three pair kersy stockings, 8 shillings.
One pair Venetians, of Kentish broad cloth, with buttons, loops, and lining of linnen, thirteen shillings, 4 pence.

In Summer.

Two shirts of Osnabridge and 2 falling Holland bands, 7 shillings.
Two pair neats leather shoes, 4 shillings, 8 pence.
One pair of stockings, 2 shillings, 8 pence.
A hat cap coloured, 3 shillings.

Thus, friend Thomas, her Majesty, with wonted grace hath graced our bodies, and may heav'ns grace cloath her in everlasting robes of righteousness, and "on earth peace" to her who alway sheweth "good will toward all men."

So resteth thy loving Master,

John Harington.

10

To Justice Carey

[Ireland, October, 1599].

Having expected shipping till the 8th of this month [October], and meeting with none convenient, (in respect that all were taken up with sick souldiers, or with my Lord Lieutenant's horses,) I was desirous to make some use of the time that I should stay here, and therefore was easily persuaded to go with Sir William Warren, my kind friend, with whom I had been formerly acquainted in England, and to see some part of the realme northward, and the arch-rebel himself, with whom Sir William was to treat.

But staying at Dundalk till the 15th of this month, and no

news certain of the earl's coming, I went to see the Newry, and from thence to Darlingford by the narrow water, and was hindred by waters that I could not come back to Sir William Warren before his first meeting with the Earl Tyrone, which was on the 17th day; what time how far they proceeded I know not, but it appeard that the earl was left in good dysposition, because he kept his hour so well, the next morning: and, as I found after, Sir William had told him of me, and given such a report of me above my desert, that next day, when I came, the earl used far greater respect to me than I expected; and began debasing his own manner of hard life, comparing himself to wolves, that fill their bellies sometime, and fast as long for it; then excused himself to me that he could no better call to mind myself, and some of my friends that had done him some courtesy in England; and been oft in his company at my Lord of Ormond's; saying, these troubles had made him forget almost all his friends.

After this he fell to private communication with Sir William, to the effecting of the matters begun the day before; to which I thought it not fit to intrude myself, but took occasion the while to entertain his two sons, by posing them in their learning, and their tutors, which were one Fryar Nangle, a Franciscan; and a younger scholer, whose name I know not; and finding the two children of good towardly spirit, their age between thirteen and fifteen, in English cloths like a nobleman's sons; with velvet gerkins and gold lace; of a good chearful aspect, freckle-faced, not tall of stature, but strong, and well set; both of them [learning] the English tongue; I gave them (not without the advice of Sir William Warren) my English translation of "Ariosto," which I got at Dublin; which their teachers took very thankfully, and soon after shewed it the earl, who call'd to see it openly, and would needs hear some part of it read. I turn'd (as it had been by chance) to the beginning of the 45th canto, and some other passages of the book, which he seemed to like so well, that he solemnly swore his boys should read all the book over to him.

Then they fell to communication again, and, (calling me to him) the earl said, that I should witness, and tell my Lord Lieutenant, how, against all his confederates wills, Sir William had drawn him to a longer cessation, which he would never have agreed to, but in confidence of my lord's honourable dealing with him; for, saith he, "now is my harvest time, now have my men their six weeks pay afore-hand, that they have nothing to do but fight; and if I omit this opportunity, and you shall prepare to invade me the mean time, I may be condemned for a fool."

Also one pretty thing I noted, that the paper being drawn for him to sign, and his signing it with O'Neal, Sir William (though with very great difficulty) made him to new write it, and subscribe, Hugh Tyrone. Then we broke our fasts with him, and at his meat he was very merry, and it was my hap to thwart one of his priests in an argument, to which he gave reasonable good ear, and some approbation. He drank to my lord's health, and bade me tell him he loved him, and acknowledgd this cessation had been very honourably kept. He made likewise a solemn protestation that he was not ambitious, but sought only safety of his life, and freedom of his conscience, without which he would not live, though the Queen would give him Ireland.

Then he asked of Sir Henry Harington, and said he heard he had much wrong, to have an imputation of want of courage, for the last defeat at Arkloo; protesting, that himself had known Sir Henry serve as valiantly as ever any man did, naming the time, place, and persons, all known to Sir William Warren.

Other pleasant and idle tales were needless and impertinent, or to describe his fern table and fern forms, spread under the stately canopy of heaven. His guard, for the most part, were beardless boys without shirts; who, in the frost, wade as familiarly through rivers as water-spaniels. With what charm such a master makes them love him I know not, but if he bid come, they come; if go, they do go; if he say do this, they do it. He makes apparent show to be inclinable to peace; and some of his nearest followers have it buzzed amongst them, that some league of England, with Spain or Scotland, or I know not where, may endanger them. But himself, no doubt, waits only to hear what my Lord Lieutenant intends, and according to that will bend his course.

Fryar Nangle swears all oaths, that he will do all the good he can, and that he is guiltless of the heinous crimes he is indited of; for, if he had his pardon, perhaps there might be made good use of him.

This is all I remember any way worthy the writing to you, not doubting but Sir William Warren, that had the sole charge of this business, will give you much better account of the weightier affairs than I, that only went to see their manner of parting.

I remain, in much duty,

John Harington.

11

To Sir Anthony Standen

[Kelston, February 20, 1600].

Sir,

It is not a lake of Lethe, that makes us forget our friends, but it is the lack of good messengers; for who will write, when his letters shall be opened by the way, and construed at pleasure, or rather displeasure?—Some used this in Ireland, that perhaps have repented it since in England. I came to court in the very heat and height of all displeasures: after I had been there but an hour, I was threatened with the Fleet; I answered poetically, "that coming so late from the land-service, I hoped that I should not be prest to serve in her Majesty's fleet in Fleet-street." After three days every man wondered to see me at liberty; but though, in conscience, there was neither rhyme nor reason to punish me for going to see Tyrone; yet if my rhyme had not been better liked of then my reason, (I mean when I gave the young Baron of Dungannon an Ariosto,) I think I had lain by the heels for it. But I had this good fortune, that, after four or five days, the Queen had talked of me, and twice talked to me, though very briefly. At last she gave me a full and gracious audience in the withdrawing chamber at Whitehall, where herself being accuser, judge, and witness, I was cleared, and graciously dismissed. What should I say! I seemed to myself, for the time, like St. Paul, rapt up in the third heaven, where he heard wordes not to be uttered by men; for neither must I utter what I then heard: until I come to heaven, I shall never come before a statelier judge again, nor one that can temper majesty, wisdom, learning, choler, and favour, better than her Highness did at that time. In the discourse you were not unspoken of her. You shall hear ere long, but not by writing, for I will send a man. Thus much I adventure to write by this boy; but I trust him with no messages. I omitted no opportunity of mentioning and gracing, the best I could, all my friends while I staid at London. In December I came hither, but since, I hear little and do nothing but sit by a good fire, and feed my lean horses, and hearken for good news, but hear none, save the certain expectation of peace with Spain.

My Lord Keeper is a widdower. Doctor *Eaton* hath *eaten* the bishoprick of Ely; all the clergy wish him choaked with it. Master Edmondes hath been with the Dutchess of Burgundy, and well used; and she speaketh much honour of the Queen, which moves great hope of the league. You wonder I write nothing of *one:*—believe me I hear nothing; but *he* is where he was, and I think must be, till these great businesses be concluded. Let this suffice from a private country knight, that lives among clouted shoes, in his frize jacket and galloshes, and who envies not the great commanders of Ireland, but hereby commends himself to them.

Your true friend,

John Harington.

Kelston, near Bath,
Feb. 20, 1600.

12

To Sir Robert Cecil

[Greenwich, June 25, 1600.]

Ryght honorable

Thowghe the greatest part of wisdom I can challenge to my selfe, ys but to bee a dilligent observer of the wisdome of others, and the cheefe knowledge I hav' attayned, ys but to know that I know litle, yet owt of my trewe zeale to her majesties sarvyce, I presume, in a matter now in hand, to present to your honorable consyderacion, my slender reasons, thowgh suddenly yet perhaps not unsowndly conceaved, for differring and yf yt shall so seem good, for dyvertinge the cowrse entended, for the proclamacion abowt knights, and yf I fortune to be mistaken, as one that doe but grope in the darke, and see, but somtymes, by other mens lyghts; yet to encorage mee, I learnd last day this lesson. *Et quod patet, et quod latet, amor implet.*

I thinke thear are few witts so dull, and no herts so undewtifull, but doe both see and acknowledge, how Royally her Majestie hath hetherto proceeded, concerning all the last yeers errors in Ierland; with soche an admirable temper of high magnanimitye with princely clemency, of fyrme resolucion with moste mylde prosecution, that all must confesse, no one thing to have been donne or guyded, *ab impetu, a perturbacione, ab iracundia,* but *ex judicio ex ratione* and *pro imperio et statu* (for with whose words can I better expresse yt, then with those that promised, nay rather prophecyed thease deeds?)

Now thear ys a secret brute muttered amongst many, that all the knights knighted in Awgust and synce, shalbee publyshed in her Majesties name to bee no knights. (I name the tyme, becawse yowr honor shall see thearby I speake free from passyon for my selfe, thowghe not without compassyon of others). Yf yt wear a thing past, obedyence showld make mee sylent, but beinge (as I wysh yt ever may bee,) to come, I may speake with pardon, thowgh not with applawse. Yowr honor remembers I thinke that I once used this comparyson, that knighthood doth impresse a character of honor in to evry parson, how mean so ever, as babtisme dothe a marke of Christianitye. I will not stand longe uppon this poynt, yet becawse yt ys a cheefe poynt, I will be so bolde thus sleyghtly to poynt at yt.

I have read that Saint Ambrose being a chylde, and babtysinge the chyld of a Jew, as yt wear in play with water that ranne in the street, and using withall the word *Ego te Babtizo, etc.* That reverent Churche pronownced the Chylde to be babtysed, and by no means wold permit him to bee rebabtised. I have herd that kinge Edward, knighting a boy in sport, that asked him how knights wear made, and a man by error, taking him for an other that was recommended, yet the Harrolds affyrmd them both to bee knights, soche vertue hath water and the word in the sacrament of owr sowls, soch forse hath the Royall sword and the word, for the sacred dignitye of knighthood, for thowgh a small error in the Princes patent may frustrat the seale, yet this manyfest error in the pattent of honor cannot frustrat the sword. And yt seems to hold with good reason, for yf the sword by error shold cut of a wrong hed yt can never bee set on agayn, so yf yt lay honor by lyke error, on an unfitte showlder, it cannot bee taken of agayn. And thowgh I do in this argue but *a Simili,* yet yf leysure wold permit mee I cold bring arguments *a fortiore* and *a Tutiore,* why this cowrse at this tyme ys exceeding unconvenient to bee taken.

The lyke was expected in November last, and yf it must bee donne, had been better to have been then donne, by how moche a man ys lesse greeved to be disposessed of a howse, whear hee hath layn but a weeke then whear he hath setled many months. Evn then did I heer your honor, and the moste noble Lord Admyrall marvellowsly commended for contesting agaynst that dawngerows example, which, yf I know any thinge, ys now more dawngerous. I wold bee affrayd to wryte thus, yf a greater fear expelld not the lesse, thowgh no fear shall ever let mee for speaking the trewth and doing my dewty humbly beseechinge your honor evn with my sowle, to continew your honorable endever yet, whyle yt may bee donne, to stay this proclamacion, which (to omitte many more seriows consyderacions,) will be accompanyed with the secreat and most bitter curses of dyvers and some very fayr Ladyes, who are not yet so good philosophers as to neglect honor, and embrace paciens, or at least, to have a *proviso,* that the ladyes may still hold theyr places, and so moste humbly I take my leave this 25 of June from Greenwitch.

Your honors at comawndment,

John Haryngton.

13

To Sir Robert Cecil

[July 3, 1600.]

Ryght honorable.

I was very lately charged, by a noble parson, before as noble a person, and from a great Lady, to have been the informer to her Majestie of the names and number of those knights, that wear made after the 4th of awgust as thowgh I had, only uppon my memory presumed to set down the certayn tyme when they wear made. I doe not often boste of my memory, to remember more then others can remember, I cold rather boste that I can forget that which few use to forget (I mean a shrewd turne). But to discharge mee of that suspicion that some mens malles or at least misconstruccion, hath sowght to lay uppon mee, I have acquaynted the two great Lords (I mean the Erls of Northumberland and Rutland,) how earnestly I had dealt with yowr honor, and how very honorably yow dellt with us all in that matter, and for theyr pryvat satisfaccion I have undertaken to show them, both the note I gave yowr honor, and the letter I wrote to yowr honor in that busynesse, which yf yt might please yow to favor mee so moche, to let mee have, I wear moche bownd to yowr honor thearfore, and so moste humbly take my leave the third of July 1600.

Yowr honors at commawndment

John Haryngton.

14

To ———

[1600]

I sent Letters by a messenger that Master Rydman appoynted, and thearin certefyed your Honour how Nevell my adversaries man by Advyce of Judge Walmsley came to me; Master Nevel I fynde very forward to offer his Servyce in hope of some greate rewarde to persuade his Master to part with the Reversion of Brierley to me and my heyrs, and to bring it to some speedy Arbiterment.

But I must not admytt neyther the Judge nor any manne an Arbitrator in the matter. Now thearfore to hasten the busyness the more, or to bring it to Tryal, I have taken owt process for (W. Drugg) of whose Howse I sealed a Lease, and have also procured the Shreeves warrant with a Blank to put in what special Baylies we lyst to serve him, that yt may be speedyly retorned into the Kings Bench. They tell me we may have a Tryal in Lent next and that I reste at your honours Commande

John Haryngton.

15

To Sir John Stanhope

[November 20, 1600].

Right Honourable

Master Rydman hathe imparted to me as far as I have been hereupon Confydent, to make an offer of money to her majestie, thowgh my Council are not very forward to advise it, which they count too hazardous a Course; But that your Honour may not doubt that I will be as trew to you as to myself, I doe in that and will in all thinges else follow your Honours Dyrections and I hope to be able to certyfy you shortly how well it succeeds.

I have procured Master Rydman to recommend the furderawnce of my busyness in general Terms to some of your Honours good Friends here, and I shall humbly pray your Honour when you wryte to any of them to second the same, and concerning my Cowrse of proceedings with Master C. T. Master Cuthbert —— Surveyor now of the Cowrt of Wardes and one sometyme of Master Talbots Cownsel, hath offered to deal with him to make composytion with me, in that very forme as your Honour wrytes of to Master Rydman. It will be tedyous and obscure to delyver all the particular parts of my proceedings in these matters, but all ys and shall bee to this effect to bring Brierly to be yours in Yorkshire for a reasonable pryce.

I will make Master Rydman able, at his coming down, to enforme you of all Circumstances, so I humbly take leave.

16

To ———

[December 8, 1600].

Most honourable and my specyal good Lady

Suche news as are here I have wrytten to my Lord, and such as I wryte not I suppose the bearer will supply, for my matter in which your —— to serve me must be my Sheet Anker. I am in good hope that I shall have the Feesimple for 1000 li. which I have adventured to offer upon your Honourable word, which I protest I count more —— than the Lord Mayor of London's bonde. Before it came to sealinge I purpost to have Advyce of some of your Council which you shall Appoynt for the passinge of it, and I doubt not but those means will be found that shall be lawful to deal in yt without fear of —— or —— so for this tyme I humbly take leave praying your Ladyship to be assured that you shall never find me dishonest but ever thankfull and always at your Servyce.

John Haryngton.

17

To ———

[1600]

Sir

Of a Tedyous and Dangerous and Chargeable Jorney I have

yet made this use, I have entered into the Haringtons Lands and by help of those gracious Letters you procured me in her Majesties name, I did it with less Peryl, though in one place I had lyke to have been beaten.

If I make anything at all of the Tytle I must acknowledge yt only of her Majesties goodness that first gave yt my Father, and now by this her Favor continues it to me. And I heartily desyer and vow to spend yt wholly in her Majesties servyce, and —— for the present howsoever Dyvers great Lawyers and judges deem yt a broken and discontinued Tytle and —— but for my sturring in yt, yt had been perpetually concealed from the Crown, as well as yt ys detayned from the Ryght Heyre. Yet I will adventure to give her Majestie 500 li. in money, and some prety Jewel or garment, as you shall advyse, only praying her Majestie will be pleased to refer the consyderation of this my offer to some one or Two of her Majesties Council for Expedition which I pray you find some good Tyme to move in it.

18

To Lady Jane Rogers

[December 19, 1600.]

To the right vertuous and his kynde Mother in law, the Ladie Jane Rogers.

Madam I have sent you my long promisd Orlando, and that it maie properly belonge to you and your heire femall, I have added to it as manie of the toyes I have formerly written to you and your daughter, as I could collect out of my scatterd papers; supposing (though you have seene some of them long since) yet now to revew them againe, and remember the kynde, and sometime the unkynde occasions, on which some of them were written, will not be unpleasant, and because there was spare roome, I have added a few others that were showd to our Soveraigne Lady, and some, that I durst never show any Ladie, but you two. And so wishing you to lock me up as safe in your love, as I know you will lay up this booke safe in your Chest I commend me to you.

19 December
1600

Your sonne in law and in Love
John Haryngton.

19

To the Countess of Bedford

[December 19, 1600.]

To the trulie Noble and right vertuous Ladie, Lucie Countess of Bedford.

Right Honorable, and my most honored good Ladie, I have sent you heere the devine, and trulie devine translation of three of Davids psalmes, donne by that Excellent Countesse, and in Poesie the mirrois of our Age; whom, as you are neere unto in blood, of lyke degree in Honor; not unlyke in favore; so I suppose none coms more neere hir then your self in those, now rare, and admirable guifts of the mynde, that clothe Nobilitie with vertue.

I have presumed to fill up the emptie paper with som shallowe meditations of myne owne; not to conjoyne theis with them; for that were to piece sattin with sack-cloth, or patch leade upon golde; much lesse to compare them; that are but as foyle to a dyamond; but as it were to attend them. So as being bothe of meaner matter, and lighter manner, yett maie serve to waite as a wanton page is admitted to beare a torche to a chaste matrone. But as your cleare-sighted judgement shall accept or praise them, I shall hereafter be embouldned to present more of them, and to entytle som of them to your Honorable name, unto which I vowe to rest an ever much devoted servant.

Jhon Haryngton.
19 December 1600.

20

To Sir Robert Cecil

[January 31, 1600/1601.]

Ryght honorable.

I was gevn to understand by Sir John Stanhop, both that I ame bownd to yow in generall for yowr good opinion, and particulerly, that uppon the deceasse of Dr. James, yowr honor did name mee as one yow thowght fit to bee a reeder to her Majestie. Also I must not bee unmyndfull of yowr favorable letters yow wrate for mee when I went to the North, to Master Attorney of the Wards who thearuppon hath been exceeding redy ever since to do mee pleasure, and moch strengthneth my hope of good successe in that busynes.

For thease favors my best requytall I can yet yeeld, ys trewly to honor yow, and to make all those in whome I can challenge any interest to doe the lyke; which I must confess without any pryvat respect wee wear bownd to doe for yowr open and honorable cowrse in strengthing Justice with awtorytye, and gracing meryts with favor, (a vertue, in which all men of vertue have an Interest.) Howbeyt yf yowr honor shall proceed to second mee with yowr good word when I shall get her highnes moved for soch a place, as nature, and breeding, and my earnest desyre make mee think my selfe fit for, I shall retayn soch a memory thearof, as yowr honor shall see I cownt no vyce more fowl then Ingratitude, nor no oblygacion greater then a benefit so I humbly take my leave, this last of January. 1600.

Yowr honors at commawndment

John Haryngton.

21

To Sir Robert Cecil

[September 7, 1601.]

Right honorable.

Yt may please yowr honor to remember I once moved yow

concerning Master Arthur Hoptons place of a Coronell in this Cownty of somerset, which was then lyke to be voyd by his dawngerows sycknes, and hee ys now remooved from yt for his weaknes and infyrmitye.

I thowght yt my dewty now to offer my selfe to the Lord Levetenant for the place, and I must confesse, by antyquytye, by opportunytye of dwellinge, by some experyence, by choyse of the worthyest of the cowntrye, and of the trayned sowldyers them selves I thowght yt partly dew to mee. Howbeyt some lettre from the Pryvy chamber (to use my Lords own word) ys lyke to make a yownger preferred afore mee. Yet I heer his Lordship will refer the choyse to yowr honors the Lords of the cowncell, whear I moste humbly and earnestly beseeche yowr honor to way indifferently trew desarts and not to harken to fallse and mallicyows suggestions and I wold not dowbt to have all ryght.

My Lord Levetenant told mee (concealing the awtor) that hee had been told in this cowntry by one: that I was backward in relligion, which his lordship pretends to be some let to my desyre; But I hope yowr honor except thear be proofe will not believe bare reports, for wee have some pure speryted fellows that will not sticke to say as moche of yowr honor and the best in the Realme.

I protest before god to yowr honor I ame no papist neyther in lyfe or thowght, I allow and use the book of common prayer, which many of owr forward men doe not, I beleeve 12 articles of the creed and they beleeve skant 11. and thowgh yt ys unusuall in Choyce of a Collonell to examin him by his Catachysme, yet yf I cannot geve accownt of both dutyes better then my ryvall can of eyther, let me loose all place and all good opinion.

I hope your honor will bear with this my boldnes grownded on truthe and stirred up with injurye.

I have ever been assystawnt to Master Hopton in the place, and in the yeer 88. my Cowntry can witnesse my forwardnes, and the last 8th of february yowr honor was an ey witnesse of my redynesse, and I will ever bee as forward and as redy to serve agaynst all the world with my powr my purse and my prayer, my soveraygn my benefactor and my godmother, and so I humbly take my leave this viith of September. 1601.

Yowr honors to commawnd,

John Haryngton.

22

To Sir Hugh Portman

[Kelston, October 9, 1601.]

My honoured Friend,

I humblie thank you for that venison I did not eat, but my wife did it much commendation. For six weeks I left my oxen and sheep, and venturd to Court, where I find many lean-kinded beastes, and some not unhorned. Much was my comfort in being well received, notwithstanding it is an ill hour for seeing the Queen. The madcaps are all in riot, and much evil threatend. In good soothe I feard her Majestie more than the rebel Tyrone, and wishd I had never received my Lord of Essex's honor of knighthood. She is quite disfavourd, and unattird, and these troubles waste her muche. She disregardeth every costlie cover that cometh to the table, and taketh little but manchet and succory potage. Every new message from the city doth disturb her, and she frowns on all the ladies. I had a sharp message from her brought by my Lord Buckhurst, namely thus, "Go tell that witty fellow, my godson, to get home: it is no season now to foole it here." I liked this as little as she dothe my knighthood, so tooke to my bootes and returned to the plow in bad weather. I must not say much, even by this trustie and sure messenger; but the many evil plots and designs have overcome all her Highness' sweet temper. She walks much in her privy chamber, and stamps with her feet at ill news, and thrusts her rusty sword at times into the arras in great rage. My Lord Buckhurst is much with her, and few else since the city business; but the dangers are over, and yet she always keeps a sword by her table. I obtained a short audience at my first coming to courte, when her Highness told me, "If ill counsel had brought me so far from home, she wish'd Heaven might marr that fortune which she had mended." I made my peace in this point, and will not leave my poor castle of Kelston, for fear of finding a worse elsewhere, as others have done. I will eat Aldborne rabbits, and get fish (as you recommend) from the man at Curry-Rival; and get partridge and hares when I can, and my venison where I can; and leave all great matters to those that like them better than myself. Commend me to your ladie and all other ladies that ever heard of me. Your books are safe, and I am in liking to get Erasmus for your entertainmente.

John Harington.

From Kelston, Oct. 9.
1601.

I coud not move in any suit to serve your neighbour B. such was the face of things; and so disorderd is all order, that her Highness hathe worne but one change of raiment for many days, and swears much at those that cause her griefs in such wise, to the no small discomfiture of all about her, more especially our sweete Lady Arundel, that *Venus plus quam venusta.*—

23

To Sir Robert Cecil

[London, June 7, 1602.]

Right honorable.

Being this last weeke in Notinghamshyre, abowt busynes of my own, I retorned by Grantam, whear I herd the tragicomedy of the Maypole and the minister in which women wear soch agents as the men wear at last forced to be pacient. All so in the same sheer I herd of a more seryows ryot agaynst one Capten Lovell that drayneth the fenns thear in which the women wear to ympacient, and worse may come of yt yf wysdome prevent yt not.

Coming to Stamford I was showd yowr moste worthy fathers

tombe, a most bewtyfull monument of his happy lyfe and deathe. In my way thence hether I saw bothe the Pallace of Burleghe and the paradyce of Theballs, and thowgh yt wear owt of my way I cowld not balk Cambridge, the Nursery of all my good breedinge.

In this unyversytye I saw, not onely the colledges increased in nomber, bewtyfyed and adorned in buyldings, but all orders so dewly observed, disputacions so well performed, all old controversyes both with the town and amonge them selves so appeased, as I rejoyced at moch, and gratulated theyr happy choyse of so worthy a chawncellor. And I thowght they might well call yow as one of theyr learnedest doth in an epistle theyr *felix* that ympart unto them so moche felycyty by yowr honorable care and provydence. How deerly wellcome yowr sweet sonne ys to that unyversitye I need not tell yowr honor thowgh many of them told yt mee. But that I may tell yowr honor all the news that may concern yow, not far beyond Theballs I met with an old Norfolk gentleman, who told mee hee herd yow wold sell Theballs. Uppon which I wysht him to goe with mee to see yt, whether yt wear kept lyke a howse the master was wery of. But when I behelde the sommer roome I thowght of a verse in Aryostos enchauntments.

But which was straung whear earst I left a wood
A wondrous stately pallace now thear stood.

and the syght of yt enchawnted me so as I thinke the roome not to be matcht yf yow will put two verses more of Aryosto to the chamber in the same Canto.

And unto this a lardg and lyghtsom stayr
Without the which no roome ys truly fayr.

To conclude I came thence hether, full of delyght, of honor and admyracion of yow and all yowr fathers howse by that I observed in this Jornye, and in this cogytacion, a man of myne own comes to me post from myne own poor howse with a letter from my eldest sonne (of 12 yeer old) with news that my wyfe was delyverd of a sonne, and becawse my sonne must *patrisare* hee wrytte yt in this verse. *Gaude pater, quartum genetrix peperit tibi natum,* which moved mee to make this suyt to yowr honor to be pleasd to be his godfather that hee may bear yowr name.

My desyre heerin I make my pledg of my love and honor to yow, and the grawnting of yt I shall take as an assewrance of yowr favor and good opinion of mee, which I wold both desarve and confyrme by all means I may and so I humbly take leave this

7 of June 1602.

Channon row.

Yowr honors at commawndment,

John Haryngton.

24

To Sir Robert Cecil

[London, June 22, 1602.]

Ryght honorable.

I have sent yowr honor by the bearer hereof a homely present, and thowgh the mettle thearin bee neyther gold nor sylver, yet yf Master Controller of the works or I can judg owght yt will bee worth gold and sylver to yowr howse. In my ydle discowrse on this subject (, yf yowr honor can remember), I valewd this devyse for my own poor howse to bee worth one hunderd pownds, and in Theballs (as myght be in proportion) worth a thousand.

But seryowsly yowr honor shall fynde, for yowr howse in the Strand, as well for yowr pryvat lodgings, as for all the famuly, the use of yt commodyows and necessary, and above all in tyme of infeccion most holsome.

The errors of some dull workmen have made that in some places yt hath not done so well as yt myght, but Master Basyll and my selfe will geve that dyrection for yowrs as neyther fayr nor fowl wether shall annoy.

And so praying yowr honor, that the frendly mynde of the gever, with the good use of the guifte, may excuse the meanesse thearfore, I humbly take leave till my retowrn out of the cowntry which shall god willing bee very shortly.

Channon row the 22
of June. 1602.

Yowr honors at commawndment

John Haryngton.

25

To Gilbert Talbot, Earl of Shrewsbury

[Greenwich, July, 1602.]

Right Honourable,

I went to Master Hammond, according as I promised, and at that instant, as I understood by him, he was sending to me for the same cause by your Lordship's direction. I found by the conveyance of the house that the architects of this last age had been much more careful than the former to avoid as much of the inconvenience as they could; and I saw they had spared no costs, for I found fair cisterns of lead, of which we must now raise new uses, for these, to speak in the lawyers phrase, are good but for a moiety, specially where they are. Your Lordship will bear with me if in this text I write obscurely, because so it is most mannerly.

Concerning Court news I can say little that is like to be news to your Lordship. This day I heard Master Secretary tell at dinner that Biron is dead, and died very desperate—a suitable end to one that had been a great blasphemer, and that had killed many scores with his own hands in cold blood. He accused his accusers to have been the first suggesters of his treasons. For Low Country news, Sir Edward Conway, of the Brill, arrived here yesternight; and out of his speeches we that are of the Court, but not of the Council, do gather that, either for lack of victuals or of spirit, there hath yet been no fighting. For Irish news: the Spaniards are still expected, and Sir Oliver Sentjohn is presently to repair into Ireland, as some think to supply Sir John Barkley's place, Serjeant Major, who was lately slain in a

——— but where nor how is not known. For home news; one Mistress Thwaits, if I mistake not the name (she is sister to Master Clifford's wife) follows an appeal against Master Manners, and my Lord Monteagle, and others that have the Queen's pardon, for the death of her husband, and as freshly as if it were but yesterday; but both she and her counsel, if they can be known, are like to be committed for their manifest contempt. The progress holds still, where it was, and as it was. My Lord Admiral is sick, and only hopeth to meet the Queen at the Earl of Hertford's. My Lady Ambassadress of France was entertained by the Queen yesterday very graciously, and gave among the Queen's maids French purses, fans, and masks, very bountifully.

This is all I had, and more than is worth the writing; and so, desiring to be most humbly recommended to my Lady; and most kindly to Sir Charles Cavendish, who shall have cause to thank me for his chamber in Broad Street,

I remain, humbly at your Lordship's service.

John Harrington.

Greenwich, of July, 1602.

Postscript. I must remember in a postscript how Master Secretary made a great boast this day at dinner, that my Lord and my Lady of Shrewsbury had commended his river.

26

To Richard Langley

[December 3, 1602.]

To Master Richard Langley
Schoolmaster of Eaton

Because my sonne should not loose all his tyme beeing with mee heer at the court I have ymployed him in exercyses to the queen and some of my Lords, and yf they seeme a litle to rype for a boy of the fift forme in Eaton yow must suppose that a trewant once in the sixt forme thear hath prompted him, and trewly since I came from Cambridge (which ys now 20 yeeres)

I cannot remember that I have written any latten verses yet by this occasion of teaching my sonne I see I have not quite forgotten them. But for him I fynd him apt enough to verses, and I desire not hee showld bee much addicted to them least yt hinder him (as yt hath done mee) of better studies. So I bid yow farewell.

this 3 of December
1602

Your loving Frend

Jo. Har.

27

To Lady Mary Harington

[December 27, 1602.]

Sweet Mall,

I herewith send thee, what I woud God none did know, some ill bodings of the realme and its welfare. Oure deare Queene, my royale godmother, and this state's natural mother, dothe now bear shew of human infirmitie, too faste for that evil which we shall get by her dethe, and too slowe for that good which shee shall get by her releasement from pains and miserye.

Deare Mall, how shall I speake what I have seene, or what I have felt?—Thy good silence in these matters emboldens my pen. For, thanks to the swete god of silence! thy lips do not wanton out of discretion's path, like the many gossipping dames we coud name, who lose their husband's fast hold in good friends, rather than hold fast their own tongues. Nowe I will truste thee with greate assurance, and whilst thou doste broode over thy young ones in the chamber, thou shalte read the doinges of thy greiving mate in the cowrte.

I finde some lesse mindfull of whate they are soone to lose, than of what they may perchance hereafter get. Nowe, on my owne parte, I cannot blote from my memorie's table, the goodnesse of our Sovereigne Ladie to me, even (I will saie) before borne; her affectione to my mother who waited in privie cham-

SIR JOHN HARINGTON
AND
LADY HARINGTON

ber, her betterring the state of my father's fortune (which I have, alass! so much worsted,) her watchings over my youthe, her likinge to my free speech, and admiration of my little learninge and poesy, which I did so muche cultivate on her commande, have rootede such love, suche dutyfull remembraunce of her princelie virtues, that to turne askante from her condition withe tearlesse eyes, woud staine and foule the springe and founte of gratitude.

It was not manie daies since I was bidden to her presence. I bleste the happy momente; and founde her in moste pitiable state. She bade the archbishope aske me if I had seene Tyrone? I replied, with reverence, that "I had seene him withe the Lord Deputie." She lookede up, with much choler and greife in her countenance and saide, "Oh, nowe it mindeth me that you was *one* who sawe this manne *elsewhere:*"—and hereat, she droppede a teare, and smote her bosome. She helde in her hande a goldene cuppe, whiche she often put to her lippes; but, in soothe, her hearte seemethe too fulle to lacke more fillinge. This sighte movede me to thinke on whate paste in Irelande; and I truste she did not lesse thinke on *some* who were busier there than myselfe. She gave me a message to the Lord Deputie, and bade me come to the chamber at seven o clocke. Hereat some who were aboute her did marvel, as I do not holde so highe place as those she did not chuse to do her commandes. Deare Mall, if I gette no profitte, I shall gette some envie, and this businesse maye turne to some accounte withe the Lord Deputie. Her Majestie enquirede of some matters whiche I had written; and as she was pleasede to note my fancifulle braine, I was not unheedfull to feede her humoure, and reade some verses, whereat she smilede once, and was pleasede to saie;—"When thou doste feele creepinge tyme at thye gate, these fooleries will please thee lesse; I am paste my relishe for suche matters: thou seeste my bodilie meate dothe not suite me well; I have eaten but one ill tastede cake since yesternighte." She rated moste grievouslie, at noone, at some who minded not to bringe uppe certaine matters of accounte. Several menne have been sente to, and when readie at hande, her Highnesse hathe dismissede in anger; but who, dearest Mall, shall saye, that *"youre Highnesse hathe forgotten."*

I was honourede at dinner with the archbishoppe and several of the churche pastors, where I did finde more corporeal than spiritual refreshmente, and though oure ill state at cowrte maie, in some sorte, overcaste the countenance of these apostolical messengers; yet were some of them well anointed with the oyl of gladnesse on Tuesdaie paste. Hereof thou shalt in some sorte partake. My Lorde of Salisburie had seizen his tenantes corne and haye, with sundrie husbandrie matters, for matters of money due to his lordshippes estate: hereat the aggrievede manne made suite to the bishoppe, and requestede longer time and restitution of his goodes:—"Go, go, (saithe the bishoppe) I heare ill reporte of thie livinge, and thou canst not crave mercie; thou comeste not to churche service, and haste not receivede confirmation; I commande thee to attend my ordinance and be confirmed in thy faithe at Easter nexte cominge."—"I crave your lordshippes forgivenesse, (quothe the manne,) in goode soothe I durste not come there, for as youre lordshippe hathe lain your hande on all my goodes, I thinke it full meete to take care of my heade!"—Suche was parte of oure discourse at dinner. So thou seeste, sweete Mall, although the bishoppes hande was heavy, oure pesantes head was not weake, and his lordshippe said he woude forego his paymente.

Nexte monthe I will see thie swete face, and kiss my boys and maids, which I praie thee not to omitte on my accounte. Send me up, by my manne Combe, my Petrarche. Adeiu, swete Mall.

I am thine ever lovinge

John Harington.

28

To Lord Thomas Howard

[April, 1603.]

My Lorde,

Touchynge our matters here, and what hathe fallen oute

sithence you departede, maye perchance not be unpleasante to you to heare. Manie have beene the mad caps rejoicinge at oure new Kynges cominge, and who (in good trothe) darede not have set forthe their good affection to him a monthe or two agoe: but, alas! what availethe truthe, when profite is in queste? Yow were true and leige bondsman to her late Highnesse, and felte her sweete bounties in full force and good favour. Nor did I my poor selfe unexperience her love and kyndness on manie occasions; but I cannot forbeare remembringe my dread at her frownes in the Iryshe affaire, when I followede my generall (and what shoude a captaine doe better?) to Englande a little before his tyme. If Essex had met his "appoyntede tyme" (as Davide saithe) to die, it had fared better, than to meet his follie and his fate too.

But enoughe of olde tales; a new kynge will have new soldiers, and God knowethe what men they will be. One saith he will serve him by daie, another by nighte; the women (who love to talke as they lyke) are for servynge him bothe daye and nyghte. It pleasethe me to thynke I am not under their commande, whoe offer so bountyfullie what perchance they woulde be gladde to receive at others handes: but I am a cripple, and not made for sportes in newe cowrtes. Sir Robert Cary was prime in his Scottysh intelligence of the Queenes deathe. Some will saye that bad tydinges travel faste; but I maye call Sir Roberts no ill borden to Edenborrow.—St. Paul hathe saide, that "the race is not alwaie givene to the swyfte:"—I dowte Sir Robert will give the Sainte the lie, for he is like to get both *race* and *prize,* and (as fame goethe) creepethe not a little into favoure.

I am now settynge forthe for the countrie, where I will read Petrarch, Ariosto, Horace, and such wise ones. I will make verses on the maidens, and give my wine to the maisters; but it shall be such as I do love, and do love me. I do muche delight to meete my goode freindes, and discourse of getting rid of our foes. Each nighte do I spende, or muche better parte thereof, in counceil with the aunciente examples of lerninge; I con over their histories, their poetrie, their instructions, and thence glean my own proper conducte in matters bothe of merrimente or discretion; otherwyse, my goode Lorde, I ne'er had overcome the rugged pathes of Ariosto, nor wonne the highe palme of glorie, which you broughte unto me, (venture to saie it) namely, our late Queenes approbation, esteeme, and rewarde. Howe my poetrie maye be relishde in tyme to come, I will not hazard to saie. Thus muche I have livede to see, and (in good soothe) feel too, that honeste prose will never better a mans purse at cowrte; and, had not my fortune been in *terra firma,* I might, even for my verses, have daunced bare foot with Clio and her school-fellowes untill I did sweat, and then have gotten nothinge to slake my thirste, but a pitcher of Helicons well. E'en let the beardless god Apollo dip his own chin in such drinke; a haire of my face shall have better entertainmente.

I have made some freindes to further my suite of favour withe the Kynge, and hope you will not be slacke in forwardeing my beinge noticede in proper season: but, my goode Lorde, I will walke faire, tho a cripple; I will copie no mans steps so close as to treade on his heel; if I go at all, it shall be verily uprightely, and shall better my selfe in thus saieing, *Sequar—sed passibus æquis.*—Nowe, my Lorde, farewell! and truste his worde who venturethe to honour himselfe in the name of

Youre friende,

John Harington.

When you can fairely get occasion, I entreate a worde touchynge your doinges at Cowrte. I will pointe oute to you a special conveyance, for, in these tymes, discretion must stande at oure doores, and even at our lippes too. Goode caution never comethe better, than when a man is climbinge; it is a pityfull thinge to sett a wronge foote, and, insteade of raisinge ones heade, to falle to the grounde and showe ones baser partes.

29

To Lord Cecil of Essingdon

[London, May 21, 1603].

My very good Lord

I hope yowr Lordship never had cawse to have yll opinion of mee and of late yow seemd to enterpret kyndely and as I ment yt, my just dealing with yow in an accydent that happend. I ame now in distresse, in an honest cawse. I looke for no releefe but from the King. Yowr Lordships good word may hasten yt. Yt will cost yow lytle, yt may avayl mee moche. Yf the world would, god would not forsake mee in so just a matter. Yet expedycion dubles both the Justyce and benefyte. Breefly yt ys thus.

I that never committed cryme in my lyfe (let all my enemyes object what they can) am betrayd by my kin into a det of 4000[li] and thinking to prop up a howse not contemtible, and allyed to yow, beying to weake a prop yt ys all falln on mee, and so must lye heer. Whyle John Skinner floryshes at Barwyke and flyes with my fethers, old Markham dotes at home, and his honest sonne Sir Griffin yowr kynsman, lyke an Eneas that would cary his father owt of the flames, ys lyke to burn yn yt with him, the lubber ys so heavy to ly on his maymed sonnes showlders. I beseech yow show yowr selfe a frend to us both in this so in hast I end free in mynde, and innocency, thowghe a prisoner in body and fortune and

At yowr lordships servyce

21 May. 1603.

John Haryngton.

30

To Lord Cecil of Essingdon

[London, June, 1603].

Ryght honorable

I would have been glad to have herd some comfortable awnswer eyther by lettre or message in this my distresse; I was to forward in an unfortunat frendship to my uncle to be bownd for him in his declyning state; and yet I hope (yf wee may have speedy Justyce,) neyther shall his howse bee quyte overthrown, and moche lesse I (that ow no peny of the dette but as a sewerty) shall bee thearby oppressed, thowgh I suffer now for my to moche kyndenes.

I humbly pray yowr Lordship to let mee know what I ame lyke to trust to and what releefe I may hope for, in a matter deserving some commiseracion; consydering the Principalls have bothe means and mynds to sell lands to pay theyr detts. Yf yt shall please yowr Lordship to geve some comfortable awnswer to the bearer who ys lyke to smart in this cawse no lesse than I, I shall bee glad to receav yt from him, so I commend yowr Lordship to th' allmyghty from my unaccustomed Lodging this vi[th] of June. 1603.

Yowr lordships to Commawnd,

John Haryngton.

31

To Lord Cecil of Essingdon

[London, June 10, 1603].

Ryght honorable and my very good Lord

I understand by Sir Griphin Markham that yowr Lordship tooke honorable care of my cawse; and that yow promised to wryte or send a man to mee, to assewr me of yowr favor heerin. Which I protest was more comfort to mee than any thinge I herd since this my restraynt, except only the most gracious message I receavd from his Maiestie by Sir Roger Ashton.

Wee crave nothing but Justyce agaynst John Skinner, I was arrested for that very mony that bowght his place at Barwyke, I ow not a farthing for my selfe; His Majestie sayd hee showld bee immedyatly sent for, and commawnded to attend the end of this cawse, that the Markhams and hee may satisfye what I stand bownd for; but I dowbt hee ys not sent for yet. Yt ys yll sollyciting busynes owt of a pryson.

I beseech yowr honor hee may bee sent for by the next packet, and so praying yowr Lordship to preserv mee in yowr good opinion I comfort my selfe with this saying *Non tormentum sed causa facit martirem.*

1603. 10. June.

Yowr Lordships humbly to comawnd,

John Haryngton.

32

To Lord Cecil of Essingdon

[London, June 27, 1603].

Ryght honorable my very good Lord.

Yesternight late a prysoner heer (Timothee Elks) that was Master Georg Brookes servant told mee the cawse of his Masters discontentment toward yowr honor in particular, grew in the Queens tyme abowt the Mastership of Saint Crosse, the missing whearof, his state decaying, by his large expence, made him a more dawngerows malcontent in this tyme, and so I perceave Sir Griphin Markham his state lykwyse decayinge, (and hee missing his parks,) in a simpathy of discontent accorded with him.

As I had wrytten this moche and was thinking to wryte furder of this matter I was interrupted by the unlookd for coming to mee of my Lady Markham (a desolate Lady god knows and worse then widdow).

She useth many perswasyons to mee that her husband may bee innocent in thease practyses, in which the voyce ys hee ys a principall; only thus far her speech prevayls with mee, to make mee thinke that she may bee ygnorant of his purposes in yt, and thearfore I undertake on her importunytye, to wryte to yowr honor her protestacion in this kynde, and that shee ys now at her unkles Master Sebastyan Harvye in Lyme Street, whear she wold exspect the end of her husbands tryall, yf yowr lordship will so permit, which request being in my understanding very reasonable I presume to joyn with her in.

Sir Thomas Erskin and other my honorable Frends send mee word his Majesties gracyows favor to mee ys soch, that to the releefe of my distresse by the Markhams, hee hath sayd in his princely word I shall have theyr forfeyture, the which his gracyows goodnes, as I take yowr honor to have in part procured, so I humbly pray the same to continew yt and I shall ever rest unfaynedly

27 of July
1603

At yowr Lordships Servyce
John Haryngton.

33

To Lord Cecil of Essingdon

[October, 1603.]

Right honorable and I hope, still my speciall good Lord:

My wyfe sent mee your Lordships lettre written to her from Kensington, which at the fyrst syght did troble mee, both fearing shee had gevn your Lordship some just offence, and fynding some phrases in yt tasting of some passyon in behalfe of your offycer, and I wysh men in your Lordships place voyd of all passyon but compassyon, and so I beseeche you bee in reeding myne answer.

Fyrst my wyfe, who in all kynde of truth I dare swear ys trewer then Dobbinson, affirms shee sayd nothing but this that shee thought your Lordship nor no Lord of the cownsell wowld condemne my eskape consydering the dawnger, and moch lesse offer her that indignytye to break open her doors as Dobbinson did. And though your Lordships warrant as a Cownsellor and principall secretary of the State ys above any pryviledge and undisputable: yet her neyborors tell her that but for treasons no officer can enter a howse in Channon Row. And I ame sewr yt was wont to be far from your honors Cowrse to lend the cowntenance of state to soche a wrangle of det. I have herd yt noted in your father as a great note of wysdome that the second tale prevayld more with him then the fyrst, and I hope when yow shall heer my complaynt after theyrs, your honor will judge I have offerd them more kyndenes then they can deserve, and that they are of kin to the old serpent, that accust myne Eve to have spoken eyther so unadvysedly of your lordship or so untrewly of mee thowgh I have reason to forgeve her a greater fawlt, that hath endewrd xxi weeks plage and imprysonment allmost for my sake besyde the pawning of her plate and 140li. of her Joynture.

But whear your honor wrytes I used an elloquent figure to engage yow to get mee Sir Griphin Markhams forfeyture your lordship doth in that phrase but retowrne my sonns verse:

> Tu quoque maturo pollens facunde Cecili consilio, patriae fida columna tuae.

But in playn trewth withowt figures. Yf Sir Griph. Markham have been a traytor to mee and so many frends and last to his Prince, Yf his mother and some of hers have been both spytefull and skornfull to yow and all your kin, Yf shee now with a murthering mynde to mee (for I can call yt no better) cawsd new accions to bee layd on mee to hold mee in prison, for meer malles, becawse I charged her with misgoverning of her husbands estate, thease 8 yeers, and cosening him of 8000 marks, Yf her own sonne told my Lord of London, that the Jesuyts had tawght her to pay no dette but unto recusants: Yf all this my adversyty and crosse and afflyccion (for good my lord call yt not mysery) have falln on mee meerly by theyr dette, I doe not unconscionably to begge theyr land, the Kyng doth most graciowsly to grawnt yt and your Lordship shall doe justly and honorably to furder yt, as yow have promist favorably in your former lettres, and thear ys rather more cawse then lesse now in that I doe evydently for your Lordships only sake releeve them that cared not, for xli. to rewin mee and thearfore in this respect yow will geve mee leave to rely somwhat more of your favor then evry other Cownsellor. To omitt that to my powr I have been allways respectyve to my Lord your Brother, to your nephews and neeces more then ordinary. My eskape was an honest eskape, I shunned the plage and not the dette and I was strawngely used and yowr Lordships name strongly abusd as your Lordship may see by this note enclosed.

They confesse now I ame not in execucion nor was not thease ten weeks, they cannot deny the plage to bee in the gatehowse and vi ded and the vii[th] sycke: and thearfore I myght thinke him as moche my frend wold wysh mee to the gallows as to the Gatehowse and ame sory for my two poor Cosens (betrayd by theyr brother) thowgh I love not theyr mother, whose lyves your Lordship hath saved from one dawnger. Yet they remayn still in an other, and yf some commiseracion wear extended to all them that are capable of yt yt wear honorable to the world and charytable before god. For as Dydo sayd *Non ignara mali miseris succurrere disco,* so may I say. As for the poverty eyther of the Credytors or the offycers, whear your lordship seems greatly to pitty bothe: under favor thear ys cawse of neyther, but moche of me and nyne children. The Credytors are Brabson Hare and Scory. Yf they had one to make fowr I wold say they wear the *Cater pillers* of the Common welth. As for your offycer Dobbinson hee hath bond of Okey of 2000[li.] And Okey him selfe braggs that in .88. hee had 1000[li.] in the bottom of a close stoole which with the good fees hee takes and the good use hee makes, and some good misteryes hee practyses (for I will bee no promooter) may well bee by this tyme according to his own computacion 4000[li.] and hee hath no chylde to Care for.

Trew yt ys hee makes very dilligent search after mee, whearby your honor may see how moche more dilligent proffit makes, then dewty, for when the Fryer eskaped last day, whome Okey affermd to bee a traytor and a moste dawngerous papist, they never searched howse for him. Only for a culler he threttend to send to newgate his man Symon that let him owt, and so I concluded that the fryer committed Symony.

As for mee hee never trusted mee, lockt mee all nyght, new

barrd his windows, had watch over mee howerly, and farder I told him yf the plage increast I would bee gone.

Whearfore I beseech you reproove them as they are worthye; bothe for theyr Covetows crewellty, and one for his indiscrecion and neglygence, and for mee beleeve that I will doe as becomes an honest man allways, and in this, as your Lordship or any you will appoynt will thinke good, and yf you will refer yt to Sir Willim Wade and Sir Walter Cope I will send that, and them that shall satisfye them. And after I ame so sufficiently ayrd that I may withowt offence repayr to the Cowrt I will in evry poynt so satisfy your Lordship as I dowbt not but you will restore mee to your good opinion or rather I hope you will thinke the better of mee for this cowrse I have taken, and so I wish your Lordship all helth and happynes.

34

To Dr. John Still, Bishop of Bath and Wells

[Bath or Kelston, October (?) 1603].

My Worthie Lorde.

I have lived to see that damnable rebel Tir-Owen broughte to Englande, curteouslie favourede, honourede, and well likede. Oh! my Lorde, what is there which doethe not prove the inconstancie of worldlie matters! How did I labour after that knave's destruction! I was callede from my home by hir Majesties commaund, adventurede perils by sea and lande, endurede toil, was near starvinge, eat horse-fleshe at Munster; and all to quell that man, who nowe smilethe in peace at those that did hazarde their lives to destroy him. Essex tooke me to Irelande; I had scante tyme to putte on my bootes; I followede withe good wyll, and did returne wyth the Lorde Leiutenante to meet ill wyll; I did beare the frownes of hir that sente me; and, were it not for hir good lyking, rather than my good deservynges, I had been sore discountenancede indeede. I obeyede in goinge wythe the Earle to Irelande, and I obeyede in comynge wythe him to Englande. But what did I encounter thereon? Not his wrathe, but my gracious Soveraigns ill humour. What did I advantage? Why, trulie, *a knighthood;* whych had been better bestowede by hir that sente me, and better sparede by him that gave it. I shall never put oute of remembraunce hir Majestie's displeasure:—I enterd her chamber, but she frownede and saiede, "What, did the foole brynge *you* too? Go backe to your businesse." In soothe, these wordes did sore hurte hym who never hearde soche before; but heaven gave me more comforte in a daie or twoe after; hir Majestie did please to aske me concernynge our northerne jorneyes, and I did so well quite me of the accounte, that she favourede me wyth such discourse that the Earle hymself had been well glad of. And now dothe Tyr-Owen dare us old commanders wyth hys presence and protection.

I doubte not but some state businesse is well nighe begunne, or to be made out; but these matters pertain not to me nowe. I muche feare for my good Lord Grey and Raleigh. I hear the plot was well nighe accomplyshede to disturb our peace and favour Arabella Stuart, the Prince's cousin. The Spaniardes beare no good wyll to Raleigh, and I doubte if some of the Englyshe have muche better affectione towarde hym; God delyver me from these desygns. I have spokene wyth Carewe concerninge the matter; he thynkethe ill of certaine people whome I knowe, and wishethe he coude gaine knowledge and further inspectione hereof, touchynge those who betrayede thys busynesse. Cecil dothe beare no love to Raleighe, as you well understande in the matter of Essex. I wyste not that he hathe evyll desygn in pointe of faithe or relygion. As he hathe ofte discoursede to me wyth moch lerynge, wysdom, and freedome, I knowe he dothe somewhat dyffer in opynyon from some others; but I thynke alsoe his hearte is welle fixed in everye honeste thynge, as farre as I can looke into hym. He seemethe wondrouslie fitted, bothe by arte and nature, to serve the state, especiallie as he is versede in foraign matters, his skyll thereyn being alwaies estimable and prayse-worthie. In relygion, he hathe showne (in pryvate talke) great depthe and goode readynge, as

I once experyencede at hys owne howse, before manie lernede men. In good trothe, I pitie his state, and doubte the dyce not fairely thrown, if hys lyfe be the losynge stake: but hereof enowe, as it becomethe not a poore countrye knyghte to looke from the plow-handle into policie and pryvacie. I thanke Heavene, I have been well nighe driven heretofore into narrowe straits, amongste state rocks and sightless dangers; but if I have gained little profitte and not moche honoure, I have not adventured so far as to be quite sunken herein. I wyll leave you all now to synke or swym, as seemethe beste to your owne lykinge; I onlie swym nowe in oure bathes, wherein I feel some benefyt and more delyghte. My lameness is bettered hereby, and I wyll shortlie set forwarde to see what goethe on in the citie and prie safelie amonge those that truste not mee, neither wyll I truste to them: newe prynces begete newe lawes, and I am too well strycken in yeares and infirmyties to enter on newe courses. God commend and defend your Lordshippe in all youre undertakynges. He that thryvethe in a courte muste put halfe his honestie under his bonnet; and manie do we knowe that never parte that commoditie at all, and sleepe wyth it all in a bag. I reste your lordshippes trew friende,

John Harington.

35

To Sir Amias Paulet

[December, 1603?]

My lovynge cosene,

It behovethe me now to recite my journal, respectynge my gracious commande of my Sovereigne Prince, to come to his closet; which matter as you so well and urgentlie desyer to heare of, I shall, in suchwyse as suitethe myne beste abilitie, relate unto you, and is as followethe.—When I came to the presence-chamber, and had gotten goode place to see the lordlie attendants, and bowede my knee to the Prince; I was orderde by a specyal messenger, and that in secrete sorte, to waite a whyle in an outwarde chamber, whence, in near an houre waitinge, the same knave ledde me up a passage, and so to a smale roome, where was good order of paper, inke, and pens, put on a boarde for the Prince's use. Soon upon this, the Prince his Highnesse did enter, and in muche goode humour askede, "If I was cosen to lorde Haryngton of Exton?" I humblie repliede,—"His Majestie did me some honour in enquiringe my kin to one whome he had so late honourede and made a barone;" and moreover did adde, "wee were bothe branches of the same tree." Then he enquyrede muche of lernynge, and showede me his owne in suche sorte, as made me remember my examiner at Cambridge aforetyme. He soughte muche to knowe my advances in philosophie, and utterede profounde sentences of Aristotle, and suche lyke wryters, whiche I had never reade, and which some are bolde enoughe to saye, others do not understand: but this I must passe by. The Prince did nowe presse my readinge to him parte of a canto in "Ariosto;" praysede my utterance, and said he had been informede of manie, as to my lernynge, in the tyme of the Queene. He asked me "what I thoughte pure witte was made of; and whom it did best become? Whether a Kynge shoulde not be the beste clerke in his owne countrie; and, if this lande did not entertayne goode opinion of his lerynge and good wisdome?" His Majestie did much presse for my opinion touchinge the power of Satane in matter of witchcraft; and askede me, with muche gravitie,—"If I did trulie understande, why the devil did worke more with anciente women than others?" I did not refraine from a scurvey jeste, and even saide (notwithstandinge to whom it was saide) that —"we were taught hereof in scripture, where it is tolde, that the devil walketh in dry places." His Majestie, moreover, was pleasede to saie much, and favouredelye, of my good report for merth and good conceite: to which I did covertlie answer; as not willinge a subjecte shoulde be wiser than his Prince, nor even appeare so.

More serious discourse did next ensue, wherein I wantede roome to continue, and sometime roome to escape; for the Queene his mother was not forgotten, nor Davison neither. His Highnesse tolde me her deathe was visible in Scotlande before it did really happen, being, as he said, "spoken of in secrete by those whose power of sighte presentede to them a bloodie heade dancinge in the aire." He then did remarke muche on this gifte, and saide he had soughte out of certaine bookes a sure waie to attaine knowledge of future chances. Hereat, he namede many bookes, which I did not knowe, nor by whom written; but advisede me not to consult some authors which woulde leade me to evile consulations. I tolde his Majestie, "the power of Satan had, I muche fearede, damagede my bodilie frame; but I had not farther will to cowrte his friendshipe, for my soules hurte." —We nexte discoursede somewhat on religion, when at lengthe he saide: "Now, Sir, you have seen my wisdome in some sorte, and I have pried into yours. I praye you, do me justice in your reporte, and in good season, I will not fail to add to your understandinge, in suche pointes as I maye find you lacke amendmente." I made courtesie hereat, and withdrewe downe the passage, and out at the gate, amidst the manie varlets and lordlie servantes who stoode arounde.

Thus, you have the historie of your neighbour's highe chaunce and entertainmente at cowrte; more of whiche matter, when I come home to my owne dwellynge, and talk these affaires in a corner. I muste presse to *silence* hereon, as otherwyse all is undone. I did forget to tell, that his Majestie muche askede concerninge my opinion of the new weede tobacco, and said "it woud, by its use, infuse ill qualities on the braine, and that no lernede man ought to taste it, and wishede it forbidden." I will nowe forbeare further exercise of your tyme, as Sir Robertes man waitethe for my letter to beare to you, from

Youre olde neighboure,
friend, and cosene,

John Harington.

36

To Gilbert Talbot, Earl of Shrewsbury

[March 31, 1604.]

My very good Lord

I have sent your Lordship the particuler rates of Lenton which yf your Lordship will do mee the favor to recommend to a good chapman, yt wold bee a means of my speedy delyvery owt of this thraldome.

I hope Sir Griphin Markham and I shall agree frendly, and that hee will learn to know and use his frends.

Now I ame to desyre your Lordship yf ever servyce and love of any Markham was acceptable to yow; yf my long professed dewty may presume to challenge yt, to favor us in our bill agaynst Sir John Skinner, whose frawd, wastfullnes, and willfullnes, hathe been the fyrst concussyon, and ys lyke to bee the fynall rewin of the Markhams credyt.

Your Lordship promist mee to move my Lord Tresorer and my Lord of Northampton and my Lord Cecill on this behalfe. I pray your Lordship let mee add my Lord Chawncellor; who may stryke the greatest stroke thear-yn. And so, praying your Lordships favor that I may speake with your Lordship yf yow passe by, I take leave this xxxi[th] of March, 1604.

Your Lordships at commaund,

John Haryngton.

37

To Lord Cecil of Essingdon

[May 20, 1604.]

Right Honorable my very good Lord

Yt is not unknowne to your Lordshipp and the rest of my Lords what great distresse of ymprisonment and sicknes, I have indured for my Unckle Thomas Markham, which being by Gods goodnes and the Kings allmost overblowne; My sonns Unckle, my wyves owne and only Brother pursews me in the *Starr Chamber* with a desyer rather then hope utterly to disgrace mee.

I have sowght all good meanes of Attonement, with him, soch as noe Christianity, or rather no humanity could refuse from a man in my Case.

But all offers being rejected, I must appeale to the Justice of that Honorable Court, where I earnestly intreat your Lordshipps presence to morrow, and where I aske no favor but free and full hearing.

I will speake nothing to the disgrace of my adversary but lett the matter it selfe speake. The Constancy and kyndnes of his sister to mee in all my Adversitie makes me forbear him, and sorrow to thinck that either I must be disgraced or doe him disgrace that is brother to her who hath deserved of me what soever a faithfull wife can deserve of a kynd Husband.

The breife of the Chardge and my aunswer is here sett downe, so I take leave the xxth of May 1604.

Your Lordshipps at commaundement
unfaynedly
John Haryngton.

Edward Rogers esquior Playntive.

That Sir John Harington in the 44th Eliz: foreknowing that the Lady Rogers his wyves mother lying then at Bath could not live above fowr days did take the keys of her howse at Cannington 30 myle distant against her will and there in ryotouse manner ryfled the said Howse and caryd thence in plate and mony 5000^{li} which belonged of right to Edward Rogers esquire, and to sonne Fræuncis, That after the decease of the said Lady Rogers, the same Sir John Harington came in lyke ryotous manner to the same howse and there burned and razed the Evidences of the said Edward Rogers.

Sir John Harington Defendant.

To the First the defendant answereth he went with the privity of the Lady Rogers and by her appointment, and the said Lady had not any Plate or money at that howse to the vallew of 20li.

That his second coming was peaceable as Executor in ryght of his wyfe, and that none of Master Rogers evidence wear then burned to his knowledge.

38

To Lord Cecil of Essingdon

[London, June 7, 1604].

Ryght honorable my very good Lord.

I hope now I shall honestly discharge those detts for which I have been so longe trobled, being now redy to performe so moche as I offerd to yowr Lordship for sale of my land in Nottinghamshyre.

I have fownd an honest gentleman that will buy yt, wee are agreed of the pryce, his mony lyes by him both to his hindrawnce and myne, and because his cownsell advyses him to this kynde of assewrawnce, contayned in this enclosed, Master Attorney requyres a warrant in that fowrme, and hath cawsd his own men to draw yt for yowr Lordships hand.

I assewr yowr Lordship, and I have made good proofe thearof the land ys better by 1000li that I passe to the King then that I passe from him, but that yt lyeth in the Cowntry whear I have dwelt all my lyfe.

I will troble yowr Lordship no farther, but trust yowr Lordship shall fynde my endeavors, and what so ever ys or shold lye in my powr, honest and just, howsoever my successe and fortune that ys in other mens powr may bee hard and unpleasawnt so I take humble leave

From the baylyvs howse:
1604. 7. June.

Yowr Lordships at commawndment

John Haryngton.

39

To Lord Cecil of Essingdon

[London, June 12, 1604].

Right honorable my verie good Lord

Master Atturney hath given me dispatch upon your Lordships last Warrant, not onely with expedition but even with bounty.

Now if it maie please your Lordship to recommend theise to Sir Thomas Lake to hasten his Majesties sygnature I should soone be a free man, but ever acknowledge myself highlie bounde to your Lordship.

Yet one earnest and just request I make now to your Lordship that yow will been pleasd at my humble sute to bee at the Starre Chamber to morrow, to heare a Cause that hath been in deed chiefe cause of all this my trouble in which I am defendant against my wives onely and naturall (yet to unnaturall) brother.

A good Fyne may rise to the king out of it for if I bee guiltie I deserve yt (though never worse able to paie it) but if I bee innocent, as my conscience tells me, and I hope the Evidence will tell your Lordships then a Fyne is dew from a false and mallicious and verie riche Accuser. And even so I humblie take my leave,

the xii[th] of June. 1604.

Your Lordships humbly at Commandement

John Haryngton.

40

To Lord Cecil of Essingdon

[June 17, 1604.]

Ryght honorable my very good Lord.

My Cawse in the starchamber hath had a very honorable and full heeringe, between my wyves brother and mee, and by the generall consent of the whole Cowrt uppon the speciall mocion of my Lord Chawncellor seconded most honorably by my Lord of Northampton and other of my Lords the sentence ys respyted for a tyme and the matter referd to the Arbytrement of my Lord of Shrewsbury

Lord Knolls
Lord Wotton
Justyce Fenner
Justyce Yelverton

My Wyfe ys an earnest sutor to his Majestie, to allow and awtoryse this cowrse of arbiterment by his most gracious lettre and beseecheth your Lordship to recommend the procuring thearof to Sir Thomas Lake, who ys allso purposd to morrow to procure the dispatch of the books your Lordship delyverd him uppon which, Master Michell Hix will presently discharge my execucions, and I myght by your honorable favor have a speedy end of a chargable and unkynde sute so I humbly take leave this

17 of June.
1604

Your Lordships at commawndment

John Haryngton.

41

To Lord Cecil of Essingdon

[July 8, 1604.]

Right honorable my good Lord.

This bearer can certefy your Lordship not only how justly I have discharged the det I lay in execucion for, but also how respectyvely I have delt with your Lordships officer, who I must confesse since my coming to his howse hath used mee very well.

Now my ernest suyt to your Lordship ys, that having discharged this det, having ended my unkynde suyt with my wyves brother, and being restored to the presence of my most graciows soveraygne, (to whose speciall goodnes, the successe of my busynes ys to bee referred,) that I may allso be receaved into your Lordships good favor and opinion in soch measure as I was afore my trobles, and I shall sencearly labor to deserve yt, and so I humbly take leave

the .8. of July.
1604

Your Lordships at Commawndment,

John Haryngton.

42

To Viscount Cranborne

[November 13, 1604.]

Right honorable and my very good Lord.

After my escape out of the gatehouse Master Okey by the name of your Lordships officer came with your Lordships warrant to take mee at Hampton Court. I was assured by Councell that by the law of the Land I could not be taken out of another mans house after my escape; but having no purpose to contest with your Lordship and lesse to make dishonest advantage of my escape, I gave Okey a bond of 2000li at Hampton court to dischardge all the debt and whatsoever covenants he would put in: not daring to refuse any, rather then in that contagious tyme to go to the Gatehouse agayn.

Since this tyme (as I hope Master Haughton your steward and Master Dobbinson have certefied your Lordship) I have paid the debt, discharged all the dew fees of the execution, and yet now Master Okey most wrongfully sews this bond in the kings bench to my great charge and trouble, and presuming on some favor thear, refuses all offers that are made on my behalfe and denies in his plea to be your lordships officer, only with some perswasyon (and doubting least I would call him into the starchamber for some misdemeanors of his) he said he would referr the matter (between him and mee) to any two your Lordship would name. These are thearfore humbly to pray your Lordship to sygnify to him your Lordships pleasure heerin, and to referr the hearing as well of his complaynt as mine to some

two of these undernamed, and so I humbly take my leave, the 13th of November
1604

Yowr Lordships at Commawndment

John Haryngton.

Sir Walter Cope
Sir Michel Hix
Sir Hugh Beeston
Master Richard Haughton

43

To Viscount Cranborne

[Kelston, April 20, 1605].

Right honorable my very good Lord.

Your lordship hath been pleased in tymes past to reed some discowrces of myne and to geve them better allowance then men of meaner Judgment. Now I am bold to entreat your Lordship with the lyke favorable approbacion to read this short relation (for yt ys to long for a lettre) contayning my humble and zelows offer for his Majesties sarvyce in Ierland.

When your Lordship hath read yt, I make but one request more, and that in a word ys but this, that what successe soever yt shall please god to send to yt, my offer may have as yt deservs an honorable and favorable interpretacion.

So I humbly take leave from Kellston
20 April 1605.

Your Lordships at comawndment,

John Haryngton.

44

To Secretary Barlow

[Theobalds, July, 1606].

My good Friend,

In compliance with your asking, now shall you accept my

poor accounte of rich doings. I came here a day or two before the Danish King came, and from the day he did come untill this hour, I have been well nigh overwhelmed with carousal and sports of all kinds. The sports began each day in such manner and such sorte, as well nigh persuaded me of Mahomets paradise. We had women, and indeed wine too, of such plenty, as woud have astonishd each sober beholder. Our feasts were magnificent, and the two royal guests did most lovingly embrace each other at table. I think the Dane hath strangely wrought on our good English nobles; for those, whom I never could get to taste good liquor, now follow the fashion, and wallow in beastly delights. The ladies abandon their sobriety, and are seen to roll about in intoxication. In good sooth, the parliament did kindly to provide his Majestie so seasonably with money, for there hath been no lack of good livinge; shews, sights, and banquetings, from morn to eve.

One day, a great feast was held, and, after dinner, the representation of Solomon his Temple and the coming of the Queen of Sheba was made, or (as I may better say) was meant to have been made, before their Majesties, by device of the Earl of Salisbury and others.—But, alass! as all earthly thinges do fail to poor mortals in enjoyment, so did prove our presentment hereof. The Lady who did play the Queens part, did carry most precious gifts to both their Majesties; but, forgetting the steppes arising to the canopy, overset her caskets into his Danish Majesties lap, and fell at his feet, tho I rather think it was in his face. Much was the hurry and confusion; cloths and napkins were at hand, to make all clean. His Majesty then got up and woud dance with the Queen of Sheba; but he fell down and humbled himself before her, and was carried to an inner chamber and laid on a bed of state; which was not a little defiled with the presents of the Queen which had been bestowed on his garments; such as wine, cream, jelly, beverage, cakes, spices, and other good matters. The entertainment and show went forward, and most of the presenters went backward, or fell down; wine did so occupy their upper chambers. Now did appear, in rich dress, Hope, Faith, and Charity: Hope did assay to speak, but wine renderd her endeavours so feeble that she withdrew, and hope the King would excuse her brevity: Faith was then all alone, for I am certain she was not joyned with good works, and left the court in a staggering condition: Charity came to the King's feet, and seemed to cover the multitude of sins her sisters had committed; in some sorte she made obeysance and brought giftes, but said she would return home again, as there was no gift which heaven had not already given his Majesty. She then returned to Hope and Faith, who were both sick and spewing in the lower hall. Next came Victory, in bright armour, and presented a rich sword to the King, who did not accept it, but put it by with his hand; and, by strange medley of versification, did endeavour to make suit to the King. But Victory did not tryumph long; for, after much lamentable utterance, she was led away like a silly captive, and laid to sleep in the outer steps of the anti-chamber. Now did Peace make entry, and strive to get foremoste to the King; but I grieve to tell how great wrath she did discover unto those of her attendants; and, much contrary to her semblance, most rudely made war with her olive branch, and laid on the pates of those who did oppose her coming.

I have much marvalled at these strange pegeantries, and they do bring to my remembrance what passed of this sort in our Queens days; of which I was sometime an humble presenter and assistant: but I neer did see such lack of good order, discretion, and sobriety, as I have now done. I have passed much time in seeing the royal sports of hunting and hawking, where the manners were such as made me devise the beasts were pursuing the sober creation, and not man in quest of exercise or food. I will now, in good sooth, declare to you, who will not blab, that the gunpowder fright is got out of all our heads, and we are going on, hereabouts, as if the devil was contriving every man shoud blow up himself, by wild riot, excess, and devastation of time and temperance. The great ladies do go well-masked, and indeed it be the only show of their modesty, to conceal their countenance; but, alack, they meet with such countenance to uphold their strange doings, that I marvel not at ought that happens. The Lord of the mansion is overwhelmed in preparations at Theobalds, and doth marvelously please both Kings, with good meat, good drink, and good speeches. I do often say (but not aloud) that the Danes have again conquered the Britains, for I see no man, or woman either, that can now command himself or herself. I wish I was at home:—*O rus, quando te aspiciam?*—And I will; before the Prince Vaudemont cometh.

I hear the uniting the kingdoms is now at hand; when the Parliament is held more will be done in this matter. Bacon is to manage all the affair, as who can better do these state jobs. My cosin, Lord Harington of Exton, doth much fatigue himself with the royal charge of the princess Elizabeth; and, midst all the foolery of these times, hath much labour to preserve his own wisdom and sobriety. If you would wish to see howe folly dothe grow, come up quickly; otherwise, stay where you are, and meditate on the future mischiefs of those our posterity, who shall learn the good lessons and examples helde forthe in these days. I hope to see you at the Bathe, and see the gambols you can perform in the hot waters, very speedily; and shall reste your assured friend in all quiet enjoyments and hearty good affections.

John Harington.

45

To Robert Markham

[1606]

My goode Cosin,

Herewithe you will have my Journale wyth our Historie, duringe our marche against the Irishe rebells. I did not intend any eyes should have seen thys discourse, but my own childerns; yet, alas! it happened otherwyse: for the Queen did so aske, and, I may saye, demande my accounte, that I coude not withholde shewing it; and I, even nowe, almoste tremble to rehearse hir

Highnesse displeasure hereat. She swore, "by God's Son, we were all idle knaves, and the Lord Deputy worse, for wasting our time and hir commandes, in such wyse as my Journale dothe write of." I coude have tolde hir Highnesse of suche difficulties, straites, and annoyance, as did not appear therein to her eyes; nor, I founde, coude not be broughte to her eare; for her choler did outrun all reasone, tho I did meete it at a seconde hande. For what shewe she gave at firste to my Lorde Deputy, at his return, was far more grievous, as wyll appear in goode tyme. I marvell to thynk what strange humors do conspire to patch up the natures of some myndes. The elements do seem to strive which shall conquer and rise above the other. In good soothe, our late Queene did enfolde them all together. I blesse her memorye, for all hir goodnesse to me and my familie; and now wyll I shewe you what strange temperament she did sometyme put forthe. Hir mynde was oftime like the gentle air that comethe from the westerly pointe in a summer's morn; 'twas sweete and refreshinge to all arounde her. Her speech did winne all affections, and hir subjectes did trye to shewe all love to hir commandes; for she woude saye, "hir state did require her to commande, what she knew hir people woude willingely do from their owne love to hir." Herein did she shewe hir wysdome fullie: for who did chuse to lose hir confidence; or who woude wythholde a shewe of love and obedience, when their Sovereign said it was their own choice, and not hir compulsion? Surely she did plaie well hir tables to gain obedience thus wythout constraint: again, she coude pute forthe suche alteracions, when obedience was lackinge, as lefte no doubtynges whose daughter she was. I saie thys was plain on the Lorde Deputy's cominge home; when I did come into hir presence, she chaffed muche, walkede fastly to and fro, looked with discomposure in her visage; and, I remember, she catched my girdle when I kneelede to hir, and swore, "By God's Son I am no Queen; that *man* is above me;—Who gave him commande to come here so soon? I did sende hym on other busynesse." It was longe before more gracious discourse did fall to my hearynge; but I was then put oute of my trouble, and bid "Go home." I did not stay to be bidden twise; if all the Iryshe rebels had been at my heels, I shoude not have had better speede, for I did now flee from one whom I both lovede and fearede too.

Hir Highnesse was wont to soothe hir rufflede temper wyth *readinge* every mornynge, when she had been stirred to passion at the council, or other matters had overthrown hir gracious disposition. She did much admire Seneca's wholesome advisinges, when the soul's quiet was flown awaie; and I saw muche of hir translating thereof. By art and nature together so blended, it was difficulte to fynde hir right humour at any tyme. Hir wisest men and beste counsellors were oft sore troublede to knowe hir wyll in matters of state: so covertly did she pass hir judgemente, as seemed to leave all to their discreet management; and, when the busynesse did turn to better advantage, she did moste cunningly commit the good issue to hir own honour and understandinge; but, when ought fell oute contrarie to hir wyll and intente, the council were in great straite to defende their owne actinge and not blemyshe the Queen's goode judgmente. Herein hir wyse men did oft lacke more wysdome; and the Lorde Treasurer woude ofte shed a plenty of tears on any miscarriage, well knowynge the difficulte parte was, not so muche to mende the matter itself, as his mistresse's humor: and yet he did most share hir favour and good wyll; and to his opinion she woude oft-tyme submit hir owne pleasure in great matters. She did keepe him till late at nyghte in discoursinge alone, and then call oute another at his departure, and try the depthe of all arounde hir sometyme. Walsingham had his turn, and each displaied their witte in pryvate.

On the morrowe, everye one did come forthe in hir presence and discourse at large; and, if any had dissembled withe her, or stood not well to hir advysinges before, she did not let it go unheeded, and sometymes not unpunishede. Sir Christopher Hatton was wont to saye, "The Queene did fishe for men's souls, and had so sweete a baite, that no one coude escape hir network." In truthe, I am sure hir speeche was suche, as none coude refuse to take delyghte in, when frowardness did not stand in the way. I have seen her smile, soothe with great semblance of good likinge to all arounde, and cause everie one to open his moste inwarde thought to her; when, on a sudden, she woud ponder in pryvate on what had passed, write down all their opinions, draw them out as occasion required, and sometyme disprove to their faces what had been delivered a month before. Hence she knew every one's parte and by thus *fishinge,* as Hatton sayed, she caught many poor fish, who little knew what snare was laid for them.

I will now tell you more of hir Majestys discretion and wonder-working to those about her, touchynge their myndes and opinions. She did oft aske the ladies around hir chamber, If they lovede to thinke of marriage? And the wise ones did conceal well their liking hereto; as knowing the Queene's judgment in this matter. Sir Mathew Arundel's fair cosin, not knowing so deeply as hir fellowes, was asked one day hereof, and simply said—"she had thought muche about marriage, if her father did consent to the man she lovede."—"You seeme honeste, i'faithe, said the Queen; I will sue for you to your father."—The damsel was not displeased hereat; and, when Sir Roberte came to cowrte, the Queene askede him hereon, and pressede his consentinge, if the match was discreet. Sir Roberte, muche astonied at this news, said— "he never heard his daughter had liking to any man, and wantede to gain knowledge of hir affection; but woude give free consente to what was moste pleasinge to hir Highnesse wyll and advyse."—"Then I will do the reste;" saith the Queene. The ladie was called in, and the Queene tould her father had given his free consente. "Then, replied the ladie, I shall be happie and please your Grace."—"So thou shalte; but not to be a foole and marrye. I have his consente given to me, and I vow thou shalte never get it into thy possession: so, go to thy busynesse. I see thou art a bolde one, to owne thy foolishnesse so readilye."

I coude relate manye pleasante tales of hir Majestie's outwittinge the wittiest ones; for few knew how to aim their shaft against hir cunninge. We did all love hir, for she said she loved us, and muche wysdome she shewed in thys matter. She did well temper herself towards all at home, and put at variance those abroad; by which means she had more quiet than hir neighbours. I need not praise her frugality; but I wyll tell a storie that fell oute when I was a boye. She did love riche cloathynge, but often chid those that bought more finery than became their state. It happenede that Ladie M. Howarde was possessede of a rich border, powderd wyth golde and pearle, and a velvet suite belonginge thereto, which moved manie to envye; nor did it please the Queene, who thoughte it exceeded her owne. One daye the Queene did sende privately, and got the ladies rich vesture, which she put on herself, and came forthe the chamber amonge the ladies; the kirtle and border was far too shorte for her Majesties heigth; and she askede every one, "How they likede her new-fancied suit?" At lengthe, she askede the owner herself, "If it was not made too short and ill-becoming?" which the poor ladie did presentlie consente to. "Why then, if it become not me, as being too shorte, I am minded it shall never become thee, as being too fine; so it fitteth neither well." This sharp rebuke abashed the ladie, and she never adorned her herewith any more. I believe the vestment was laid up till after the Queenes death.

As I did bear so much love towarde hir Majestie, I know not well how to stop my tales of hir virtues, and sometimes hir faults, for *nemo nascitur sine*—, saith the poet; but even her errors did seem great marks of surprizing endowments.—When she smiled, it was a pure sun-shine, that every one did chuse to baske in, if they could; but anon came a storm from a sudden gathering of clouds, and the thunder fell in wondrous manner on all alike. I never did fynde greater show of understandinge and lerninge, than she was bleste wyth; and whoever liveth longer than I can, will looke backe and become *laudator temporis acti.* Yet too, will I praise the present tymes, or I should be unmindfull of many favours receivede from manie handes.

Nowe will I trye to stop, and give your patience a breathingetime from my historie; but the subject of the letter wyll excuse my tedious reciting. I write from wonder and affection. I have nowe passed my storms, and wishe for a quiet harbour to laye up my bark; for I growe olde and infirme. I see few friendes, and hope I have no enemies. So nowe adieu, good cosin, and read my tale which I penned of our marches, ambuscades, culverins, and such-like matters; which if it give you no more pleasure in the readynge than it did me in the enduringe, I muste thinke it a sorry tale trulye.

I reste your lovynge Cosin,
John Harington.

Send me Petrarche by my man, at his returne.

46

To Prince Henry (?)

[1606?]

Right Gracious and inestimably deere Prince.

For your pleasures sake and my promise I present your Highnes this collection or rather confusion of all my ydle Epigrams, some of which some guilty minds might perhaps take in some despyte, but *Candidi et Cordati Lectores,* cleer minded and worthy reeders I know will peruse with good disport. The common lycense or rather lycensiowsnes of Poets may be my excuse yf not my warrant, as well for some sharpe reprehensions as for some broad phrases in them. For I have endevored so to sawse the matters, that though yowr Highnes and all noble minds may find some delectacion in the verse yet yt shall breed rather detestacion of the vice reprooved in the verse.

I subscribe yt thus with this picture rather then my name becawse so light and ingloriows a worke was fitter for those yowng years and the *barbatula* or french *Pe*[*cke*] *Devaunt,* then for *questas barbas* (as the Spaniardes call yt) that should bring with gray hairs more grave thoughts. Which thoughts shall think their master no longer worthie of life then he remayns

Most faithfully devoted
to your Highnes

47

To Prince Henry

[1606]

Most noble and honoured Sir,

I here sende by my servant such matter as your Highness did covet to see, in regard to Bishop Gardener of Winchester, which I shall sometime more largely treat of, and lay at your feet. I may truly say, this prelate did persecute me before I was born; for my father was by his command imprison'd in the Tower for eleven months, for only carrying a letter to the Princess Elizabeth; and my mother was taken from her presence, and obliged to dwell with Master Topcliff, as an heretic. My poor father did send many petitions to the Bishop, but in vain, as he expended one thousand pounds to get his liberty. Nor had they any comfort but their consciences to beguile this affliction, and the sweet wordes and sweeter deeds of their mistress and fellow prisoner. But, not to rail only, I will inform your Highness what old Sir Matthew Arundel was wont to say, touching these times—"that Bonner was more to blame than Gardener, who used to call him ass, and other scurvy names, for dealing so cruelly by honest men." I was moved to say so much against this judgment, that Sir Matthew said, my father ought to have lain in prison much longer, for sending such a saucy sonnet to Gardener: in truth it was not over civil, but after fair wordes ill taken, such deeds are not foul; and, considering those unrefin'd times, the poetry is not badly conceived; as your Highness may judge in due season, when I bring it before you, and here have sent no ill written letter to beg mercy of the Bishop; of which my father gave me copies, with many others in his own justification. In humble consideration of your Highness favour and countenance,

I remain, to all commande,

John Harington.

48

To Thomas Sutton

[June, 1607.]

Master Sutton,

I ame more ashamed than afrayd to come to you, being in your det 200[li] for myselfe, and 50[li] for sir John Skinner, and able to pay neyther till Camps be sold. With moche suyt and no little charge I procurd the act of parliament to passe, and that in so good fashyon (as Master Moore and Master Hyde, and other of counsell with yt and of the comittee for yt, wear of opynion) that all encombrances wear wypte of, saving Wines, which ys excepted. My hope was then that you shold buy yt, who I was sewr wold deal justly and pay trewly, and not wysh to buy yt undersolde.

June, 1607.

49

To Thomas Sutton

[November 6, 1607.]

Master Sutton.

There is an old verse, "*ter pulsare licet, si non aperitur abito.*" I have formerly written two long lettres to you, (yet I wysh you shold not think them too long): in them I recommended two commendable matters unto you, devotion and honor, which have been sometyme lawfully maryed together, though now some mayntayn an opinion that they are devorced. I have yet receaved no dyrect answer of them, but only a summons to come speedyly up, which I obayd before I receaved yt. I know both in your kyndnes and good maners you will thinke fit to answer so many lynes so frendly written to you under my hand, with a few under yours. I need not amplyfy unto you or repeat the worthynes of the thinges I perswade; only I protest to you on my salvation, the wysest men I have spoken with, the godliest and learnedest dyvynes I do meet with, approve my motion in bothe, and will eyther by conference or wryting confyrm as moche to you. I only wysh you not to undervallew your self, pluck up your speryts, linger not in good purposes, rejecte not friendly advyses, *hilarem datorem diligit Deus;* God loveth a cheerful giver; and God's deputyes on earth participat of that among other dyvyne qualytyes, namely in bountefull geving favors, and in gratefull accepting good actions, and somtyme good intentions; and so wyshing you (as to myselfe) good success in your good desyres, I commit you to God.

Your assured trewe frend,

John Haryngton.

From my lodging this foul Fryday
morning, 6th November, 1607.

50

To the Earl of Salisbury

[November 9, 1607].

Right Honorable my very good Lord

When I told your Lordship at Winsor of my purpose of dealing with Master Sutton, yt pleas'd yow to allow my endevors thearin as good and commendable, uppon which I have proceeded confydently, and comfortably, myne owne conscyence being 1000 wittnesses of my cleer intention therein. The Wysest and Oldest have sparks of ambition, though it be lyke a yowng Maid that blusshes, and will say nay, and is glad to seeme forst. *Vim licet Apelles grata est vis illa puellis.* And Horace sayth of a wyse man. *Præcipue sanus nisi quum pituita molesta est.* The comment calls this Rewm, Ambition.

Therefore I pray your Lordship let such a writt be made as I moved, and such a letter or Message, as suddenly and secretly as a matter of this Nature requyreth. And uppon my Alleadgeance, yf I bring not a deed seald of *Dominium et Maneriam de Castle Camps* to Duke Charles and his heires after the old mans lyfe that is above lxx, I will bring back the letter and cancell the

Writt, and hazard the Censure of my Wit for attempting that I fayld to performe. And yf I can once make this entry, having well batterd the place with long letters and many discourses, Camps cannot come to this sweet Duke, naked nor alone.

Good my Lord give me expedytion in this, as I know yow deerely love the King and his Chilldren. I have set a rest uppon yt; and, yf all I have dellt with, play fayr and above boord, I will get rest by it. Yf it misse, no bodyes labor is lost but myne, and a have a strong beleefe I shall not loose yt. But as the Italian sayth

> Servire e non aggradire
> E una cosa da morire

which death I wold be loth to dye. And so humbly take leave of your Lordship this ix[th] of November.

Your Lordships ever to be commaunded

John Haryngton.

51

To Thomas Sutton

[Greenwich, June 13, 1608.]

Sir,

Your strange message, first by my man, after by my son, now seconded with your speach to myself, did greatlie trouble me. That I have undone you, overthrown your estate, disturbed your designes: that no man dare buy any land of you, be your feoffee, nor take any trust from you; so as that which you had ordained to good uses, and to redeem your sins, was now so incombered, as you were skant master of your own; and all by means of a bruit among your friendes, raised as you supposed by me, "That you have made Duke Charles your heir, and the King your executor."

Far be it from me to abuse or misreport either so princelie and pious an intention as I know his Majestie hath to further all good works, or so godlie a purpose, as you intend to do some;

but "God cannot be mocked," though we may dissemble with men. The letter is still extant which was my warrant. I have spoken nothing but within compass of that, and that very sparinglie to your private friends; in which letter seeing you yourself would needs in your sense read a caveat to refuse honour because of age; which, in my construction, was an incouragement to take the honor due to your abilities and years; I have been since, and will be silent about it.—For the suit you would make to his Majesty (which I will not so much as guess at,) I will say what I thinke: you will make no suite, but such as will find favour and expedition; and, seeing you suppose I wronged you before, I would be glad to make you amends now by any endevor of mine. Onlie, my old friend, you may not forgett to be a benefactor to Bath church in your life-time; for alms, in one's life, is like a light borne before one, whereas alms after death is like a candle carried behind one.

Do somewhat for this church; you promised to have seen it e're this; whensoever you will go to Bathe, my lodgings shall be at your commandmente: the baths would strengthen your sinews, the alms would comfort your soule.

The tower, the quire, the two isles, are allready finished by Master Billett, executor to the worthie Lord Treasurer Burleigh: the walls are up ready for covering.

The leade is promised by our bountifull bishop, Dr. Montague; timber is promised by the earl of Shrewsburie, the earle of Hartford, the lord Say, Master Robert Hopton, and others.

There lacks but monie for workmanship, which if you would give, you should have many good prayers in the church now in your life-time, when they may indeed doe you good, and when the time is to "make friends of the mammon of iniquity, (as Christ bids us,) that we may be received into everlasting tabernacles;" to which God send us, to whose protection I leave you, &c.

From Greenwich, this
13th of June, 1608.

John Harington.

52

To Prince Henry

[Kelston, June 14, 1608]

May it please your Highnesse to accepte in as goode sorte what I nowe offer, as hath been done aforetyme; and I may saie, *I pede fausto:* but, havinge goode reason to thinke your Highnesse had goode will and likinge to reade what others have tolde of my rare dogge, I will even give a brief historie of his good deedes and straunge feats; and herein will I not plaie the curr myselfe, but in goode soothe relate what is no more nor lesse than bare verity. Althowgh I mean not to disparage the deedes of Alexander's horse, I will match my dogge against him for good carriage, for, if he did not beare a great *Prince* on his back, I am bolde to saie he did often bear the sweet wordes of a greater *Princesse* on his necke.

I did once relate to your Highnesse after what sorte his tacklinge was wherewithe he did sojourn from my house at the Bathe to Greenwiche Palace, and deliver up to the cowrte there such matters as were entrusted to his care. This he hathe often done, and came safe to the Bathe, or my house here at Kelstone, with goodlie returnes from such nobilitie as were pleasede to emploie him; nor was it ever tolde our Ladie Queene, that this messenger did ever blab ought concerninge his highe truste, as others have done in more special matters. Neither must it be forgotten, as how he once was sente with two charges of sack wine from the Bathe to my howse, by my man Combe; and on his way the cordage did slackene; but my trustie bearer did now beare himselfe so wisely as to covertly hide one flasket in the rushes, and take the other in his teethe to the howse; after whiche he wente forthe, and returnede with the other parte of his burden to dinner. Hereat your Highnesse may perchance marvele and doubte; but we have livinge testimonie of those who wroughte in the fieldes, and espiede his worke, and now live to tell they did muche longe to plaie the dogge, and give stowage to the wine themselves; but they did refrain, and watchede the passinge of this whole businesse.

I neede not saie how muche I did once grieve at missinge this dogge; for, on my journie towardes Londonne, some idle pastimers did diverte themselves with huntinge mallards in a ponde, and conveyd him to the Spanish ambassadors, where (in a happie houre) after six weeks I did heare of him; but suche was the cowrte he did pay to the Don, that he was no lesse in good likinge there then at home. Nor did the householde listen to my claim, or challenge, till I rested my suite on the dogges own proofes, and made him performe such feats before the nobles assembled, as put it past doubt that I was his master. I did send him to the hall in the time of dinner, and made him bring thence a pheasant out of the dish, which created much mirthe; but much more, when he returnede at my commandment to the table, and put it again in the same cover. Herewith the companie was well content to allow me my claim, and we bothe were well content to accepte it, and came homewardes. I coud dwell more on this matter, but *jubes renovare dolorem:* I will now saie in what manner he died. As we traveld towardes the Bathe, he leapede on my horses necke, and was more earneste in fawninge and courtinge my notice, than what I had observed for time backe; and, after my chidinge his disturbinge my passinge forwardes, he gave me some glances of such affection as moved me to cajole him; but, alas! he crept suddenly into a thorny brake, and died in a short time.

Thus I have strove to rehearse such of his deedes as maie suggest much more to your Highnesse thought of this dogge. But, having saide so much of him in prose, I will say somewhat too in verse, as you may finde hereafter at the close of this historie. Now let Ulysses praise his dogge Argus, or Tobite be led by that dogge whose name doth not appear; yet coud I say such things of my *Bungey,* (for so was he styled,) as might shame them both, either for good faith, clear wit, or wonderful deedes; to say no more than I have said, of his bearing letters to London and Greenwiche, more than an hundred miles. As I doubt not but your Highnesse would love my dogge, if not myselfe, I have been thus tedious in his storie; and again saie, that of all the dogges near your father's courte, not one hathe more love, more diligence to please, or less pay for pleasinge, than him I write of; for verily a bone would contente my servante, when some expecte greater matters, or will knavishly find oute a bone of contention.

I nowe reste your Highnesse friend, in all service that maye suite him,

John Harington.

P.S. The verses above spoken of, are in my book of Epigrams in praise of my dogge Bungey to Momus. And I have an excellente picture, curiously limned, to remaine in my posterity.

Kelstone, June 14, 1608.

53

To Thomas Sutton

[Bath, September 5, 1608.]

Master Sutton,

I long to heer how you doe, and long more to see you heer, whear I keep my lodging for you according to my promise, and wyll whyll thear ys any hope of your cominge. I sent you word I had not forgotten the charge you gave mee; now I say to you the mocyon ys made to the King allredy (I mean for your mortmayn) and hee hath promist yt; and furder, being told that perhaps my Lord Tresorer wold bee agaynst yt, his Majestie made awnswer, that yf yt concerned the crown land, or land in his possession, or of his Fee, yt might bee he wold shew reason agaynst yt; but in this to so godly an entent he sholde not crosse yt. Let me heer of you, and think not that I love you as those that wold gayn by you, but I wold gayn you and myselfe to God. I have, for all my losses, more left then I am worthy of, and thowsands more worthy want yt, and as the *yeer fraues* are lyke to want. You rich men should open your barnes; geve, lend, distribute to the poore, and lay up thresore in Heaven; Fayth ys good, hope is good, but charity ys the cheefer, "*major horum caritas.*" Heer are lawyers at Bathe; justice Willimes, an honest and stout judge; heer ys sir Henry Montacu, recorder; Master Francis Moore. Heer be devynes, heer bee physicians, and heer is saynt Billet the benefactor of this church, and founder of the new hospital for lame pilgrims. Heer ys the young lord Norrys, whome sycknes hath allmost made olde. And heer bee lame old men whome the Bath hath almoste made younge. Believe me, I think yt wold do you much good, and because I wish you much good, I wysh you heer. I can let you have honest roome, and cost me never a peny. So fareyewell,

Your trew Frend,

John Haryngton.

From Bath, this 5th of September, 1608.

54

To Prince Henry

1609

Moste Noble Prince,

It was sometyme since your wyll, that I should sende unto you suche scraps and fragments of witte and poesie as I mighte, from my poore braine; but as respecte is due to crowned heads, and as soche sholde be honorede before clownishe heads, I have here sent to your Highnesse a prettie verse, made by that unfortunate, and yet in his godlinesse I wist, moste fortunate King, Henrie the Sixthe; it hathe often caused much griefe to thinke on the perilous state of that goode Kinge, not forgetting to remark how he framed his lyfe to meet his death. I met with this verse in a book of my grandfather's writing, whose father was so moche in the trobles and warres of York and Lancaster, as to lose all his landes for being a commander on the wrong side, and among the traitors, if so I may say; and yet thus saith a poet:

Treason dothe never prosper;—What's the reason?
Why;—if it prosper, none dare call it Treason.

But this is not King Henry's verse. My ancestor Sir James Haryngton did once take prisoner, with his party, this poor Prince; for which the House of York did graunt him a parcel of lands in the northern counties, and which he was fool enough to lose again, after the battle of Bosworth, when King Henry the Seventh came to the crown; and methinks I feel his follie to this tyme, for, on forfeiture of twenty-five rich manors, it was time for our house to travel to southward, where, if they brought no landes, they founde some, from the goodness of Henrie the Eight.

The verse I did mean to presente your Highnesse wyth is as doth now followe, and well suteth the temper and condition of him who made it:

"Kingdomes are but cares;
State ys devoyd of staie;
Ryches are redy snares,
And hastene to decaie.

"Plesure ys a pryvie prycke
Wich yvce doth styll provoke;
Pompe, unprompt; and fame, a flame;
Powre, a smouldryng smoke.

"Who meenethe to remoofe the rocke
Owte of the slymie mudde,
Shall myre himselfe, and hardlie scape
The swellynge of the flodde."

Soe much for poor King Henrie's verse; and nowe take (if your Highnesse will excuse it) some of his prose: for I find written under this, in the same hand, the following sentences; and no doubte they were not given as his without good credit and groundes:

Patyence ys the armore and conqueste of the godlie: thys merytythe mercie, when cawslesse ys soffered sorrowe.

Nougte els ys warre bote furie and madnesse, whereyn ys not advyse bote rashnesse; not ryghte bote rage, rulethe and raignethe.

HENRIE.

And none so trulie coud speake thus as our poore author, under his piteous imprisonment, his bloody kingdom, his distressed kyndred; from all which God hath now most marvelously freed and deliverd these realms.

As I have thus given your Highnesse a short ensample of royal poetrie, I will not in haste forsake the matter, and descend from high to low; but will now venture to send to your readinge a special verse of King Henry the Eight, when he conceived love for Anna Bulleign. And hereof I entertain no doubt of the author; for, if I had no better reason than the rhyme, it were sufficient to think that no other than suche a King could write suche a sonnet; but of this my father oft gave me good assurance, who was in his household. This sonnet was sunge to the lady, at his commaundment, and here followeth:

The eagle's force subdues eache byrd that flyes;
What metal can resyst the flaminge fyre?
Dothe not the sunne dazle the cleareste eyes,
And melte the ice, and make the froste retyre?
The hardest stones are peircede thro wyth tools;
The wysest are, wyth Princes, made but fools.

Thus have I given your Highnesse another ensample of royal poetrie; nor, if time did serve, or your time woud permit, shoud I omit some prettier verses of our late Princesse, of blessed remembrance; but enow at this time.

I have complied with your requeste, and sente my "Ariosto," for your Highnesse entertainment, humbly suing for some special marke of your approbation in returne, from the hand and head of that Prince who claymeth the dutyful obeysance and unequalled estimation of

His honoured Servant,

John Harington.

55

To the Earl of Salisbury

[November 15, 1609.]

Right honorable my singular good Lord.

Whearas I understand your Lordship hath lately made enquyry concerning his Majesties Castles in Wales or the borders thearof, that have fees allowed to the constables, and yet are of small importawnce and use being now quyte owt of reparacions.

It may please yowr Lordship to bee advertised that I hold by Queen Elisabeths gratiows grawnt, the constableship of Carnarvon in Northwalls, with .LX.li fee to the same, being grawnted mee in reward of my father and mothers .22. years servyce.

Which Castle I confesse now to bee of no use at all but for the gaole of the Cowntry, and that by usurpacion.

The havn ys a barrd havn skant safe for fysher boats.

This tyme .9. yeer I left good store of Lead thear, and I allow a deputy .10.li a yeer to looke to yt.

The timber ys all rotton having not been repayred since Edward the fyrst his tyme that built yt.

The walls are still exceeding good, and wold soone bee made to serve for a garryson, yf cawse (as god forbid) shold requyre.

The fee I shall bee willing to surrender into his Majesties hand yf his Majestie by your Lordships good means will favor mee with some offyce in possessyon or reversyon that my son and I may bee capable of, and wee shall bee both bownd to pray for yowr Lordships prosperitye.

Allso I canne enforme your Lordship of good proffit to be made of Bristow Castle when your Lordship shalbee pleased that I shall attend your Lordship thearabowt.

15. November. 1609.

Yowr Lordships humbly to commaund

John Haryngton.

56

To Thomas Sutton

[December 21, 1609]

Master Sutton,

I was booted and spurd to have gon out of London on Satirday; but understanding your interrogatoryes wear not then in, I tooke occasyon to put off my going down till this day; which being the latest I could possibly stay, I hope you will have mee excused, and the rather becawse indeed I can say just nothing of the matter, which I think ys the cawse my lady Skinner forbeareth to serve process on me, though she said she wold. I heer now that my lady Arbella ys fallen sicke of the small pox, and that my lady Skinner attendeth her, and taketh great payns about her. Yf you think yt import you so moche as yt bee worth my comming up, I will stay till the parlement begin, which I heer will hold the 18th of February, or thereabout; agaynst which tyme make redy your bill for the mortmayn, and I can assewr you yt shall passe, yf you will bee as good as your word, and so I am bidden to tell you. In the mean tyme I will provyde your lodging at Bath, warm and clenly, good dry wood for your fyre; the town hath ever good beefe and bredde; and when you see the place and fynde (as I wysh) that God geve you helth, that then let God work with you for the good of the church and poore thear; by whose prayr your lyfe and helth may bee continewd yet seavn yeer at least, so you wold bee cheerful and not vex your selfe with the paltry dealing of such as sir John Skinner: and so I will end with this distich that my father taught mee above 40 yeer since,

> In doing good use no delay,
> For tyme ys swift, and slydes away.

21 December 1609

Your trew loving frend,

John Haryngton.

57

To Thomas Sutton

[February 5, 1609/1610.]

Sir,

Yt is not one of the least signes of God's favour unto you, that hee hath taken out of this world the man that above all others, without cause or desert, did seke your disturbance and defamation. But that he should dye in such miserie as ys reported, under the arrest of the sheriffs baylfes; and that in his life tyme hee should bee playd uppon the stage soe extreme scornfully; which, I suppose, of all the rest did most breake his heart; this ys to my thoughts a fearfull example of God's judgments, that even in this world sometimes punisheth men in the same kynd and measure they offend; one particular of which concerninge yourselfe I will reserve till I meete you. And soe of him now no more, but wish you to forgive him as I doe, and be good to his wife, who had no fault but being too good for him, and though I knowe how litle shee loves mee, and how muche shee hath wronged both you and mee heretofore, yet, I suppose, the man beinge gone, the mynd will alter, and she will proove herselfe and her owne nature.

But the speciall cause of my wryting to you ys to remember you now the Parlament draws nyghe of your mortmayn you appoynted [me] to bee a sewtor for; which as you know I did by your appoyntment mocion on your behalfe and, after by your lyke requeste, crave a special bill of Parlament, which now being come I ame calld uppon to know your resolucion thear in, that yt may bee accordingly proceded in. That ys all at this tyme I will wryte to you meaning shortly to visit you.
this 4th of febr. 1609.

58

To ———

[February 5, 1609/1610].

Right honorable

Whether Master Nevell did misreport or your honor misunderstand the offer was made by him selfe for Eamston in behalfe of Master Basset I know not, nor yt becomes not mee to conjecture.

But this I am well assewred that 4000li was the pryce hee offred and that hee assewred mee of great thanks from your honor for that which he knows full well I did evn to my own prejudice in the busynes.

59

To Lord Compton

[1610?]

Right honorable my very good lord.

I ame exceding glad to heer of your recovery specially whear I did heer yt which was from the mowth of the king him selfe, whose moste gracious care of your Lordship in this your sicknes hath made yt known how deer you have ever been to him.

And for mee I protest I have prayd for you in my soule which ys the best of my part I cold doe, and that not only because I knew you formerly in generall to bee of a noble and Joviall disposycion and welbeloved of all sorts, but in my perticuler when you did so earnestly and hartely set forward that same honest stratagem of myne for Duke Charles with words that I will not often repeat but yet I can never forget.

And now my Lord yf god have herd all our prayers that wisht you well let mee geve you the best I can which ys frendly advyse to shew your selfe gratefull to god agayn for this preciowse guift of helth which ys more worth then the welth of the world, with some work of Charytye and herein I must comend to you a place to which you have heretofore this come for your helth and may do hereafter a place to which your fatherinlaw promised some faver at being the cheifest and most famous clothing place of England and nere to which hee hathe left you goodly lands. I mean the Cytty and Church of Bathe.

The later of which in what case yt stands, in how open an ey of all travellers and strawngers to the shame of over 52 yeers peace in England your Lordship hath been an ey witnes. Let mee perswade your Lordship to vow somwhat to this godly and goodly worke which cannot but beer a sweet savor to his devyne Majestie, and severall in the world.

I did in the greatest of all Sicknesses that brought me for a tyme to worse state then I have herd of your Lordships sicknes vow a vow, and I hope to perform yt.

I send your Lordship here a list of theyr worthy names. Put what you liste down.

My Lord Byshop hath —— allredy.

60

To —— Sheldon

[1610?]

Cosen Sheldon,

Cutler ys broken with us absurdly and now yt appeers hee was from the beginning but a broker for my Lady Candish, but I have yet found a chapman thowgh abating moch of the pryce, who upon soch warrant agaynst my Lady Markhams Joynture as was formerly offerd from you and mee will go thorow. Whearfore now I pray you let us Joyn and remember the quyet that grows partly to you of being discharged of the Claym of 500li of Sir M. Hicks which Sir griph. by his lettres from beyond sea wold have layd on Kerby, of Stannopes 300li and of Skinners recog[nizance] for which I lost .100li to Skynner him selfe, and so wee may conclude with this proverbe. evn reck[oning] makes long frends.

61

To ——

[1612?]

May it please your Grace

Yf sicknes had not hindered mee, I had attended your grace long ere this, as well as to show my selfe thankfull, for the favour yow showd my sister in reconcyling her in so good termes to her husband, as allso to have had your graces direction for publishing all or som of these selected psalms, which his Majestie hath due tytle too yf it may stand with his gracious pleasure to accept it.

I have rais'd my selfe a mighty enmitie by offering my service in this kynd.

For as the fathers call these psalms darts to drive away devills, so I have been an instrument to sharpen up som of them that seem'd to bee dull poynted, and overgrown with rust, have thearby, I think, offended the cheife enemy of mankynd; whearby (god having permitted him) he hath at this howr layd more crosses upon my health, and consequently upon my wealth, then I had indured these 7 years before. But I comfort my selfe that impairing in this world is preparing for another. Yet I desire ere I dy to have this revenge to see the work published to gods honor and the kings, having no thought of any privat ambition to my selfe, and doubting greatly least if I dy the rashnes of som, and zeale of gaine rather then of godlines, will precipitat the publishing of them, which I would as much as I could prevent by your graces good favour.

62

To King James

[1612?]

That your Majestie will be pleased to referr the examynacion of this woorcke of the Psalms drawing so nere to an end to some of your learned chaplains now resyding abowt London, and the resolucion of all doubtfull places to my Lord Bishop of Elie. And whereas I fynde Master Aton your Majesties servant very judicious in this kynde and by whose advyce I must ingenuously acknowledge I have receaved some furtherance in this worck, yt may please your Majestie to joyne him also as well as for the revew of the same as for the ordring of the convenyent publishing of yt to your Majesties best lykinge.

And whereas your Majestie most nobly and publykly professeth withowt all parcyallitie to love vertue for vertue, I beseech your Majestie that my honest worke herein may fynde your gracious Acceptance, presuming to say this much that but few devynes in your Majesties dominions could so soone have accomplisht such a worcke of holly poetry, and fewer poetts could so faythfully have delyverde in smooth verse pure devinity.

EPIGRAMS

THE EPISTLE TO ALL

Readers, that Epigrams must bee read attentiuely, that *Legere & non intellegere, est negligere.*

1 *When in your hand you had this Pamphlet caught,*
Your purpose was to post it ouer speedie,
But change your minde, and feede not ouer-greedy:
Till in what sort, to feede you first be taught.
Suppose both first and second course be done,
No Goose, Porke, Capon, Snites, nor such as these,
But looke for fruit, as Nuts, and Parma-cheese,
And Comfets, Conserues, Raisons of the Sunne.
Then taste but few at once, feede not too fickle,
So shall you finde some coole, some warme, some biting,
Some sweet in taste, some sharpe, all so delighting,
As may your inward taste, and fancie tickle.
But though I wish Readers, with stomacks full,
Yet fast or come not, if your wits be dull.
  For I had liefe you did sit downe and whistle,
  As reading, not to reede. So ends th' Epistle.

1 14 Yet fast or come not, A] Yet fast nor come not, 1618 etc.

Booke I

Against MOMVS.

1 *That his Poetrie shall be no fictions, but meere truths.*

2 Scant wrate I sixteene lines, but I had newes,
Momus had found one fault, past all excuse,
That of *Epistle* I the name abuse.
No, gentle *Momus,* that is none abuse,
Without I call that *Gospel* that ensues,
But read to carpe, as still hath been thine vse;
Fret out thine heart to search, seeke, sift and pry,
Thy heart shall hardly giue my pen the ly.

2 *Against* Sextus, *a scorner of Writers.*

3 Of Writers, *Sextus* known a true despiser,
Saith that uppon our writings oft he lookes,
And yet confesseth he growes ne're the wiser.
But *Sextus,* where's the fault? not in our bookes.
No sure, tis in your selfe (Ile tell you why, sir)
Bookes giue not wisedome where was none before.
But where some is, there reading makes it more.

3 *Against* Lesbia, *both for her patience and impatience.*

4 *Lesbia,* I heard, how ere it came to passe,
That when old *Peleus* call'd thy Lord an Asse,
You did but smile; but when he cald him Oxe,
Straight-waies you curst him with all plagues & pox.
There is some secret cause why you allow
A man to scorne his braine, but not his brow.

3 [2] Saith that uppon A] Affirmes, that on 1618 etc. [3] And yet confesseth A] And confesseth 1618 etc. [5] why, sir) A] wherefore) 1618 etc.

4 *Of a poynted Diamond giuen by the Author to his wife, at the birth of his eldest sonne.*

5 Deare, I to thee this Diamond commend,
In which, a modell of thy selfe I send,
How iust vnto thy ioynts this circlet sitteth,
So iust thy face and shape my fancy fitteth.
The touch will try this Ring of purest gold,
My touch tries thee as pure, though softer mold.
That metall precious is, the stone is true,
As true, as then how much more precious you?
The Gem is cleare, and hath nor needes no foyle,
Thy face, nay more, thy fame is free from soile.
Youle deem this deere, because from me you haue it,
I deem your faith more deer, because you gaue it.
This pointed Diamond cuts glasse and steele,
Your loues like force in my firme heart I feele.
    But this, as all things else, time wasts with wearing,
    Where you, my Iewels multiply with bearing.

5 *Against Writers that carpe at other mens bookes.*

6 The Readers, and the Hearers like my bookes,
But yet some Writers cannot them digest.
But what care I? For when I make a feast,
I would my Guests should praise it, not the Cookes.

6 *Of a young Gallant.*

7 You boast, that Noble men still take you vp,
That when they bowle or shoot, or hawke or hunt,
In Coach, or Barge, on horse thou still art wont,
To runne, ride, row with them, to dine or sup:
This makes you scorne those of the meaner sort,
And thinke your credit doth so farre surmount;
Whereas indeed, of you they make no count,

5 [4] fancy A B] fancies 1618 etc. [7] true, B] true 1618, [11] deere, A] dear, B cleere, 1618 deare, 1633.

But as they doe of hawkes and dogges, for sport.
    Then vaunt not unto us this vayn renowne,
    Lest we both take you vp, and take you downe.

7 *To my Lady* Rogers, *the Authors wiues mother, how Doctor* Sherwood *commended her house in Bathe.*

8 I newly had your little house erected,
In which I thought I had made good conueiance,
To vse each ease, and to shunne all annoyance,
And prayd a friend of iudgement not neglected,
To view the roomes, and let me know the faults.
He hauing view'd the lodgings, staires, and vaults,
Said all was excellent well, saue here and there.
You thinke he praysd your house. No, I doe sweare,
    He hath disgrac'd it cleane, the case is cleere,
    For euery roome is either there, or here.

8 *Of* Lesbia, *a great Lady.*

9 *Lesbia* doth laugh to heare sellers and buyers
Cald by this name, Substantiall occupyers:
Lesbia, the word was good while good folke vsd it,
You mard it that with *Chawcers* iest abusd it:
    But good or bad, how ere the word be made,
    Lesbia is loth perhaps to leaue the trade.

9 *Of one that begd nothing, and had his sute granted.*

10 When thou dost beg, and none begs more importunate,
And art deny'd, as none speeds more infortunate,
With one quaint phrase thou doost inforce thy begging,
My mind vnto thy suite in this sort egging.
Alas, sir this? Tis nothing, once deny me not.

7 9 Then vaunt not unto us this vayne renowne, A] Then vaunt not thus of this your vaine renowne, 1618 etc.

8 Heading Sherwood A B] Sherehood 1618 etc.

Well then, for once content, henceforth bely me not.
    Your words so wisely plaste, doe so inchaunt me,
    Sith you doe nothing aske, I nothing graunt yee.

10 *Another of asking nothing.*

11 Some thinke thee *Lynus* of a Fryer begotten,
For still you beg where nothing can be gotten;
Yet oft you say, for so you haue been taught,
Sir, graunt me this, tis but a thing of nought.
And when indeed you say so, I belieue it,
As nought, vnto a thing of nought I giue it.
Thus with your begging, you but get a mock,
And yet with begging, little mend your stock.
    Leaue begging *Lynus* for such poore rewards,
    Else some will begge thee in the Court of Wards.

11 *Of liberality in giuing nothing.*

12 I heare some say, and some belieue it too,
That craft is found eu'n in the clouted shoo:
Sure I haue found it with the losse of pence,
My Tenants haue both craft and eloquence.
For when one hath a suite before he aske it,
His Orator pleades for him in a basket.
Well Tenant well, he was your friend that taught you
This learn'd Exordium, *Master, here cha brought you.*
For with one courtesie and two Capons giuing,
Thou sauest ten pounds in buying of thy liuing.
    Which makes me say, that haue obseru'd this quality,
    In poore men not to giue, is liberallity.

12 *Of learning nothing at a Lecture, vpon occasion of Dr.* Reynolds *at Oxford, afore my Lord of Essex, and diuers Ladies and Courtiers, at the Queenes last beeing there, on these words: Idolum nihil est, An Idol is nothing.*

11 [8] begging, little A] begging little, 1618 1625 begging little 1633.
12 [12] liberallity. A] niggerality. 1618 etc.

13 While I at Oxford stay'd, some few months since,
To see, and serue our deare & Soueraigne Prince,
Where graciously her Grace did see and show
The choisest fruits that learning could bestow,
I went one day to heare a learned Lecture
Read (as some said) by *Bellarmines* correcter,
And sundry Courtiers more then present were,
That vnderstood it well saue here and there:
Among the rest, one whom it least concerned,
Askt me what I had at the Lecture learned?
I that his ignorance might soone beguile,
Did say, I learned nothing all the while.
Yet did the Reader teach with much facilitie,
And I was wont to learne with some docilitie.
What learn'd you, Sir, (quoth he) in swearing moode?
I nothing learn'd, for nought I vnderstood,
I thanke my Parents, they, when I was yong,
Barr'd me to learne this Popish Romane tong,
And yet it seemes to me, if you say true,
I without learning learn'd the same that you.
    Most true, said I, yet few dare call vs Fooles,
    That this day learned nothing at the Schooles.

13 A Paradox of Doomes day.

14 Some Doctors deeme the day of Doome drawes neere:
But I can proue the contrary most cleere,
For at that day our Lord and Sauiour saith,
That he on earth shall scant finde any faith,
But in these daies it cannot be denyde,
All boast of onely faith and nought beside:
    But if you seeke the fruit thereof by workes,
    You shall finde many better with the Turkes.

14 Against a foolish Satyrist called Lynus.

15 Helpe, friends, I feele my credit lyes a bleeding,
For *Lynus,* who to me beares hate exceeding,

I heare against me is eu'n now a breeding
A bitter Satyr all of Gall proceeding:
Now sweet *Apollos* Iudge, to be his speeding,
For what he writes, I take no care nor heeding,
For none of worth wil think them worth the reeding.
  So my friend *Paulus* censures them who sweares,
  That *Lynus* verse suits best with *Mydas* eares.

15 Of a faire woman; translated out of Casaneus his Catalogus gloriae mundi.

16 These thirty things that *Hellens* fame did raise,
A Dame should haue that seeks for beuties praise:
Three bright, three blacke, three red, 3. short, 3. tall,
Three thick, three thin, three close, 3. wide, 3. small:
Her skin, and teeth, must be cleare, bright, and neat,
Her browes, eyes, priuy parts, as blacke as Ieat:
Her cheekes, lips, nayles, must haue vermillian hiew,
Her hands, hayre, height, must haue ful length to view.
Her teeth, foote, eares, all short, no length allowes,
Large brests, large hips, large space betweene the browes,
A narrow mouth, small waste, streight ( )
Her fingers, hayre, and lips, but thin and slender:
Thighs, belly, neck, should be full smooth and round,
Nose, head and teats, the least that can be found.
  Sith few, or none, perfection such attaine,
  But few or none are fayre, the case is plaine.

16 Of a Hous-hold fray friendly ended.

17 A man & wife stroue earst who should be masters,
And hauing chang'd between them hous-hold speeches,
The man in wrath broght forth a pair of wasters,—
& swore those 2. shuld proue who ware the breeches.
She that could break his head, yet giue him plasters,
Accepts the challenge, yet withall beseeches,

17 [1] masters, A] master, 1618.

That she (as weakest) then might strike the first,
And let him ward, and after doe his worst.
He swore that shuld be so, as God should blesse him,
And close he lay him to the surest locke.
She flourishing as though she would not misse him,
Laid downe her cudgell, and with witty mocke,
She told him for his kindnes, she would kisse him,
That now was sworne to giue her neuer knocke.
You sware, said she, I should the first blow giue.
And I sweare I'le neuer strike you while I liue.
Ah flattring slut, said he, thou dar'st not fight.
I am no Larke, quoth she, man, doe not dare me,
Let me point time and place, as 'tis my right
By Law of challenge, and then neuer spare me.
Agreed, said he. Then rest (quoth she) to night,
To morrow at Cuckolds hauen, I'le prepare me.
Peace, wife, said he, wee'le cease all rage and rancor,
Ere in that Harbor I will ride at Ancor.

17 Of Blessing without a crosse.

18 A Priest that earst was riding on the way,
Not knowing better how to passe the day,
Was singing with himselfe Geneua Psalmes.
A blind man hearing him, straight beg'd an almes.
Man, said the Priest, from coyne I cannot part,
But I pray God blesse thee, with all my heart.
O, said the man, the poore may liue with losse,
Now Priests haue learn'd to Blesse without a crosse.

18 Of writing with a Double meaning.

19 A certaine man was to a Iudge complaining,
How one had written with a Double meaning.
Foole, said the Iudge, no man deserueth trouble,
For Double meaning, so he deale not Double.

17 10 surest A] sured 1618 etc.

19 *Against* Cosmus *a great Briber.*

20 This wicked age of ours complaines of Bribing,
The want of iustice most to that ascribing:
When Iudges, who should heare both with equalitie,
By one side brib'd, to that shew partialitie.
But *Cosmus* in this case doth well prouide,
For euer he takes Bribes, of euery side:
Wherefore on him complaine can no man rightly,
But that he still may sentence giue vprightly.
I first would chuse one that all Bribes doth loath,
I next could vse him that takes bribes of both.

20 *Of a Precise Tayler.*

21 A Taylor, thought a man of vpright dealling,
True, but for lying, honest, but for stealing,
Did fall one day extremely sicke by chance,
And on the sudden was in wondrous trance.
The Fiends of hell mustring in fearfull manner,
Of sundry coloured silke display'd a banner,
Which he had stolne, and wish't as they did tell,
That one day he might finde it all in hell.
The man affrighted at this apparision,
Vpon recouerie grew a great Precision.
He bought a Bible of the new translation,
And in his life, he shew'd great reformation:
He walked mannerly, and talked meekely;
He heard three Lectures, and two Sermons weekely;
He vowed to shunne all companies vnruly,
And in his speech he vsde none oath, but truely:
And zealously to keepe the Sabboths rest,
His meate for that day, on the e'ue was drest.
And lest the custome, that hee had to steale,

21 [1] A Taylor, thought a man of vpright dealling, A] A Tayler a man of an vpright dealing, 1618 etc.

Might cause him sometime to forget his zeale,
He giues his iourneymen a speciall charge,
That if the stuffes allowance being large,
He found his fingers were to filch inclin'd,
Bid him but haue the Banner in his minde.
This done, I scant can tell the rest for laughter,
A Captaine of a Ship came three daies after,
And brought three yards of Veluet, & three quarters
To make Venetians downe below the garters.
He that precisely knew what was enuffe,
Soone slipt away three quarters of the stuffe.
His man espying it, said in derision,
Remember, Master, how you saw the vision.
    Peace (knaue) quoth he, I did not see one ragge
    Of such a colour'd silke in all the flagge.

21 *Of one* Paulus *a great man that expected to be followed.*

22 Proud *Paulus* late aduanc't to high degree,
Expects that I should now his follower be.
Glad I would be to follow ones direction,
By whom my honest suits might have protection.
But I sue *Don Fernandos* heyre for land,
Against so great a Peere he dare not stand.
A Bishop sues me for my tithes, that's worse,
He dares not venter on a Bishops curse.
Sergeant Erifilus beares me old grudges,
Yea but, saith *Paulus, Sergeants* may be Iudges.
Pure *Cinna* o're my head would begge my Lease,
Who? My Lord—? Man, O hold your peace.
Rich widdow *Lesbia* for a slander sues me.
Tush for a womans cause, he must refuse me.
Then farewell frost: *Paulus,* henceforth excuse me,
    For you that are your selfe thrall'd to so many,
    Shall neuer be my good Lord, if I haue any.

22 [12] Who? My Lord—? A] Who my Lord.—1618 etc.

22 Of a terrible Temporall non-resident.

23 Old *Cosmus* hath of late got one lewd qualitie,
To rayle at some that haue the cure of soules,
And his pure sprite their auarice controules,
That in their liuings is such inequalitie,
That they that can, keepe no good hospitalitie,
And some that would, whose fortune he condoles,
Want meanes: which comes, he sayes, in generalitie,
Because of these same *Totquots,* and Pluralitie;
Affirming as a sentence full discust,
One Clergie man haue but one liuing must.
But he, besides his sundry ciuill offices,
Hath bought in fee, fiue fat Impropriations,
Twelue Patronages, rights, or Presentations,
All which he keepes, yet preaches not nor prophesies.
Wel *Cosmus* hold thy tong, else some wil scoffe at this.
Thoud'st haue vs thinke a Priest should haue but one,
Wee'le thinke, nay say, nay sweare thou shouldst haue none.
Ill suites it thee to blame them for *non Residents,*
That giuest thereof such foule and shamefull Presidents.

23 A Tale of a Rosted Horse.

24 One Lord, 2. Knights, 3. Squires, 7. Dames at least,
My kind friend *Marcus* bade vnto his Feast,
Where were both Fish and Flesh, and all acates,
That men are wont to haue that feast great States.
To pay for which, next day he sold a Nagge,
Of whose pace, colour, Raine, he vs'd to bragge.
Well, Ile ne're care for red, or fallow Deere,
If that a horse thus cookt can make such cheere.

23 5 can, keepe A] can keepe, 1618 1625 can keepe 1633.
12 bought A] brought 1618 1625.
18 Ill suites it thee to blame them for *non Residents,* A] Il sutes it thee to blame, then for *non-Residents* 1618 1625.
24 8 If that a horse A] And if a horse 1618 etc.

24 *Of Madam* Dondrages *with her faire brest.*

25 A Fauorite of *Charles* late King of France,
Disporting with the King one day by chance,
Madam *Dondrages* came among the rest,
All bare, as still she vsed, all her brest.
The King would needs haue notice of his Minion;
Of this free Dame what was his franke opinion?
I say, and dare affirme, my liege, quoth he,
That if the crupper like the pettrell be,
  None but a king I worthy can acount,
  Vpon so braue a trapped beast to mount.

25 *The Author to his wife, of a womans eloquence.*

26 My *Mall,* I mark that when you mean to proue me
To buy a Veluet gowne, or some rich border,
Thou calst me good sweet heart, thou swearst to loue me,
Thy locks, thy lips, thy looks, speak all in order,
Thou think'st, and right thou think'st, that these doe moue me,
That all these seuerally thy sute do forder:
  But shall I tell thee what most thy suit aduances?
  Thy faire smoothe words? no, no, thy faire smooth hanches.

26 *Of* Peleus *ill-fortune in burying his friends.*

27 Old *Peleus* plaines his fortune and ill chaunce,
That still he brings his friends vnto the graue.
Good *Peleus,* I would thou hadst led the daunce,
And I had pointed thee what friends to haue.

25 [9] None but a king I worthy can acount, A] A King a Loue I worthy can account, 1618 etc.

26 [5] me, A] me 1618 etc. [6] forder: A] furder: B further: 1618 etc.

27 [3] Good A] God 1618.

27 *To my Lady* Rogers, *of breaking her bitches legge.*

28 Last night you laid it (Madam) in our dish,
How that a mayd of ours, whom we must check,
Had broke your bitches legge, I straight did wish
The baggage rather broken had her neck:
You tooke my answer well, and all was whish.
  But take me right, I meant in that I said,
  Your baggage bitch, and not my baggage mayd.

28 *Of Paying.*

29 A Captaine late arriu'd from losse of *Sluce,*
Hearing some friend of mine did him abuse,
Vow'd he would pay him when he met him next.
My friend with these great threats nothing perplext,
  Prayd that the promise faild not of fulfilling,
  For three yeeres past he lent him fortie shilling.

29 *The Author, of his own fortune.*

30 Take fortune as it falles, as one aduiseth:
Yet *Heywood* bids me take it as it riseth:
And while I think to doe as both doe teach,
It falles and riseth quite beside my reach.

30 *Of the cause of dearth.*

31 I heare our Country neighbors oft complaine,
Their fruits are still destroyd with too much raine:
Some gesse by skill of Starres, and Science vaine,
Some watry Planet in the heauens doth raigne:
No, Sinne doth raigne on earth, the cawse is plaine;
Which if we would repent, and then refraine,
The skyes would quickly keepe their course againe.
  Now that with lewdnesse we be luld asleepe,
  The heauens, to see our wickednesse, doe weepe.

31 [5] cawse A] case 1618 etc.

31 To Sir Hugh Portman, *in supping alone in too much company.*

32 When you bade forty guests, to me vnknowne,
I came not, though you twice for me did send,
For which you blame me as a sullen friend.
Sir, pardon me, I list not suppe alone.

32 Of Sextus, *a bad husband.*

33 Had I, good *Sextus,* well considered first,
And better thought on phrases of ciuilitie,
When I said, you of husbands were the worst,
I should haue said, excepting the Nobilitie.
Well, now, to speak more mannerly and true,
The Nobles, and great States-men, all foreprised,
An husband worse then you, I neuer knew.
Then mend, yet thus in mending be aduised:
  Be no good husband, for as some haue thought,
  Husbands that will be good, make huswifes nought.

33 Of writing with double pointing. It is said, that King Edward *of Carnaruan lying at Berkly Castle prisoner, a Cardinall wrote to his Keeper,* Edwardum occidere noli, timere bonum est, *which being read with the point at* timere, *it cost the King his life. Here ensues as doubtfull a point, but I trust, not so dangerous.*

34 Dames are indude with vertues excellent?
What man is he can proue that they offend?
Daily they serue the Lord with good intent:
Seld they displease their husbands: to their end
Alwaies to please them well they doe intend.
  Neuer in them one shall finde shrewdnes much.
  Such are their humors, and their grace is such.

33 5 Well, now, A] Well, none, 1618 etc.

34 To my Lady Rogers.

35 Good Madame, in this verse obserue one point,
That it seemes the Writer did appoint
With smoothest oyle of praise your eares to noynt;
Yet one his purpose soone may disappoint.
For in this verse displacing but a point,
Will put this verse so clearely out of ioynt,
That all this praise will scant be worth a point.

35 To her Daughter, vpon the same point, reading the same verse with another point.

36 Dames are indude with vertues excellent?
What man is he can proue that? they offend
Daily: they serue the Lord with good intent
Seld: they displease their husbands to their end
Alwaies: to please them well they doe intend
Neuer: in them one shall find shrewdnesse much.
Such are their humors, and their graces such.

36

37 My *Mall,* the former verses this may teach you,
That som deceiue, some are deceiu'd by showes.
For this verse in your praise, so smooth that goes,
With one false point and stop, did ouer-reach you,
And turne the praise to scorne, the rimes to prose,
By which you may be slanderd all as Shrowes:
And some, perhaps, may say, and speake no treason,
The verses had more rime, the prose more reason.

37 Comparison of the Sonnet, and the Epigram.

38 Once, by mishap, two Poets fell a-squaring,
The Sonnet, and our Epigram comparing;
And *Faustus,* hauing long demurd vpon it,

35 [5] displacing A] disparting 1618 etc.

Yet, at the last, gaue sentence for the Sonnet.
Now, for such censure, this his chiefe defence is,
Their sugred taste best likes his likresse senses.
  Well, though I grant Sugar may please the taste,
  Yet let my verse haue salt to make it last.

38 *Of an accident of saying grace at the Lady* Rogers, *who vsed to dine exceeding late. Written to his wife.*

39 My *Mall,* in your short absence from this place,
My selfe here dining at your mothers bord,
Your little sonne did thus begin his grace;
The eyes of all things looke on thee, ô Lord,
And thou their foode doost giue them in due season.
Peace boy, quoth I, not more of this a word,
For in this place, this Grace hath little reason:
When as we speake to God, we must speake true.
And though the meat be good in taste and season,
This season for a dinner is not due:
Then peace, I say, to lie to God is treason.
Say on, my boy, saith shee, your father mocks,
Clownes, and not Courtiers, vse to goe by clocks.
Courtiers by clocks, said I, and Clownes by cocks.
  Now, if your mother chide with me for this,
  Then you must reconcile vs with a kisse.

39 *Of Don* Pedro *and his Poetry.*

40 Sir, I shall tell you newes, except you know it,
Our noble friend *Don Pedro,* is a Poet.
His verses all abroad are read and showne,
And he himselfe doth sweare they are his owne.
His owne? tis true, for he for them hath paid
Two crownes a Sonnet, as I heard it said.
So *Ellen* hath faire teeth, that in her purse
She keepes all night, and yet sleepes ne're the worse.

So widdow *Lesbia,* with her painted hide,
Seem'd, for the time, to make a handsome bride.
    If *Pedro* be for this a Poet cald,
    So you may call one hairie that is bald.

40 *A comfort for poore Poets.*

41 Poets, hencefoorth for pensions need not care,
Who call you beggers, you may call them lyers,
Verses are growne such merchantable ware,
That now for Sonnets, sellers are, and buyers.

41 *Against a foolish Satyrist.*

42 I read that Satyre thou intitlest first,
And I layd aside the rest, and ouer-past,
And sware, I thought, that th' author was accurst,
That that first Satyre had not been his last.

42 *An Epitaph in commendation of* George Turberuill, *a learned Gentleman.*

43 When rimes were yet but rude, thy pen endeuored
To pollish Barbarisme with purer stile:
When times were grown most old, thy heart perseuered
Sincere & iust, vnstaind with gifts or guile.
Now liues thy soule, though from thy corps disseuered,
There high is blisse, here cleare in fame the while;
    To which I pay this debt of due thanks-giuing,
    My pen doth praise thee dead, thine grac'd me liuing.

43 *To the Queenes Maiestie, when shee found fault with some particular matters in* Misacmos Metamorphosis.

44 Dread Soueraign, take this true, though poore excuse,
Of all the errors of *Misacmos* Muse,
A hound that of a whelpe my selfe hath bred,

41 [1] hencefoorth A] hereafter, 1618 1625 hereafter 1633.

And at my hand and table taught and fed,
When other curres did fawne and flatter coldly,
Did spring and leape, and play with me too boldly:
For which, although my Pages check and rate him,
Yet stil my self doth much more loue then hate him.

44 To the ladies of the Queenes Priuy-Chamber, at the making of their perfumed priuy at Richmond, *The Booke hanged in chaines saith thus:*

45 Faire Dames, if any tooke in scorne, and spite
Me, that *Misacmos* Muse in mirth did write,
To satisfie the sinne, loe, here in chaines,
For aye to hang, my Master me ordaines.
Yet deeme the deed to him no derogation,
But deign to this deuice new commendation,
Sith here you see, feele, smell that his conueyance
Hath freed this noysome place from all annoyance.
Now iudge you, that the work mock, enuie, taunt,
Whose seruice in this place may make most vaunt:
If vs, or you, to praise it, were most meet,
You, that made sowre, or vs, that make it sweet?

45 To Master Cooke, *the Queenes Atturney, that was incited to call* Misacmos *into the Starre-chamber, but refused it; saying, he that could giue another a Venue, had a sure ward for himselfe.*

46 Those that of dainty fare make deare prouision,
If some bad Cookes marre it with dressing euill,
Are wont to say in iest, but iust derision,
The meat from God, the Cookes came from the diuell.
But, if this dish, though draffe in apparision,
Were made thus sawst, a seruice not vnciuill,
Say ye that taste, and not digest the Booke,
The Dee'le go with the meat, God with the Cooke.

45 [4] me A] he 1618 etc. [6] deign A] doome 1618 etc.

46 *Against* Lynus, *a Wryter, that found fault with the* Metamorphosis.

47 *Lynus,* to giue to me a spightfull frumpe,
Said that my writings sauourd of the Pumpe,
And that my Muse, for want of matter, takes
An Argument to write of from the Iakes.
Well, *Lynus,* speake each Reader as he thinks,
Though thou of Scepters wrat'st, and I of sinks,
Yet some will say, comparing both together,
My wit brings matter thence, thine matter thither.

47 *Of Garlick to my Lady* Rogers.

48 If Leekes you like, and doe the smell disleeke,
Eate Onions, and you shall not smell the Leeke:
If you of Onions would the sent expell,
Eate Garlick, that will drowne th' Onyons smell.
But sure, gainst Garlicks sauour, at one word,
I know but one receit, what's that? (go looke.)

48 *A dish of dainties for the Diuell.*

49 A godly Father, sitting on a draught,
To doe as need, & Nature hath vs taught,
Mumbled, as was his manner, certaine prayers:
And vnto him, the Diuell straight repaires,
And boldly to reuile him he begins,
Alleaging, that such prayers are deadly sinnes;
And that it prou'd he was deuoyd of grace,
To speake to God in so vnfit a place.
The reuerend man, though at the first dismayd,
Yet strong in faith, thus to the Diuell said;
Thou damned Spirit, wicked, false, and lying,
Despayring thine owne good, and ours enuying:
Each take his due, and me thou canst not hurt,
To God my prayer I meant, to thee the durt.
Pure prayer ascends to him that high doth sit.
Downe falls the filth, for fiends of hell more fit.

49 Of Don Pedro *his sweet breath.*

50 How ist, *Don Pedros* breath is still perfum'd,
And that he neuer like himselfe doth smell?
I like it not, for still it is presum'd;
Who smelleth euer well, smells neuer well.

50 Misacmos *against his Booke.*

51 The Writer and the matter well might meet,
Were he as eloquent, as it is sweet.

51 Of Cloacina *and* Sterquitius.

52 The Romanes euer counted superstitious
Adored with high titles of Diuinitie,
Dame *Cloacina,* and the Lord *Sterquitius,*
Two persons in their State of great affinitie.
But we, that scorne opinions so pernitious,
Are taught by Truth well try'd, t'adore the Trinitie.
And, who-so care of true Religion takes,
Wil think such Saints wel shrined in A I A X.

52 To the Queene when she was pacified, and had sent Misacmos *thankes for the inuention.*

53 A Poet once of *Traian* begd a Lease,
(*Traian,* terror of Warre, mirror of Peace)
And doubting how his writings were accepted,
'Gainst which he heard some Courtiers had excepted,
He came to him, and with all due submission,
Deliuered this short Verse, with this Petition:
Deare Soueraigne, if you like not of my Writings,
Grant this sweet cordiall to a spirit daunted.
But if you reade, and like my poore enditings,
Then for reward let this small sute be granted.
Of which short Verse, I finde insu'd such fruit,
The Poet of the Prince obtain'd his sute.

53 [4] excepted, A] excepted; 1618 etc. [12] Poet A] Poet, 1618.

53 A Poets Priuiledge.

54 Painters and Poets claime by old enroulement,
A Charter, to dare all without controulement.

54 To Faustus.

55 *Faustus* findes fault, my Epigrams are short,
Because to reade them, he doth make some sport:
I thanke thee, *Faustus,* though thou iudgest wrong,
Ere long I'll make thee sweare they be too long.

55 Against Faustus.

56 What is the cause, *Faustus,* that in dislike
Proud *Paulus* still doth touch thee with a Pike?
It breedeth in my minde a great confusion,
To thinke what he should meane by such allusion.
Trowst thou hee meanes, that thou mightst make a Pike-
man?
That cannot be, for that thou art no like man.
Thy crazed bones cannot endure the shocke,
Besides, his manner is to speake in mocke.
Or ist, because the Pike's a greedy Fish,
Deuoures as thou dost many a dainty Dish?
And in another sort, and more vnkinde,
Wilt bite, and spoile those of thy proper kinde;
Or doth he meane thou art a quarrell-piker,
That amongst men, wert neuer thought a striker?
In this he sayes, thou art a Christian brother,
That stricken on one eare, thou turnest tother.
Or doth he meane that thou would'st picke a thanke?
No sure, for of that fault I count thee franke.
How can thy tale to any man be gratefull,
Whose person, manners, face and all's so hatefull?
Then *Faustus,* I suspect yet one thing worse,
Thou has pickt somwhat else. What's that? a purse?

56 [4] allusion. A] elusion. 1618 etc. [16] turnest tother. A] turnest the other. 1618 1625 turn'st the other. 1633.

56 Of *mis-conceiuing.*

57 Ladies you blame my verses of scurrilitie,
While with the double sense you were deceiu'd.
Now you confesse them free from inciuilitie,
Take heede henceforth you be not misconceiu'd.

57 How the Bathe is like Purgatory.

58 Whether it be a Fable, or a Story,
That *Beda* and others write of Purgatory:
I know no place that more resemblance hath
With that same Purgatory, then the Bathe.
Men there with paines, doe purge their passed sinnes,
Many with paines, purge here their parched skins:
Frying and freezing are the paines there told,
Here the chiefe paine, consists in heate and cold.
Confused cryes, vapour and smoke and stinke,
Are certaine here: that there they are, some thinke.
There fire burnes Lords and Lowts without respect,
Our water for his force workes like effect:
Thence none can be deliuered without praying,
Hence no man is deliuered without paying.
    But once escaped thence, hath sure saluation,
    But those goe hence, still feare recidiuation.

58 Of going to Bathe.

59 A common phrase long vsed here hath beene,
And by prescription now some credit hath:
That diuers Ladies comming to the Bathe,
Come chiefely but to see, and to be seene.
But if I should declare my conscience briefely,
I cannot thinke that is their Arrant chiefely.
    For as I heare that most of them haue dealt,
    They chiefely came to feele, and to be felt.

58 10 thinke. A] thinke 1618.

59 *Of Plaine dealing.*

60 My writings oft displease you: what's the matter?
You loue not to heare truth, nor I to flatter.

60 *Against* Paulus.

61 Because in these so malecontented times,
I please my selfe with priuate recreation;
In reading or in sweetest contemplation,
Or writing sometime prose, oft pleasant rimes:
Paulus, whom I haue thought my friend sometimes,
Seekes all he may to taint my reputation:
Not with complaints, nor any haynous crimes,
But onely saying in his scoffing fashion,
These writers that still sauour of the schooles,
Frame to themselues a Paradice of fooles.
But while he scornes our mirth and plaine simplicitie,
Himselfe doth sayle to *Affricke* and to *Ind.*
And seekes with hellish paines, yet doth not finde
That blisse, in which he frames his wise felicitite.
    Now which of twaine is best, some wise man tell,
    Our Paradice, or else wise *Paulus* hell.

61 *Of* Caius *hurts in the warre.*

62 *Caius* of late return'd from Flemmish warres,
Of certaine little scratches beares the skarres,
And for that most of them are in his face,
With *tant plus beau* hee showes them for his grace.
Yet came they not by dint of Pike, or Dart,
But with a pot, a pint, or else a quart.
    But he ne're makes his boast, how, and by whom
    He hath receiu'd a greater blow at home.

61 [12] to *Ind.* A] *Ind.* 1618. [15] man A] men 1618.
62 [7] whom A] whom, 1618.

62 *Of two Welsh Gentlemen.*

63 I heard among some other pretty Tales,
How once there were two Gentlemen of Wales,
Of Noble bloud, discended of his House
That from our Ladies gowne did take a Louse.
These two (thus goes the tale) vpon a day,
Did hap to trauell vpon London way;
And for 'twas cumbersome to weare a boote,
For their more ease, they needs would walke afoote.
Their fare was dainty, and of no small cost,
For euery meale they call'd for bak't and rost.
And lest they should their best apparell lacke,
Each of them bore his Wardrobe at his backe.
Their Arrant was, but sore against their wils,
To Westminster to speake with Master *Milles.*
No maruell men of such a sumptuous Dyet,
Were brought vnto Star-chamber for a Ryot.
These Squires one night arriued at a towne,
To looke their lodgings, when the Sun was downe.
And for the Inne-keeper his gates had locked,
In haste, like men of some account they knocked.
The drowsie Chamberlaine doth aske who's there.
They told that Gentlemen of Wales they were.
How many, quoth the man, is there of you?
Quoth they, Here is *Iohn ap Rice, ap Iones, ap Hue,*
And *Nicholas ap Steuen, ap Giles, ap Dauy.*
Then Gentlemen, adue, quoth he, God saue ye.
    Your Worships might haue had a bed or twaine,
    But how can that suffice so great a traine?

63 *To Master* Maior *of Bathe, that Bathe is like Paradice.*

64 Sir, if you either angry were or sory,
That I haue lik'ned Bathe to Purgatory:
Loe, to re-gaine your fauour in a trice,

63 3 House A] House, 1618 16 vnto A] into the 1618 etc.

I'le proue it much more like to Paradice.
Man was at first in Paradice created,
Many men still in Bathe are procreated.
Man liu'd there in state of Innocence,
Here many liue in wit, like Innocents.
There sprang the heads of foure most noble streames:
From hence flow springs, not matcht in any Realmes.
Those springs & fruits, brought helpe for each disease.
These vnto many maladies bring ease.
Man, there was monylesse, naked and poore.
Many goe begging here from dore to dore.
Man there did taste the Tree he was forbidden.
Here many men taste fruits, makes them be chidden.
Angels dwell there in pure and shining habit.
Angel-like faces some this place inhabit.
Angels let in all are admitted thither,
Angels keepe in all are admitted hither.
If hymnes wer thear by Adam sung and Heva,
Heer knights and ladies psalmes sing of Geneva.
Many are said to goe to heauen from thence,
Many are sent to heauen, or hell, from hence.
    But in this one thing likenesse most is fram'd,
    That Men in Bathe goe naked, not asham'd.

64 *Of* Don Pedro's *debts.*

65 *Don Pedro's* out of debt, be bold to say it,
For they are said to owe, that meane to pay it.

65 Of one that vow'd to dis-inherit his sonne, and giue his goods to the poore.

66 A citizen that dwelt neere Temple-barre,
By hap one day fell with his Sonne at Iarre;

64 [18] Angel-like faces A] Angels like faces, 1618 1625 Angels-like faces 1633 [21] and [22] A are omitted 1618 etc.

Whom for his euill life, and lewd demerit,
He oft affirm'd, he would quite dis-inherit,
And vow'd his goods, and lands, all to the poore.
His sonne what with his play, what with his whore,
Was so consum'd at last, as he did lacke
Meate for his mouth, and clothing for his backe.
O craftie pouerty! his father now
May giue him all he hath, yet keepe his vow.

66 *Of a Precise Cobler, and an ignorant Curat.*

67 A Cobler, and a Curat, once disputed
Afore a Iudge, about the Queenes Iniunctions,
And sith that still the Curat was confuted,
One said 'twas fit that they two changed functions.
Nay, said the Iudge, that motion much I lothe,
But if you will, wee'le make them Coblers both.

67 *Of* Lynus *Poetrie.*

68 When *Lynus* thinkes that he and I are friends,
Then all his Poems vnto me he sends:
His Disticks, Satyrs, Sonnets, and Exameters,
His Epigrams, his Lyricks, his Pentameters.
Then I must censure them, I must correct them,
Then onely I must order, and direct them.
I read some three or foure, and passe the rest,
And when for answere, I by him am prest,
I say, that all of them, some praise deserue,
For certaine vses I could make them serue.
But yet his rime is harsh, vneu'n his number,
The manner much, the matter more, doth cumber.
His words too strange, his meanings are too mistick,
But at one word, I best indure his Disticke:
And yet, might I perswade him in mine humor,

66 [5] poore. A] poore, 1618 etc. [9] now A] now, 1618.
68 [12] more, A] both 1618 etc.

Not to affect vaine praise of common rumor,
  Then should he write of nothing: for indeede,
  Gladly of nothing I his verse would reade.

68 *Of one that seekes to be stellified being no Pithagorian.*

69 An vse there was among some Pithagorians,
If we giue credit to the best Historians:
How they that would obserue the course of Starres,
To purge the vapors, that our cleere sight barrs,
And bring the braine vnto a settled quiet,
Did keepe a wondrous strict and sparing dyet,
Drinke water from the purest heads of springs,
Eate Hearbs and Flowers, not taste of liuing things:
And then to this scant fare, their bookes applying,
They call'd this sparing Dyet, Stellifying.
Then thinkest thou, professed Epicure,
That neuer couldest vertuous paines endure,
That eat'st fat Venson, bowzest Claret Wine,
Do'st play till twelue, and sleepe till after nine,
  And in a Coach like *Vulcans* sonne dost ride,
  That thou art worthy to be stellified?

69 *Against* Momus.

70 Lewd *Momus* loues mens liues and lines to skan,
Yet said (by chance) I was an honest man.
But yet one fault of mine, he strait rehearses,
Which is, I am so full of toyes and verses.
True, *Momus,* true, that is my fault, I grant.
Yet when thou shalt thy chiefest vertue vaunt,
  I know some worthy Sprites one might entice,
  To leaue that greatest Vertue for this Vice.

69 [4] barrs, A] tarres, 1618 etc.
70 [1] loves A] loves, 1618. [8] Vertue A] Vertue, 1618.

70 *Of* Galla, *and her Tawny fanne.*

71 When *Galla* and my selfe doe talke together,
Her face she shroudes with fanne of tawny Fether,
And while my thought somewhat thereof deuiseth,
A double doubt within my minde ariseth:
As first, her skin or fanne which looketh brighter,
And second whether those her looks be lighter,
Then that same Plume wherwith her looks were hidden.
But if I cleer'd these doubts, I should be chidden.

71 To his Wife for striking her Dogge.

72 Your little Dogge that barkt as I came by,
I strake by hap so hard, I made him cry,
And straight you put your finger in your eye,
And lowring sate. I askt the reason why.
Loue me, and loue my Dogge, thou didst reply:
Loue as both should be lou'd. I will, said I,
And seald it with a kisse. Then by and by,
Cleer'd were the clouds of thy faire frowning sky.
Thus small euents, great masteries may try.
For I by this, doe at their meaning ghesse,
That beate a Whelpe afore a Lyonesse.

72 Against a Wittall Broker that set his wife to sale.

73 I see thee sell Swords, Pistols, Clokes, and Gowns,
With Dublets, Slops, & they that pay thee crowns
Doe, as 'tis reason, beare away the ware,
Which to supply, is thy continuall care.
But thy wiues ware, farre better rate doth hold,
Which vnto sundry chapmen's dayly sold.
Her Fayre lasts all the yeere, and doth not finish,
Nor doth her ware ought lessen, or diminish.

72 [4] sate. I A] sate, and 1618 etc.
73 [2] crowns A] crowns; 1618 crownes, 1633.

73 *Of his translation of* Ariosta.

74 I spent some yeeres, & months, & weeks, and dayes,
In Englishing the Italian *Ariost.*
And straight some offered Epigrams in praise
Of that my thankelesse paines, and fruitlesse cost.
But while this offer did my spirits raise,
And that I told my friend thereof in boste:
He disapprou'd the purpose many wayes,
And with this prouerbe prou'd it labour lost:
Good Ale doth need no signe, good Wine no bush,
Good verse of praisers, need not passe a rush.

74 *Of* Cinna's *Election.*

75 Pvre *Cinna* makes no question he's elect,
Yet lewdly liues: I might beleeue him better,
If he would change his life, or change one letter,
And say that he is sure he is eiect.
An holy, true, and long preserued purity,
May hap, and but perhap breede such securitie.

75 *The Author to a Daughter of nine yeere olde.*

76 Though pride in Damsels is a hatefull vice,
Yet could I like a Noble-minded Girle,
That would demand me things of costly price,
Rich Veluet gownes, pendents, and chaines of Pearle,
Carknets of Aggats, cut with rare deuice,
Not that hereby she should my minde entice
To buy such things against both wit and profit,
But I like well she should be worthy of it.

76 *To the Earle of Essex, of one enuious of* Ariosto *translated.*

77 My Noble Lord, some men haue thought me proud,
Because my *Furioso* is so spred,
And that your Lordship hath it seene and read,

74 [6]boste: A] post: 1618 etc. [10]need A] needs 1618 etc.

And haue my veine, and paine therein alowd.
No sure, I say, and long time since haue vowd,
My fancies shall not with such baits be fed,
Nor am I fram'd so light in foote or head,
That I should daunce at sound of praises crow'd:
Yet I'le confesse this pleas'd me when I heard it,
How one that euer carpes at others writings,
Yet seldome any showes of his enditings:
With much adoe gaue vp this hungry verdit,
'Twas well he said, but 'twas but a translation.
Is't not a Ramme that buts of such a fashion?

77 *Of a speechlesse woman. To his wife.*

78 A curst wife, of her husbands dealings doubting,
At his home comming silent was and mute,
And when with kindnesse he did her salute,
She held her peace, and lowring sate and pouting,
Which humor that he thought to check with flouting:
He caus'd one secretly to raise a brute
That she lay speechlesse: straight the Bell doth toule,
And men deuoutly giuen, pray'd for her soule.
Then some kinde Gossips made a speciall sute
To visit her, her hard case to condole:
She wondred at the cause: but when she knew it,
From that time forward, so her tongue did role,
That her good man did wish he had been breechlesse,
When first he gaue it forth, that she was speechlesse.
Well then, my *Moll,* lest my mis-hap be such,
Be neuer dumbe, yet neuer speake too much.

78 *Of a donne Horse.*

79 When you and I, *Paulus,* on Hackneyes hyred,
Rode late to *Rochester,* my Hackney tired:

77 [9] Yet A] Yes 1618.
79 Heading *Of a donne Horse.* A] *Of a dumbe Horse.* 1618 1625 *Of a dun horse.* 1633 [1] on Hackneyes hyred, A] once Hackneys hired, 1618 etc.

You that will lose a friend, to coine a iest
Play'd thus on me, and my poore tyred beast.
Marke, in *Misacmos* Horse a wondrous change,
A sudden Metamorphosis most strange.
His horse was bay at rising of the Sunne,
And now you plaine may see his Horse is donn.
Well, *Paulus,* thus with me you please to sport,
But thus againe, your scoffe I can retort.
Your haire was blacke and therein was your glory:
But in two yeeres, it grew all gray and hoary.
Now like my Hackney worne with too much trauell,
Mired in the clay, or tired in the grauell.
  While two yeere more ouer your head are runne,
  Your haire is neither blacke nor gray, 'tis dunne.

79 *Of* Leda *that plaid at Tables with her Husband.*

80 If tales are told of *Leda* be not Fables,
Thou with thy Husband do'st play false at Tables.
First, thou so cunningly a Die canst slurre,
To strike an Ace so dead, it cannot sturre.
Then play thou for a pound, or for a pin,
High men or low men, still are foysted in.
Thirdly though, for free entrance is no fearing,
Yet thou dost ouerreach him still at bearing:
If poore Almes-ace, or Sincts, haue beene the cast,
Thou bear'st too many men, thou bear'st too fast.
Well, *Leda,* heare my counsell, vse it not,
Else your faire game may haue so foule a blot,
  That he to lose, or leaue, will first aduenture,
  Then in so shamefull open points to enter.

79 [7] His horse was bay A] His horseway lay 1618 1625 His horse was gray 1633 [8] donn. A] downe. 1618 1625 dun. 1633.

80 [6] High men or A] High men are 1618. [7] though,] through, 1618 etc.

80 Of Soothsaying, to the Queene of England.

81 Might Queenes shun future mischiefe by foretelling,
Then among Soothsayers 'twere excellent dwelling:
But if there be no means, such harms expelling,
Knowledge makes the grief, the more excelling.
Well, yet deare Liege, my soule this comfort doth,
That of these Soothsayers very few say sooth.

81 How an Asse may proue an Elephant.

82 It hath beene said, to giue good spirits hope,
A Knight may proue a King, a Clarke, a Pope.
But our yong spirits disdaining all old Rules,
Compar'd by holy Writ, to Horse and Mules:
'Tis vaine with ancient Prouerbs, to prouoke
To vertuous course, with these such beare no stroke.
Then their old pride, let my new Prouerb dant,
An Asse may one day proue an Elephant.

82 Of a Precise Lawyer.

83 A Lawyer call'd vnto the Barre but lately,
Yet one that lofty bare his lookes, and stately,
And how so e're his minde was in sinceritie,
His speech and manners shew'd a great austeritie.
This Lawyer hapt to be a bidden ghest,
With diuers others to a Gossips feast.
Where though that many did by entercourse,
Exchange sometimes from this, to that discourse:
Yet one bent brow, and frowne of him was able,
To gouerne all the talke was at the table.
His manner was, perhaps to helpe digestion,
Still to Diuinitie to draw each question:
In which his tongue extrauagant would range,
And he pronounced Maxims very strange.
First, he affirmd, it was a passing folly,
To thinke one day more then another holy.

83 5 hapt A] hop'd 1618 etc.

If one said Michaelmas, straight he would chide,
And tell them they must call it Michaels tide.
If one had sneezde to say (as is the fashion)
Christ helpe, 'twas witchcraft, & deseru'd damnation.
Now when he talked thus, you must suppose,
The Gossips cup came often from his nose.
And were it the warme spice, or the warme wether,
At last he sneezed twice or thrice together.
A pleasant ghest, that kept his words in minde,
And heard him sneeze, in scorne said, Keepe behinde.
At which the Lawyer taking great offence,
Said, Sir, you might haue vs'd saue reuerence.
I would quoth th'other, saue I feard least you
Would then haue cal'd saue reuerence witchcraft too.

83 *A Prophesie when Asses shall grow Elephants.*

84 1 When making harmful gunnes, vnfruitfull glasses,
Shall quite consume our stately Oakes to ashes:
2 When Law fils all the land with blots and dashes,
3 When land long quiet, held concealed, passes.
4 When warre and truce playes passes and repasses,
5 When Monopolies are giu'n of toyes and trashes:
6 When courtiers mar good clothes, with cuts & slashes,
7 When Lads shal think it free to ly with Lasses,
8 When clergy romes to buy, sell, none abashes,
9 When fowle skins are made fair with new found washes,
10 When prints are set on work, with *Greens & Nashes,*
11 When Lechers learn to stir vp Lust with lashes,
When plainnesse vanishes, vainenesse surpasses,
Some shal grow Elephants, were knowne but Asses.

84 *To my Lady* Rogers *of her seruant* Paine.

85 Your seruant *Payne,* for Legacies hath sued
Seuen yeeres. I askt him how his matter passes.

83 24 last A] least 1618 etc. 29 feard least you A] fear'd you 1618 1625 feared you 1633.

He tels how his Testator left not assets.
By which plea him th'executor would elude.
I, in this Lawyers French both dull and rude,
Replide, the plea my learning farre surpasses.
Yet when reports of both sides I had view'd
In *Forma pauper,* this I did conclude;
He was left *Paine,* and all his Counsell asses:
Yet you would giue a hundred crownes or twaine,
That you could cleare discharge your seruant *Paine.*

84 *Of one that is vnwilling to lend money.*

86 When I but buy two suites of rich apparrell,
Or some faire ready horse against the running,
Rich *Quintus,* that same Miser, slye and cunning,
Yet my great friend, begins to pick a quarrell,
To tell me how his credit is in perill;
How some great Lord (whose name may not be spoken,)
With him for twenty thousand crownes hath broken.
Then, with a fained sigh, and signe of sorrow,
Swearing he thinks these Lords will quite vndoe him,
He cals his seruant *Oliuer* vnto him,
And sends to the Exchange, to take on vse
One thousand pounds, must needs be paid to morrow.
Thus would he blind mine eyes with this abuse,
And thinks, though he was sure I came to borrow,
That now I needs must shut my mouth for shame.
Fie *Quintus,* fie, then when I speak deny me.
But to deny me thus, before I try thee,
Blush and confesse that you be too too blame.

85 *Against Promoters.*

87 Base spies, disturbers of the publike rest,
With forged wrongs, the true mans right that wrest:
Packe hence exil'd to desart lands, and waste.

85 4 elude. A] allude. 1618 etc. 8 *pauper* A] *paper* 1618 etc. 9 *Paine,* A] *Pauper,* 1618 etc.

And drinke the cup that you made others taste.
But yet the Prince to you doth bounty show,
That doth your very liues on you bestow.

86 Against too much trust.

88 If you will shrowde you safe from all mis-haps,
And shunne the cause of many after-claps:
Put not in any one, too much beliefe:
Your joy will be the lesse, so will your griefe.

87 Of dangerous reconciling.

89 *Dicke* said, Beware a reconciled foe,
For, though he sooth your words, he seekes your woe:
But I would haue my friend late reconciled,
Beware thee *Dicke,* lest he be worst beguiled.

88 Of Leda *that saies she is sure to be saued.*

90 Since *Leda* knew that sure she was elected,
She buyes rich clothes, fares well, and makes her boast:
Her corps, the Temple of the Holy Ghost,
Must be more cherrished, and more respected:
But *Leda* liueth still to sinne subiected.
Tell *Leda,* that her friend *Misacmos* feares,
That till she get a mind of more submission,
And purge that corps with Hysope of contrition,
And wash that sinful soule with saltish tears,
Though Quailes she eates, though Gold & Pearle she weares,
Yet sure she doth with damned *Core & Dathan,*
But feed and clad a Synagogue of Sathan.

89 To the Lady Rogers, *of her vnprofitable sparing.*

91 When I to you sometimes make friendly motion,
To spend vp your superfluous prouision,

89 4 thee A] then 1618 etc.

Or sell the same for coyne, or for deuotion,
To make thereof among the poore diuision;
Straight you answere me, halfe in derision,
And bid me speake against your course no more:
For plenty you doe loue, store is no sore.
But ah, such store is enemy to plenty,
You waste for feare to want, I dare assume it:
For, while to sell, spend, giue, you make such dainty,
Keepe corne and cloth, till rat and rot consume it,
Let meat so mould, till muske cannot perfume it,
And by such sparing, seeke to mend such store,
Sore is such store, and God offending sore.

90 Against Church-robbers, vpon a picture that hangs where it is worthy.

92 The Germans haue a by-word at this houre,
By *Luther* taught, by Painters skill exprest,
How Sathan daily Fryers doth deuoure,
Whom in short space he doth so well disgest,
That passing downe through his posterior parts,
Tall souldiers thence he to the world deliuers,
And out they flie, all arm'd with pikes and darts,
With halberts, & with muskets and caliuers.
According to these *Lutheran* opinions,
They that deuoure whole Churches and their rents,
I meane our fauourites and Courtly Minions,
Void Forts and Castles, in their excrements.

91 A Tale of a Bayliffe distraining for rent. To my Ladie Rogers.

93 I heard a pleasant tale at Cammington,
There where my Lady dwelt, cald The faire Nun,
How one that by his office was Deceiuer,
(My tongue oft trips) I should haue said Receiuer,

92 Heading 1615 *How the Devill eates Friers.* 9 these A] which 1615 this 1618 etc.

Or to speake plaine and true, an arrant Baylie,
Such as about the Country trauell daily,
That when the quarter day was two daies past,
Went presently to gather rents in hast.
And if, as oft it hapt, he brake good manner,
He straight would plead the custome of the Mannor,
Swearing he might distraine all goods and chattell,
Were it in moueables, or else quick cattell.
This Bayliffe, coming to a tenement,
In the Tenants absence, straynd his wife for rent;
In which the beast so pliable he found,
He neuer needes to driue her to the pound.
The Tenant, by intelligence, did ghesse,
The Bayliffe taken had a wrong distresse:
And to the Bayliffes wife he went complaining,
Of this her husbands vsage in distraining;
Requesting her like curtesies to render,
And to accept such rent as he would tender.
She, whether moued with some strange compassion,
Or that his tale did put her in new passion,
Accepts his payment like a gentle wench;
All coyne was currant, English, Spanish, French:
And when she taken had his sorrie pittance,
I thinke, that with a kisse she seal'd the quittance.
When next these husbands met, they chaft, they curst,
Happy was he that could cry Cuckold furst.
From spightfull words, they fell to daggers drawing,
And after, each to other threatned lawing.
Each party seekes to make him strong by faction,
In seuerall Courts they enter seuerall action,
Actions of Battery, actions in the Case,
With riots, routes, disturbed all the place.
Much bloud, much money had been spilt and spent,
About this foolish straining for the rent;
Saue that a gentle Iustice of the Peace,
Willing to cause such foolish quarrels cease,

Preuail'd so with the parties by entreatie,
Of concord both agreed to haue a treatie:
And both refer'd the matter to the Iustice,
Who hauing well obserued what a Iest tis:
To thinke two Cuckolds were so fairely parted,
Each hauing tane the blow, that neuer smarted,
He charged each of them shake hands together,
And when they meet, to say, Good morrow, brother.
Thus each quit other all old debts and dribblets,
And set the Hares head, 'gainst the Gooses giblets.

92 Of casting out Spirits with fasting, without Prayer.

94 A vertuous Dame that for her state and qualitie,
Did euer loue to keepe great Hospitalitie,
Her name I must not name in plaine reciting,
But thus the chiefest instrument in writing,
Was, by Duke *Humfreys* ghests so boldly haunted,
That her good minde thereby was shrewdly daunted.
She sighing said one day to a carelesse Iester,
These ill bred ghests my boord and house so pester,
That I pray God oft times with all my heart,
That they would leaue this haunt, and hence depart:
He that by his owne humor hap'ly ghest,
What manner sprite these smel-feasts had possest,
Told her, the surest way such spirits out-casting,
Was, to leaue prayer awhile, & fall to fasting.

93 Against Itis *a Poet.*

95 *Itis* with leaden sword doth wound my Muse,
Itis whose Muse in vncouth termes doth swagger,
What should I wish *Itis* for this abuse,
But to his leaden sword, a woodden dagger.

93 44 obserued what a Iest tis: A] obserued what a Iest is: B obseru'd what a iest is: 1618 1625 observed what a jest is: 1633.
94 13 her, A] him, 1618 1625.
95 3 What A] For 1618 1625.

94 Of Wittoll.

96 *Cayus,* none reckned of thy wife a poynt,
While each man might, without all let or cumber,
But since a watch o're her thou didst appoint,
Of Customers she hath no little number.
Well, let them laugh hereat that list, and scoffe it,
But thou do'st find what makes most for thy profit.

Booke II

1 *To the Lady* Rogers, *th'authors wiues Mother.*

97 If I but speake words of unpleasing sound:
Yea though the same be but in sport and play,
You bid me peace, or else a thousand pound,
Such words shall worke out of my childrens way.
When you say thus, I haue no word to say.
Thus without Obligation, I stand bound,
Thus, wealth makes you command, hope me obay.
But let me finde this true another day:
Else when your body shall be brought to ground,
    Your soule to blessed *Abrahams* bosome, I
    May with good manners giue your soule the lye.

2 *Of the Bishopricke of Landaffe.*

98 A learned Prelate late dispos'd to laffe,
Hearing me name the Bishop of Landaffe:
You should say, he aduising well hereon,
Call him Lord *Aff:* for all the land is gone.

3 *Of* Don Pedro's *Dyet drinke.*

99 *Don Pedro* drinkes to no man at the boord,
Nor once a taste doth of his cup affoord.
Some thinke it pride in him: but see their blindnesse!
I know therein, his Lordship doth vs kindnesse.

4 *Of* Leda *and* Balbus.

100 *Leda* was *Balbus* queane, yet might shee haue denide it.
She weds him, now what meanes hath *Leda* left to hide it?

97 [1] unpleasing A B] a pleasing 1618 etc. [10] I A] I. B 1618 1625.

5 *Of* Cinna *his Gossip Cup.*

101 When I with thee, *Cinna,* doe dine or sup,
Thou still do'st offer me thy Gossips cup:
And though it sauour well, and be well spiced,
Yet I to taste thereof am not enticed.
Now sith you needs will haue me cause alledge,
While I straine curt'sie in that cup to pledge:
One said, thou mad'st that cup so hote of spice,
That it had made thee now a widdower twice.
I will not say 'tis so, nor that I thinke it:
But good Sir, pardon me, I cannot drinke it.

6 *Of* Leda's *Religion.*

102 My louely *Leda,* some at thee repining,
Askt me vnto what sect thou art inclining?
Which doubts shall I resolue among so many,
Whether to none, to one, to all, to any?
Surely one should be deem'd a false accusant,
That would appeach *Leda* for a Recusant.
Her fault according to her former vsing,
Was noted more in taking, then refusing.
For Lent, or Fasts, she hath no superstition,
For if she haue not chang'd her old condition:
Be it by night in bed, in day in dish,
Flesh vnto her more welcome is then Fish.
Thou art no Protestant, thy fals-hood saith,
Thou canst not hope to saue thy selfe by faith.
Well, *Leda,* yet to shew my good affection,
I'le say thy sect is of a double section.
A Brownist louely browne, thy face and brest,
The Families of Loue, in all the rest.

7 *That fauorites helpe the Church.*

103 Of late I wrote after my wanton fashion,
That fauourites consume the Churches rents:

But mou'd in conscience with retraction,
Ile shew how sore that rashnes me repents.
For noting in my priuate obseruation,
What rents and schismes among vs dayly grow:
No hope appeares of reconciliation,
By helpe of such as can, or such as know.
    My Muse must sing, although my soule laments,
    That Fauorites increase the Churches rents.

8 Of Cinna *his courage.*

104 Pvre *Cinna* saith, and proudly doth professe,
That if the quarrell he maintaines be good:
No man more valiant is to spend his bloud,
No man can dread of death, of danger lesse.
But if the cause be bad, he doth confesse,
His heart is cold, and cowardly his moode.
Well, *Cinna,* yet this cannot be withstood,
Thou hast but euill lucke, I shrewdly gesse,
    That biding whereas brawles are bred most rife,
    Thou neuer hadst good quarrell all thy life.

9 Of a Lawyer that deseru'd his fee.

105 *Sextus* retain'd a Sergeant at the Lawes,
With one good Fee in an ill-fauor'd cause.
The matter bad, no Iudge nor Iury plyent,
The verdit clearely past against the Clyent.
With which he chaft, and swore he was betray'd,
Because for him the Sergeant little said:
And of the Fee, he would haue barr'd him halfe.
Whereat the Sergeant wroth, said, Dizzard Calfe,
Thou would'st, if thou hadst wit, or sence to see,
Confesse I had deseru'd a double Fee,
That stood and blushed there in thy behalfe.

10 *Of* Don Pedro.

106 A Slaue thou wert by birth, of this I gather,
For euer more thou sai'st, my Lord, my Father.

11 *Against* Lynus *a writer.*

107 I heare that Lynus growes in wondrous choller,
Because I said, he wrote but like a scholler.
If I haue said so, *Linus,* I must grant it,
Yet to regain thy loue thus I recant it:
What ere I speake thy scholler-ship concerning,
I neuer thought, or meant, that thou hast learning:
But that hereof may grow no more recitall,
I'le teach the how to make mee full requitall.
Say thou to breed me equall spight and doller,
Misacmos neuer writes, but like a scholler.

12 *Of* Don Pedros *bonds.*

108 *Don Pedro* cares not in what bonds he enter.
Then I to trust *Don Pedro* soone will venter.
For no man can of bonds stand more secure,
Then he that meanes to keepe his paiment sure.

13 *Against* Cayus *that scorn'd his Metamorphosis.*

109 Last day thy Mistris, *Cayus,* being present,
One hapt to name, to purpose not vnpleasant,
The Title of my mis-conceiued Booke:
At which you spit, as though you could not brooke
So grosse a Word: but shall I tell the matter
Why? If one names a Iax, your lips doe water.
There was the place of your first loue and meeting,
There first you gaue your Mistris such a greeting,
As bred her scorne, your shame, and others lafter,

107 4 A Missing in 1618 etc. 7 no more] some more 1618 1625 some small 1633. 9 doller, A] choller, 1618 etc.

And made her feele it twenty fortnights after:
Then thanke their wit, that make the place so sweet,
That for your *Hymen* you thought place so meet.
  But meet not Maids at Madam *Cloacina,*
  Lest they cry nine moneths after, Helpe *Lucina.*

14 Against an Atheist.

110 That heau'ns are voide, & that no gods there are,
Rich *Paulus* saith, and all his proofe is this:
That while such blasphemies pronounce he dare,
He liueth here in ease, and earthly blisse.

15 Of Cosmus *heyre.*

111 When all men thought old *Cosmus* was a dying,
And had by Will giu'n thee much goods & lands,
Oh, how thc littlc *Cosmus* fcll a crying!
Oh, how he beat his brestes & wrong his hands!
How feruently for *Cosmus* health he pray'd!
What worthy Almes he vow'd, on that condition:
But when his pangs a little were allayd,
And health seem'd hoped, by the learn'd Physicion,
  Then though his lips, all loue, and kindnesse vanted,
  His heart did pray, his prayer might not be granted.

16 Of Faustus, *a stealer of Verses.*

112 I heard that *Faustus* oftentimes reherses,
To his chaste Mistris, certaine of my Verses:
In which with vse, so perfect he is growne,
That she poore foole, now thinkes they are his owne.
I would esteeme it (trust me) grace, not shame,
If *Dauis,* or if *Daniel* did the same.
For would I thanke, or would I quarrell pike,
I, when I list, could doe to them the like.

111 4 beat his brestes & wrong A] beates his brests, and wring 1618 1625 beats his brests, and wrings 1633.

But who can wish a man a fowler spight,
Then haue a blinde man take away his light?
A begging Theefe, is dangerous to my purse:
A baggage Poet to my Verse is worse.

17 Misacmos *of himselfe.*

113 Mvse you, *Misacmos* failes in some endeuour.
Alas, an honest man's a Nouice euer.
Fie, but a man's disgrac'd, noted a Nouice.
Yea, but a man's more grac'd, noted of no vice.

18 *Of the corne that rained.*

114 I handled, tasted, saw it with mine eyes,
The graine that lately fell downe from the skies:
Yet what it tok'ned could I not deuise,
And many doubts did in my minde arise.
At last, I thus resolu'd, it signifies
That this is our sole meane, to mend this dearth,
To aske from heau'n, that we doe lacke on earth.

19 *To his wife, at the birth of his sixt Child.*

115 The Poet Martiall made a speciall sute
Vnto his Prince, to grant him vnder seale,
Right of three children, which they did impute
A kinde of honour, in their Common-weale.
But for such sute, my selfe I need not trouble,
For thou do'st seale to me this Patent double.

20 *Against Feasting.*

116 Kinde *Marcus,* me to supper lately bad,
And to declare how well to vs he wishes,
The roome was strow'd with Roses, not with Rushes,

116 [3] Roses, not A] Roses and 1618 etc.

And all the cheere was got, that could be had.
Now in the midst of all our dainty dishes,
Me thinke, said he to me, you looke but sad.
Alas (said I) 'tis to see thee so mad,
To spoile the skies of Fowles, the seas of fishes,
The land of beasts, and be at so much cost,
For that which in one houre will all be lost.
That entertainment that makes me most glad,
Is not the store of stew'd, boyl'd, bak't and rost.
But sweet discourse, meane fare; & then beleeue me,
To make to thee like cheere, shall neuer grieue me.

21 *Against* Cosmus *couetousnesse.*

117 *Cosmus,* when I among thine other vices,
That are in nature foule, in number many,
Ask thee what is the reason thee entices,
To be so basely pinching for thy penny?
Do'st thou not call vpon thy selfe a curse,
Not to enioy the wealth that thou hast wonne:
But saue, as if thy soule were in thy purse?
Thou straight reply'st, I saue all for my sonne.
Alas, this re-confirmes what I said rather:
Cosmus hath euer beene a Penny-father.

22 *Against Vintners in Bathe.*

118 If men ought those in dutie to commend,
That questions of Religion seeke to end,
Then I to praise our Vintners doe intend.
For Question is twixt Writers old and latter,
If wine alone, or if wine mixt with water,
Should of the blessed Sacrament be matter?
Some ancient Writers wish it should be mingled,
But latter men, with much more zeale inkindled,
Will haue wine quite and cleane from water singled.

118 [4] Writers A] Writer 1618 etc.

Our zealous Vintners here, growne great Diuines,
To find which way antiquitie enclines,
For pure zeale mix with water all our wines.
  Well, plainly to tell truth, and not to flatter,
  I find our wines are much the worse for water.

23 To Passifie his wiues mother, when shee was angry.

119 Madam, I read to you a little since,
The story of a Knight that had incurd
The deep displeasure of a mighty Prince:
For feare of which, long time he neuer sturd,
Till watching once the King that came from Chappel,
His little sonne fast by him, with his Gardon,
Entic'd the Infant to him with an apple;
So caught him in his armes, and su'd for pardon:
  Then you shall turne your angry frown to lafter
  As oft as in mine armes you see your daughter.

24 To his wife, of Poppea Sabynas *faire heyre.*

120 *Mall* once I did, but doe not now enuy
Fierce *Neroe's* blisse, of faire *Poppeas* rayes,
That in his lap, koming her locks would lye,
Each hayre of hers, a verse of his did praise,
But that prais'd beauty, fruitlesse spent her daies.
No yong *Augustus* euer cal'd him Dad.
No small *Poppeas* with their prettie playes,
Did melt their hearts, and melting make them glad:
But thou in this, do'st passe his faire *Sabyna,*
That hast seuen times beene succor'd by *Lucina.*
Thy wombe in branches seau'n, it selfe displayes.
  Then leaue I *Nero,* with *Poppeas* heyres:
  To ioy, and to inioy thee, and thine heyres.

119 Heading *Passifie* A] Bassify, 1618. 9 to lafter A B] from lafter, 1618 etc.

25 *Against* Lalus *an ill Preacher.*

121 Yong *Lalus* tooke a Text of excellent matter,
And did the same expound, but marre the latter,
His tongue so vainely did and idly chatter,
The people nought but hem, & cough and spatter.
Then said a Knight not vs'd to lye or flatter:
Such Ministers doe bring the Diuels blessing,
That marre vs so good meate, with so ill dressing.

26 *Against* Paulus *an Atheist.*

122 Lewd *Paulus,* led by *Sadduces* infection,
Doth not beleeue the bodies resurrection:
And holds them all in scorne, and deepe derision,
That tell of Saints or Angels apparision;
And sweares, such things are fables all, and fancies
Of Lunatiques or Fooles, possest with franzies.
I haue (said he) trauail'd both neere and farre,
By sea, by land, in time of peace and warre,
Yet neuer met I sprite, or ghost, or elfe,
Or ought (as is the phrase) worse then my selfe.
Well, *Paulus,* this, I now beleeue indeede,
For who in all, or part, denies his Creede;
Went he to sea, land, hell, I would agree,
A Fiend worse then himselfe, shall neuer see.

27 *Of* Galla *going to the Bathe.*

123 When *Galla* for her health goeth to the Bathe,
She carefully doth hide, as is most meete,
With aprons of fine linnen, or a sheete,
Those parts, that modesty concealed hath:
Nor onely those, but eu'n the brest and necke,
That might be seene, or showne, without all checke.
But yet one foule, and vnbeseeming place,
She leaues uncouered still: What's that? Her face.

122 1 *Paulus,* A] *Lalus,* 1618.
123 Heading *Of* Galla A] *To* Galla 1618 etc.

28 *To one that had meate ill drest.*

124 King Mithridate to poysons so inur'd him,
As deadly poysons, damage none procur'd him.
So you to stale vnsauorie foode and durtie,
Are so inur'd, as famine ne're can hurt yee.

29 *Of giuing much credit.*

125 Of all the Towne old *Codros* giues most credit:
Who he, poore soule! Alas that ere you sed it.
How can he credit much, and is so poore?
Hee's blinde: yet makes he loue to euery whore.

30 *Of honest Theft. To my good friend Master* Samuel Daniel.

126 Proud *Paulus* late my secrecies reuealing,
Hath told I got some good conceits by stealing.
But where got he those double Pistolets,
With which good clothes, good fare, good land he gets?
Tush, those, he saith, came by a man of warre,
That brought a Prize of price, from countries farre.
Then, fellow Thiefe, let's shake together hands,
Sith both our wares are filcht from forren lands.
    You'le spoile the Spaniards, by your writ of Mart:
    And I the Romanes rob, by wit, and Art.

31 *Against* Faustus.

127 In skorne of writers, *Faustus* still doth hold,
Nought is now said, but hath beene said of old:
Well, *Faustus,* say my wits are grosse and dull,
If for that word, I giue not thee a Gull:
Thus then I proue thou holdst a false position,
I say, thou are a man of fayre condition,

127 [5] thou holdst A] that holds 1618 etc.

A man true of thy word, tall of thy hands,
Of high disent, and left good store of lands,
Thou with false dice and cards hast neuer plaid,
Corrupted neuer Widdow, Wife nor Maid,
And as for swearing none in all this Reame,
Doth seldomer in speech curse or blaspheme.
In fine, your vertues are so rare and ample,
For all our sonnes thou maist be made a sample.
    This I dare sweare, none euer said before,
    This I may sweare, none euer will say more.

32 Of Free will.

128 I know a foolish fellow hath a fashion,
To proue that all is by Predestination,
And teach's, nor man, nor spirit hath free will
In dooing, no, nor thinking good or ill.
I am no Doctor at this disputation,
Nor are deepe questions fit for shallow skill:
Yet I'le renounce, with learn'd men reputation,
If I disproue not this by demonstration:
Ile proue so plaine, as none can it resist,
That in some things, three things do what they list:
    The wind, saith Scripture, where it list doth blow,
    His tongue talkes what it lists, his speeches showe,
    My heart beleeues him as it list, I know.

33 Of a drunken Paracelsian.

129 When *Pilo* other trades of thrift had mist,
He then profest to be an Alcumist,
That's all too much, Chimist you might him call,
And so I thinke twere true, and leaue out all:
He takes vpon him, he can make a mixture,
Of which he can extract the true elixar,
Tinctur of Pearle and Currall he doth draw,
And Quintessence the best that ere you saw,

He hath the rare receit *Aqua Mirabilis,*
Only he wants some drams *Auri potabilis,*
He doth of nature so the secret ferrit,
That he of euery thing can draw the spirit:
Spirits of wines, spirits of stones and herbes,
Whose names can scant be told with nownes and verbes,
But of all spirits my spirit doth diuine,
His spirit best doth loue the spirit of wine.

34 Of Misacmos *his successe in a suite.*

130 *Misacmos* hath long time a suter beene,
To serue in some neere place about the Queen:
In which his friends to work his better speede,
Doe tell her Highnesse, as tis true indeede,
That hee's a man well borne and better bred,
In humane studyes seene, in stories read,
Adding vnto an industry not small,
Pleasant conceit and memory withall,
And chiefely that he hath been from his youth,
A zealous searcher of Eternall Truth:
Now neuer wonder, he his suite doth misse:
What I haue told you, that the reason is.

35 A Groome of the Chambers religion in King Henry *the eights time.*

131 One of King *Henries* Fauorites beganne,
To moue the King one day to take a man,
Whom of his Chamber he might make a Groome,
Soft, sayd the King, before I graunt that roome,
It is a question not to be neglected,
How he in his Religion stands affected.
For his Religion, answered then the Minion,
I doe not certaine know whats his opinion:

129 [9] rare receit A] cure, except 1618 etc. [10] some drams A] drammes 1618 etc. [13] wines, A] mynes, 1618 etc.

But sure he may, talking with men of learning,
Conforme himselfe in lesse then ten days warning.

36 *To Doctor* Haruey *of Cambridge.*

132 The prouerbe sayes, who fights with durty foes,
Must needs be soyld, admit they winne or lose.
Then think it doth a Doctors credit dash,
To make himselfe Antagonist to *Nashe.*

37 *An infallible rule to rule a wife. To his wiues mother.*

133 Concerning th'wiues hold this a certaine rule,
That if at first, you let them haue the rule,
Your selfe at last, with them shall haue no rule,
Except you let them euer-more to rule. *Probatum est.*

38 *Why* Paulus *takes so much Tobacco.*

134 When our good Irish neighbours make repaire,
With Lenton stuffe vnto Bridgewaters Faire,
At euery Boothe, and Alehouse that they come,
They call for Herring straight, they must haue some.
Hostis, I pree dee hast tee any Herring?
Yea, sir: O passing meat! a happy Herring.
Herring they aske, they praise, they eate, they buy;
No price of Herring can be held too hie.
But, when among them it is closely mutter'd,
Those Herrings that they bought to sell are vtter'd,
Then giue them Herring, Poh, away with these:
Pree dee good Hostis, giue's some English Cheese.
Hence I haue learn'd the cause, and see it clearely,
Why *Paulus* takes Tobacco, buyes it dearely,
At Tippling-houses, where he eates and drinks,
That euery roome straight of Tobacco stinks.
He swears tis salue for all diseases bred,

132 [2] soyld, A] foyld, 1618 etc. [4] *Nashe.* A] *Nash?* 1618.
134 [10] bought to sell A] bought, to sell 1618.

It strengthens ones weake back, comforts the head,
Dulls much flesh-appetite, tis cordiall durable,
It cures that ill, which some haue thought incurable.
Thus while proud *Paulus* hath Tobacco praised,
The price of eu'ry pound, a pound is raised.
And why's all this? because he loues it well?
No: but because himselfe hath store to sell.
  But hauing sold all his, he will pronounce
  The best of *Cane* not worth a groat an ounce.

39 Of a formall Minister.

135 A Minister, affecting singularitie,
And preaching in the Pulpit of his theame,
Borne with the current of the common streame,
Extolled faith and hope, forgetting charitie.
For while he was most busie in his Text,
He spyde a woman talking with her next,
And straight he crid to her, Dame, leaue thy babbling.
Wherewith the good poore woman shrewdly vext,
Could hold no longer, but fell flat to squabbling:
  Beshrew thy naked heart, she doth reply.
  Who babbled in this place more? thou, or I?

40 Of a lawfull wife.

136 At end of three yeeres law, and sute, and strife,
When Canon lawes, & common both command her,
Cys married thee; now sue them for a slaunder,
That dare deny she is thy lawfull wife.

41 Against Feasting.

137 Last day, I was vnto your house inuited,
And on the bord were forty diuers dishes,
Of Sallets, and of flesh & fowles and fishes,

134 [26] of A] in 1618 etc.
135 [4] Extolled A] Extolling 1618 etc.

With which (God knowes) I little am delighted.
    Before I came, I tooke that you did bid me,
    But now, I rather thinke, you did forbid me.

42 *Against* Lynus, *that said the Nobility were decayed.*

138 You *Lynus,* say, that most of our Nobilitie
Are much decayd in valour and in wit:
Though some of them haue wealth, and good ability,
Yet very few for gouernment are fit.
Foole, seest thou not, that in our stately buildings,
Plaine massy stones the substance doth sustaine,
Yet colloms wreath'd & caru'd, set out with guildings,
Must in high ranke for ornament remaine:
    So men of noble birth, the State adorne,
    But by the wise, stout, learnd, the sway is borne.

43 *To* Itis, alias Ioyner, *an vncleanly token, conuayd in cleanly tearmes.*

139 *Torquato Tasso,* for one little fault,
That did perhaps deserue some small rebuke,
Was by his sharp and most vngratefull Duke,
Shut vp close prisoner in a loathsome vault;
Where wanting Pen and Inke by Princes order,
His wit, that wals of Adamant could pierce,
Found meanes to write his mind in excellent verse:
For want of Pen and Inke, with pisse and ordure.
But thy dull wit damn'd by *Appollos* crew,
To dungeon of disgrace, though free thy body,
With pen, nay Print, doth publish like a noddy
Base taunts, that turn'd vpon thy selfe, are true.
And wanting salt thy wallowish stile to season,
And being of vncouth tearmes a senslesse coyner,
Thou call'st thy selfe vnproperly, a Ioyner,

137 5 Before A] Became, 1618 1625 Because 1633.
138 7 caru'd, A] staid, 1618 etc.
139 11 noddy A] noddy. 1618 etc. 12 true. A] true, 1618 1625 true; 1633.

Whose verse hath quite disseuer'd rime and reason:
    Deseruing for such rayling, and such bodging,
    For this, *Torquatos* Inke, for that, his Lodging.

44 *To his wife.*

140 When I to thee my Letters superscribe
Thus, To mine own; *Leda* thereat doth iybe.
And aske her why? she saith, because I flatter.
But let her thinke so still, it makes no matter:
If I doe flatter, onely thou canst try,
Suffiseth me, I think I doe not lye.
    For, let her husband write so, for my life,
    He flattereth himselfe more then his wife.

45 *Sir* Iohn Raynsfords *confession.*

141 *Raynsford,* a Knight, fit to haue seru'd king *Arthur,*
And in Queene *Maries* dayes a demy Martyr:
For though both then, before, and since he turn'd,
(Yet sure, *per ignem hanc,* he might be burn'd.)
This Knight agreed with those of that profession,
And went, as others did, to make confession:
Among some *Peccadilios,* he confest,
That same sweet sinne, that some but deeme a Iest,
And told, how by good helpe of bawdes and varlets,
Within 12. months he had sixe times twelue harlots.
The Priest, that at the tale was halfe astonished,
With graue & ghostly counsell him admonished
To fast, and pray, to driue away that diuell,
That was to him causer of so great euill,
That the lewd spirit of Lecherie, no question,
Stird vp his lust, with many a lewd suggestion:
A filthy Fiend, said he, most foule and odious,
Nam'd, as appeares, in holy writs, *Asmodius.*
Thus, with some Pennance that was ne're performed,

140 [6] I think A B] thou think'st 1615 etc.

Away went that same Knight, smally reformed.
Soone after this, ensued religions change,
That in the Church bred alteration strange,
And *Raynsford,* with the rest, follow'd the streame.
The Priest went rouing round about the Realme.
This Priest, in clothes disguis'd himselfe did hide,
Yet *Raynsford,* three yeers after him had spyde,
And layd vnto his charge, and sorely prest him,
To tell if 'twere not he that had confest him.
The Priest, though this Knights words did sore him daunt,
Yet what he could not wel deny, did grant,
And prayd him not to punish, or controule
That he had done for safety of his soule.
No, knaue, quoth he, I will not harme procure thee,
Vpon my Worship here I doe assure thee:
I onely needs must laugh at thy great folly,
That would'st perswade with me to be so holy;
To chastise mine owne flesh, to fast, and pray,
To driue the spirit of Lechery away.
'Sownds, foolish knaue, I fasted not, nor prayd,
Yet is that spirit quite gone from me, he said:
If you couldst helpe me to that spirit againe,
Thou shouldst a hundred pound haue for thy paine.
    That lustie Lord of Lecherie *Asmodius,*
    That thou cal'st odious, I doe count commodious.

46 A pretty questions of Lazarus *soule well answered.*

142 Once on occasion two good friends of mine
Did meete at meate, a Lawyer and Diuine:
Both hauing eaten well to helpe digestion,
To this Diuine, the lawyer put this question:
When *Lazarus* in graue foure dayes did stay,
Where was his soule? in heauen, or hell I pray?
Was it in hell? Thence no redemption is.
And if in heauen: would Christ abate his blisse?
Sir, said the Preacher, for a short digression,

First, answere me one point, in your profession:
If so his heyres and he had falne to strife,
Whose was the land, if he came backe to life?
This latter question mou'd them all to lafter,
And so they drunke one to another after.

47 *Against long suits in Law.*

143 In Court of Wards, Kings Bench, & Common place
Thou follow'd hast one sute, this seu'n yeeres space.
Ah wretched man, in mothers wombe accurst,
That could'st not rather lose thy sute at furst.

48 *Of an importunate prater, out of* Martiall.

144 He that is hoarse, yet still to prate doth prease,
Proues he can neither speake, nor hold his peace.

49 *Against Ielousie. To my friend.*

145 Right terrible are windes on waters great,
Most horrible are tempests on the sea,
Fire mercilesse, that all consumes with heat,
Plagues monstrous are, that Citties cleane decay:
Warre cruell is, and pinching famine curst:
Yet of all ills, the ielouse wife is worst.

50 *Against* Quintus, *that being poore and prodigall, became rich and miserable.*

146 Scant was thy Liuing, *Quintus,* ten pound cleare,
When thou didst keepe such fare, so good a table,
That we thy friends praid God thou might'st be able,
To spend, at least, an hundred pounds a yeare.
Behold, our boone God did benignly heare.

142 12 to life?] from life? 1618 etc.
143 4 That A] Thou 1618 etc.
144 1 prease,] please, 1618 etc.

Thou gotst so much by Fortune fauourable,
And foure friends deaths to thee both kind and deare:
But suddenly thou grew'st so miserable,
We thy old friends to thee vnwelcome are,
Poore-Iohn, and Apple-pyes are all our fare.
No Salmon, Sturgeon, Oysters, Crab, nor Cunger.
What should we wish thee now for such demerit?
I would thou might'st one thousand pounds inherit,
Then, without question, thou wold'st starue for hunger.

51 *To my Lady* Rogers.

147 Good Madam, with kind speech & promise faire,
That from my wife you would not giue a rag,
But she should be Exector sole, and heyre.
I was (the more foole I) so proud and brag,
I sent to you against S.*Iames* his Faire,
A Teerce of Claret-wine, a great fat Stagge.
You straight to all your neighbors made a feast,
Each man I meet hath filled vp his panch,
With my Red-deere, onely I was no ghest,
Nor euer since did taste of side or haunch.
Well, Madam, you may bid me hope the best,
That of your promise you be sound and staunch,
Else, I might doubt I should your Land inherit,
That of my Stagge did not one morsell merit.

52 *Of* Sextus *mis-hap comming from a Tauerne.*

148 Now *Sextus* twice hath supt at *Sarazens* head,
And both times, homewards, comming drunk to bed:
He by the way his Pantoffles hath lost,
And grieu'd both with the mocke, and with the cost,
To saue such charges, and to shun such frumps,
He goes now to the Tauerne in his Pumps.

147 8 meet A B] met 1618 etc.

53 *How* Sextus *laid claime to an Epigram.*

149 When *Sextus* heard my Rime of Rainsford reeding,
With laughter lowd he cries, and voice exceeding,
That Epigram was mine, who euer made it.
I told him that conceit, from me, he had it.
Ah barbarisme, the blinder still the bolder!
Will *Sextus* ne're grow wiser growing older?
When *Phidias* framed had in marble pure,
Ioues goodly Statue, would a man endure
A Pyoner to challenge halfe the praise,
That from the quarr the ragged stone did raise:
Or should a Carman boast of his desart,
Because he did vnload it from his Cart:
I thinke that *Sextus* selfe would neuer say't.
So in like manner, *Sextus,* that conceit
    Was like a rugged stone, dig'd from thy foolish head,
    Now 'tis a Statue caru'd by vs, and polished.

54 *Of an Alborne Rabbet.*

150 Late comming from the Palace of the best,
(The centre of the men of better sence)
My purse growne low, by ebbe of long expence:
And going for supplyes into the West,
My hoast to whom I was a welcome ghest,
Makes me great cheere, but when I parted thence,
My trustie seruant *William* tooke offence:
(Though now God wot, it was too late to spare)
That in the shot things too high prized are.
And namely for two Rabbets twenty pence.
The Tapster well enur'd to prate and face,
Told they were white, and yong, and fat, and sweet:
New kill'd, and newly come from Alborne chase:

149 6 wiser A] wise? 1618 etc. older? A] older, 1618 etc. 13 say't. A] say't, 1618 etc.
150 Heading *Alborne* 1633] *Aborne* A 1618.

For that good fare, good paiment is most meete.
I willing to make short their long debate,
Bade my man pay the reck'ning at his rate:
Adding, I know, a miser of his money,
Giues more then ten pence for an Alborne Coney.

55 Of hearing Masse.

151 Men talking, as oft times it comes to passe,
How dangerous 'tis now to heare a Masse;
A valiant Knight swore for a thousand pound,
He would not present at a Masse be found.
A Noble Lord stood by, and hearing it,
Said, Sir, I then should much condemne your wit.
For were you found, and follow'd ne're so nearely,
You gaine nine hundred pound & vpward clearely.

56 Of a Preacher that sings Placebo.

152 A smooth-tong'd Preacher that did much affect
To be reputed of the purest sect,
Vnto these times great praises did afford,
That brought, he said, the sunne-shine of the Word.
The sunne-shine of the Word, this he extold,
The sunne-shine of the Word, this still he told.
But I that well obseru'd what slender fruits
Haue growne of all their preaching and disputes,
Pray God they bring vs not, when all is done,
Out of Gods blessing, into this warme sunne.
For sure, as some of them haue vs'd the matter,
Their sunne-shine is but moone-shine in the water.

57 Of the naked Image that was to stand in my Lo: Chamberlaines Gallery.

153 *Actæon,* guiltelesse vnawares espying
Naked *Diana,* bathing in her bowre,
Was plagu'd with horns, his dogs did him deuoure.

Wherefore take heede, ye that are curious prying,
    With some such forked plague you be not smitten,
    And in your foreheads so your faults be written.

58 Of the same to the Ladies.

154 Her face vnmask't, I saw, her corps vnclad,
No vaile, no couer, her and me betweene:
No ornament was hid, that beauty had,
I blusht that saw, she blusht not that was seene.
    With that I vow'd neuer to care a rush,
    For such a beauty, as doth neuer blush.

59 Of Don Pedroe's *threats.*

155 *Don Pedro* thinkes I scorne him in my Rime,
And vowes, if he can proue I vse detraction,
Of the great scandall he will haue his action:
I that desir'd to cleere me of the crime,
When I was askt, said, No, my Lord, I haue not.
Then sweare, said he, Not so, my Lord, I cannot.
    Since that I neuer heard newes of this action:
    Wherefore, I thinke, he hath his satisfaction.

60 Against brauery.

156 When Romane *Mutius* had in contryes quarrell,
The seruant killed, to the Masters terror:
What time his eye deceiu'd with rich apparell,
Did cause his hand commit that happy error:
The King amaz'd at so rare resolution,
Both for his safety, and his reputation:
Remou'd the fire, and stay'd that execution:
And for his sake, made peace with all his Nation.
    Perhaps it is from hence the custome springs,
    That oft in Court Knaues goe as braue as Kings.

153 6 foreheads so your A] foreheads your 1618.
156 1 contryes A] countries 1615 countrey 1618 etc. 10 braue A 1615] well 1618 etc.

61 *Of* Leda's *vnkindnesse.*

157 Faire *Leda* late to me is growne malicious,
At all my workes in prose or verse repining:
Because my words, she saith, makes men suspitious,
That she is to the Puritanes inclining.
Leda, what ere I said, I did suspect,
Thou wert not pure enough, in one respect.

62 Of an Abbot that had beene a good fellow.

158 An Abbot that had led a wanton life,
And cited now, by deaths sharpe Sumner, sicknesse,
Felt in his soule, great agony and strife,
His sinnes appearing in most hideous likenesse.
The Monkes that saw their Abbot so dismaid,
And knew no lesse his life had been lasciuious:
Yet for his finall comfort, thus they said,
Thinke not, deare Sir, we will be so obliuious,
But that with fasting, and with sacred ringing,
And prayer, we will for you such grace attaine,
That after *requiem* and some Dirges singing,
You shall be freed from Purgatories paine.
Ah, thankes my sonnes, said he, but all my feare
Is onely this, that I shall ne're come there.

63 Against Cinna *a Brownist, that saith he is sure to be saued.*

159 If thou remaine so sure of thine election,
As thou said'st, *Cinna,* when we last disputed,
That to thy soule, no sinne can be imputed:
That thy strong Faith, hath got so sure protection,
That all thy faults are free from all correction.
Heare then my counsell, to thy state well suted,
It comes from one, that beares thee kinde affection,

'Tis so infallible, that no obiection
There is, by which it may be well confuted.
Leaue, *Cinna,* this base earth with sinne polluted.
And to be free from wicked mens subiection,
And that the Saints may be by thee saluted,
Forsake wife, friends, lands, goods & worldly pelfe,
And get a halter quickly, and goe hang thy selfe.

64 To Master Bastard, *a Minister that made a pleasant Booke of English Epigrams.*

160 Though dusty wits of this vngratefull time,
Carpe at thy booke of Epigrams, and scoffe it:
Yet wise men know, to mix the sweet with proffit
Is worthy praise, not onely void of crime.
Then let not enuy stop thy veine of Rime:
Nor let thy function make thee shamed of it:
A Poet is one step vnto a Prophet:
And such a step, as 'tis no shame to clime.
You must in Pulpit treat of matters serious:
As best beseemes the person, and the place,
There preach of Faith, Repentance, hope and grace,
Of Sacraments, and such high things mysterious.
But they are too seuere, and too imperious,
That vnto honest sports will grant no space:
For these our minds refresh, when those do wery vs,
And spurre our dulled spirit to swifter pace.
The wholsom'st meates that are, will breed satietie,
Except we should admit of some varietie.
In musike notes must be some high, some base.
And this I note, your Verses haue intendment,
Still kept within the lists of good sobrietie,
To work in mens ill manners, good amendment.
Wherefore if any thinke such verse vnseasonable:
Their Stoicke mindes are foes to good societie,

160 3 proffit A] profit. 1618. 15 those do wery A] those weary 1618 etc. 16 dulled A] doubled 1618 etc. 17 satietie, A] sacietie, 1618 etc.

And men of reason may thinke them vnreasonable.
It is an act of vertue and of pietie,
To warne vs of our sinnes in any sort,
In prose, in verse, in earnest, or in sport.

65 Of a kinde vnkinde Husband.

161 A rich old Lord did wed a rich yong Lady,
Of good complexion, and of goodly stature,
And for he was of kinde and noble nature,
He lou'd to see her goe as braue as may be.
A pleasant Knight one day was so presumptuous,
To tell this Lord in way of plaine simplicitie,
'Tis you, my Lord, that haue this worlds felicitie:
To haue a Dame so yong, so sweet, so sumptuous.
Tush, said the Lord, but these same costly Gownes,
With Kirtles, Carknets, plague me in such sort,
That euery time I taste of *Venus* sport,
I will be sworne, cost me one hundred Crownes.
Now, fie Sir, said his wife, where is your sence;
Though 'tis too true, yet say not so for shame,
For I would wish to cleere me of the blame:
That each time cost you but a hundred pence.

66 Of Galla's *goodly Periwigge.*

162 You see the goodly hayre that *Galla* weares,
'Tis certain her own hair, who would haue thought it?
She sweares it is her owne: and true she sweares:
For hard by Temple-barre last day she bought it.
So faire a haire, vpon so foule a forehead,
Augments disgrace, and showes the grace is borrowed.

67 Of Master Iohn Dauies *Booke of Dancing. To himselfe.*

163 While you the Planets all doe set to dancing,
Beware such hap, as to the Fryer was chancing:

Who preaching in a Pulpit old and rotten,
Among some notes, most fit to be forgotten;
Vnto his Auditory thus he vaunts,
To make all Saints after his pype to daunce:
In speaking which, as he himselfe aduances,
To act his speech with Iestures, lo, it chances,
Downe fals the Pulpit, sore the man is brused,
Neuer was Fryer, and Pulpit more abused.
Then beare with me, though yet to you a stranger,
To warne you of the like, nay greater danger.
For though none feare the falling of those sparkes,
(And when they fall, 'twill be good catching Larkes)
Yet this may fall, that while you dance and skip
With Female Planets, sore your foote may trip,
That in your lofty Caprioll and turne,
Their motion may make your dimension burne.

68 *To* Paulus.

164 To loue you, *Paulus,* I was well enclin'd:
But euer since your honour did require,
I honor'd you, because 'twas your desire:
But now to loue you, I doe neuer minde.

69 *Of Table-talke.*

165 I had this day carroust the thirteenth cup,
And was both slipper-tong'd, and idle-brain'd,
And said by chance, that you with me should sup.
You thought hereby, a supper cleerely gain'd:
And in your Tables you did quote it vp.
Vnciuill ghest, that hath been so ill train'd!
Worthy thou art hence supperlesse to walke,
That tak'st aduantage of our Table-talke.

163 7 In speaking which, as A] It speaking, which as 1618 etc.
165 1 thirteenth A] thirteene 1618.

70 *Of the commodities that men haue by their Marriage.*

166 A fine yong Clerke, of kinne to Fryer *Frappert,*
Prompt of his tongue, of person neat and dappert:
Not deepely read, yet were he put vnto it,
One that could say his seruice, and would doe it.
His markes & haire, show'd him of excellent carriage:
This man one day hap'ned to talke of marriage,
And prou'd not onely, that 'tis honorable,
But that the ioyes thereof are admirable.
He told the tale to me, and other friends,
And straight I learn'd it at my fingers ends.
Which ioyes that you may better vnderstand,
I'le place one on each finger of my hand.
Foure ioyes, he said, on married Priest be cast,
A wife, and friends, and coyne, and children last.
And first the wife, see how at bed, at boord,
What comfort, and what ioyes, she doth affoord.
Then for her friends, what ioy can be more deare,
Then louing friends, dwell they farre off or neare.
A third ioy then it is, to haue the portion,
Well got, and void of strife, fraud or extortion.
And fourthly, those sweet Babes, that call one Dad,
Oh, how they ioy the soule, and make it glad!
But now, Sir, there remaines one obseruation,
That well deserues your due consideration.
Marke then againe, I say, for so 'twere meete,
Which of these ioyes are firme, and which doe fleete.
First, for the wife, sure no man can deny it,
That for most part, she stickes most surely by it.
But for thy friends, when they should most auaile you,
By death, or fortunes change, oft times they faile you.
Then for the portion, without more forecast,
Whiles charge encreaseth, money failes as fast.

166 [12] place one on A] place on 1618 place them on 1633. [13] be cast, A] he casts, 1618 I cast, 1633. [21] one Dad, A] on Dad, 1618 etc.

And last the children, most of them out-liue you,
But ill brought vp, they often liue to grieue you.
Now marke vpon the fingers, who remaine,
The Children and the Wife, onely these twaine.

71 *To* Marcus *that would borrow.*

167 You sent to me, *Marcus,* for twenty marke:
But to that sute, I would by no meanes harke:
But straight next day, you sent your man in post,
To tell me how a Lord with you would host.
And I must lend, to entertaine this State,
Some Basons, Ewres, and some such other plate.
Are you a Foole? Or thinke you me a foole,
That I should now be set againe to schoole?
Were not my wisedome, worthy to be wondred,
Denying twenty markes, to lend one hundred?

72 *To his wife after they had been married 14 yeers.*

168 Two Prentiships with thee I now haue been,
Mad times, sad times, glad times, our life hath seen,
Souls we haue wroght 4.payre since our first meeting
Of which, 2.soules, sweet soules, were to be fleeting.
My workemanship so well doth please thee still,
Thou wouldst not graunt me freedome by thy will:
And Ile confesse such vsage I haue found,
Mine heart yet ne're desir'd to be vnbound.
But though my selfe am thus thy Prentice vow'd,
My dearest *Mall,* yet thereof be not proud,
Nor claime no Rule thereby; ther's no such cause:
For *Plowden,* who was father of the Lawes
Which yet are read and rul'd by his Enditings,
Doth name himselfe a Prentice in his writings,

168 Heading *14 yeers.* A B] *foure yeere.* 1618. [4] fleeting. A B] fleeting, 1618 etc.

And I, if you should challenge vndue place,
Could learne of him to alter so the case:
I plaine would proue, I still keep due priority,
And that good wiues are still in their minority:
But far from thee, my deare, be such Audacitie:
I doubt more thou dost blame my dul Capacitie,
That though I trauaile true in my vocation,
I growe yet worse and worse at th'occupation.

73 *Of a Bequest without a Legacy.*

169 In hope some Lease or Legacy to gaine,
You gaue old *Titus* yeerely ten pound pension.
Now he is dead, I heare thou dost complaine,
That in his will of thee he made no mention.
Cease this complaint that shewes thy base intention.
He left thee more, then some he lou'd more deerely,
For he hath left thee ten pound pension yeerely.

74 *Of one that lent money on sure band.*

170 When *Lynus* little store of coyne is spent,
And no supply of office or of Rent,
He comes to *Titus* knowne a wary spender,
A pleasant wit, but no great money-lender,
And prest him very hard for twenty pound,
For which small kindnesse he were greatly bound,
And lest (quoth he) you deeme it my presumption,
If I should offer you my bare assumption,
I sweare All-hallows, I wil make repayment,
Yea though I pawne mine Armour and my Rayment,
And for your more assurance, you shall haue
What Obligation you your selfe will craue,
Or Bill or Bond your payment to performe,
Recognizance, Statute or any forme.
Now *Titus* by report so well did know him,

168 [17] keep A] kept B 1618 etc.
170 [7] my A] might 1618 1625 were 1633.

That he might scant trust him so far as throw him,
And said he should haue so much at his hands,
Forthwith if he might poynt the forme and bands.
Agree'd, quoth *Lynus* straight, and doth him thanke.
But *Titus* brings a Foorme of foure Inch-Plancke,
Two of the Gard might scantly well it lift,
And ere that *Lynus* well perceiu'd the drift,
Fast to that Foorme he bound him hands and feete:
Then brought the mony forth and let him see't,
And sware till he his fashions did reforme,
None other bands could serue nor other forme.

75 *Of light Merchandize.*

171 In Rome a Cryer had a Wench to sell,
Such as in Common Stewes are wont to dwell,
Her name, nor his, I shall not neede to tell.
But hauing held her long at little price,
And thinking thus some chapman to entice,
He clipt her in his armes as nothing nice,
And so he kist her more then once or twice.
What might he gaine, thinke you, by this deuice?
One that before had offered fifty shilling,
To giue one fift part, seemed now vnwilling.

76 *Of father* Peleus *stable.*

172 Old *Peleus* burn'd a Stable to the ground,
Which new to build doth cost three hundred pound:
That's but one Gennets price with him, no force,
A Stable? No: He did but lose a horse.

77 *Of a censurer of English writers.*

173 That Englishmen haue small, or no inuention,
Old *Guillam* saith, and all our workes are barren,

170 23 bound A] bindes 1618 binds 1633. 25 till A] till, 1618.
171 5 thus A] that 1618 1625 so 1633.
172 2 new A] now 1618 etc.

But for the stuffe, we get from Authors forren.
Why, *Guillam,* that same gold thou tak'st in pension,
Which makes thee loue our Realm more then your own
And follow still our English Court, and camp,
Now that it hath our dearest Soueraignes stampe,
Is English coine, though once 'twere *Indian* growne.
  Except not then 'gainst English wits, I pray,
  You that accept so well of English pay.

78 Of Titus *boasting.*

174 A kinde companion *Titus* all his daies,
And till his last, a pleasant wit and tongue;
If he had heard a man his owne strength praise,
Would tell what he would doe when he was yong.
And hauing, with oathes, his speeches bound:
Thus would he speak: I would at twelue score pricks,
Haue shot all day an arrow of a pound,
Haue shot the flight full fortie score and sixe,
I would haue ouer-lifted all the Gard,
Out-throwne them at the barre, the sledge, the stone,
And he that is in wrestling held most hard,
I would in open plaine haue ouerthrowne.
Now, say some by, Was *Titus* e're so strong?
Who he? the weakest man hundreds among.
Why tels he then such lyes in serious sort,
What he could do? Nay, sure 'twas true, though sport.
  He said not he could doe. That were a fable.
  He said, He would haue done, had he beene able.

79 To Doctor Sherwood, *how Sack makes one leane.*

175 I marueld much last day, what you did meane,
To say that drinking Sack, will make one leane:

173 [6] camp, A] campe. 1618 etc.
174 [14] hundreds A] a hundred 1618 etc.
175 Heading Sherwood, A] Sherhood 1618, Sheerhood, 1633.

But now I see I then mistooke you cleane.
For my good neighbour *Marcus* who I tro,
Feares fatnesse much, this drinke hath plyde him so,
That now except he leane, he cannot goe.
Ha, gentle Doctor, now I see your meaning,
Sacke will not leaue one leane, 'twill leaue him leaning.

80 *Of swearing first betweene the wife and the Husband.*

176 *Cis,* by that Candle, in my sleepe, I thought,
One told me of thy body thou wert nought:
Good husband, he that told you, lyde, she sed,
And swearing laid her hand vpon the bread.
Then eate the bread (quoth he) that I may deeme
That fancie false, that true to me did seeme.
Nay Sir, said she, the matter well to handle,
Sith you swore first, you first must eate the Candle.

81 *To his Wife.*

177 Because I once in verse did hap to call
Thee by this louing name, my dearest *Mall,*
Thou think'st thy selfe assured by the same,
In future ages, I haue giu'n thee fame.
But if thou merit not such name in veritie,
I meane not so to mis-informe posteritie.
For I can thus interpret if I will,
My dearest *Mall,* that is, my costliest ill.

82 *To a prattling Epicure.*

178 If thou loue dainty fare at others tables,
Thou must their humor and their houres endure:

175 [3] see I then A] see, and then 1618 etc.

Leaue arg'ments, controulings, thawrts and brables.
Such freedome sutes not with an Epicure.

83 *Of* Don Pedro.

179 The wise *Vlisses* loathing forraine Iarres,
Fain'd himselfe mad, to keepe him from the wars:
But our *Don Pedro* sees our Martiall schooles
Prefer before wise cowards Martiall fooles.
And fearing faining mad will not suffice,
To stay him from the warres, faines himselfe wise.

84 *To Master* Bastard, *taxing him of Flattery.*

180 It was a saying vs'd a great while since,
The subiects euer imitate the Prince,
A vertuous Master, makes a good Disciple,
Religious Prelates breede a godly people.
And euermore the Rulers inclination,
Workes in the time the chawnge and alteration.
Then what's the reason, *Bastard,* why thy Rimes
Magnifie Magistrates, yet taunt the times?
I thinke that he to taunt the time that spares not,
Would touch the Magistrate, saue that he dares not.

85 Ouids *confession translated into English for Generall* Norreys. 1593.

181 To liue in Lust I make not my profession,
Nor in my Verse, my vices to defend:
But rather by a true and plaine confession,
To make men know my meaning is to mend.
I hate, and am my selfe that most I hate.
I load my selfe, yet striue to be discharged,

178 3 controulings, thawrts A] contouling thwarts 1618 1625 controuling thwarts 1633.

179 3 sees A 1615] seekes 1618 etc. schooles A] schooles, 1615 etc. 4 Prefer A] Preferre 1615 Prefers 1618 1625 Preferres 1633.

180 6 chawnge A] workes 1618 etc.

Like sterelesse ship vnstai'd, runnes my estate,
Bound by my selfe, I sue to be enlarged.
No certaine shape, my fancies doth enflame:
A hundred causes kindle my affection,
If sober looke doe show a modest shame,
Straight to those eyes my soule is in subiection.
A wanton looke, no lesse my heart doth pierce,
Because it showes a pleasant inclination.
If she be coy like *Sabines* sharpe and fierce,
I thinke such coynesse, deepe dissimulation.
If she be learn'd, I honour gifts so rare,
If ignorant, I loue a milde simplicitie.
If she doe praise my writings, and compare
Them with the best, in her I take felicitie.
If she dispraise my Verses, and their Maker,
To win her liking, I my loue would lend her.
Goes she well grac't? Her gate would make me take her:
If ill, perhaps to touch a man, would mend her.
Is shee well tun'd in voice, a cunning singer?
To snatch a kisse, eu'n thus I feele a will.
Playes she on Lute with sweete and learned finger?
What heart can hate a hand so full of skill?
But if she know with art her armes to moue,
And dance Carantoes with a comely grace,
T'omit my selfe that quickly fall in loue,
Hippolitus would haue *Priapus* place,
Like th'ancient *Heroynes* I count thee tall,
Me thinkes they fill a braue roome in the bed:
Yet comlier sports are found in statures small,
Thus long and short haue aye my liking bred.
If she goe plaine, then what a piece were this?
Were she attyr'd, if braue, I loue her brauery,
Fayre, nut-browne, sallow, none doth looke amisse,
My wanton lust is thrald in so great slauery.

181 29 art A] heart 1618 etc. 33 *Heroynes* A] *Heroyes* 1618 1625 *Heroes* 1633.

If hayre like Iet, her neck like Ivory couer,
Ledas was blacke, and that was *Ledas* glory.
With yellow lockes, *Aurora* pleas'd her louer.
Loe thus my fancie sutes to euery story:
The Matron graue, the greene yong girle and pritty,
I like for age, for manners vnsuspicious,
In fine, to all in Country, Court and City,
My loue doth presse to proue it selfe ambitious.

86 *A witty speech of* Heywood *to the Queene.*

182 When good Queen *Mary* with much pain & anguish,
Did on deaths bed in lingring sicknesse languish:
Old pleasant *Heywood* came her Grace to visite:
For mirth to such doth oft more good then Phisicke,
Whom, when the gracious Princesse had espyde,
Ah, *Heywood!* here they kill me vp, she cryde:
For, being smotherd quite with too much heate,
Yet my Physicians proue to make me sweat;
But it doth proue so painefull to procure it,
That first Ile die before I will endure it.
Heywood, with cheerefull face, but cheerelesse soule,
Thus her bad resolution did controule.
    Sweet Lady, you must sweat, or else, I sweare it,
    We shall all sweat for it, if you forbeare it.

87 *To my wife, from Chester.*

183 When I from thee, my deere, last day departed,
Summoned by Honor to this Irish action,
Thy tender eyes shed teares: but I, hard-harted,
Tooke from those teares a ioy, and satisfaction.
Such for her Spouse (thought I) was *Lucrece* sadness,
Whom to his ruine Tyrant *Tarquin* tempted.
So mourned she, whose husband feined madnes,

182 [1] good A] old 1618 etc. anguish, A] languish, 1618 etc. [5] gracious A] sickly 1618 etc.

Thereby from Troian warres to stand exempted.
Thus then I doe reioyce in that thou greeuest,
And yet, sweet foole, I loue thee, thou beleeuest.

88 *Against lying* Lynus.

184 I wonder *Lynus,* what thy tongue doth ayle,
That though I flatter thee, thou still doost raile?
Thou think'st, I ly, perhaps thou think'st most true:
Yet to so gentle lyes, pardon is due.
A lie, wel told, to some tastes is restoritie;
Besides, we Poets lie by good authoritie.
But were all lying Poetry, I know it,
Lynus would quickly proue a passing Poet.

89 Of lending on Priuy-seales.

185 A friend of mine, to me made mickle mone
About some moneyes lending in the lone;
Alleaging, that to lend, were little griefe,
If of repayment men haue firme beleefe.
But other mens examples make vs dread,
To speed as some in other times haue sped.
For if one faile, who then will care for vs?
Now I, to comfort him, replyed thus,
While God preserues the Prince, ne're be dismayd,
But, if she faile, be sure we shall be payd.

90 In defence of Lent.

186 Ovr belly-gods dispraise the *Lenton* fast,
And blame the lingring daies, and tedious time,
And sweare this abstinence too long doth last,

184 [5] A lie, wel told, to some tastes is A] A lie, wel told to some, tastes ill 1618 etc.

185 Heading *Of lending on* A] *Of lending our* 1618 etc. [8] him, A] them, 1618 etc.

186 [3] last, 1633] last A B last. 1618 1625.

Whose folly I refute in this my rime.
Methusalem, nine hundred yeares was fed
With nought but herbes, and berries of the field;
Iohn Baptist thirty yeeres his life had led
With Locusts and wild Honey woods did yeeld.
He that the Israelites from Egypt brought,
Where they in slauish thraldome long did dwell,
He whome to heau'n the firie Chariot raught,
Yea, Christ himselfe, that saues vs all from Hell:
These three, as holy Scripture doth repeate,
In forty daies did neither drinke, nor eate.
Why then should we against this Law repine,
That are permitted euery kind of Fish?
Are not forbid the tastes of costly Wine,
Are not debard of many a daintie dish:
Both Sugar, Ginger, Pepper, Cloues, and Mace,
And Sinnamon, and Spice of euery kind,
And Reysons, Figs and Almonds in like case,
To please the taste, and satisfie the mind:
And yet forsooth, we thinke we should be mard,
If we from flesh but forty dayes be bard.

91 Malum bene positum ne moueas.

187 A Iudge, to one well studied in the Lawes,
That was too earnest in his Clyents cause,
Said, Stir't no more; for as the cause doth sinke
Into my sense, it seemeth like a stinke.

92 Of King Dauid. *Written to the Queene.*

188 Thou Princes Prophet, and of Prophets King,
Growne from poore Pastoralls, and Shepheards fold,
To change the sheephooke to a Mace of gold,
Subduing sword and speare, with staffe and sling:

186 [4] rime. B] rime A rime, 1618 1625 rime; 1633. [11] whome A] whom B home 1618 etc. raught, B] raught A rought; 1618 etc.

188 Heading *Of King* Dauid. *Written to the Queene.* B] *To King* Dauid. A 1618 etc.

Thou that didst quell the Beare and dreadful Lyon,
With courage vnappald, and actiue lymmes;
Thou that didst praise in yet induring Himmes
With Poetry diuine the God of *Syon;*
Thou sonne in Law to King & Prince appointed:
Yet, when that king by wrong did seek thy harme,
Didst helpe him with thy Harp, and sacred charme:
And taught not once to touch the Lords Anointed.
Thou, thou great Prince, with so rare gifts replenished
Could'st not eschew blind Buzzard *Cupids* hookes,
Lapt in the bayt of *Bersabees* sweet lookes:
With which one fault, thy faultles life was blemished.
Yet hence we learne a document most ample,
That faln by fraillty we may rise by fayth,
And that the sinne forgiuen, the penance staieth;
Of Grace and Iustice both a sweet example.
Let no man then himselfe in sinne imbolden
By thee, but thy sharpe penance, bitter teares,
May strike into our harts such godly feares,
As we may be thereby from sin with-holden.
Sith we, for ours, no iust excuse can bring,
Thou hadst one great excuse, thou wert a King.

93 Of Monsters. To my Lady Rogers.

189 Strange-headed Monsters, Painters haue described,
To which the Poets strange parts haue ascribed,
As *Ianus* first two faces had assign'd him
Of which, one look't before, tother behind him:
So men, may it be found in many places,
That vnderneath one hood can beare two faces.
Three-headed *Cerberus,* Porter of Hell,
Is faind with *Pluto,* God of wealth to dwell.

188 7 in yet A B] in it, 1618 etc. 12 taught not once A] taught'st not once B taught, no not 1618 etc. 18 That faln by fraillty we may rise by fayth, A] That faln by fraylty we may rise by faith, B Our flesh then strongest is, when weak'st our faith. 1618 etc.

So still with greatest States, and men of might,
Dogs dwell, that doe both fawne, and bark, & bite.
Like *Hydras* heads, that multiply with wounds,
Is multitude, that mutinie confounds:
On what seu'n-headed beast the Strumpet sits,
That wears the skarlett, poseth many wits,
Whether seu'n sinnes be meant, or else seu'n hils,
It is a question fit for higher skils.
  But then of these, if you can rightly conster,
  A headlesse woman is a greater Monster.

94 Of a pleasant Broker.

190 A broker that was hyr'd to sell a Farme,
Whose seat was very sound, fruitful and warme,
Thinking to grace the sales man with the tale,
Said thus: Friends, *Marius* sets this land to sale;
But thinke not this for debt or need to sell:
For as for money he is stor'd so well,
He hath at all times ready in his chest,
And some beside, he hath at interest.
Then were the chapmen earnestly in hand,
To question of the Title of the land:
Why should one sell, say they, that lets to vse?
The Broker driuen to seeke some new excuse,
Did study first, and smyling, thus replide,
His Worships beasts, and sheepe, and Hindes there dyde;
Since which, he neuer could the place abide.
Now though in this the foolish Broker lyde,
  Yet the report thereof did so much harme,
  That now, poore *Marius* cannot sell his Farme.

95 To the Lady Rogers.

191 To praise my wife, your daughter (so I gather)
Your men say, she resembleth most her father.

189 14 That wears the skarlett, poseth A] That weares the scarfe, sore troubleth 1618 etc.

191 Heading *To the Lady* Rogers. A B] *To the L.* Ro. 1618.

And I no lesse, to praise your sonne, her brother,
Affirme that he is too much like his mother.
I know not if we iudge aright, or erre:
But let him be like you, so I like her.

96 To his wife, in excuse he had call'd her foole in his writing.

192 A man in show that scornes, in deede enuies
Thy feruent loue, and seeks the same to coole,
Findes fault, that in a Verse I call'd thee Foole:
And that it could be kindly tane, denies.
But thou didst kindly take it, then he lyes.
Well, therefore I wish him a wife most wise,
Noble descended from great *De la Poole:*
Learn'd to set her husband still to schoole,
So faire to draw to her all amorous eyes.
Let flattering tongues protest she doth deserue,
That great Commanders her should sue to serue:
Then let him walke and with *Acteons* lucke,
Amid the Herd, say, *Welcome, fellow Bucke.*
Meane while, my *Mall,* thinke thou 'tis honorable,
To be my Foole, and I to be thy Bable.

97 Of the growth of Trees. To Sir Hugh Portman.

193 At your rich Orchard, you to me did show,
How swift the Trees were planted there, did grow:
Namely, an Elme, that in no long abode,
Did of a twigge, grow vp to be a loade.
But you would quite condemne your trees of slouth,
Compar'd to our trees admirable grouth.
Our planters haue found out such secret skils,
With pipe and barrel-staues, and iron Mils;
That Okes, for which none ten yeeres since were willing

193 Heading *To Sir* Hugh Portman. A] *to Sir* H. Port. 1618 etc. 9 willing A] willing, 1618 etc.

To giue ten groats, are growne worth thirty shilling,
At which I waxt so wood, I said in rage,
That thirst of Gold, makes this an Iron age.

98 *Against promoting* Lynus.

194 Thou, *Linus,* that louest still to be promoting,
Because I sport, about King *Henries* marriage:
Think'st this will proue a matter worth the carriage.
But let it alone, *Lynus,* it is no booting.
While Princes liue, who speakes, or writes & teaches
Against their faults, may pay for speech, and writing:
But being dead, dead men, they say, leaue biting:
Their eyes are seal'd, their armes haue little reaches.
Children they are, and fooles that are afeard,
To pull, and play, with a dead Lyons beard.

99 *The Story of* Marcus *life at Primero.*

195 Fond *Marcus* euer at *Primero* playes,
Long winter nights, and as long Summer dayes:
And I heard once, to idle talke attending,
The Story of his times, and coines mis-spending.
As first, he thought himselfe halfe way to heauen,
If in his hand he had but got a seu'n.
His Fathers death set him so high on flote,
All rests went vp vpon a seu'n, and coate.
But while he drawes for these gay coats & gownes,
The gamesters from his purse draw all his crownes.
And he ne're ceast to venter all in prime,
Till of his age, quite was consum'd the prime.
Then he more warily, his rest regards,
And sets with certainties vpon two cardes,
On sixe and thirtie, or on seu'n and nine,
If any set his rest, he saith (and mine):

194 [4] booting. A] booting, 1618 etc.
195 [9] gay A] gray 1618 etc. [14] two cardes, A] the Cards 1618 etc. [16] he saith (and mine): A] and saith, and mine: 1618 etc.

But seeld with this, he either gaines or saues,
For either *Faustus* prime is with three knaues
Or *Marcus* neuer can encounter right,
Yet drew two Ases, and for further spight,
Had colour for it with a hopefull draught,
But not encountred, it auail'd him naught.
Well, sith encountring, he so faire doth misse,
He sets not till he nine and fortie is.
And thinking, now his rest would sure be doubled,
He lost it by the hand, with which sore troubled,
He ioynes now all his stocke, vnto his stake,
That of his fortune, he full proofe may make.
At last both eldest hand and fiue and fifty,
He thinketh now or neuer (thriue vnthrifty.)
Now for the greatest rest he hath the push:
But *Crassus* stopt a Club, and so was flush:
And thus what with the stop, and with the packe,
Poore *Marcus,* and his rest goes still to wracke.
Now must he seeke new spoile to set his rest,
For here his seeds turne weeds, his rest, vnrest.
His land, his plate he pawnes, he sels his leases,
To patch, to borrow, and shift, he neuer ceases.
Till at the last, two Catch-poles him encounter,
And by arrest, they beare him to the Counter.
    Now *Marcus* may set vp, all rests securely:
    For now he's sure to be encountred surely.

100 Lesbias *rule of praise.*

196 *Lesbia,* whom some thought a louely creature,
Doth sometimes praise some other womans feature:
Yet this I do obserue, that none she praises,
Whome worthy fame by bewties merrits rayses.
But onely of their seemely parts she tels,

196 [4] Whome worthy fame by bewties merrits rayses. A] Whom worthy fame, by beauties merits praises. 1618 etc.

Whom she doth sure beleeue, her self excels.
    So, *Linus* praises *Churchyard* in his censure,
    Not *Sydney, Daniel, Constable,* nor *Spencer.*

101 *Another of Table-talke.*

197 Among some Table-talke of little weight,
A friend of mine was askt by one great Lady:
What sonnes he had? My wife (saith he) hath eight.
Now fie, said she, 'tis an ill vse as may be.
I would you men would leaue these fond conditions,
To put on vertuous wiues such wrong suspitions.
Tush, said her Lord, you giue a causelesse blame,
The Gentleman hath wisely spoke, and well:
To reckon all his sonnes perhaps were shame,
His wiues sonnes therefore he doth onely tell.
    Behold, how much it stands a man in steede,
    To haue a friend answere in time of neede.

102 *Of old* Haywoods *sonnes.*

198 Old *Haywoods* sons did wax so wild & youthfull,
It made their aged father sad and ruthfull.
A friend one day, the elder did admonish
With threats, as did his courage halfe astonish,
How that except he would begin to thriue,
His Sire of all his goods would him depriue.
For whom, quoth he? Eu'n for your yonger brother.
Nay then, said he, no feare, if't be none other.
My brother's worse then I, and till he mends,
I know, my father no such wrong intends,
    Sith both are bad, to shew so partiall wrath,
    To giue his yonger vnthrift that hee hath.

197 6 To put on A] T'enure on 1618 etc.
198 2 ruthfull. A] wrathfull. 1618 etc.

Booke III

1 *Yong* Haywoods *answere to my Lord of Warwicke.*

199 One neere of kinne to *Heywood* by his birth,
And no lesse neere in name, and most in mirth,
Was once for his Religions sake committed,
Whose case a Noble Peere so greatly pittied:
He sent to know what things with him were scant,
And offered frankely to supply his want.
  Thankes to that Lord, said he, that wills me good,
  For I want all things sauing hay and wood.

2 *To the great Ladies of the Court.*

200 I haue beene told, most Noble courtly Dames,
That ye commend some of my Epigrams:
But yet I heare againe, which makes me pensiue,
Some of them are, to some of you offensiue.
Those that you like, I'le giue, and aske no guerdon,
So that you grant those you mislike, you pardon.
  Both are the fruitlesse fruits of idle houres,
  These for my pleasure reade, and those for yours.

3 *Of a Lady that giues the cheek.*

201 Is't for a grace, or is't for some disleeke,
Where others kisse with lip, you giue the cheeke?
Some note that for a pride in your behauiour:
But I should rather take it for a fauour.
For I to show my kindnesse, and my loue,
Would leaue both lip and cheek, to kisse your Gloue.
  Now with the cause, to make you plain acquainted,
  Your gloue's perfum'd, your lip & cheek are painted.

199 [4] greatly A] lately 1618 etc. [7] wills A] will 1618 etc.
201 Heading *cheek.* A] *cheeke.* 1615 *checke.* 1618. [2] others 1615] other A 1618 etc.

4 *Of* Balbus *a Poet.*

202 *Balbus* of Writers reck'ning vp a Rable,
Thinks their names are by him made honorable:
And not vouchsafing me to name at all,
He thinkes that he hath greeu'd me to the gall.
I galld? no, simple fellow, thou art gulled,
To thinke I weigh the praise of such a dull head.
Those that are guilty of defect, and blame,
Doe neede such testimonials of their fame.
  Learne then, vntaught, learn then you enuious elues,
  Books are not praised, that do not praise themselues.

5 *To* Leda.

203 In Verse, for want of Rime, I know not how,
I cald our Bathes the pilgrimage of Saints,
You *Leda* much the praise do disallow,
And thinke this touch your pure Religion taints.
  Good *Leda,* be not angry, for God knowes,
  Though I did write of Saints, I meant of shrowes.

6 *To* Sextus, *an ill Reader.*

204 That Epigram that last you did rehearse,
Was sharpe, and in the making, neat and tearse,
But thou doost read so harsh, point so peruerse,
It seemd now neither witty nor a vearse.
  For shame poynt better, and pronounce it cleerer,
  Or be no Reader, *Sextus,* be a Hearer.

7 *Of Bathes cure vpon* Marcus.

205 The fame of *Bathe* is great, and still endures,
That oft it worketh admirable cures.

202 [5] I galld? no, simple fellow, thou art gulled, 1615] I galled? simple soule no thou art gulled A I galled? Simple foole! nor yet gulled, 1618 etc. [6] I weigh the praise of 1615] I way the praise of A I may thee pray for 1618 etc.

204 [4] seemd now neither witty nor a vearse. A] seemed now neither witty nor verse. 1618 etc.

The barren by their vertue haue conceiu'd,
The weake and sick, haue health & strength receiu'd;
And many Cripples that came thither carried,
Go sound from thence, when they a while haue tarried.
But yet one cure on *Marcus* lately showne,
My Muse doth thinke most worthy to make known;
For, while he bathes with Gascoyne wines & Spanish,
Thereby old aches from his lymmes to banish,
Hunts after youthfull company, entycing
Them to the sports of bowling, carding, dycing:
His wantonnesse breeds want, his want enforces
Marcus, by one and one to sell all his horses.
  Lo, how the Bathe hath searcht his sicknes roote,
  He can, nay more, he must goe thence afoote.

8 *Of a Lady that sought remedy at the Bathe.*

206 A Lady that none name, nor blame none hath,
Came the last yeere with others to the Bathe:
Her person comely was, good was her feature,
In beauty, grace and speech, a louely creature.
Now as the Lady in the water staid,
A plaine man fell a talking with her maid,
That lean'd vpon the rayle, and askt the reason,
Why that faire Lady vs'd the Bathe, that season?
Whether 'twere lamenesse, or defect in hearing,
Or some more inward euill, not appearing?
No, said the Maid to him, beleeue it well,
That my faire Mistris sound is as a Bell.
But of her comming, this is true occasion,
An old Physician mou'd her by perswasion,
These Bathes haue power to strengthen that debility,
That doth in man or woman breed sterrilitie.
Tush, said the man with plaine & short discourse,
Your Mistris might haue tane a better course.

205 [8] make known; A] be known; 1618 etc. [14] to sell A] sell 1618 etc.

Let her to Oxford, to the Vniuersitie,
Where yong Physicians are, and such diuersitie
Of toward spirits that in all acts proceede,
Much fitter then the Bathe is for the deede.
No, no, that will not serue, the Maid replide,
For she that Physike hath already tride.

9 To Sir Morris Barkly.

207 Your father gaue me once a Dormant warrant:
But sending at Saint *Iames* tide to the keeper,
My men came backe as from a sleeuelesse Arrant,
And in a boxe, I laid my warrant sleeper.
You Noble Sir, that are his heyre apparant,
Will giue henceforth, I hope, a waking Warrant.

10 Of Faustus *the Fault-finder.*

208 Of all my Verses, *Faustus* still complaines,
I writ them carelesly: and why forsooth?
Because, he saith, they goe so plaine and smooth.
It showes that I for them ne're beat my braines.
I, that mens errors neuer loue to sooth,
Said, they that say so, may be thought but noddies.
For sample marke, said I, your Mistris bodies,
That sit so square, and smooth down to her raines,
That, that fine waste, thy wealth and wit doth waste,
Thinke you her Taylor wrought it vp in haste?
No: aske him, and heele say he took more paines
Then with old *Ellens* double-welted frock,
That sits like an old felt on a new block.
Who cannot write, ill iudge of Writers vaines.
The worke of Taylers hands, and Writers wits,
Was hardest wrought, when as it smoothest sits.

206 24 For she A] For her, 1618.
208 9 thy A] that 1618 etc. doth waste, A] doth waste. 1618 etc.

11 Of an ill Physician for the body, that became a worse Surgeon for the soule.

209 A certaine Mountebanke, or paltry Leach,
Finding his Physick furdred not his thrift,
Thought with himselfe to find some further drift.
And though the skill were farre aboue his reach,
He needs would proue a Priest, and falls to preach.
But patching Sermons with a sorry shift,
As needs they must that ere they learne will teach:
At last, some foes so neerely doe him sift,
And of such words and deeds did him appeach,
As from his Liuing quite they did him lift,
And of the Patron straight they begd the gift:
And so the Mountebanke did ouer-reach.
Who when he found he was pursu'd so swift,
Gaue place vnto so sharpe and fierce a breach:
Shutting vp all with this shrewd muttering speach,
Well, though, said he, my Liuing I haue lost,
Yet many a good mans life this losse shall cost.
A stander by, that would be thought officious,
Straight, as an heynous matter of complaint,
Doth with his speech the Iustices acquaint:
Alleaging, as it seem'd, indeed suspicious,
That to the State his meaning was pernitious.
The Leech thus touched with so shrewd a Taint,
Yet in his looke nor answer did not faint;
Protesting, that his mind was not malicious.
But if the course that he must take be vicious,
He flat affirmed it was curst constraint:
For, of my Liuing hauing lost possession,
I must, said he, turne to my first profession;
In which, I know too well, for want of skill,
My medcines many an honest man will kill.

209 24 did not A] did, nor 1618 etc. 31 My medcines many an honest man will kill. A] My Medicines will many a man kill. 1618 1625 My Medicines will many a good man kill. 1633.

12 *Of Sir* Philip Sydney.

210 If that be true the latten Prouerbe sayes,
Laudari a laudatis is most praise;
Sydney, thy works in *Fames* bookes are enrold,
By Princes pennes, that haue thy works extold,
Whereby thy name shall dure to endlesse dayes.
But now, if rules of contrary should hold,
Then I, poore I, were drownd in deepe dispraise,
Whose works base Writers haue so much debased,
That *Lynus* dares pronounce them all defaced.

13 *Of impudent* Lynus.

211 Not any learning, *Lynus,* no, God knowes,
But thy brute boldnes made some to suppose,
That thou might'st haue been bred in *Brazen-nose.*
A murren on thy pate, 'twould doe thee grace,
So were thine head so arm'd in euery place,
A Steele scull, Copper nose, and Brazen face.

14 *Against an vnthrifty* Lynus.

212 Many men maruaile *Lynus* doth not thriue,
That had more trades then any man aliue;
As first, a Broker, then a Petty-fogger,
A Traueller, a Gamster, and a Cogger,
A Coyner, a Promoter, and a Bawde,
A Spy, a Practicer in euery fraude:
And missing thrift by these lewd trades and sinister,
He takes the best, yet proues the worst, a Minister.

15 *Of* Faustus.

213 I find in *Faustus* such an alteration,
He giues to *Paulus* wondrous commendation:
Is *Paulus* late to him waxt friendly? No.
But sure, poore *Faustus* faine would haue it so.

210 [1] latten A] latter 1618 etc.

16 Of a deuout Vsurer.

214 A Merchant, hearing that great Preacher, SMITH,
Preach against Vsury, that art of byting,
The Sermon done, embrac'd the man forth-with,
Vnto his bord most friendly him inuiting.
A friend of his, hoping some sweet aspersion
Of grace would moue him to some restitution,
Wisht him, in token of his full Conuersion,
Release some Debters, held in Execution.
Foole, said he, thinke you Ile leaue my trade?
No: but I thinke this Preacher learn'd and painefull,
Because the more from it he doth perswade,
'Tis like to proue to me more sweet and gainefull.
Was euer Iew of Malta, or of Millain,
Then this most damned Iew, more Iewish villain?

17 Of a reformed Brother.

215 In studying Scriptures, hearing Sermons oft,
Thy mind is growne so plyable and soft,
That though none can attaine to true perfection,
Thy works come neere the words of their direction.
They counsell oft to fast, and euer pray,
Thou louest oft to feast, and euer play:
Sackcloth and Cinders they aduise to vse,
Sack, Cloues, and Sugar, thou wouldst haue to chuse:
They wish our works, and life, should shine like light,
Thy workes and all thy life is passing light,
They bid vs follow still the Apostles lore,
Apostata's thou follow'st euermore.
They bid refresh the poore with Almes-deedes,
Thou rauish dost the poore with all misdeedes.
They promise ioyes eternall neuer wasting,
You merit noyes infernall euerlasting.

214 [7] Wisht A] Wist 1618 1625 Wish'd 1633.
215 [5] They A] Thy 1618. [15] promise A] promist 1618 1625 promis'd 1633. 1618 etc.

18 Of Sheepe turned Wolues.

216 When hearts obdurate make of sin an habite,
High frowning *Nemesis* was wont to send
Beares, Lions, Wolues, and Serpents, to this end,
To spoyle the coasts where so bad folke inhabite.
Now since this age, in habite and in act,
Excels the sinnes of euery former age,
No maruaile *Nemesis* in her iust rage,
Doth like, or greater punishment exact.
And for this cause, a cruell beast is sent,
Not only that deuoures and spoyles the people,
But spares not house, nor village, Church nor Steeple,
And makes poore widdowes mourn, Orphants lament.
You muse (perhaps) what beasts they be that keepe
Such beastly rule as seld was seene before!
Tis neither Beare, nor Lyon, Bull, nor Bore:
But Beasts, then al these beasts, more harmfull, sheep.
Loe then, the mystery from whence the name
Of Cotsold Lyons first to England came.

19 Of Lynus, *borrowing.*

217 When *Lynus* meets me, after salutations,
Courtsies, and complements, and gratulations,
He presseth me, euen to the third deniall,
To lend him twenty shillings, or a royall:
But of his purpose, of his curtsie fayling,
He goes behind my backe, cursing and rayling.
Foole, thy kind speeches cost not thee a penny,
And more foole I, if they should cost me any.

20 Of one Master Carelesse.

218 Where dwels Mr. *Carelesse?* Iesters haue no dwelling.
Where lies he? in his tongue by most mens telling.

216 [4] bad A] good 1618 etc. [13] keepe A] keepe, 1618. [16] harmfull, 1633] harmfull A harmeful 1618 1625.

Where bords he? there where feasts are found by smelling.
Where bites he? all behind, with all men yelling.
Where bides the man? oh sir, I mist your spelling.
Now I will read, yet well I doe not wot:
But if that I to him shall point his lot,
  In Shot-ouer, at Dogs-head in the pot.
  For in that signe his head's oft ouer-shot.

21 *Against* Momus, *in praise of his dogge* Bungey.

219 Because a witty Writer of this time,
Doth make some mention in a pleasant rime,
Of *Lepidus* and of his famous dogge,
Thou *Momus,* that dost loue to scoffe and cogge,
Prat'st among base companions and giue'st out,
That vnto me herein, is meant a flout.
Hate makes thee blinde, *Momus,* I dare be sworne,
He meant to me his loue, to thee his scorne,
Put on thy enuious spectacles and see,
Whom doth he scorne therein, the dogge or mee:
The Dogge is grac't, compared with great Bankes,
Both beasts right famous, for their pretty prankes,
Although in this, I grant, the dogge was worse,
He onely fed my pleasure, not my purse:
Yet that same Dogge, I may say this and boast it,
Hath found my purse with gold when I haue lost it.
Now for my selfe, some fooles like thee may iudge,
That at the name of *Lepidus* I grudge,
No sure: so farre I thinke it from disgrace,
I wishe it cleave to me and to my race:
Lepus or *Lepos,* I in both haue part,
That in my name I beare, this in mine heart.
But, *Momus,* I perswade my selfe that no man,
Will deigne thee such a name, English or Roman,

218 [9] head's A] head 1618 etc.
219 [6] a flout. A] aflout. 1618. [16] Hath A] He 1618 etc. [20] cleave A] cleare 1618 etc.

Ile wage a But of Sack, the best in Bristo,
Who calls me *Lepido* will count thee *Tristo.*

22 Of Faustus.

220 Now *Faustus* saith, long Epigrams are dull.
Lowt, Larks are lothsom when ones panch is full.
Yet whom the short doe please, the long not weary,
I wish them neuer weary, euer merry.

23 Of summum bonum.

221 While I of *summum bonum* was disputing,
Propounding some positions, som confuting,
Old *Sextus* sayes that we were all deluded,
And that not one of vs aright concluded.
Knowledge, sayth he, is only true felicity,
Straightwayes a stranger askt me in simplicity,
Is *Sextus* learned? no quoth I, by this light.
Then without light, how iudgeth he so right?
He doth but ayme, as poore men vallew wealth,
The feeble value strength, the sicke man health.

24 To Mall, *to comfort her for the losse of her Children.*

222 When at the window thou thy doues are feeding,
Then thinke I shortly my Doue will be breeding,
Like will loue like, and so my liking like thee,
As I to doues in many things can like thee.
Both of you loue your lodgings dry and warme,
Both of you doe your neighbours little harme,
Both loue to feede vpon the finest graine,
Both of your liuings take but little paine,
Both murmur kindly, both are often billing,
Yet both to *Venus* sports will seeme vnwilling;

219 [26] Who calls me *Lepido* will count thee *Tristo.* A] Who calls me *Lepid,* I will call him *Tristo.* 1618 etc.
221 [7] light. A] light, 1618.
222 [4] thee. A B] thee, 1618. [7] finest A B] firmest 1618 etc.

Both doe delight to looke your selues in Glasses,
You both loue your own houses as it passes;
Both fruitfull are, but yet the Doue is wiser,
For, though she haue no friend that can aduise her,
  She, patiently can take her young ones losse,
  Thou, too impatiently doost beare such crosse.

25 *Of the excuse of* Symony.

223 *Clerus,* I heare, doth some excuse alledge
Of his and all his fellows sacriledge:
As namely, that 'tis sore against their wills,
That men are bound to take the lesse of ills;
That they had rather (no man needs to doubt it)
Take livings with the lands than thus without it:
And therefore we must lay this haynous crime,
Not vnto them forsooth, but to the time.
Alas! a fault confest, were halfe amended,
But sinne is doubled that is thus defended.
  I know, a right wise man saies and beleeues,
  Where no Receiuers are, there be no Theeues.

26 *In commendation of Master* Lewkners *booke of the description of Venice, Dedicated to Lady* Warwick. 1595.

224 Lo, here's describ'd, though but in little roome,
Faire Venice, like a Spouse in *Neptunes* armes;
For freedome, emulous to ancient Rome,
Famous for counsell much, and much for Armes:
Whose stories earst written with Tuscan quill,
Lay to our English wits, as halfe conceal'd,

223 [2] Of his and all his fellows A] Of his, and other fellowes 1618 etc. [3] 'tis sore A] to some, 1618 etc. [5] (no man needs to doubt it) A] no man need to doubt, 1618 etc. [6] Take livings with the lands than thus without it: A] Take Liuings whole, then such as his without: 1618 etc. [11] saies A] sings 1618 etc.

224 Heading Lewkners *booke of the description* A] Lewkeners *sixt description* 1618 etc.

Till *Lewkners* learned trauaile and his skill,
In well grac'd stile and phrase hath it reueald.
Venice, be proud, that thus augments thy fame;
England, be kind, enricht with such a Booke,
Both giue due honor to that noble Dame,
For whom this taske the Writer vnder-tooke.

27 *Of one that gaue a Benefice.*

225 A Squire of good account, affirm'd he meant
A learned man a Liuing to present:
But yet that Squire, in this did breake the square,
He purposed thereof to keepe a share;
To set two sonnes to schoole, to make them Clarks,
He doth reserue each yeere an hundred markes.
    Ah, said the Priest, this card is too too cooling,
    I set your sonns? nay, they set me to schooling.

28 *Of* Faustus *fishing.*

226 With siluer hooke *Faustus* for flesh was fishing,
But that game byting not vnto his wishing,
He said, he did (being thus shrewdly matcht)
Fish for a Roach, but had a Gudgen catcht.
Faustus, it seemes thy luck therein was great,
For sure the Gudgen is the better meat.
    Now bayt againe, that game is set so sharpe,
    That to that Gudgen, thou mayst catch a Carpe.

29 *To his friend. Of his Booke of* Aiax.

227 You muse to find in me such alteration,
That I, that maydenly to write was wont,
Would now set to a Booke so desperate front,
As I might scant defend by ymitation.
My Muse that time did need a strong Purgation,

225 [1] meant A] went, 1618 etc. [3] the square, A] no square, 1618 etc. [8] sonns? A] sonnes; 1618 1625 sons? 1633.
227 [4] ymitation. A] incitation. 1618 etc.

Late hauing tane some bruse by lewd reports;
And when the Physick wrought, you know the fashion
Whereto a man in such a case resorts:
And so my Muse, with good *decorum* spent
On that base titled Booke, her excrement.

30 Of a Seller of Time.

228 When of your Lordship I a Lease renew'd,
You promis'd me before we did conclude,
To giue me time, namely, twice twelue months day,
For such a Fine as I agreed to pay.
I bade a hundred pound, 'twas worth no more.
Your Lordship set it higher by a score.
Now, since I haue by computation found,
That two yeeres day cost me this twenty pound.
Sir, pardon me, to be thus plainely told it,
Your Lordship gaue not two yeeres day, you sold it.

31 Of the Earle of Essex.

229 Great Essex, now of late incurred hath
His Mistris indignation and her wrath:
And that in him she chiefly dissalouth,
She sent him North, he bent him to the South:
Then what shall Essex do? Let him henceforth,
Bend all his wits, his power and courage North.

32 Of himselfe.

230 Because in this my selfe-contenting vaine,
To write so many Toyes I borrow leasure,
Friends sorrow, fearing I take too much paine,
Foes enuy, swearring I take too much pleasure.
I smile at both, and wish, to ease their griefes,
That each with other would but change beliefs.

230 [4] swearring A] swearing 1615 swearing, 1618. [6] beliefs A] beleefe 1615 reliefs 1618 etc.

30 *To Doctor* Sherwood, *of Bathe.*

231 Because among some other idle glances,
I, of the Bathes say sometimes as it chances,
That this an onely place is in this age,
To which faire Ladies come in pilgrimage,
You feare such wanton gleekes, and ill report,
May stop great States that thither would resort.
No, neuer feare it, pray but for faire weather:
Such speech as this, will bring them faster thither.

31 *Of* Marcus *courtesie.*

232 When I some little purchase haue in hand,
Straight *Marcus* kindly offers me his band.
I tell him, and he takes it in great snuffe,
His is a Falling Band, I weare a Ruffe.
But if you maruaile I his helpe refuse,
And meane herein some meaner mans to vse:
The cause is this, I fear within a weeke,
That he of me like courtesie will seeke.

32 *Of one that had a blacke head, and a gray Beard.*

233 Though many search, yet few the cause can finde,
Why thy beard gray, thy head continues blacke:
Some thinke thy Beard more subiect to the winde.
Some think that thou dost vse that new-found knack,
Excusable to such as haire doe lacke:
A quaint Gregorian to thy head to binde.
Some thinke that with a combe of drossie Lead,
Thy siluer locks doe turne to colour darke:
Some thinke 'tis but the nature of thy head:
But we thinke most of these haue mist the marke.
For this thinke we, that thinke we thinke aright.
Thy beard and yeeres are graue, thy head is light.

232 7 fear within a weeke, A] meane, within a weeke, 1618 etc.

33 Against an old Lecher.

234 Since thy third curing of the French infection,
Priapus hath in thee found no erection:
Yet eat'st thou Ringoes, and Potato Rootes,
And Caueare, but it little bootes.
Besides the beds-head a bottle lately found,
Of liquor that a quart cost twenty pound.
For shame, if not more grace, yet shew more wit,
Surcease, now sinne leaues thee, to follow it.
Some smile, I sigh, to see thy madnesse such,
That that which stands not, stands thee in so much.

34 To his wiues Mother, reprouing her vnconstancie.

235 Last yeere while at your house I hapt to tarry,
Of all your goods, you tooke an Inuentory:
Your Tapistry, your linnen, bedding, plate,
Your sheepe, your horse, your cattle you did rate:
And yet one moueable you did forget,
More moueable then theis therein to set.
Your wauering minde, I meane, which is so moueable,
That you for it, haue euer beene reproueable.

35 Of a Cuckold that had a chaste Wife.

236 When those Triumvers set that three mans song,
Which stablished in Rome a hellish Trinity,
That all the towne, and all the world did wrong,
Killing their friends, and kinne of their affinity,
By tripartite Indenture, parting Rome,
As if the world for them had wanted roome,
Plotyna wife of one of that same hundred,
Whom *Anthony* prescrib'd to lose their life,

234 [1] curing A] carriage 1618 etc. [10] which stands A] withstands 1618.
235 [6] theis B] this A this, 1618 etc.

For beauty much, for loue to be more wondred,
Su'd for her Spouse, and told she was his wife.
The Tyrant pleasd to see so faire a suter,
Doth kisse her, and imbrace her, and salute her.
Then makes, nay mocks, a loue too kinde, too cruell:
She must, to saue her husband from proscription,
Grant him one night, her husbands chieftest Iewell:
And what he meant, he shewd by lewd description:
Vowing, except he might his pleasure haue,
No meanes would serue, her husbands life to saue.
Oh motion! mouing thoughts, no thoughts, but thorns,
Either he dies, whom she esteemes most dearely:
Or she her selfe subiect to thousand scornes.
Both feares doe touch a Noble Matron neerely.
Loe, yet an act, performed by this woman,
Worthy a woman, worthy more a Romane:
To show more then her selfe she lou'd her Spouse,
She yeelds her body to this execution.
Come, Tyrant, come, performe thy damned vowes,
Her single heart hath doubled thy pollution.
Thou pollute her? No, foole, thou are beguiled:
She in thy filthy lap lies vndefiled.
Honour of Matrons, of all wiues a mirror!
I'le sweare with thee, thy husband weares no horne:
Or if this act, conuince mine oath of error,
Twas a most precious one, an Vnicorne.
　　If ought I know by hearing or by reading,
　　This act *Lucretias* deed is farre exceeding.

36 Of the Lady that lookt well to her borders: To Sir John Lee.

237 A Lady of great Birth, great reputation,
Clothed in seemely, & most sumptuous fashion

236 [10] her A] his 1618 1625 [11] pleasd A] pleasant 1618 etc. [19] mouing A] louing 1618 etc.
237 Heading *To Sir* John Lee. A only.

Wearing a border of rich Pearle and stone,
Esteemed at a thousand crownes alone,
To see a certaine Interlude, repaires,
To shun the press, by dark and priuat staires.
Her Page did beare a Torch that burnt but dimly.
Two cozening mates, seeing her deckt so trimly,
Did place themselues vpon the stayres to watch her,
And thus they laid their plot to cunny-catch her:
One should as 'twere by chance strike out the light;
While th'other that should stand beneath her, might
Attempt, (which modestie to suffer lothes)
Rudely to thrust his hands vnder her clothes.
That while her hands repeld such grosse disorders,
His mate might quickly slip away the borders.
Now though this act to her was most vnpleasant,
Yet being wise (as womens wits are present:)
Straight on her borders both her hands she cast,
And so with all her force she held them fast.
Villaines, she cryde, you would my borders haue:
But I'le saue them, tother it selfe can saue:
Thus, while the Page had got more store of light,
The coozening mates, for fear slipt out of sight.
    Thus her good wit, their cunning ouer-matcht,
    Were not these conycatchers conycatcht?

37 *The Hermaphrodite.*

238 When first my mother bore me in her wombe,
She went to make inquirie of the gods,
First of my birth, and after of my tombe.
All answerd true, yet all their words had ods.
Phoebus affirm'd, a Male childe should be borne:
Mars said it would be female, *Iuno* neither:

237 [6] To shun the press, by dark and priuat staires A] Through a great prease vp a darke paire of staires. 1618 etc. [17] vnpleasant, A] displeasant, 1618 etc. [20] And so with A] And with 1618 etc. [22] them, A] them 1618 [24] fear A] scare 1618 feare 1625 1633.

But I came forth, alas, to natures scorne,
Hermaphrodite, as much as both together.
Then for my death, *Iuno* foretold the sword:
Phoebus assign'd me drowning for my fate:
Mars threatned hanging, each perform'd their word,
As note how all prou'd true in seuerall rate.
A Tree fast by a brooke I needs would clime,
My sword slipt out, and while no heede I tooke,
My side fell on the point, and at that time,
My foote in boughs, my head hang'd in the brooke:
That I thus borne a Male, a Female, neither,
Dyde drown'd, & hang'd, & wounded all together.

38 Of a sicknesse grew with a Tobacco pipe.

239 Vnto a gentle Gentlewomans chamber,
A Pedler came, her husband being thence,
To sell fine linnen, Lawnes and Muske and Amber.
She franke of fauours, sparing of expense,
So bargain'd with him, ere he parted thence,
That for ten Ells of Holland, fiue of Lawne,
To grant dishonest pleasures, she was drawne.
Next day the man repenting of his cost,
Did studie meanes, to get him restitution:
Or to be paid for that he there had lost,
And thus he puts his thought in execution:
He turnes to her, with settled resolution,
And in her husbands presence vnawares,
He asketh fifty shillings for his wares.
Her husband ignorant what cause had bred it,
My wife, said he, had you so spent your store,
You must with petty chapmen runne on credit?
Now for my Honors sake, doe so no more.

238 12 all A] well 1618 etc. 15 at that time, A] at that same time, 1618 etc. 17 Female, A] Female 1618.
239 2 A Pedler A] Her Pedler 1618 etc. 5 him A] her 1618 her 1625 1633. 9 restitution:] resolution: 1618 etc.

No Sir (quoths he) I meant it to restore.
I took it of him onely for a tryall,
And finde it too high prised by a ryall.
Thus neuer changing countenance, she doth rise
With outward silence, inward anger choking.
And going to her closet, she espies
Tobacco in a pype, yet newly smoking.
She takes the pype, her malice her prouoking,
And laps it in his linnen, comming backe,
And so the Pedler putts it in his packe,
And packes away, and ioyes that with his wyle,
He had regayn'd the stuffe, yet gayn'd his pleasure.
But hauing walked scarcely half a mile,
His packe did smoke, and smell so out of measure,
That opening it vnto his great displeasure,
He found by that *Tobacco* pype too late,
The fiery force of feeble female hate.
And seeking then some remedy by lawes,
Vnto a neighbour Iustice he complaines:
But when the Iustice vnderstood the cause,
In her examination taking paines,
And found 'twas but a fetch of womens braines:
The cause dismist, he bids the man beware,
To deale with women that can burne his ware.

39 A good answere of a Gentlewoman to a Lawyer.

240 A vertuous Dame, that saw a Lawyer rome
Abroad, reprou'd his stay so long from home:
And said to him, that in his absence thence,
His wife might want her due beneuolence.
But he to quit himselfe of such disgrace,
Answer'd it thus, with putting of a case.

239 [21] by a ryall. A] for a Royall. 1618 etc. [28] putts A] put 1618 etc. [42] can A] could 1618 etc.
240 [5] to A] straight 1618 etc. [6] of A] off 1618 etc.

One owes one hundred pounds, now tell me whether
Is best? To haue his paiment all together:
Or take it by a shilling, and a shilling,
Whereby the bagge should be the longer filling?
Sure, said the Dame, I grant 'twere little losse,
If one receiu'd such payments all in grosse.
Yet in your absence this may breede your sorrow,
To heare your wife for want might twelue pence borrow.

40 *Of one that tooke thought for his wife.*

241 No sooner *Cynnas* wife was dead and buried,
But that with mourning much and sorrows wearied,
A Maid, a seruant of his wiues, he wedded,
And after hee had boorded her, and bedded,
And in her Mistris roome had fully plast her,
His wiues old seruant waxed his new master.

41 *Sir* Iohn Rainsfords *choyce of a man.*

242 *Rainsford,* whose acts were many times outragious,
Had speciall care, to haue his men couragious:
A certaine friend of his one day began,
Vnto his seruice to commend a man,
One well approued, he said, in many iarres,
Whereof in head, armes, hands, remain'd the skarres.
The Knight the man, his markes and manners view'd,
And flat refusing him, did thus conclude:
This is no man for me, but I suppose,
Hee's a tall fellow that gaue him all these blowes.

42 *Of* Linus *and his Mistris.*

243 Chaste *Linus,* but as valiant as a Gander,
Came to me yet, in friendly sort as may be:

241 [4] bedded, 1615] bedded A bedded. 1618 1625 bedded, 1633.
242 Heading Rainsfords A] Baunsfords 1618. [6] head, 1633] head A 1618 1625. [10] Hee's A] He is 1618 etc.

Lamenting that I rais'd on him a slander,
Namely, that he should keepe a gallant Lady.
Begge me (said I) if I proue such a babie,
To let my tongue, so false and idly wander.
    Who sayes that you keepe her, lyes in his throte,
    But she keepes you, that all the world may note.

43 *In praise of my Lady and her Musike.*

244 Vpon an Instrument of pleasing sound
A Lady playd more pleasing to the sight.
I being askt in which of these I found
Greatest content, my senses to delight?
    Rauisht in both at once, as much as may be,
    Said, Sweet was Musike, sweeter was the Lady.

44 *Of Riding-rimes.*

245 Faire *Leda* reads our Poetry sometimes,
But saith she cannot like our Ryding-rimes;
Affirming that the Cadens falleth sweeter,
When as the Verse is plac'd between the Meeter.
Well, *Leda,* leaue henceforth this quarrel-piking,
And sith that one between is to your liking,
    You shall haue one betweene; yet some suppose,
    Leda hath lou'd both Riding-rime, and Prose.

45 *Of deuout Parents and children.*

246 A husband and a wife oft disagreeing,
And either weary of th'other, being
In choller great, either deuoutly prayes
To God, that he will shorten th'others dayes:
    But more deuout then both, their sonne and heire
    Praies God that he wil grant them both their pray'r.

243 7 his throte, A] her throate, 1618 etc.
244 Heading *my Lady* A] *a Lady* 1618 etc. 2 more A] More 1618 etc.

46 *In commendation of two valiant Scottish Knights, that defended their King from the Earle* Gowry: *Sir* Thomas Erskin, *Sir* Iohn Ramsey.

247 The Persian Monarch, who by faithfull spyall
Was safe preseru'd from slaues intended slaughter,
By him whose Cousin and adopted daughter
Vnwares he did endow with scepter royall;
When reading in his bed a good while after,
He found in true records that seruice loyall,
Then with most gratefull mind to make requitall,
By large edict o're all his chiefest towne
Of so great merritts he doth make recytall:
And to increase *Mardoches* great renowne,
Vpon his head (such was their vse that season)
He caused to be set his royall Crowne.
　　But greater should be your reward in reason;
　　He but reueal'd, but you reueng'd a Treason.

47 *In prayse of the Countesse of Darby, married to the Lord Keeper.*

248 This noble Countesse liued many yeeres
With Darby, one of Englands greatest Peeres:
Fruitfull and faire, and of so cleare a fame,
As all the Brittish Ile admirde her Name.
But this braue Peere, extinct by hastned Fate,
She stayd (ah too too long) in widdowes state:
And in that state, tooke so sweet State vpon her,
All eares, eyes, tongues, heard, saw, & told her honor:
Yet finding this a saying full of veritie,
'Tis hard to haue a Patent of prosperitie,
　　Shee found her wisest way and safe to deale,
　　Was to consort with him that keepes the Seale.

247 [8–9] A only.

248 Heading *Lord Keeper.* A] *Lord Chauncellor.* 1618 etc. [3] fame, A] name, 1618 etc. [4] As all the Brittish Ile admirde her Name. A] That all this Region marueld at her fame. 1618 etc.

48 *Of* Cosmus, *that will keepe a good house hereafter.*

249 Old *Cosmus* to his friends thus out doth giue,
After awhile, he like a Lord will liue.
After awhile, hele end all troublous suites,
After awhile, retaine some men of qualitie,
After awhile, of riches reape the fruits,
After awhile, keepe house in some formality,
After awhile, finish his beautious building,
After awhile, leaue off his busie buying:
Yet all the while he liues but like a hilding,
His head growes gray with fresh vexations tryeng.
Well, *Cosmus,* I beleeue your heire doth smile,
To thinke what you will doe after awhile:
For sure, the Prouerbe is more true then ciuill,
Blest is the sonne whose Sire goes to the Diuell.

49 *Of neate* Galla.

250 The pride of *Galla* now is growne so great,
She seekes to be surnam'd *Galla* the neat,
But who their merits shall, and manners scan,
May thinke the terme is due to her good man.
Ask you, Which way? Methinks your wits are dull:
My Shoomaker resolue you can at full,
Neats Leather is both Oxe-hide, Cow, and Bull.

50 *Of reuersing an error.*

251 I did you wrong, at least you did suppose,
For taxing certaine faults of yours in Prose:
But now I haue the same in Ryme reherst,
My error, nay your error is reuerst.

249 [10] tryeng. A] toyling. 1618 etc.
250 [6] Shoomaker A] Shoomakes 1618.

51 *Of good Sauce.*

252 I went to suppe with *Cinna* tother night,
And to say true (for giue the diuell his right)
Though scant of meat we could a morsell get,
Yet here with store of passing sauce we met.
You aske what sauce, where pittance was so small?
This, Is not hunger the best sauce of all?

52 *Of a slaunder.*

253 On *Lesbya, Lynus* raysed had a slander,
For which when as she thought to take an action,
Yet by request she tooke this satisfaction,
That being drunke, his tongue did idly wander:
Came this from *Viderit vtilitas?*
Or else from this, *In Vino veritas?*

53 *Of a Lady early vp.*

254 *Lesbya,* that wonted was to sleepe till noone,
This other morning stirring was at fiue:
What did she meane, thinke you, to rise so soone?
I doubt we shall not haue her long aliue.
Yes: neuer feare it, there is no such danger,
It seemes vnto her course you be a stranger:
For why, at dauncing, banquetting, and play
And at Carowsing many a costly cup,
She sate the night before, vntill twas a day,
And by that meane, you found her early vp.
Oh, was it so? why then the case is cleere,
That she was early vp, and ne're the neere.

254 7 at A] a 1618.

Booke IV

1 To an ill Reader.

255 The verses, *Sextus,* thou doost read, are mine;
But with bad reading thou wilt make them thine.

2 In lectorem inuidum.

256 Who reades our verse, with visage sowre and grim,
I wish him enuy me, none enuy him.

3 Of Table friends. To Sir Hugh Portman.

257 You thinke his faith is firme, his friendship stable,
Whose first acquaintance grew but at your Table:
He loues your venison, snytes, quailes, larks, not you:
Make me such fare, and take my friendship too.

4 The Authour to his wife, of partition.

258 Some Ladies with their Lords diuide their states,
And liue so when they list, at seuerall rates;
But I'le endure thee, *Mall,* on no condition,
To sue with me a writ of such partition.
Twice seuen yeeres since, most solemnly I vow'd,
With all my worldly goods I thee endow'd.
Then house, plate, stuffe, not part, but all is thine:
Yet so, that thou, and they, and all are mine.
Then let me goe, and sue my writ of dotage,
If I with thee part house, or close, or cottage.
For, where this is my Lords, and that my Ladies,
There some, perhaps, think likewise of their babies.

257 Heading *To Sir* Hugh Portman. A only.
258 [1] states, A B] state, 1615 etc. [2] rates; A B] rate; 1615 etc. [6] endow'd. A B] endow'd, 1615 etc.

5 *Of Treason.*

259 Treason doth neuer prosper, what's the reason?
For if it prosper, none dare call it Treason.

6 *Of the warres in Ireland.*

260 I prays'd the speech, but cannot now abide it,
That war is sweet, to those that haue not try'd it:
For I haue prou'd it now, and plainely see't,
It is so sweet, it maketh all things sweet.
At home Canarie wines and Greeke grow lothsome:
Here milke is Nectar, water tasteth toothsome.
There without bak't, rost, boyld, it is no cheere.
Bisket we like, and Bonny Clabo heere.
There we complaine of one reare rosted chicke:
Heere viler meat, worse cookt, ne're makes me sicke.
At home in silken sparuers, beds of Downe,
We scant can rest, but still tosse vp and downe:
Heere I can sleepe, a saddle to my pillow,
A hedge the Curtaine, Canopy a Willow.
There if a child but cry, oh what a spite!
Heere we can brooke three larums in one night.
There homely roomes must be perfum'd with Roses:
Here match and powder ne're offends our noses.
There from a storme of raine we run like Pullets:
Heere we stand fast against a showre of bullets.
Lo then how greatly their opinions erre,
That thinke there is no great delight in warre:
    But yet for this (sweet warre) Ile be thy debter,
    I shall for euer loue my home the better.

7 *Of Women learned in the tongues.*

261 You wisht me to a wife, faire, rich and young,
That had the Latine, French and Spanish tongue.
I thank't, and told you I desir'd none such,
And said, One Language may be tongue too much.

Then loue I not the learned? yes as my life;
A learned mistris, not a learned wife.

8 *The Author of his wife, of the twelue Signes, how they gouerne.*

262 Marke here (my *Mall*) how in this dozen lines,
Thus placed are the twelue celestiall Signes:
And first, the *Ram* beares rule in head and face,
The stiffe-neckt *Bull* in neck doth hold his place,
The *Twins* mine armes and hands do both imbrace,
Then *Cancer* keepes the small ribs and the brest,
And *Leo* back and heart hath aye possest.
Then *Virgo* claimes the entrailes and the panch,
Libra the nauell, reynes, and either hanch.
Scorpio pretends power in the priuy parts,
Both thighes are pierst with *Sagitaries* darts.
Then *Capricorne* to knees his force doth send.
Aquarius doth to legges his vertue lend.
Pisces beneath vnto the feet discend.
Thus each part is possest; now tell me, *Mall,*
Where lies thy part? in which of these? In all.
In all? content. Yet sure thou art more iealous
Of *Leo's* part and *Scorpio's,* then their fellowes.

9 *Against Swearing.*

263 In elder times an ancient custome was,
To sweare in weighty matters by the Masse.
But when the Masse went downe (as old men note)
They sware then by the crosse of this same grote.
And when the Crosse was likewise held in scorne,
Then by their faith, the common oath was sworne.
Last, hauing sworne away all faith and troth,
Only God dam'n them is their common oath.
Thus custome kept *decorum* by gradation,
That losing Masse, Crosse, Faith, they find damnation.

10 *Of little pitie.*

264 When noble *Essex, Blount* and *Danuers* died,
One saw them suffer, that had heard them tried:
And sighing, said; When such braue souldiers dye,
Is't not great pitie, thinke you? No, said I:
There is no man of sense in all the citie,
Will say, 'Tis great, but rather little pitie.

11 *In praise of a book cald the gentle craft written by a shoomaker.*

265 I past this other day through *Pauls* Church-yard,
And heard some reade a booke, and reading laught,
The title of the booke was Gentle Craft.
The proiect was, as by their speech I heard,
To proove among som less important things
That shomakers and sowters had been kings.
But when I markt the matter with regard,
A new-sprung branch it in my minde did grafte,
And thus I said, Sirs, scorne not him that writ it:
A gilded blade hath oft a dudgeon haft,
And well I see, this writer roues a shaft
Neere fairest marke, yet happily not hit it.
For neuer was the like booke sold in Poules,
If so with Gentle Craft it could perswade
Great Princes midst their pompe to learne a trade,
Once in their liues to worke, to mend their soules.

12 *Of the games that haue beene in request at the Court.*

266 I heard one make a pretty Obseruation,
How games haue in the Court turn'd with the fashion,
The first game was the best, when free from crime,
The Courtly gamesters all were in their prime:

265 Heading *In praise of a book cald the gentle craft written by a shoomaker.* A] *Of a Booke called the Gentle Craft.* 1615 etc. 4–6 A only 8 it in my minde did grafte, A] that in my minde did grafte, 1615 etc.

The second game was Post, vntill with posting
They paid so fast, 'twas time to leaue their boasting.
Yet oft the gamesters all have been so fair,
That with one Carde one hath been sett a pair.
Then thirdly follow'd heauing of the Maw,
A game without Ciuility or Law,
An odious play, and yet in Court oft seene,
A sawcy knaue to trump both King and Queene.
Then was tres Cozes next a game whose number
The women gamsters at the first did cumber;
For at this game a looker on might see
Yf one made not a pair, yet two made three.
Then follow'd Lodam, hand to hand or quarter,
At which some maids so ill did keep the Quarter,
That vnexpected, in a short abode
They could nor cleanly beare away their load.
Now Noddy follow'd next, as well it might,
Although it should haue gone before of right.
At which I saw, I name not anybody,
One neuer had the knaue, yet laid for Noddy.
The last game now in vse is Bankerout,
Which will be plaid at still, I stand in doubt,
    Vntill, *Lauolta* turne the wheele of time,
    And make it come about againe to Prime.

13 The Author to Queene Elizabeth, *in praise of her reading.*

267 For euer deare, for euer dreaded Prince,
You read a verse of mine a little since,
And so pronounst each word, and euery letter,
Your gracious reeding grac't my verse the better:
Sith then your Highnes doth by gift exceeding,
Make what you read, the better in your reading,
    Let my poore Muse your paines thus far importune,
    To leaue to read my verse, and read my fortune.

266 7–8 and 13–16 A only 25 Bankerout, A 1615] Bankerupt, 1618 etc.
267 4 gracious reeding A] Gracious reading 1615 Gracious reading, 1618 etc.

14 *Of King* Henries *wooing.*

268 Vnto a stately great outlandish Dame,
A Messenger from our King *Henry* came,
(*Henry* of famous memory the eight)
To treat with her in matter of great weight;
As namely, how the King did seeke her marriage,
Because of her great vertue and good carriage.
She (that had heard the King lou'd change of pasture)
Repli'de, I humbly thanke the King, your Master,
    And would, (such loue his fame in me hath bred,)
    My body venter so, but not my head.

15 *Two witty answers of Bishop* Bonner.

269 Fatt *Bonner* (late that bishop was of London)
Was bid by one, *Good morrow Bishop quondam:*
He with the scoffe, no whit put out of temper,
Reply'd incontinent, *Adieu knaue Semper.*
Another in suche kinde of scoffing speeches,
Would beg his tippet, needs, to line his breeches.
    Not so (quoth he) but it may be thy hap,
    To haue a foolish head to line thy cap.

16 *Of* Lynus *borrowing.*

270 *Lynus* came late to me, sixe crownes to borrow,
And sware God damn him, hee'd repai't to morrow.
I knew his word, as currant as his band,
And straight I gaue to him three crownes in hand;
    This I to giue, this he to take was willing,
    And thus he gaind, and I sau'd fifteene shilling.

17 *To the learned byshop of Bathe and Welles.*

271 The pleasant learn'd *Italian Poet Dant,*
Hearing an Atheist at the Scriptures iest,

269 [1] Fatt *Bonner* (late that bishop was of London) A] *Bonner,* that late had Bishop beene of London, 1615 etc.

271 Heading *To the learned byshop of Bathe and Welles.* A] *A good answere of the Poet* Dant *to an Atheist.* 1615 etc.

Askt him in sporte, which was the greatest beast?
He simply said; he thought an Elephant.
Then *Elephant* (quoth *Dant*) it were commodious,
That thou wouldst hold thy peace, or get thee hence,
Breeding our Conscience scandall and offence
With thy prophaned speech, most vile and odious.
Oh Italy, thou breedst but few such *Dants,*
I would our England bred no Elephants.

18 Of Quintus *almes.*

272 When *Quintus* walketh out into the street,
As soone as with some begger he doth meete,
Ere that poore soule to aske his almes hath leasure,
He first doth chafe and sweare beyond all measure,
And for the Beadle all about he sends,
To beare him to *Bridewell,* so he pretends.
The Begger quickly out of sight doth goe,
Full glad in heart he hath escaped so.
Then *Quintus* laughes, and thinks it is lesse charges,
To sweare an oath or two, then giue a larges.

19 Of Marcus *his drunken feasting.*

273 When *Marcus* makes (as oft he doth) a feast,
The Wine still costs him more then all the rest.
Were water in this towne as deare as hay,
His horses should not long at liuery stay.
But tell me, is't not a most foolish tricke,
To drinke to others healths till thou be sicke?
Yet such the fashion is of Bacchus crue,
To quaffe and bowze, vntill they belch and spue.
Well, leaue it, *Marcus,* else thy drinking health,
Will proue an eating to thy wit and wealth.

271 [3] sporte, A] iest 1615 etc. [8] prophaned A] profan'd 1615 etc.

20 A good iest of a Crow.

274 A Baron and a Knight, one day wear walking
On Richmond greene, & as they were in talking,
A Crow, that lighted on the raile by Fortune,
Stood becking, and cry'd *kaw* with noise importune.
This bird, the Baron said, doth you salute,
Sir Knight, as if to you he had some sute.
Not vnto me, the Knight reply'd in pleasance,
'Tis to some Lord he makes so low obeysance.

21 Of kissing the foote.

275 A Courtier, kinde in speech, curst in condition,
Finding his fault could be no longer hidden,
Went to his friend to cleere his hard suspition,
And fearing left he might be more then chidden,
Fell to a flattering and most base submission,
Vowing to kisse his foote, if he were bidden.
My foote? (said he) nay, that were too submisse,
But three foote higher you deserue to kisse.

22 Of a sawcy Cator.

276 A Cator had of late some wild-fowle bought,
And when vnto his Master them he brought,
Forthwith the Master smelling nigh the rump,
Said, Out, thou knaue, these sauour of the pump.
The man (that was a rude and sawcy Lout)
What Sir, said he, smell you them thereabout?
Smell your faire Lady there, and by your fauour,
You fortune may meete with a fulsome sauour.

274 [1] day wear walking A] day were walking 1615 day walking 1618 etc.
275 [7] nay, that were too A] that were too 1615 1618 1625 that were too too 1633.
276 [8] You A 1615] Your 1618 etc.

23 *Of a certaine Man.*

277 There was (not certain when) a certaine preacher,
That neuer learn'd, and yet became a Teacher,
Who hauing read in Latine thus a Text
Of *erat quidam homo,* much perplext,
He seem'd the same with study great to scan
In English thus; *there was a certaine man.*
But now (quoth he) good people, note you this,
He saith there was, he doth not say there is:
For in these daies of ours, it is most certaine,
Of promise, oth, word, deed, no man is certaine:
Yet by my text you see it comes to passe,
That surely once a certaine man there was.
But yet I thinke, in all your Bible no man
Can finde this text; *there was a certaine woman.*

24 *Of* Lesbia.

278 Old widdow *Lesbia,* after husbands fiue,
Yet feeleth *Cupids* flames in her reuiue,
And now she takes a gallant youth and trim.
Alas for her, nay, nay, a lasse for him.

25 *The horne Cinque-apace.*

279 Who wishes, hopes, and thinks, his wife is true,
To him one horne, or vnicorne is due.
Who sees his wife play false, and will not spy it,
He hath two hornes, and yet he may deny it.
The man that can indure when all men scorne,
And pardon open faults, hath treble horne;
Who brings fine Courtiers oft to see his bride,
He hath one paire of hornes on either side.
But he that sweares hee did so happy wiue,
He can be none of these, let him haue fiue.

278 [4] a lasse A] alas 1615 etc.

26 Of cursing Cuckolds.

280 A Lord that talked late in way of scorne,
Of some that ware inuisibly the horne,
Said he could wish, and did (as for his part)
All Cuckolds in the Thames, with all his heart.
 But straight a pleasant Knight reply'd to him,
 I hope your Lordship learned hath to swimme.

27 Of the pillars of the Church.

281 In old time they were Call'd the Churches pillars,
That did excell in learning and in piety,
And were to youth examples of sobriety,
Of Christ's faire field the true and painefull tillers:
But where are now the men of that society?
Are all those tillers dead? those pillars broken?
No, God forbid such blasphemy be spoken;
 I say, to stop the mouthes of all ill-willers,
 God's field hath harrowers still, his Church hath pillars.

28 Of Exchange.

282 Old *Caius* sold a wench, to buy a barke.
Yong *Titus* gaue the ship, to haue the slut.
Who makes the better mart, now let vs marke,
T'one goes to roue, the tother goes to rut.

29 Of Lesbias *kissing craft.*

283 *Lesbia* with study found a meanes in th'end,
In presence of her Lord to kisse her friend,
Each of them kist by turnes a little Whelpe,
Transporting kisses thus by puppies help.
 And so her good old Lord she did beguile:
 Was not my Lord a puppy all the while?

281 1 were Call'd the A] were the 1615 etc.
282 4 T'one goes A 1615] Th'one loues 1618 etc.

30 Of sixe sorts of Fasters.

284 Sixe sorts of folkes I find vse fasting dayes,
But of these sixe, the sixt I onely praise.
The sicke man fasts, because he cannot eate.
The poore doth fast, because he hath no meate.
The miser fasts, with minde to mend his store.
The glutton, with intent to eate the more.
The hypocrite, thereby to seeme more holy.
The vertuous, to preuent or punish folly.
    Now he that eateth fast, and drinkes as fast,
    May match these fasters, any but the last.

31 Of Cinna.

285 Pvre *Cinna* gets his wife a maiden Cooke
With red cheecks, yellow locks, & cheerfull looke.
What might he meane hereby? I hold my life,
She dresseth flesh for him, not for his wife.

32 Of Claudia.

286 *Claudia,* to saue a noble Romans blood,
Was offred by some friends that wisht his good,
A iewell of inestimable price;
But she would not be won by this deuice:
    For she did take his head, and leaue the iewell.
    Was *Claudia* now more couetous, or cruell?

33 A rule to Play.

287 Lay down your stake at play, lay down your passion:
A greedy gamester still hath some mis-hap.
To chafe at luck proceeds of foolish fashion.
No man throws still the dice in fortunes lap.

287 [3] luck A] play, 1615 etc.

34 Of a drunken tobacco taker.

288 When *Marcus* hath carrowst March Beere and Sack,
And that his brains grow dizzy therewithall,
Then of Tobacco he a pipe doth lacke,
Of Trinidade in cane, in leafe, or ball,
Which tane a little, he doth spit and smacke,
Then laies him on his bed for feare to fall,
And on Tobacco layes the blame of all.
But that same pipe which *Marcus* braine did lade,
Was of *Medera,* not of Trinidade.

35 Tristis es et felix, sciat hoc fortuna Caueto.
To a Lady.

289 Froward yet fortunate? if fortune knew it,
Beleeue me, Madam, she would make you rue it.

36 A Salisbury tale.

290 Faire *Sarum's* Church, beside the stately tower,
Hath many things in number aptly sorted,
Answering the yeere, the month, weeke, day & houre,
But aboue all (as I haue heard reported,
And to the view doth probably appeare)
A piller for each houre in all the yeere.
Further, this Church of *Sarum* hath beene found,
To keepe in singing seruice so good forme,
That most Cathedrall Churches haue beene bound,
Themselues *ad vsum Sarum* to conforme:
I am no Cabalist to iudge by number,
Yet that this Church is so with pillers fill'd,
It seemes to me to be the lesser wonder,
That *Sarums* Church is euery hower pill'd.
And sith the rest are bound to *Sarums* vse,
What maruell if they taste of like abuse?

288 Heading *tobacco taker.* A] *Tobacconist.* 1615 etc. 7 And on Tobacco layes the blame of all. A] And poore Tobacco beares the name of all. 1615 etc.

37 *Of a faire Shrew.*

291 Faire, rich, and yong? how rare is her perfection,
Were it not mingled with one foule infection?
I meane, so proud a heart, so curst a tongue,
As makes her seeme, nor faire, nor rich, nor yong.

38 *Of Gods part.*

292 One that had farm'd a fat Impropriation,
Vs'd to his neighbours often exhortation,
To pay to him the tithes and profits duely,
Affirming (as he might affirme most truely)
How that the tithes are God Almighties part,
And therefore they should pay't with all their heart.
But straight replyed one amongst the rest,
(One that had crost him oft, but neuer blest),
  It is Gods part indeed, whose goodnes gaue it;
  But yet oft times we see the Diuell haue it.

39 *Of* Lalus *simoniacall horse-coursing.*

293 Pvre *Lalus* gat a benefice of late,
Without offence of people, Church, or State;
Yea but aske eccho how he did come by it,
Come buy it? No with oathes he will deny it.
He nothing gaue direct, or indirectly.
Fie, *Lalus,* now you tell vs a direct lye:
Did not your Patron for an hundred pound,
Sell you a horse was neither yong nor sound,
No Turke, no Courser, Barbary, nor Iennit?
Simony? No, but I see money in it.
  Well, if it were but so, the case is cleere;
  The Benefice was cheape, the Horse was deare.

292 8 blest), A] blest.) 1615 etc.
293 1 gat A 1615 1625 1633] gate 1618.

40 *An addition to the same Epigram.*

294 *Peter* for Westminster, and *Paul* for London,
Lament, for both your Churches will be vndone,
If Smithfield find a fetch forth of a stable,
Lawes to elude, and Lords of Councell table.

41 *Of* Cinna.

295 Fiue yeeres hath *Cinna* studied Genesis,
And knowes not yet what *in Principio* is;
And greeu'd that he is graueld thus, he skips,
Ore all the Bible, to th'Apocalips.

42 *Of bagge and baggage.*

296 A man appointed, vpon losse of life,
With bag and baggage at a time assign'd,
To part a towne; his foule vnweildly wife,
Desired him that she might stay behind.
Nay, quoth the man, Ile neuer be so kind,
As venture life, for such an vgly hag
That lookes both like a baggage and a bag.

43 *Of a womans kindness to her husband.*

297 One that had liued long by lewdest shifts,
Brought to the Court that Corne from cockle sifts,
Starchamber, that of Iustice is the mirror,
Was senten'st there, and for the greater terrour,
Adiudged, first, to lye a yeere in fetters,
Then burned in his forhead with two letters,
And to disparage him with more disgrace,
To slit his nose, the figure of his face.
The prisoners wife with no dishonest mind,
To shew her selfe vnto her husband kind,

294 4 elude, A] delude, 1615 etc.
295 2 not yet what A] not what 1615 etc.

Sued humbly to the Lords, and would not cease,
Some part of this sharp rigour to release.
He was a man (she said) had seru'd in warre,
What mercy would a Souldiers face so marre?
What though he wear with some few crimes entangled,
Twear pitty that a man should be so mangled.
Thus much said she: but grauely they replied,
It was great mercy that he thus was tried:
His crimes deserue he should haue lost his life,
And hang in chaines. Alas, repli'd his wife,
The grief of his disfiguring is such
His hanging would not grieve me halfe so much:
    If you disgrace him thus, you quite vndoe him,
    Good my Lords hang him, pray be good vnto him.

44 *Of* Don Pedro.

298 *Don Pedro* neuer dines without red Deere;
If red Deere be his guests, grasse is his cheere:
I, but I meane, he hath it in his dish,
And so haue I oft what I doe not wish.

45 The Author to his wife.

299 *Mall,* once in pleasant company by chance,
I wisht that you for company would dance,
Which you refus'd, and said, your yeeres require,
Now, Matron-like, both manners and attire.
Well *Mall,* if needs thou wilt be Matron-like,
Then trust to this, I will a Matron like:
Yet so to you my loue may neuer lessen,
As you for Church, house, bed, obserue this lesson.
Sit in the Church as solemne as a Saint,
No deed, word, thought, your due deuotion taint.
Vaile (if you will) your head, your soule reueale
To him, that onely wounded soules can heale.

297 15–16, 21–22 A only.

Be in my house as busie as a Bee,
Hauing a sting for euery one but mee,
Buzzing in euery corner, gathering hony.
Let nothing waste, that costs or yeeldeth mony.
And when thou seest my heart to mirth incline,
The tongue, wit, bloud, warme with good cheere and wine,
And that by lawfull fancy I am led,
To clyme my neast, thy vndefiled bed
Then of sweet sports let no occasion scape,
But be as wanton, toying as an Ape.

46 Of Lelia.

300 When louely *Lelia* was a tender girle,
She hapt to be deflowred by an Earle;
Alas, poore wench, she was to be excused,
Such kindnesse oft is offered, seld refused.
But be not proud; for she that is no Countesse,
And yet lies with a Count, must make account this,
All Countesses in honour her surmount,
They haue, she had, an honourable Count.

47 Of a drunken Smith.

301 I heard that *S M V G* the Smith, for ale and spice
Sold all his tooles, and yet he kept his vice.

48 Of Soothsaying.

302 Might Kings shun future mischief by foretelling,
Then amongst Soothsayers 'twere excellent dwelling;
But if there be no means such harmes repelling,
The knowledge makes the sorrow more excelling.
But this, deare Soueraigne, me comfort doth,
That of these Sooth-sayers, very few say sooth.

299 19–20 B only.

49 A good request of a Lawyer.

303 A pleasant Lawyer standing at the barre,
The Causes done, and day not passed farre,
A Iudge to whom he had profest deuotion,
Askt him in grace, if he would haue a motion:
Yes Sir, quoth he, but short, and yet not small,
That whereas now of Sarieants is a call,
I wish (as most of my profession doe)
That there might be a call of Clyents too:
For sure it brings vs Lawyers mickle cumber,
Because of them we find so small a number.

50 Of Friendship.

304 New friends are no friends; how can that be true?
The oldest friends that are, were sometimes new.

51 Of Caius *increase in his absence.*

305 While *Caius* doth remaine beyond the Seas,
And followes there some great important suit,
His Lands bare neither Oates, nor Beanes, nor Pease,
But yet his wife beares faire and full-growne fruit.
What is the cause that brings his Lands sterility,
And his wiues fruitfulnes and great fertility?
His Lands want occupyers to manure them,
But she hath store, & knows how to procure them.

52 Of a toothlesse Shrew.

306 Old *Ellen* had foure teeth as I remember,
She cought out two of them the last December;
But this shrewd cough in her raign'd so vnruly,
She cought out tother two before twas Iuly.
Now she may cough her heart out, for in sooth,
The said shrewd cough hath left her ne're a tooth.
But her curst tongue, wanting this common curbe,
Doth more then erst the houshold all disturbe.

53 To Doctor Sharpe.

307 Late I tooke leaue of two right noble dames,
And hasted to my wife as I protested:
You will'd me stay awhile, and thus you iested:
You Sir, may please your Wife with Epigrams.
Well said, 'twas Doctor-like, and sharply spoken,
No friendship breakes, where iests so smooth are broken.
But now you haue new orders tane of late,
Those orders, which (as you expound Saint *Paul*)
Are equall honourable vnto all;
I meane of marriage the holy state,
I hope, in Lent, when flesh growes out of date,
You will, in stead of tother recreation,
Be glad to please your wife with some Collation.

54 Of the Papists Feasts, and the Brownists Fasts.

308 A Papist dwelling to a Brownist neere,
Their seruants met, and vanted of their cheere.
And first, the Papists man did make his bost,
He had each festiuall both bak't and rost,
And where (said he) your zealous sort allow,
On Christmasse day it selfe to goe to plow,
We feast, and play, and walke, and talk, and slumber,
Besides, our holy dayes are more in number:
As namely, we do keepe with great festiuity,
Our Ladies, both assumption and natiuity;
S. *Pauls* conuersion, S. *Iohns* decollation,
S. *Laurence* broyld, S. *Swithens* moyst translation,
S. *Peters* chaines, and how with Angels vision
He brake the prison, quite without misprision.
I grant, the tother said, you seeme more gainesome,
But for your sport, you pay too deare a ransome.
We like your Feasts, your Fastings bred our greeues,
Your Lents, your Ember weekes, and holy Eeues.
But this coniunction I should greatly praise,
The Brownists fasts, with Papists holy daies.

55 Of Milo *the glutton.*

309 *Milo* with haste to cram his greedy gut,
One of his thumbs vnto the bone had cut:
Then straight it noysed was about by some,
That he had lost his stomack with his thumb.
To which one said, No worse hap fall vnto him:
But if a poore man finde it, 'twill vndoe him.

56 Of Fortune.

310 Fortune, men say, doth giue too much to many:
But yet shee neuer gaue enough to any.

57 Of deuotion and promotion.

311 I met a Lawyer at the Court this Lent,
And asking what great cause him thither sent,
He said, that mou'd with Doctor *Androes* fame,
To heare him preach, he onely thither came:
But straight, I wisht him softly in his eare,
To find some other scuse, else some will sweare,
Who to the Court come onely for deuotion,
They in the Church pray onely for promotion.

58 Of a painted Lady.

312 I saw dame *Leda's* picture lately drawne,
With haire about her eares, transparent Lawne,
Her Iuory paps, and euery other part,
So limd vnto the life by Painters Art,
That I that had been long with her acquainted,
Did thinke that both were quick, or both were painted.

59 Of Galla's *gallantry.*

313 What is the cause our *Galla* is so gallant,
Like ship in fairest wind, top and top gallant?

Hath she of late been courted by some Gallant?
No sure: How then? *Galla* hath quaft a gallon.

60 *In Cornutum.*

314 *A Thais?* no, *Diana* thou didst wed:
For she hath giuen to thee *Acteons* head.

61 *Of* Paulus, *a Flatterer.*

315 No man more seruile, no man more submisse,
Then to our Soueraigne Lady *Paulus* is.
He doth extoll her speech, admire her feature,
He calls himselfe her vassall, and her creature.
Thus while he dawbes his speech with flatteries plaster,
And calls himselfe her slaue, he growes our Master,
Still getting what he list without controle,
By singing this old song, *re mi fa sol.*

62 *Of* Lynus, *an ill ghest.*

316 Aske you what profit *Kew* to me doth yeeld?
This, *Lynus,* there I shal see thee but seeld;
For as good ghests may make a cottage gratefull,
So such as thou do make a Palace hatefull.

63 *Against* Pius Quintus, *that excommunicated Queene* Elizabeth.

317 Are Kings your Foster-Fathers, Queens your nurses,
Oh Roman Church? Then why did *Pius Quintus*
With Basan bulls (not like one *pius intus*)
Lay on our sacred Prince vnhallowed curses?
It is not health of soules, but wealth of purses
You seek, by such your hell-denouncing threats,
Oppugning with your chaire, our Princes seats,

316 [3] For as good A] For where good 1615 etc. make a cottage A] take a cottage 1615 etc. [4] So such A] There, such 1618 1625 There such 1615 1633.

Disturbing our sweet peace; and that which worse is,
You suck out blood, and bite your Nurses teats.
    Learne, learne, to ask your milk, for if you snatch it,
    The nurse must send your babes pap with a hatchet.

64 *Of finding a Hare.*

318 A Gallant full of life, and voyd of care,
Yet lov'd all coursing game and bought it deerly,
Came to his friend earst in a morning early,
And ask'd his friend if he would find a Hare?
He that for sleepe more then such sports did care,
Affirm'd that business toucht him nothing neerly,
    Said, Goe your waies, and leaue me here alone;
    Let them find Hares that lost them, I lost none.

65 *Of Merit, and Demerit.*

319 A Knight, and valiant seruitor of late,
Playn'd to a Lord and Councellor of State,
That Captaines in these dayes were not regarded,
That onely Carpet Knights were well rewarded:
For I, saith he, with all my hurts and maimes,
Get not the recompence my merit claimes.
Good Cousin (said the Lord) the fault is yours,
Which you impute vnto the higher Powers,
For where you should in *Pater noster* pray,
Giue vnto vs our daily bread to day;
    Your misdemeanors this petition needs,
    Our trespasses forgiue vs, and misdeeds.

66 *Of* Faustus, *Esquire.*

320 *Faustus,* for taking of a wrong possession,
Was by a Iustice bound vnto the Session:
The Cryer the Recognizance doth call,
Faustus, Esquire, come forth into the Hall.

318 2–3, 6 A only.

Out (said the Iudge) on all such foolish Cryers,
Diuels are Carpenters, where such are Squires.

67 *Of* Peleus *friendship.*

321 When *Peleus* is brought vp to London streets,
By Proces iust to answer waighty sutes,
Oh then how kind he is to all he meets!
How friendly by their names he them salutes!
Then one shall haue a Colt of his best race,
Another gets a warrant for a Buck:
Some deeper brib'd, according as their place
May serue his turne, to worke or wish good luck.
But when his troubles all to end are brought
By time, or friendly paines on his behalfe,
Then straight (as if he set vs all at nought)
His kindnes is not now so much by halfe.
Sith then his suites in Law his friendship doubles,
I for his friendships sake could wish him troubles.

68 *Of inclosing a Common.*

322 A Lord, that purpos'd for his more auaile,
To compasse in a Common with a rayle,
Was reckoning with his friend about the cost
And charge of euery reule, and euery post:
But he (that wisht his greedy humour crost)
Said, Sir, prouide you posts, and without fayling,
Your neighbors round about wil find you rayling.

69 *To his Wife when she was sick of the sullens.*

323 Late hauing been a fishing at the Foord,
And bringing home with me my dish of Trouts,
Your minde that while, did cast some causelesse doubts:

321 [2] iust] first 1615 etc.
323 Heading *To his Wife when she was sick of the sullens.* A B] *The Author to his wife, of too much stomack.* 1615 etc.

For while that meat was set vpon the boord,
You sullen silent, fed your selfe with powts.
I twice sent for you, but you send me word,
　　How that you had no stomack to your meat.
　　Well I fear'd more, your stomack was too great.

70 *A witty choice of a Country fellow.*

324 A rich Lord had a poore Lout to his ghest,
And hauing sumptuous fare, and costly drest,
Caru'd him a wing of a most dainty Bird;
Affirming seriously vpon his word,
Those birds were sent him from his louing cosen,
And were well worthy twenty marks a dozen.
He that for such great dainties did not care,
Said, I like well your Lordships courser fare:
　　For I can eat your Beefe, Pig, Goose, and Cony,
　　But of such fare, giue me my share in mony.

71 *To a great Magistrate, in Re and in Spe.*

325 Those that for Princes good do take some paine
(Their good to whom of right all paines we owe)
Seeke some reward for seruice good to gaine,
Which oft their gracious goodnesse doth bestow:
　　I for my trauell, begge not a reward,
　　I begge lesse by a sillable, a Ward.

72 *A comparison of a Booke, with Cheese.*

326 Old *Haywood* writes, & proues in some degrees,
That one may wel compare a book with cheese;
At euery market some buy cheese to feed on,
At euery mart some men buy bookes to read on.
All sorts eate cheese; but how? there is the question,
The poore for food, the rich for good disgestion.
All sorts read bookes, but why? will you discerne?

325 [1] good A] goods 1615 etc. [2] good A] goods 1615 etc.

The foole to laugh, the wiser sort to learne.
The sight, taste, sent of cheese to some is hateful,
The sight, taste, sense of bookes to some's vngratefull,
No cheese there was, that euer pleas'd all feeders,
No booke there is, that euer lik't all Readers.

73 *A Scottish verse.*

327 *Rob, Will,* and *Dauy,*
Keepe well thy *Pater noster* and *Aue:*
And if thou wilt the better speed,
Gang no further then thy *Creed:*
Say well, and doe none ill,
And keepe they selfe in safety still.

74 *To beggers of Bookes.*

328 My friend, you presse me very hard,
my bookes of me you craue;
I haue none, but in *Pauls* Church-yard,
for mony you may haue.
But why should I my coyne bestow
such toyes as these to buy?
I am not such a foole I trowe:
forsooth no more am I.

75 *In Paulum Athaium.*

329 Proud *Paulus,* led by *Sadduces* infection,
Doth not beleeue the bodies resurrection,
But holds them all in scorne and deepe derision,
That talke of Saints or Angels apparision:
And saith, they are but fables all, and fansies
Of Lunaticks, or folkes possest with frensies.
I haue, saith he, trauell'd both neere and farre,
By land, by sea, in time of peace and warre,
Yet neuer met I spirit, or ghost, or Elfe,
Or ought (as is the phrase) worse then my selfe.

Well, *Paulus,* this I now beleeue indeed,
That who in all, or part, denyes his Creed;
Went he to sea, land, hell, I would agree,
A Fiend worse then himselfe, he could not see.

76 *Of double Fraud.*

330 A fellow false, and to all fraud inured,
In high Starchamber court was found periured,
And by iust sentence iudg'd to lose his eares:
A doome right fit for him that falsly sweares.
Now on the Pillory while he was pearching,
The Gaolor busie for his eares was searching:
But all in vaine, for there was not an eare,
Onely the places hid with locks of haire.
Thou knaue, said he, I will of thee complaine
Vnto the Lords, for cousonage againe.
Why so, said hee? their order me doth binde
To lose mine eares, not you mine eares to finde.

77 *Of taking a Hare.*

331 Vnto a Lawyer rich, a Client poore
Came early in the morning to his doore,
And dancing long attendance in the place,
At last, he gat some counsell in his case;
For which the Lawyer look't to haue beene paid:
But thus at last the poore man to him said,
I cannot giue a fee, my state's so bare:
But will it please you, Sir, to take a Hare?
He that tooke all that came, with all his hart,
Said that he would, and take it in good part.
Then must you runne apace (good Sir) quoth he:
For she this morning quite out-stripped me.
He went his way, the Hare was neuer taken.
Was not the Lawyer taken, or mistaken?

330 [5] pearching, A] preaching, 1615 etc.

78 *The Author to his Wife.*

332 Your maid *Brunetta* you with newes acquaints,
How *Leda,* (whom, her husband wanting issue,
Brought erst to Bath, our pilgrimage of Saints)
Weares her gowne veluet, kirtle, cloth of tissue,
A figur'd Sattin petticote Carnation,
With sixe gold parchment laces all in fashion.
Yet neither was Dame *Leda* nobler borne,
Nor dranke in Gossips cup by Sou'raigne sent,
Nor euer was her Highnes woman sworne,
Nor doth her husband much exceed in rent.
Then *Mall,* be proud, that thou maist better weare them.
And I more proud, thou better dost forbeare them.

79 *Of too high commendation in a meane person.*

333 A Scholler once, to win his Mistresse loue,
Compar'd her to three Goddesses aboue,
And said she had (to giue her due desarts)
Iuno's, Minerua's, and faire *Venus* parts.
Iuno so proud, and curst was of her tongue,
All men misliked her both old and yong.
Pallas so foule, and grim was out of measure,
That neither gods nor men in her tooke pleasure.
Venus vnchaste, that she strong *Mars* entices,
With yong *Adonis,* and with old *Anchises.*
How thinke you, are these praises few or meane,
Compared to a shrow, a slut, or queane?

80 *Of trusting a Captaine.*

334 An Alderman, one of the better sort,
And worthie member of our worthiest Citie;
Vnto whose Table diuers did resort,

332 [6] fashion. B 1633] fashion, A 1615 1618 1625. [7] neither A B] neuer 1615 etc.

Himselfe of stomake good, of answeres witty,
Was once requested by a Table friend,
To lend an vnknowne Captaine forty pound.
The which, because he might the rather lend,
He said he should become in statute bound.
And this (quoth he) you need not doubt to take,
For he's a man of late growne in good credit,
And went about the world with Captaine *Drake*.
Out (quoth the Alderman) that ere you sed it,
For forty pounds? no nor for forty pence.
His single bond I count not worth a chip.
I say to you (take not hereat offence,)
He that hath three whole yeeres been in a ship,
In famine, plagues, in stench, and storme, so rife,
Cares not to lye in Ludgate all his life.

81 In Cornutum.

335 What curld-pate youth is he that sitteth there
So neere thy wife, and whispers in her eare,
And takes her hand in his, and soft doth wring her,
Sliding her ring still vp and downe her finger?
Sir, tis a Proctor, seene in both the Lawes,
Retain'd by her, in some important cause;
Prompt and discreet both in his speech and action,
And doth her busines with great satisfaction.
And thinkest thou so? a horne-plague on thy head:
Art thou so like a foole, and wittoll led,
To thinke he doth the businesse of thy wife?
He doth thy business, I dare lay my life.

82 A Tragicall Epigram.

336 When doome of Peeres & Iudges fore-appointed,
By racking lawes beyond all reach of reason,
Had vnto death condemn'd a Queene anointed,
And found, (oh strange!) without allegeance, treason,

335 4 her ring A] his ring 1615 etc.

The Axe that should haue done that execution,
Shunn'd to cut off a head that had been crowned,
Our hangman lost his wonted resolution,
To quell a Queene of nobles so renowned.
Ah, is remorse in hangmen and in steele,
When Peeres and Iudges no remorse can feele?
    Grant Lord, that in this noble Ile, a Queene
    Without a head, may neuer more be seene.

83 Of reading Scriptures.

337 The sacred Scripture treasure great affoords,
To all of seuerall tongues, of sundry Realmes.
For low and simple spirits shallow Foords,
For high and learned Doctors deeper streames,
In euery part so exquisitely made,
An Elephant may swimme, a Lambe may wade.
Not that all should with barbarous audacity,
Read what they list, and how they list expound,
But each one suting to his weake capacity:
For many great Scriptureans may be found,
    That cite Saint *Paul* at euery bench and boord,
    And haue Gods word, but haue not God the word.

84 The Author to his wife: a rule for praying.

338 My deare, when in your closet for deuotion,
To kindle in your brest some godly motion,
You contemplate, and oft your eyes doe fixe
On some Saints picture, or the Crucifixe;
Tis not amisse, be it of stone or mettle,
It serueth in thy mind good thoughts to settle;
Such images may serue thee as a booke,
Whereon thou maist with godly reuerence looke,
And thereby thy remembrance to acquaint,

336 8 nobles B] noblenes A noblenesse 1615 etc.
337 1 Scripture A B] Scriptures 1615 etc.
338 1 when in A B] that in 1615 etc.

With life or death, or vertue of the Saint.
But though I do allow thou kneele before it,
Yet would I in no wise you should adore it.
For as such things well vs'd, are cleane and holy,
So superstition soone may make it folly.
All images are scorn'd and quite dis-honoured,
If the Prototype be not solely honoured.
I keepe thy picture in a golden shrine,
And I esteeme it well, because 'tis thine;
But let me vse thy picture ne're so kindly,
'Twere little worth, if I vs'd thee vnkindly.
Sith then, my deare, our heauenly Lord aboue
Vouchsafeth vnto ours to like his loue:
So let vs vse his picture, that therein,
Against himselfe we doe commit no sinne;
Nor let vs scorne such pictures, nor deride them,
Like fooles, whose zeale mistaught, cannot abide them.
But pray, our hearts, by faith's eyes be made able
To see, what mortall eyes see on a Table.
A man would thinke, one did deserue a mocke,
Should say, Oh heauenly Father, to a stocke;
Such a one were a stocke, I straight should gather,
That would confesse a stocke to be her Father.

85 Poenitentia poenitenda: Of a penitent Fryer.

339 Bound by his Church, and Trentin Catechisme,
To vow a single life, a Cloystered Frier,
Had got a swelling, call'd a Priapisme,
Which seld is swag'd, but with a femall fire.
The Leach (as oftentimes Physicians vse)
To cure the corps, not caring for the soule,
Prescribes a cordiall med'cine from the Stewes,
Which lewd prescript, the Patient did condole:

338 [11] But though I do A B] Yet doe I not 1615 etc. [12] Yet A B] Nor 1615 etc.

Yet strong in Faith, and being loth to dye,
And knowing that extremes yeeld dispensation,
He is resolu'd, and doth the med'cine trie:
Which being done, he made such lamentation,
That diuers thought he was fall'n in despaire,
And therefore for his confirmation praid.
But when that they had ended quite their prayer,
After long silence, thus to them he said:
I waile not, that I thinke my fact so vicious,
Nor am I in despaire: no, neuer doubt it;
But feeling female flesh is so delicious,
I waile, to thinke I liu'd so long without it.

86 *Of a picture with a Ferriman rowing in a tempest, with two Ladies in his boate, whereof he loued one, but she disdained him, and the other loued him, but he not her: now a voice came to his eare, that to saue his boate from beeing cast away, hee must drowne one of the Ladies: in which perplexitie hee speaketh these passions.*

In troublous seas of loue, my tender bote,
By Fates decree, is still tost vp and downe,
Ready to sinke, and may no longer flote,
Except of these two Damsels one I drowne.
I would saue both: but ah, that may not be:
I loue the tone, the tother loueth me.
Heere the vast waues are ready me to swallow.
There danger is to strike vpon the shelfe.
Doubtfull I swim betweene the deepe and shallow,
To saue th'vngrate, and be vngrate my selfe.
Thus seeme I by the eares to hold a wolfe,
While faine I would eschue this gaping gulfe.
But since loues actions, guided are by passion,
And quenching doth augment her burning fuell,

Adieu, thou Nimph, deseruing most compassion,
To merit mercy, I must shew me cruell.
   Aske you me why? oh question out of season!
   Loue neuer leisure hath to render reason.

87 *The old mans choice.*

341 Let soueraigne Reason, sitting at the Steere,
And farre remouing all eye-blinding passion,
Censure the due desert with iudgement cleere,
And say, The cruell merit no compassion.
   Liue then, kind Nimph, and ioy we two together:
   Farewell th' vnkind, and all vnkind goe with her.

88 *In Philautum.*

342 Your verses please your Reader oft, you vaunt it:
If you your selfe doe reade them oft, I grant it.

89 *To an old Batchelor.*

343 You praise all women: well, let you alone,
Who speakes so well of all, thinks well of none.

90 *Of two that were married and vndone.*

344 A fond yong couple, making haste to marry,
Without their parents will, or friends consent,
After one month their marriage did repent,
And su'd vnto the Bishops Ordinary,
That this their act so vndiscreetly done,
Might by his more discretion be vndone.
Vpon which motion he awhile did pause:
At length, he for their comforts to them said,
It had beene better (friends) that you had staid:
But now you are so hampered in the Lawes,
   That I this knot may not vntye (my sonne)
   Yet I will grant you both shall be vndone.

341 [1] Steere, A] sterne, 1615 etc.

91 *In commendation of a straw, written at the request of a great Lady, that ware a straw Hat at the Court.*

345 I vowed to write of none but matters serious,
And lawfull vowes to breake, is great offence;
But yet, faire Ladies hests are so imperious,
That with all Vowes, all Lawes they can dispence:
    Then yeelding to that all-commanding Law,
    My Muse must tell some honour of a straw.
Not of *Iack Straw,* with his rebellious crew,
That set King, Realme, and Lawes at hab or nab,
Whom Londons worthy Maior so brauely slew,
With dudgeon daggers honorable stab,
    That his successors for that seruice loyall,
    Haue yet reward with blow of weapon royall.
Nor will I praise that fruitlesse straw or stubble,
Which built vpon most precious stones foundation:
When fiery tryalls come, the builders trouble,
Though some great builders build of such a fashion,
    To learned *Androes,* that much better can,
    I leaue that stubble, fire, and straw to scan.
Nor list I with Philosophers to range,
In searching out, (though I admire the reason)
How simpathising properties most strange,
Keepe contraries in straw, so long a season.
    Yce, snow, fruits, fish, moist things, & dry & warme,
    Are long preseru'd in straw, with little harme.
But let all Poets my remembrance wipe
From out their bookes of Fame, for euer during,
If I forget to praise our Oaten pipe,
Such Musicke, to the Muses all procuring:
    That some learn'd eares preferr'd it haue before
    Both Orpharyon, Violl, Lute, Bandore.
Now if we list more curiously examine,
To search in straw some profitable points,

345 2 is great] a great 1615 etc. 19 Nor A 1633] Now 1615 1618 1625
25 wipe A 1633] wipe, 1615 1618 1625.

Bread hath beene made of straw in time of famine,
In cutting off the tender knotted ioynts:
  But yet remaines one praise of straw to tell,
  Which all the other praise doth farre excell.
That straw, which men, & beasts, & fowles haue scorned,
Hath beene by curious Art, and hand industrious
So wrought, that it hath shadowed, yea adorned
A head and face of beauty and birth illustrious.
  Now praise I? No, I enuy now thy blisse,
  Ambitious straw, that so high placed is.
What Architect this worke so strangely matcht?
An yuory house, dores Rubies, windows tuch,
A gilded roofe, with straw all ouerthatcht.
Where shall pearle bide, when grace of straw is such?
  Now could I wish, alas, I wish too much,
  I might be straw-drawne to that liuely Tuch.
But herein we may learne a good example,
That vertuous Industry their worth can raise,
Whom slanderous tongs tread vnder foot & trample.
This told my Muse; and straight she went her waies:
  Which (Lady) if you seriously allow,
  It is no toy, nor haue I broke my vow.

92 In Romam.

346 Hate, and debate, Rome through the world hath spread,
Yet *Roma Amor* is, if backward read.
Then is't not strange Rome hate should foster? No:
For out of backward loue, all hate doth grow.

345 44 dores Rubies, windows tuch, A] dores, rubies, windowes touch 1615 1618 1625 doores, wals, windowes tuch, 1633 46 grace A] place 1615 etc.

EPIGRAMS FROM ADDIT. MS. 12049

To James *the VI King of Scotland. The Dedicacion of the copy sent by Cap.* Hunter.

347 Joy to the present, hope of future ages,
Bright Northern starre, whose oryent lyght infused,
In sowth and west, stayed myndes that stood amused,
Accept a present heer of skribled pages,
A work whose method ys to be confused,
A work in which my pen yt self engages
To vse them right that have the world abused.
Yf I whear sin ys wrought, pay shame for wages,
Let your ritch grace hold my poor zeall excused;
Enormous acts move modest mindes to rages,
Which straygth a tart reproofe well gev'n asswages,
And dewly gev'n yt cannot be refused.
We do but poynt out vices and detect them;
Tis you, great prince, that one day must correct them.

My Lady Rogers *Epitaphe.*

348 Death, to make vaunt of his prepostrous powre,
First tooke away one grandchild, then his brother,
Till wayting late for his long lingred howre,
Hee sent to them their mother's aged mother.
And thus hee thinks to be owr conqueror thought,
That hath owr babes and parents thus exilde.
But, Death, hee liues that hath owr ransom wrought,
And of this triumph thou art quyte beguild.
Their soules in hands of god from death are free;
Their flesh must rise agayne to conquer thee.

Of Lynus.

349 *Lynus,* when he is fresh (which is but seld),
Fayns himselfe drunk and walks as yf hee reeld,
Laughs and talks lowd when better men speak soft,
To th'end that being drunk (which happens oft)
His frends may say to saue his reputacion,
"Hee ys not drunk, forsooth 'tis but his fashion."
Oh wondrous witt! Yet sure I rather had
Bee deemed somtymes drunk, then allways mad.

Of Don Pedro's *Pennyworth in a ritch suit of hanginge.*

350 *Don Pedro* bought within three hundred pound
A sewt of arras hanging passing ritch,
Larded with gold and silk in every stitch;
A marv'lous pennyworth doubtles he hath found.
Why? Were they worth it? Was their goodnes such?
No, nothing lyke, nor hardly halfe so much.
Yet was the pennyworth great. Then thus I rede it:
He never payes for that he takes on credit.

To my good friend Sir Hugh Portman. *Of succession.*

351 My good friend *Lynus* still ys vndermining
To know my minde in matter of succession;
And though by law it is a flat transgression
To tell which way affection is enclyning,
He sayth such law of conscience was oppression,
That all frank mindes of whatsoear profession
Against this law have shown a flat repyning.
I thus reply, "I never vse devining;
As for the prince that pleadeth now possession,
My sowle hath ever blest without disguising;
Wherfore to speak of any sonn arysing
I hold it vayn while our deer sonn ys shining;
And had I powr I should be enterprysing

To stay this sonn with Josuah from declining.
But sith the fates ar stayd by no devising,
When her live's thread shall faile with long vntwining,
I wish the future age with peace may bring
No enfant, nor no Queen! whome then? a Kinge."

Of one that had gotten a benefice and after sought for a bellypiece.

352 A country preacher aged toward fifty,
In all his life nor wanton nor vnthrifty,
Came once to me and made an ernest motion
To have a widdow thought at my devotion
By mean her lyving lying in my mannor,
Was held by widdoes state, as is the manner.
He told me first a learned tale of marriadge,
Save I perhaps have lost som in the carriadge;
But this he provd by many learned clauses,
How marriadge is allowd men for two causes:
As namely first for honest procreation,
Next to avoyd dishonest fornication;
And that late writers, men of passing piety,
Have fownd a third cause, mutuall society.
This sayd, he told how he this suit attempted
Not that to carnall lust he was much tempted,
Nor that he should by this enrich his purse,
But that his yeers required now a nurse.
"A nurse," said I, "Oh head of wisdom skarse.
Thou seekst a nurse, but thou wouldst have (an) ."
Cannot great Clarcks that hold such ghostly places,
Decline *vxores* in the gendring cases?

A Paradox. To Cinna *the Brownist.*

353 Pure *Cinna* deemes I hold a paradox,
Not to be prov'd but vnto stones and stox,

That brownists ar vnto the papists neerer
Then protestaunts: tis cleer thear's nothing cleerer.
First, *Cinna,* often I have herd thee grawnt
The Popes cheefe opposit's a Protestaunt:
Now then, to try the distance trew, compare
And make relligion either rownd or square:
Yf it be rownd, as in thease careless dayes
Yt runneth rownd (more pitty) many waies,
Place Protestaunts and Papists East and West,
And place the Brownist whear he list to rest:
Except that hee the circle quite will miss,
Hee neerer still vnto the Papist ys.
If square it be, as sewr as now tis faring,
About relligion never was more squaring,
Nor farder out of square I think twas never,
Nor fewr that to bring't in square indever,
Place th' opposites at two poynts most opposed,
And then agayn this secret ys disclosed:
For either they be quite beside all square,
Or neerer to the papistes still they are:
But be they nere so neer they need beware;
    Both sides will dawnger them except they turn them:
    The Protestants will hang, the Papists burn them.

Of a devout damsell.

354 A neighbour myne, an honest, learned Curat,
Preaching on day according to his function,
Said that their hartes wear hard and too obdurat
That in their conscience never feel compunction;
Of which, to make som playner explanacion,
With varied phrase (as schollers have the trick)
He usd som words of like signification,
A feeling, a remorse, a sting, a prick.
A zealous maid heard him with great attention,
And being pregnant of Conceit and Witt,
Calld oft to minde the wordes he last did mencion,

Which most, as seemd, did in her conscience stick.
All melancholy from the Church she went,
And comming home she laid her on her bedd,
And vnto those that wear to see her sent,
And askt what did ayl her, thus she sedd,
"The sarmon in my conscience made me sick
To heer our parson preaching of a (compunction).

To his Wyfe of womens verteues.

355 A well learnd man, in rewls of life no Stoick,
Yet one that careless Epicures derided,
Of womens vertues talking, them devyded
In three, the private, civyll, and heroyck.
And what he said of thease, to tell yow briefly,
He first began discoursing of the private,
Which each playn cuntry huswife may arrive att,
As homely and that home concerneth cheefly.
The fruit, malt, hopps, to tend, to dry, to vtter,
To beat, strip, spinn, the hemp, the wool, the flax,
And, more then all, to have good cheese and butter.
The next a step, but yet a large stepp higher,
Was civill vertue fitter for the citty,
With modest looks, good cloathes, and awnswers witty,
Those baser things not don but guided by her.
Her idle tymes and idle coyn she spends
On needle works, and when the season servs
In making dainty Iunkettes and Consarvs,
To wellcom in kind sort his deerest frends.
But farr above them all he most extolled
The statly Heroyns whose noble mynde
It self to those poor orders cannot binde,
Anomelons that still lyve vncontrolled.
These entertayn great princes; these have lerned

355 12 The next B] Then next A.

The tongues, toyes, tricks, of Room, of Spain, of Fraunce;
These can Currentos and Lavoltas dance,
And though they foot yt false tis nere discerned,
The vertues of these dames are so transcendent.
Themselvs ar learnd, and their Heroyk sperit
Can make disgrace an honor, sinn a merit.
All penns, all praysers ar on them dependent.
Well, gentle wife, thow knowst I am not Stoicall,
Yet would I wish, take not the wish in evill,
Yow knew the private vertue, kept the civill,
But in no sort aspyre to that hooroyicall.

Of certain puritan wenches.

356 Six of the weakest sex and purest sect
Had conference one day to this effect,
To change that old and popish name of preaching.
And first the first would have it called teaching;
The second, such a vulgar terme despysing,
Said it wear better call it cathecising;
The third, not full so learnd yet foole as wise,
Told that her husband calld it excercise.
The fourth, a great Magnificats corrector,
Said she allowd them best that calld it Lector.
"Nay," said the fift, "Our brethern, as I heere,
Do call it speaking in North Hampton sheere."
"Tush," said the sixt, "Then standing wear more fitt,
Sith preachers seldom in the pulpit sitt."
Now though this word was worst, yet not withstanding,
I know not why, but all likt best of standing.

Of a Zealous Ladye.

357 Two Alldermen, three Lawiers, five Phisitions,
Seavn Captains, with nine Poets, ten Musitions,
Woo'd all one wencth. She, waying all condicions

By which she might attayn to most promotion
Did take a preest at last for pure devotion.

To Mr. Bastard, *the minister that writes the pleasant Epigrams.*

358 Had yow been known to me ear yow wear maryd,
I should have wisht that single yow had taryd.
Yet of your spryte my sperit ys so awfull,
I dare not say soch marriage ys vnlawfull.
Nor dare I say men of soch holy function
Should castrat quite themselvs from such coniunction.
Nor dare I much owr saviour's speeches skann,
To whome twas spoken, "Take it they that cann."
Nor dare I say the word would work more good
Yf preachers wallowd less in flesh and bloud.
Nor dare I say such livyngs wear provided
With crosier staves, not distaves, to be guided.
Yet least I might be deemd among the dastards,
I dare say this: "Thy children shall be bastards."

That the clergy be great builders now as well as of old.

359 Was that a pryde in preests, or was yt piety?
Had those more zeall, or wer they more presumptuos
To build soch Colledges for their society,
With abbyes well endowd and Churches sumptuos?
If that wear pride, have ours too much humility?
If theirs wear zeall, have ours no godly mocion?
Yes! I can proove that ours both have abillity,
And that they build much more with more devocion.
With stone, yea, with free stones, they rear of building,
Worlds pretty, mycrocosmous, little ones,
With temples tymbred well, and som have guilding.
Shrines not of dead men's but of lively bones;
Thease buildings walk, oh! works worth admyracion,
And each beares sirname of their archytector.

And as yt ought Love layd the first foundacion,
But Love read in St. Luke with Ouids lector.
    Well, sith this building from those old one varyes,
    Som men could wish such builders had no quaryes.

The censure of a Lady in Ireland of the overthrow at Blackwater.

360 Two dames of two beleefs, the old and later,
Talkt of the loss late taken at Blackwater.
The Catholique affirmd she could not know
The hidden cause of that curst overthrow.
The tother, that professed greater purity,
Said that the cause was hidd in no obscurity;
"For God," said she, "strengthened the Rebbells arme,
Because the Papists in our campe doe swarme,
Whose erring fayth and great abhominacion
Ys cause no doubt of our great desolacion."
    "Oh, witty reason," tother strayght replyde,
    "Wear they not all Papistes on tother side?"

Of Moyses.

361 Most worthy Prophet, that by inspiration
Did tell of heavn and earth and seas creation,
That first desarvdst the name of sacred poett,
Now so prophande that fooles on fools bestow it,
Thow for they peopls liberty and good
Didst scorne the tytle of the Royall blood;
Thow that by grace obtayned from thy godd,
From Rocks deryvedst Rivers by thy rodd,
And in that rodd's true reall alteration
Didst show vndoubted transubstantiation;
Thow that didst plague all Egipt with their prince,
That tenn such plagues wear nere before nor since;
Thow that didst by thy makers speciall grace
Speak with him in the Mountanes face to face,

And thear receavdst of him ten hy behests,
In stony bookes, for our more stony brests;
Thow that twice forty dayes tookst no repast,
And gavst two samples of one Lenton fast;
Thow that in zeall reveng didst take so sore
Vppon that damned crew, Dathan and Core,
And at another time in rightfull yre
Consumedst som with sword and som with fyre;
Obtayn my pardon, if (vntoward scholler),
I proove in nothing like thee but in choller.
And now give leave vnto my awfull Muse
To tell one fault of thyne in mine excuse;
For though I needs must grante my foolish wrath
Those lawes to break somtimes me caused hath,
I breake but one and one, none for the nonce;
Thow in thy wrath didst break them all at once.

Against Leda *for carping.*

362 Last day dame *Leda* reeding in my ryme
How Moyses in his anger brake the tables,
"What! Have we byble stories ioynd with bables?
Oh sacriledg! Vnexcusable cryme!
And oh!" saith she, "the manners! oh the tyme
That feares not to confownd our fayth with fables!
Now fy, for shame on writers so prophane!"
But fly for shame; pure *Leda* ys mistane;
For he that me to speak and write enables
Knows that mine humble hart my Muse acquaints
With none but reverent thoughts of all his saints,
Who, though on earth they subiect wear to passion,
In heav'n they feele no passion but compassion.
Whearfore surcease, *Leda,* thy vain complaints;
Not saints but shrowes ar subiect vnto skorns.
For sample, *Leda,* now Ile say but this:
Thy Husband like to Moyses picture ys,
For Moyses ever painted ys with hornes.

Of Bedas *opinion of Purgatory.*

363 Pure *Cinna* sayth that *Beda* ys a lyer,
Because he writes there ys a purging place
In which men after death must stay a space
And so be sav'd yet, as yt wear by fier.
This question ys to deep for our descision,
But yet to charge a writer with a fable,
Whom all our ellders held so venerable,
I think such person worthy of derision.
But, *Cinna,* that twixt vs be no devision,
    Thus far I think we might agree togeather,
    Those that beleeve yt not shall near go thether.

Against excesse in Womans Apparrell.
To my Lady Rogers.

364 Our zealows preachers that would pride repress
Complain against Apparrells great excess;
For though the lawes against yt are express,
Each Lady like a Queen herself doth dress,
A merchaunts wife like to a barronness.
But yet preests wives, yf I aright do guess,
Offend no lawes heerin nor more nor less;
    For whie? No written law, proclaimd or printed,
    Hath our preests wives for their apparrell stinted.

Of the name Papist, Brownist, and Zwinglian.

365 Pure *Lynus* Papistry layes to my chardge,
And that my verse bewraies my thoughts, he saith.
I by deniall could myself discharge,
Yet least some think then I denyde my fayth,
Ev'n in my purest thoughts protest do I
A christian Catholique to live and dy.
As for theise names, Papist and Hugonot,
Brownist and Zwinglian, that but factions feede,

I skorn; but christian Catholique, I note
That in the scripture nam'd, this in the Creed.
But, *Lynus,* either I my mark have mist,
Or thow of theise may yet choose what thou list.

Of Galla. *To his Wife.*

366 Brave *Galla* late a lofty prelate wedding,
Sumptuous at boord but sumptuous more at bedding,
Out of her pride by all men much abhord,
When she will name her husband, saith her lorde.
Ys this a pride? Tis grace I rather guesse;
Sara did say no more, *Galla* no less.
Yet when she sayes so next, thus much say I,
Let Papist none nor Puritan be by,
For while, "My lord, my husband," she doth clatter,
Tone will deny that first, tother the latter.

Against an extream flatterer that preached at Bath on the Queens day the forteth yeer of her raign.

367 You that extoll the bliss of this our nation,
And lade our ears with stale and lothsom praise
Of forty yeares sweet peace and restfull dayes,
Which you advance with fayned admiration,
Much better would it sewt your high vocation
To beat down that your flattring tongues do raise,
And rather seeke som words of commination
For tymes abounding with abhomination.
Say that Gods wrath against vs is provoked,
And tell vs tis to vs the scripture saies,
"I forty yeers have brookt this generation."
And said, "Theis people have not known my wayes."
For law with lust, and rule with rape is yoked,
And zeall with schisme and Symony is choked.

Of an Heroicall awnswer of a great Roman Lady to her husband.

368 A grave wise man that had a great ritch Lady,
Soch as perhaps in theis dayes found thear may be,
Did think she playd him false and more then thynk,
Save that in wisdom he therat did winck.
Howbeit one time disposde to sport and play
Thus to his wife he plesantly did say,
"Sith Straungers lodge their Arrowes in thy quiver,
Deer dame, I pray you yet the cause deliver,
If you can tell the cause and not dissemble,
How all our chilldren me so much resemble."
The Lady blusht but yet this awnser made,
"Though I have vsd some traffique in the trade,
And must confess, as you have toucht before,
My bark was sometime steerd with forren ore,
Yet stowd I no mans stuff but first perswaded
The bottom with your ballast full was laded.

To my Wife.

369 Your mother layes it to me as a crime
That I so long do stay from yow sometime,
And by her fond surmise would make yow fear
My love doth grow more could or less sincear.
But let no causles doubts make you beleeue
That beeing false that beeing trew would greeve.
I, when I am from thee the farthest distance,
Doe in my soule, by my trew loves assistawnce,
In steed of sweet imbracements, dove like kisses,
Send kindest thoughts and most indeered wishes.
Then letters, then kind tokens pass, and then
My busie Muse imployes my idle penn.
Then memory in loves defence alleadges
Nine organpipes, our loves assured pleadges.

369 14 Nine A] Seavn B.

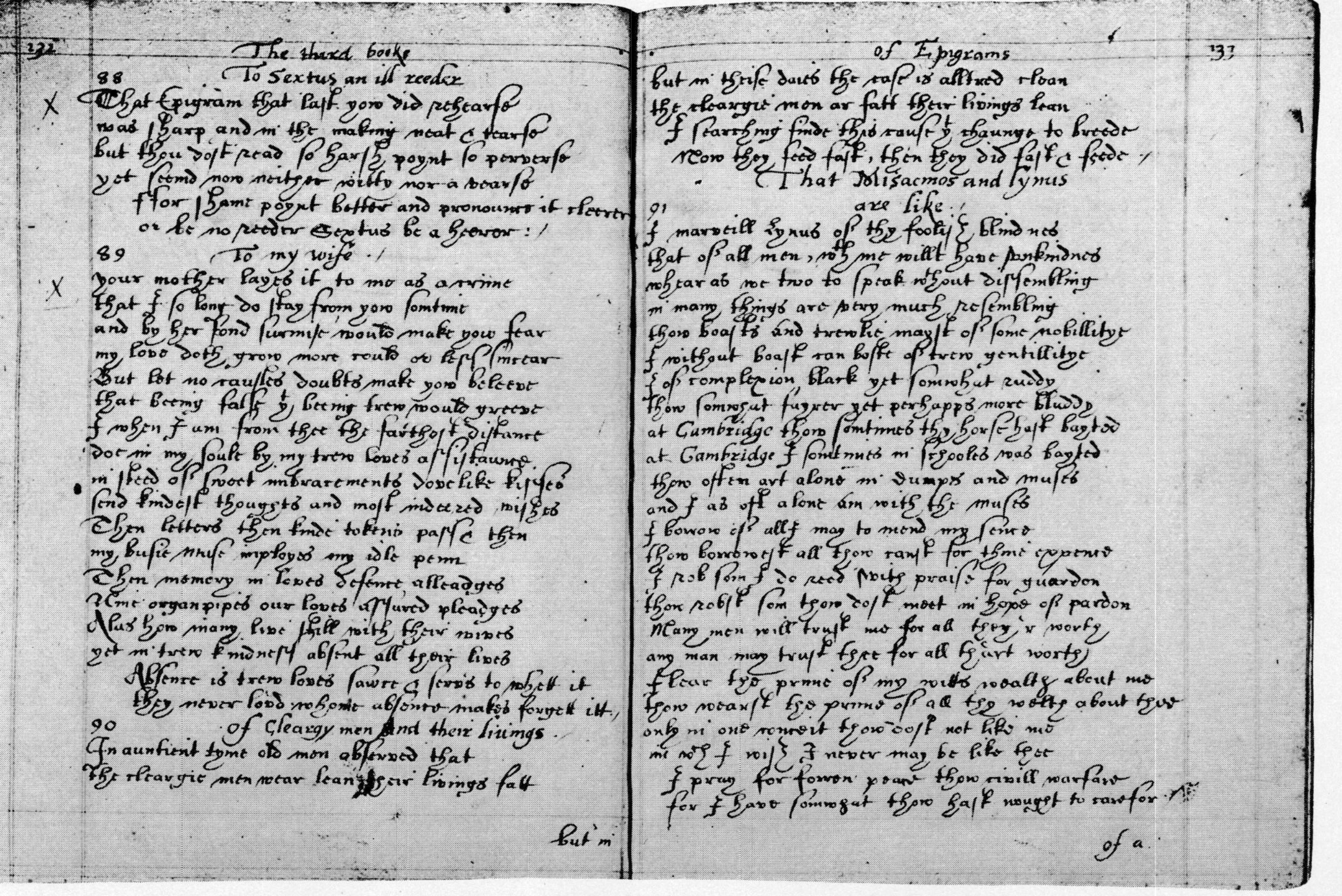
132 The third booke

88 To Sextus an ill reeder

That Epigram that last yow did rehearse
was sharp and in the making neat & tearse
but thou dost read so harsh, poynt so perverse
yet seemd now neither witty nor a wearse
Ffor shame poynt better and pronounce it clerer
or be no reeder Sextus be a hearer :/

89 To my wife ./

Your mother sayes it to me as a crime
that I so long do stay from yow somtime
and by her fond surmise would make yow fear
my love doth grow more could or less sincear
But let no causeles doubts make yow beleeve
that beeing false, wh beeing trew would greeve
I when I am from thee the farthest distance
doe in my soule by my trew loves assistance
in steed of sweet imbracements dovelike kisses
send kindest thoughts and most indeered wishes
Then letters then kinde tokens passe then
my busie muse imployes my idle pen
Then memory in loves defence alleadges
Some organpipes our loves assured pleadges
Alas how many live still with their wives
yet in trew kindness absent all their lives
Absence is trew loves sawce & serves to whett it
they never lovd whome absence makes forgett itt./

90 Of cleargy men and their livings

21. In auntient tyme old men observed that
the cleargie men wear lean their livings fatt

but in

Of Epigrams 133

but in these dayes the case is altred cleane
the cleargie men are fatt their livings lean
I searching finde this cause of chaunge to breede
Now they feed fast, then they did fast & feede ./

That Misacmos and Lynus are like ./

91
I marvell Lynus of thy foolish blindnes
that of all men, wth me will have unkindnes
whear as we two to speak without dissembling
in many things are very much resembling
thow boasts and twenty mayst of some nobillitye
I without boast can boste of trew gentillitye
I of complexion blacke yet somwhat ruddy
thow somwhat fayrer yet perhapps more bluddy
at Cambridge thow somtimes thy horse hast bayted
at Cambridge I somtimes in schooles was bayted
thow often art alone in dumps and muses
and I as oft alone am with the muses
I borow of all I may to mend my sence
thow borowest all thow canst for thie expence
I rob som I do reed with praise for guerdon
thou robst som thow dost meet in hope of pardon
Many men will trust me for all they're worth
any man may trust thee for all thow'rt worth
Ffear the prince of my witts walks about me
thow wearest the prince of all thy witts about thee
only in one conceit thow dost not like me
in wch I wish I never may be like thee
I pray for sowen peace thow civill warfare
for I have somwhat thow hast nought to care for ./

of a

FROM HARINGTON'S MANUSCRIPT (AUTOGRAPH) VOLUME OF EPIGRAMS

Alas, how many live still with their wives,
Yet in trew kindness absent all their lives.
Absence is trew loves sawce, and serv's to whett it;
They never lov'd whome absence makes forgett it.

Of Cleargy men and their liuings.

370 In auntient tyme old men observed that
The cleargie men wear lean, their livings fatt;
But in theise daies the case is alltred clean;
The cleargie men ar fatt, their livings lean.
I searching finde this cause that chaunge to breede:
Now they feed fast; then they did fast and feede.

That Misacmos *and* Lynus *are like.*

371 I marveill, *Lynus,* of thy foolish blindnes,
That of all men, with me willt have vnkindnes;
Whearas we two, to speak without dissembling,
In many things are very much resembling.
Thow boasts, and trewlie mayst, of some nobillitye,
I without boast can boste of trew gentillitye.
I of complexion black but somwhat ruddy,
Thow somwhat fayrer yet perhapps more bluddy.
At Cambridge thow somtimes thy horse hast bayted,
At Cambridge I somtimes in schooles was bayted.
Thow often art alone in dumps and muses,
And I as oft alone am with the Muses.
I borrow of all I may to mend my sence,
Thow borrowest all thou canst for thine expense.
I rob som I do reed with praise for guardon,
Thow robst som thou dost meet in hope of pardon.
Many men will trust me for all they'r worth,
Any man may trust thee for all th'art worth.
I bear the prime of my witts wealth about me,
Thow wearst the prime of all thy wealth about thee.

Only in one conceit thou dost not like me,
In which I wish I never may be like thee:
    I pray for forren peace; thow, civill warfare;
    For I have somwhat, thow hast nought to care for.

Of the parsons parte.

372 Whether it wer by chaunce, or els by arte,
You find our verse in number so well cowched
That each tenth stanze may seeme the parsons parte,
Marking the matters that therein ar towched.
But sure I am some parsons are so curst
That, though tis theirs and I bestow it freely,
Yet they of all will like that part the worste,
Yea, though yow search from Salsbury to Ely.
    For in all parsons this a fault is known:
    To lust for others good and loath their owne.

To the earle of Essex when he lay at Greys and protested to lyue retyred.

373 Oft Reeding acts admird of Charles the fyft,
Mine envious mind and captious in condicion
In his lives course discovered hath one drift
Convincing him of infinite ambycion.
For having ioynd th' Imperiall crowne to Spaine
(This grown by birth, that graunted by election),
After Conquests great he did attayn,
Getting both Indies vnder his subiection;
Sick of ambicion, that disease incurable,
Like Alexander, that more worlds would gayn,
Finding his kingdoms great but nothing durable,
Yet of an endles thirst he had to raign,
    Playnly to proove he higher still aspired
    He quite renownct all these and livd retyred.

Of two frayll saints.

374 One of the foolish family of love
That of their sure election stand so glorious
They think that ev'n their sinns are meritorious,
Did earst a sister to his pleasure move,
Alleadging, sith no sinn their soules could taint,
They might begett som prophett or a saint.
She graunted, or at least she not denide,
To give to his foule lust full satisfaction.
Yet in the midst of their venereous action,
Rapt in her flesh with zeall of sprite, she cride,
"How would the wicked and ungodly scoff it
If they should finde vs saints getting a prophett."

How England may be reformed.

375 Men say that England late is bankrout grown;
Th'effect to manifest, the cause vnknown.
Ritch Tresorors 'thath had, and wary keepers,
Fatt Judges, Councellors in gayn no sleepers;
Collectors, auditors, receavers meny,
Searchers and Customers all for the peny.
As for the Churchmen, they both pray and pay;
Soluat Ecclesia, so the courtiers pray.
Might some new officer mend old disorder?
Yes, one good *Stewart* might sett all in order.

Of two religions.

376 One by his father kept long time to schoole,
And prooving not vnlearned nor a foole,
Was earst by him demaunded one occasion
Which was the sounder Church in his perswasion,
If this Church of *Geneua* late reformed,
Or that old Catholick that theis have skorned.
Both do cyte doctors Councells, both alleadge,
Both bost the word truths everlasting pleadge.

"Then say, my sonn," quoth he. "Fear no controule.
Which of the two is safest for my soule?"
"Sure," quoth the sonn, "a man had needs be crafty
To keepe his soule and body both in safty.
But both to save, this is best way to houlde:
Live in the new, dy yf you can in th'olde."

Of Sympathy.

377 Yf, as some thinke, the sympathie of minds
Ys token of sweet love and kinde accorde,
Great sympathies and in most divers kinds
Ar between *Lesbia* and her noble Lorde.
If he to goe from home can take occasion,
Full glad ys he and doth therat reioyce:
As glad ys she and addeth her perswasion,
Nor would she have him stay to have her choyce.
Sad he returns and seeld but by compulsion;
For three dayes fish and guests ar thought vnsavory.
As sad is she; her hart feels great convulsion;
His presence checks her mirth, her sporte, her bravery.
After he hath a while at home been biding,
He chafes, he sweares, nor meat nor drink is toothsome;
As fast his loving Lady falls to chiding,
As fast she swears all cates to her are loathsome.
He shames sometimes at her new made complexions,
He feares least she should spy his secret sallyings;
She shames no less at his known imperfections,
She doubts no less lest he descry her dallyings.
On hownds and hawks he frankly spends his crowns,
And horses and such purtnances of sports;
As much she spends on kertles and on gowns
And on som ruffen that to her resorts.
Their prairs ar like, their vows but short and small;
If so it be with vocall pray'r or mentall;
Each praies to se the tothers funerall,
But neither greatly cares of dirg or trentall.

Thus in their ioy, their sorrow, and their wrath,
Their shame, their fear, their bounty, and their prayre,
All their whole life so great resemblance hath
They make a matchless match, a peerless payr.
Sweet simpathy, I know not who the devill
Should well agree yf theis agree but evill.

Of Lynus *the writer.*

378 Thow, *Lynus,* thinks thy selfe a great endyter,
And now of late thow raisest high thy lookes,
Because the stationers doe sell thy bookes.
But shall I tell thee trew? Thou art no writer;
Thou blottest papers. Only they doe write
Whose writings men of worth reede with delight.

Of Sextus *witt.*

379 To have good witt ys *Sextus* thought by many;
But sure he hides it all; he shows not any.

Of Thais *and* Clerus.

380 Fayr *Thais* skarse had a widdow been a weeke,
When *Clerus* came a match with her to seeke;
And to sett forth more statly his approach,
He hyred men and horses and a coach.
But as he was dismounting at her gate,
The porter tolde he came one hower to late,
For she was newly married that forenoone.
"Farewell!" quoth *Clerus.* "Then I came to soone."

How Faustus *lost not his Labor.*

381 When yow, fond *Faustus,* in an idle sute
Had quite consumd long tyme in little frute,
Though yow confest yow had your labour lost,
Yet yow gaind witt therby, yow made your bost.

But yf yow would indeed examin duly
Your gains and losse, and then account them truely,
Thus to transfer those words it would be fitt:
Yow gain'd the travell but yow lost the witt.

To his wife in excuse of his Absence.

382 *Mall,* in mine absence this ys still your song:
"Com home, sweet heart, yow stay from home too long."
That thow lov'st home, my love, I like yt well,
Wives should be like thy Tortas in the shell.
I love to seeke, to see, learn, know, be knowne;
Men nothing know, know nothing but their owne.
"Yea, but," yow say to me, "home homely is,
And comly thervnto." And what of this?
Among wise men, they demed are but momes
That allwayes ar abiding in their homes.
To have no home, perhapps it is a curse;
To be a prisoner at home 'tis worse.

Of a pure preaching phisition.

383 The zealows preacher, *Lalus,* as they tell,
Doth practise phisick now: tis wondrous well,
For first he taints souls with erronious spell,
And then his druggs give quick dispatch to hell.
God keepe my friends and all of our affinity
Free from his phisique, far from his devinity.

Of Goats milk and cows milk. Between a phisition and a Lady. To my Lady Rogers.

384 A learned Lady of no mean condition
Question'd one day with a more learnd phisition,
Affirming 'twas but error or presumption
That men praescribe to patients in consumption,
As they that mark it oftentimes shall note,

382 4 like B] lik A.

Somtime an Asses milke, somtimes a gote.
"But I," said shee, "for my parte doe allow
Better then both theis milks that of [a] Cow,
As having sweeter flesh and finer feeding,
And therfore better bloud and humors breeding."
The learned Leach incombred thus and troubled,
For she her words and reasons still redoubled,
"Madam," quoth he, " 'tis not so good by halfe,
Except the patient hap to be a calfe."

Misacmos *of himselfe that loves to be worst in the company.*

385 When I from schooles came to the citty first,
My Syre advisde me warely to chuse
All such as for compannions I would vse
So if I could as I might be the worst.
For why? The graver and the wiser sorte
Men like their chief compannions do esteeme,
And such they doe their inclination deeme,
And theirs ys known with whome they do consorte.
Now while I thought I had som praise deserved,
To daunt my pride heerin, I have been tolde
Faustus as strict as I this rule doth holde;
Nay, more; he cannot break it yf he would.

Of one that kept open house at Christmas.

386 This Christmas *Paulus* for his reputation
To keepe an open house makes proclamation;
To which (to make it noted) he annexes
Theis generall words: for all of both the sexes.
If *Paulus* meaning be but as he writes,
He keepes house only for Hermaphrodites.

An Epitaph on Mr: John Ashley *sometimes Mr: of the Iewells to her Maiestie. Sent to his virtuos widdow and his worthy sonne Sr:* John Ashley.

387 Loe heer in Ashes, worthy *Ashley* lies,
A Iewell to his prince, her Iewells master,
His Corps heer shrinde in tutch and allablaster,
His soule vntowcht mounts ore the marble skies;
Once happie here in courte by princes eyes,
Eyes whose aspect defend from all disaster;
Thrice happy now in heav'nly Hierarchies,
Wher his soule crownd sees his all seeing master.
By birth a squire, a Bazon by his roome,
Now is a kingdome given him by his toome.

To Mr: Iohn Dauys.

388 My deer friend *Davys,* some against vs partiall
Have found we steall some good conceits from Martiall;
So though they graunt our verse hath some Acumen,
Yet make they fooles suspect we skant ar trew men.
But *Surrey* did the same, and worthy *Wyatt,*
And they had praise and reputation by it.
And *Heywood,* whome your putting down hath raised,
Did vse the same and with the same is praised.
Wherfore yf they had witt that soe did trace vs,
They must again for their own creddits grace vs;
Or else to our more honour and their greevs
Match vs at least with honorable theevs.

To my Lady Rogers *that she loued not him, yet she loued his wife.*

389 Yow tell among your many auntient Saws,
Which you have learnd of writers of renown,
That love is heavy, still descending down;
And yet in this your selfe do break loves lawes,
For still on *Mall* yow fawn, on me yow frown.

I feele th'effect, yet cannot finde the cause.
Your love, which draws to her, from me withdraws.
But if your love be either verbe or nown,
I'le proove cleer by an vnexspected clause,
Yow then should love me first. Nay, never wonder,
For lett the harrolds set our places down,
    I hope when *Mall* and I be least asunder,
    Your daughters place is not above but vnder.

To his wife. Of loue without lust.

390 Thow tellst me, *Mall,* and I beleeve it must,
That thow canst love me much with little lust;
But while of this chaste love thow dost devise,
And lookst chaste babies in my wanton eyes,
Thy want of lust makes my lust wanton-wyse.
Then think, but say't no more; for, yf thow doest,
    Trust me I find an aptnes to mistrust;
    I cannot love thee long without my lust.

Of a Lenton dinner.

391 I din'de by hap at *Sextus* house this spring,
Where, though himselfe far'd sumptuous like a king,
With Patridge, quayles, and Ven'son all in ryott,
There was but little store of Lenton dyett;
For fish of sea or river was their none
Saving the king of fishes or poore Iohn;
Wherwith content at last to mend my cheere,
I calld to have a cupp of strong march beere.
It came and to tell trew and not to halte,
'Twas strong of Hopp and water, not of malte;
Yet twas march beer indeed, who ever made it;
The sonn was but in *Taurus* when we had it.
And take this one note more to mend my tale:
Though 'twear not stale, yet did it looke like stale.
    Well, lett my witt be matcht with a march hare
    When ear I march so farr for so ill fare.

To one of her Maiesties Phisitions in praise of the King of Scotts phisition that was knighted.

392 To swage some daungerous humors dayly surging
Each spring or fall for feare her health have harme,
You cause our Queen vse letting bloud and purging;
And many times, no great occasions vrging,
Blood Royal spins from scepter bearing Arme.
But late in North by treason most contagious,
When traytors hart his traytrous hands did arme,
With doubled weapon and with devlish charme,
To kill that oryent king with hart outragious,
And turn his spring to fall (oh haynous guilt).
His learnd phisition, awnswering that allarme,
With valient hand and with an hart coragious,
While letting others bloud his owne was spillt,
Deserv'd and gott the gilded spurr and hillt.

To one Mr: Fitzgefferies *with a Reward of French crowns for a booke he gave this Author in Latten verses.*

393 Yow write your purse wasts and consumes your stock
By reason of the crowing of some cock,
At which the Lyons Whellps take such offence
As yow suppose that reason drives them thence;
Wherfore to remedy so shrewd abuses
I without lyons send yow Flower de Luses.
Thus crost and guarded well with armes of France
The devill in your purse shall never dance.

Of Christs cote.

394 Our reverent ellders had one speciall note
That trew relligion should throughout the reame
Be kept like to our saviours wearing coate,
All of one peece and void of any seame.
How comes then this devision so extreame,
Ready to teare out one an others throte?

Who stird such waves in this still running streame,
Able to sinck St: Peeters tottring bote?
    Ist not a schisme? No, say not so: beware;
    But we have allmost worn the coate thredbare.

Of Lending money.

395 *Titus* lent *Lynus* money on his bande,
But ear that *Lynus* set therto his hande,
He was precise in setting down the place
For which the Scrivner had but left a space.
This done, they parte. In time the tyme expires;
Titus at place praefixt his crowns requiers;
But all that day of *Lynus* was no news,
No letter, man, nor friend yt to excuse.
"Well, well," quoth *Titus* with a skornfull frowne,
"Was this his care to have his place sett downe,
    To be more sure, forsooth, to think vppon it?
    Nay, nay, but to be sure to keepe him from itt."

Misacmos *of his Muse. To Sir* Iohn Ashley.

396 My Muse ys like king *Edwards* Concubine,
Whose minde did to devotion so encline
She duely did each day to church resorte,
Save yf she wer entyst to *Venus* sporte.
    So would my Muse write gravely nere the latter;
    She slipps somtimes into some wanton matter.

Of Lynus.

397 Poore *Lynus* plaines that I of late forgett him,
And saith hee'l be my guest if I will lett him.
But I so liked him last tyme I mett him
That Ile be sure do all I can to lett him.

In prayse of two worthy Translations, made by two great Ladies.

398 My soule one only *Mary* doth adore,
Only one *Mary* doth inioy my hart;
Yet hath my Muse found out two *Maryes* more
That merit endless praise by dew desart;
Two *Maryes* that translate with divers arte
Two subiects rude and ruinous before;
Both having nobless great and bewties store,
Nobless and bewty to their works imparte;
Both have ordaynde against deaths dreadfull darte
A Sheeld of fame enduring evermore.
Both works advance the love of sacred lore,
Both helpe the soules of sinners to convarte.
Their learned payn I prayse, her costly almes;
A Colledge this translates, the tother Psalmes.

To the orient king praying to neuer see him occident by any Accident.

399 Antiquitye distinguisht hath long since
Two sevrall fashions of Monarchall raigne:
A tyrant one, tother a lawfull prince,
Which by theis rules may be discerned playn.
The lawfull prince his subiects deems as sonns,
And toward them myldly himselfe behaves;
The Tyrant headlong in his fancy runs,
His will their law, his subiects counts his slaves.
Well said: yet some I knowe to fear had rather
A gentle master then a crewell father.

Of trying spiritts. A passage between two persons of great calling.

400 A Catholick had conference of late
With one of our great Prelates of the state,

Lamenting that the Church with schisme turmoyled
Had eake her buillding and revenews spoylled.
"Foole," said the prelat, "why ar yow molested
That near ar like therin to be revested?
If we retayn a portion though but small,
What's that to yow, for yow have lost it all?"
"Yet," said the tother, "we doe wish in harte
That yow might keepe it all, not spill a parte."
Now *Sollomon* be Iudge, I wish none other,
Which is the harlott, which the lawfull mother?
This side saith, "Spare my childe alyve and take it.
Lett it not perrish though I must forsake it."
    She, feelling no remorse of grace nor nature,
    Saith, "Neither thine nor mine, but *dividatur.*"

To his Wife against Women recusants.

401 The great *Asuaerus* to his royall feast
Envited *Vasti,* his beloved Queene;
But she not then disposed to be seene
Refused to come; which did him so molest
That straight, as if this had a treason beene,
Yt was aggreede his Lordes and peeres betweene
To banish her for breaking his behest.
For thus resolvd that cownsell sage and wise,
That though her face was fare, her portion ample,
Yet by so dangerous eminent example
All *Persian* ladies might their Lords despise.
Wherefore, my deerest *Mall,* I thee advise
    Ensew not *Vasties* sample but detest her,
    And rather follow her successor *Esther.*

To his wives mother.

402 When with your daughter (Madam) yow be chattring,
I finde that oft against me yow incense her;
And then forsooth my kindnes all in flattring,

My love is all but lust; this is your censure.
  Tis not my flattring her moves you thereto;
  Yt is because I will not flatter yow.

Of good Exhortation.

403 When *Faustus* is reprooved for his folly,
And warnd how such misdeeds draw on damnation,
He vows in show repentant seeming holly
Not lightly to regarde good exhortation;
But in a trice, like to the bore and dogg,
To former filth and vomitt he returns,
And from his conscience casts all care and clogg,
Still practising some lewd vngratious turns.
  Faustus observs his vow, and take him rightly,
  Not to regarde good exhortation lightly.

Of a Lady that left open her Cabbinett.

404 A vertuose Lady sitting in a muse,
As many tymes fayr vertuous Ladies vse,
Leaned her Ellbow on one knee full harde,
The other distaunt from it halfe a yarde.
Her knight, to tawnt her by a privy token,
Said, "Wife, awake, your Cabbinet stands open."
  She rose and blusht and smylld and soft doth saye,
  "Then lock it yf yow list: yow keepe the kaye."

Of Praelates that ought to be more Pontificall.

405 Great Praelates named wear in former dayes
Pontifices and had revennues large,
Because they built strong bridges and high wayes,
And kept them well repayred at their charge.
But now white apron strings tye vpp their purses;
Now Cowncells those oulde Customes doo abridge;

Simon his babes super entends and nurses;
Scant one among an hundred buillds a bridge.
    Yf those wear prowde, their pride hath had a fall;
    But I would theise were more *pontificall.*

Of repayring bridges.

406 A Squire hight *Bridges* of good reputation
Gave in his will nere halfe an hundred pounde
Onely to keepe a bridge in reparation.
Are not too few such men in our dayes founde?
    To few? No. Many soe. That is our shame,
    For every man seekes to advance his Name.

Of a Lady that goes priuate to the Bath.

407 *Lesbia,* you seeme a straunge conceyted woman
That, though thy bed to many one is common,
Yet private still yow goe into the Bathe.
We doubt your bewty some great blemish hath:
Either your brests hang bagging downe your sides;
Or else your flesh which your apparrell hides
Is with some vgly Morphew fowly tainted,
With which yow would not have vs made accquainted;
Or els your skin is black whear tis not painted.
"Not so, nor so," you say. I much mistake it,
And that yow show indeede most lovely naked.
    Then know thus doctors say of Cupid's schoole,
    "Thow hast one greater blemish: th'art a foole."

To my Lady Rogers.

408 Among the mortall sinns in number seav'n
That shutt against our soules the gates of heav'n,
Yow still doe say that letchery is worst,
Most loathd of saints and most of god accurst.
But, Madam, either yow are ill advisde,
Or in your yowth yow wear ill catechisde;

For thus learnt I of my good ghostly father,
And by his works as well as words I gather
Those sinns are least, as all the learned teach,
Whear love and charity have smallest breach;
Those sinns of which we soonest do repent vs
For those a pardon soonest shall be sent vs.
Now letchery (as showes the common sentence)
Begins with love and endeth with repentance;
Beside all those that take delight therin
Fynde it a lively not a deadly sinn.
Then lett this question be no more disputed:
Yow see how plaine your error is confuted.
    But bee't agreede thus yow and me betwix,
    Yt is the greatest sinn of seaven, save six.

To his Wife.

409 My *Mall,* if any fortune to accuse me
(As to accusing all the world is bent)
That I in lawes of wedlock do abuse me,
And secretly doe live incontinent,
Incontinent thus to thy thought excuse me:
Think envy doth for spite such lies invent;
Then note their sex and guesse at their intent.
    Yf they be men, think like themselvs they take me;
    Yf women, think that so they fain would make me.

Of Pawlus *wife and* Cayus *chilldren.*

410 One sware to me that *Pawlus* hath a wife,
Yet was he never maried all his life.
Now from this tale the reason plain I gather
How *Cayus* gets no barns, yet is a father.

Of only fayth.

411 Pure *Cinna* evermore disputing saith
That Christians saved are by only faith.

But heerin *Cinnas* speeches are abusive,
To foyst vnto our fayth a worde exclusive;
For we doe finde, marking the scriptures scope,
Sallvation comes by grace, love, fear, and hope.
Wherefore, when *Cinna* speaks fayth saveth only,
Tell him *Misacmos* saith he speaketh onely.

Of Lesbia's *censure of my verses.*

412 When some good vertuous strayne my verse inritches,
Lesbia, whose ear for wanton matter itches,
Strait way findes faults and sayes it sutes but odly
To have a wanton poett write so godly.
Thus as Musitians that, to please some Riggs,
On sober Lute and Harpe play wanton Iiggs,
So we that grasd on high *Pernassus* valley,
To please such dames soe long have vsde to dally,
That, if we tuch on goodnes and on god,
Though verse be evn, the matter semeth od.
Well, Ile be evn with them, for by their will
I see they wish I would be wanton still.

Of a pregnant pure sister.

413 I learnd a tale more fitt to be forgotten
How late a holy maide of lovs society
Was by a preacher graue with child begotten;
And when the birth drew near in great anxiety
Amid the pangs she praid with passing piety
That, sith a learned man did over reach her.
The childe she bore at least might prove a preacher.
A childe was born, and, when the throes were past,
She askt what god had sent her at the last.
The midwife made this answer, half in lafter,
"Yow may," said she, "a preacher bear heerafter,
For sure this can be none, god bless the baby;
But for a preacher heer a pullpit may bee."

Of his Wiues pye feast, to which he invited a Knight and a Lady.

414 My wife, at other times like other shrows,
Yet once a year ('tis well tis once a year)
Is kinde to me and then a fest bestows
Of dishes not farr fett nor costing deere;
The chiefe of which are pyes, not pies that chatter,
But pies of which skant twenty fill a platter.
Now, sir, I yow invite and she your Ladie
To this same feast of hers, more kinde than ample,
Where wellcom is best fare, and wher it may be
Your *Phoenix* may of mine take such example,
As now the wether lowring is enclyned,
It may grow fair when as they two have dined.

Of a preacher and his Hourglass.

415 Pure *Lalus* loves the Church but lothes the steeple.
He speaking on a day vnto the people
To th'end he might beware how time did passe,
He usd, as many doe, an hower glasse.
He entred to an ernest disputation
To prove that works are needless to sallvation,
St. Iames his doctrine he doth quite deface;
Of *Paule* and *Ebrios* he brings many a place,
Which while he cites and sifts with mickle cunning,
Out ran the glasse but his tongue still was running.
The people, with his tedious tatle cloyde,
Shrank one and one and left the chappell voide.
Well, *Lalus,* least they serve yow so hereafter,
Run yow out first and let the glass run after;
But while yow make *St. Paule* fall out with *Ieames,*
Yow trouble ours and all our neighbour reames.

To my Lady Killdare.

416 Fayr noble Lady, late I did rehearse
A story of a straw to yow in verse;

For which to grace me with our gracious prince,
My memory I heer yow praised since.
But, Madame, I would take yow more my frend
Yf yow would my forgettfullness commend.
It is no fault, I would not blush to graunt it;
And, for tis true, I need not blush to vawnt it;
That thing that lighly is forgott by no man,
That that bides firm in minde of evry woman,
    Evn that I vow I near remember long.
    What's that? Yf yow will gess aright: 'tis wrong.

Of Sextus *page.*

417 Good *Sextus,* thinke not me to yow iniurious
To say that in one choice thow art too curious,
In choosing of thy page, in which eleccion
Thou specially respectest their complexion.
    Be not so curious, for the fairest skinns
    Give oft occasion to the fowlest sinns.

Of one that could not abide the crosse.

418 Yow terme it superstition fowle and grosse
To signe a childe in baptisme with the crosse,
And say your Iudgment so much doth abhorr it
That you condem the Church of *England* for it.
    I know not, *Cinna,* why yow hate that signe,
    But thats an evill signe; beware that signe.

A good awnswer of D. Dale *to the Queene.*

419 One lately master of the Queens requests,
That wisely could mix serious things with Iests,
Came to her grace one day in winters weather,
Clad in a cloake and bootes of tanned lether.
The queen doth check him in a gratious sporte
For comming to her presence in such sorte,
To place of state, of cleanlines, and bravery,

To come in bootes vnsightly and vnsavery.
But he of ready awnswer not to seeke
Answerd her highnes in theis words or like,
"Tis not my bootes that breedes this iust offence
So to displease your highnes dainty sense,
    But tis theis bills that yeild a savor strong
    That stay vnsigned in my hand so long."

Of don Pedro.

420 Don *Pedro* loves not me, I grow so scottish;
Misacmos loves not him, he growes so sottish.
Once he did like me well, so he did vow;
Then I was ev'n with him; so I am now.

In commendation of his right vertuos cosen the Lady Hastings *maried to Mr. Iustice* Kinsmell.

421 Fair flower of *Haringtons* renowned race,
Sara, whom Venus envies for her face;
Trew *Saras* kinde that calld her husband lord,
And livde obedient and in sweet accorde;
A *Sara* did her husbands age so cheer
He grew a father at an hundred yeer.
    Looke yow to doe all this? Then looke well to itt,
    For by your looke I looke that yow should do it.

Of a grave preacher that studied in his bed.

422 A parson of stayd years and honest carriadge,
New ioyned to a modest maid in marriadge,
Yet followd still his booke with payne exceeding,
And oft at night in bed he would be reeding.
She, though she did not much allow his fashion,
Yet to performe the like in her vocation,
Calls for her linnen turn vpp to her bedd
One night: and while he reedes, she spinneth thred;
Which he reprooving, for the noyse and motion

Disturbed both his study and devotion:
"Sure, sir," said she, "I think as much he sinneth
That reedeth out of time as she that spinneth."
This speech the matter all to mirth did turne.
    He turns a leafe, she turns away the Turne.
    Was this a shrewd? No, sure, a happy turne.

Of the obiects of his satire.

423 My Lorde, though I by yow am often prest
To know the secret drift of mine entent
In these my pleasent lynes, and who are meant
By *Cinna, Lynus, Lesbia,* and the rest,
Yet pardon though I graunte not your request;
Tis such as I thereto may not assent.
What man would ask a woman he possest
Who was the father of her second daughter?
For though she lov'd him, yet so brode a Iest
Would make her blush to speake a good while after.
Theis rymes are mungrells gott on witt and lafter,
My muse the nurse that bread them at her brest;
The witt, ashamd 'twas occupide so lewdly
By Ryballds, fayn would have their names supprest,
Save her young Imps father themselves so shrewdly
That who gat some of them may soone be guest.
But as some Irish dame that false hath plaide
Will not confess her fact for threats or force,
Till death approching makes her soule afrayd
And toucheth her sick hart with sad remorse:
Then wishing she the trueth had vttred rather,
She doth her wanton deallings all discover,
And makes her chilldren know and call one father
That none had earst suspected for her lover:
    So if my wanton Muse dy penitent,
    Perhaps she then may tell yow whome she ment.

423 No title in A.

Of his Muse.

424 I near desearvd that gloriows name of Poet;
No Maker I, nor do I care who know it.
Occasion oft my penn doth entertayn
With trew discourse; let others Muses fayn;
Myne never sought to set to sale her wryting;
In part her frends, in all her selfe delighting,
She cannot beg applause of vulgar sort,
Free born and bred, more free for noble sport.
My Muse hath one still bids her in her eare;
Yf well disposd, to write; yf not, forbear.

A gratulatory Elegy of the peaceable entry of King Iames *gev'n to his Maiestie at Burlegh 1603.*

425 Come, triumphe, enter Church, courte, citty, towne;
Heer Iames the sixt, now Iames the first proclaymed.
See how all harts ar healld that earst wear maymed:
The peer is pleasd, the Knight, the clarck, the clowne;
The mark at which the mallcontent had aymed
Ys mist; succession stablisht in the crowne.
Ioy, protestaunt; let papists be reclaymed;
Leave, puritan, your supercilliows frowne,
Ioyn voice, hart, hande; all discorde be disclaymed.
Make all one flock by one great sheppard guided.
No forren woolfe can force a fould so fenced.
God for his house this *Steward* hath provided,
Right to dispose what earst was wrong dispenced.
But in my loyall love and long prepensed,
With all, yet more than all, reioyce do I
To conster *Iames primus et non vi.*

An Elegy written at the same tyme for the wellcome of Queen Ann *into England.*

426 Great Queen, belov'd and blest in heav'n and earth,
By human favor and by grace devine,

Like peacefull olive and like fruitfull vine,
Yow banish dreadfull war and barren dearth,
To bear kings born and born of kingly berth,
Whose lygnage much, whose issew more, shall shine,
Restoring Englands now long faynting merth,
And raysing vp their hopes that did decline.
Let England be your sea of blisfull pleasure
Whear yow like ship full fraught with balme and wine
With sweetly swelling sayles may swimm at leasure,
And stemm all tydes that at your course repine;
    Chaste vessell, whose deer fraught we prise and measure
    More than 10 Carricks lade with Indies tresure.

The authors farewell to his Muse written at Eaton 1603 the 14th of April.

427 Sweet wanton Muse, that, in my greatest griefe,
Wast wont to bring me solace and reliefe.
Wonted by sea and land to make me sporte,
Whether to camp or court I did resorte:
That at the plow has been my wellcom guest,
Yea to my wedlock bed hast boldly prest;
At Eton now (where first we met) I leave thee,
Heer shall my sonn and heire of me receave thee.
Now to more serious thoughts my soule aspyers,
This age, this minde, a Muse awsteare requires.
Now for those fayned joyes true joyes do spring,
When I salute my sovraigne lord and king.
Now we may tell playn truth to all that ask,
Our love may walke bare-faste without a mask.
My future age to realme and king I vow,
I may no time for wanton toyes alow.
Ever I wish, and only, him to serve,
Only his love ever I would deserve.
If he be pleasd war to proclayme with Spaine,
With such a prince I'le follow wars agayne.

If his great wisdome th' auncient peace renews,
How fayn of peace would I reporte the news.
List he give lawes to th'Irish, now well tamed,
I could give sound advises, and unblamed.
To build some statelie house is his intention,
Ah, in this kinde I had too much invention!
Will he suppress those that the land oppress,
A foe to them, myselfe I still profess.
List he to write or study sacred writte;
To heere, reade, learn, my breeding made me fitt.
    What he commaunds, I'le act without excuse,
    That's full resolvd: farewell, sweet wanton Muse!

In praise of Coryat.

428 Thou glorious Goose that kept'st the Capitoll
    Afford one quill, that I may write one storie yet
    Of this my new-come Odcome Friend, *Tom Coryet,*
Whose praise so worthy wits and pens inroll
    As (with good cause) his custome is to glory it:
    So farre am I from iudging his a sory wit,
Aboue earth, seas, ayre, fire, Ile it extoll
    To *Cinthias* spheare, the next beneath the starres.
Where his vast wit, and courage so audacious
    Of equall worth in time of peace, and warres,
(As *Rolands* erst) encombring rooms capacious
    Lie stored some in hogsheads, some in iarres.
    This makes the learn'd of late in forren parts
    Find *Phoebes* face so full of wennes and warts.

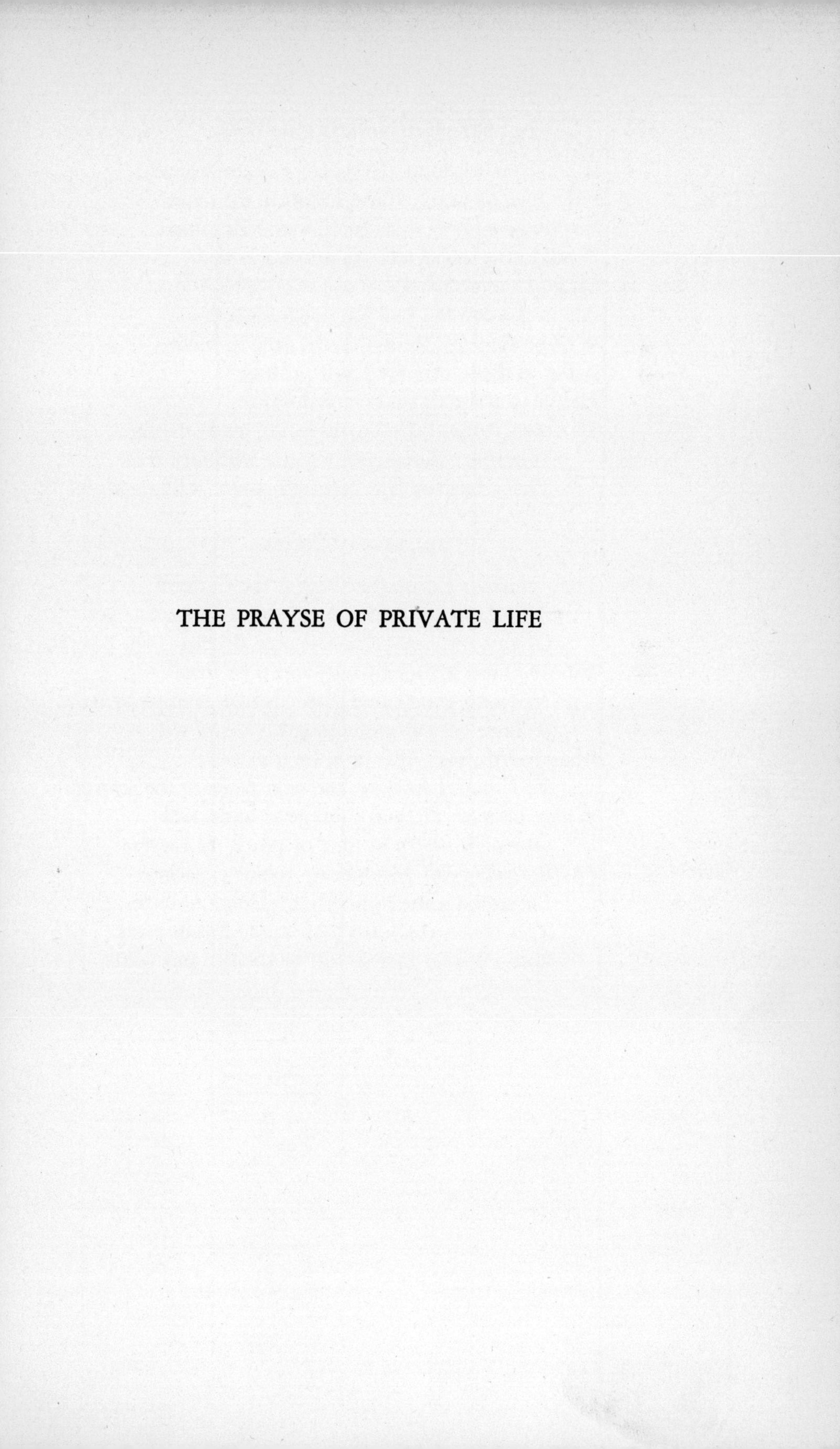

THE PRAYSE OF PRIVATE LIFE

THE PRAYSE OF PRIVATE LIFE

PROHEAME

CERTENLY I thinke, that everie Christian vertuously resolved (and by age overtaken) ought not ymploy himselfe in other affaires then suche as concerne his owne soule and the Service of God, who is the ende of all. For though present pleasures of this life, do daylie labor to diverte the mynde from so excellent a resolucion yet by Gods devine grace and honest excercises all empeachmentes maie be removed. But first it behoveth him so determined, to acquite himselfe of worldly cares and other such trobles as accompanie contynewall business, and therewith also remove himselfe also from concourse of people and tumultuous Townes; which is a matter of much difficultie. For he that is prejudicate and obstinately bent to weare out his life amonge the multytude, will not easely be wayed downe with the pour of perswation, reason or examples, but for the most part parcisteth in defence of his owne will: secretly sayinge to himselfe, "thus yt shalbe."

PART I

CA. 1.

IT semeth to me that the happines of private life and the trouble[s] which accompanie busines, shall best appeare, if we laye before us the commodities and discommodities of eyther, the one causinge quiet and rest, the other offence and laborsome care. For as the end of the one is pleasante laysor, so the other is displeasinge affaires and wearisome busines. And though casually yt cometh to passe, that some man busied doth prosper (which rarely and as a wounder hapneth), yet will I not exchange the pleasure and contente which I finde in solitarie life, for any comeforte or commoditie that business can bringe. I doe not onely commende the name of solitarines, but also highly prayse those good thinges wherewith it is accompanied: because retyringe doth much delight me, and quiet conjoyned with libertie maketh my life pleasinge. Yet am I not so inhumane as to hate the companye of Men (whom by Gods lawe I am bound to love as myselfe) but I abhor their Sinnes (and chiefly my owne) together with those cares and vexations wherewith Worldly Men are molested. Of all which I shall the more aptly be understoode yf I produce what may be said of the one and the other.

My meaninge therefore is to touch the commodities and discommodities of eyther, and thereby the diversitie shall more playnely appeare. For thinges contrarie layed together, do shewe their difference. Yet doe I wittingly first touche that which pleaseth least, to the ende the taste of the other maye seeme the sweeter. Lett eache man resolve to take that course he best liketh, and before his ende cast upp the accompte of his owne life. *Res pulcra est, consummare vitam ante Mortem.*

CA. 2.

Now let us presuppose twoe Men of these contrarie dispositions and beholdinge them with the eyes of our mynde, yt shall playnely appeare which of them leadeth a more happier life. The busied man dwelleth most commonly in Courte, Cyttie or Boorrowe Towne. He is ofte, even at midnight awaked with his owne cares, or the call of Magistrates. He is likewise by dreaminge affrighted, and some tymes terefied with night visions. His sleape also ofte tymes disturbed by ambition, covetise, or contrivinge howe to oppresse other Men: which cogitations are proper to courtiers. The Marchante museth howe to sell his wares for greatest gayne, howe to compasse the inheritance of some yonge heire, or defraude the prince of his custome. Thus publickely or privately he bayteth his brayne, by all sinister meanes to bringe to passe that which he had projected. Sometymes he thinketh to adventure to this or that Countrie, over joyed with hope; and sometymes by misadventure dejected. In the ende (as an unskillful Weaver) he worketh such a webb as intangleth himselfe and many otheres.

But the Solytarie Man riseth in the Morninge, haveinge noe busines and contenteth himselfe with moderate sleapes not broken nor troubled with fearfull and fond dreames, but sometymes at his wakeinge is saluted with a sweete songe of the Nightingale. Then openeth he his lipps and eyther by prayers or godly psalmes, devoutly desireth the Almightie to be his defendour, or as one diffident of his owne deserts ymploreth the ayde of his Creator, givinge unto his celestiall Majestie all glorie and prayse. Duringe these doings, with a tremblinge hope and secret feare, rememberinge his Sinnes, he sheddeth abundant teares whereby is expressed the sorrowes of his Soule, comforted by hope. Such is his Estate, wherewith no pleasure of the Cyttie, nor pompe of the Princes Courtes can compare. Then elevating his eyes he behouldeth the Heaven and Starres where God his maker inhabiteth, and with all his Soule he sigheth for beinge from thence excluded. After these cogitacions he setteth himselfe to studie in some good booke, or passe the tyme in vertuouse exercise, and that done, eateth his meale with good appetite, and a quiet mynde. *Tranquilitas vera, bona mens.*

CA. 3.

The day at hande, the busied man risith in the morninge to entertaine, sometymes his frendes and sometymes his foes. Then is he saluted, entreated, ymportuned, pressed, and pittifully compleyned unto. Contrariwise the private Solytarie man, at his riseinge findeth his Hall emptie, and himselfe at libertie to passe everie waie, or staye at home, at his pleasure. The busied man goeth to the Courte, to the Royal Exchange or Markett, his mynde full fraught with affaires and contentious suits. The Solytarie Man at his owne leasure walketh into the woodes, the fielde or garden, silently meditating of what he liste, and when he thinketh good retorneth home.

The busied man seeketh out the proud Pallace of Potentate, or resorteth unto the terrible tribunal of Judges, there to affirme matter of truth mixed with falsehood, endeavoringe to oppresse the innocent or incorrage the offendor and finally to mayntaine somewhat to his owne shame or the perill of another. In the meane space his Conscience byteth (which happilie by his owne stammeringe tonge appeareth). For ofte tyme thinkinge to affirme falsely, he uttereth a truth, producinge one worde for another. And so blushinge or become pale, hee telleth on his tale, and endevoringe to shewe eloquence, declareth himselfe a Drounken Dounce. At length the busines done, home he goeth, desiringe to hide himselfe. The Solytarie Man walkinge alone in holsome Fieldes, and finding a pretie hill garnished with pleasant flowers, there he setteth himselfe downe. Then beholdinge the Sommit he prayeth and prayseth God in puritie of hearte and fervor of true devotion, castinge awaie all malice and envie, with everie other vice: till seeing the Son hie, he retorneth home; desiringe of God noe more than the Satericke Poet wished, *Mens Sana, in Corpore Sano.*

CA. 4.

The busied Man at dinner tyme cometh home, and sodenly his Servantes swarme aboute him: being sett downe, they furnishe everie place with chayres and stooles, and as yt were burie him with softe guyshinges. Then shall you heare the noyse of Dogges, Men, Familiers and Flatterers. In this confusion the table is prepared, and by motion of many feete, the plate, the cheares, Stooles and Carpetts of Silke are defiled with dust. In the meane space the poore servantes attende tremblinge, then the Cookes begin to playe their partes, and sett fourth their service of fleshe and fishe, provided and fetched from Sea and Lande, from Mountaines Playnes and Rivers. Which cates boyled, baked, rosted, fryed and changed in their nature, doe raise a marvelous savor. After these preparacions, thether is brought Ale, Beare, and Wyne, both sweete and sower: with other made Drinkes to please the pallett. Besides these he entertayneth his gueastes with rare sightes: as horrible Beastes, strange Fishes, Apes, Owles, Mermasetts, Munckeys, Babbions, out-landish Birdes, and Beastes: as Woolfes, Tigers, Beares, Cockes of Turkie and I[ce]land Doggs perfumed: with other Monsters, some eatinge ravenously, and other brasting their Gorges loathsomely. So have you all sortes of delicates to please the taste and likewise other sightes to contente the eye: as it were a new Ovidian Chaos.

> Frigida pugnabunt calidis, humentia siccis,
> mollia cum duris, sine pondere habentia pondus.

Nowe amonge the multytude of these divers delicates and exquisite Cates composed of matter (in nature contrarie) reasonably may yt be doubted least poysoned or some unholsome morcell maie be taken, for discoverie whereof a taster is appointed and against other subtillties, other remeadies provided. Duringe the dinner tyme, this busie Bassa sitteth malancolie, and frowninge, as lyttle delighted with the smell and savor of so many, divers meates, and happily haveing the night before surfited, or by that morninges affayres offended, eateth without pleasure and sitteth without ease. Sweatinge, belchinge and yawninge, he tasteth of everie dishe, yet loathing all.

The Solytarie Man contented with fewe meates (and fewer

Servantes) haveinge the day before eaten moderately at his owne table and there meanly, yet cleanely furnished, ornefieth his Howse with no greater pompe then his owne presence. In steede of tumulte, he hath a small compaine, in steede of noyes, he useth silence, for want of familiers he is accompanied with himselfe. He is his owne companion: with himselfe he enterteyneth himself, and so he and himselfe doe eate together. His house is made of claye, the walles cleane, and poorely cladd. His buildinge not framed of stone, but of wood, covered with noe coste. There are noe roofes of silver or goulde, neyther be the Flores covered with carpetts or silke, yet maye he from thence behould the Heaven, which prospecte excelleth all others. Hee treadeth upon the Earth, not on purple silke: his Musike noe more then sweete Psalmes, with giving thanks to God, his purveyor noe other then a poore Baker, his Cooke a sillie woman. What they offer him thereof he eateth moderately, accomptinge yt pretious. All other Cates caught in woodes or farr fetched from fieldes and Rivers he doth not desire. Such is his fare, thankfull to God and Man: contented he is with common foode, not bought with money nor provided with muche payne: esteeminge his fare, not by the cost, but his owne appetite. He envieth noe man, nor hateth any bodie, but contente with his fortune, holdeth himselfe secure. He feareth nothinge, nor desireth any thinge. His cuppes are of earth and free from poyson. He knoweth true riches is to desire nothinge, and the most mightie commaunde to obay noe bodie. His life is pleasant and peaceable. He passeth the night in sound sleape and the daie in delightfull accion. He feasteth without feare and liveth in libertie. Att home he sitteth secure, and abroade he walketh without mistrust. He knoweth himselfe, and not his goodes to be loved. Noe man desireth his death, but euerie one wisheth him life. Neyther doth he wishe to live longe, but to die well. He careth not where he ende his daies, but how and in what sorte. The some of his endeavor is not more, but having finished the fable of life, to close the same up with a commendable ende: as the Florentine poet said. *Un bel muorire tutta la Vita honora.*

CA. 5.

The daye doth passe, and untarieinge tyme slippeth awaie. Dynner beinge done, the busied man is troubled by a multytude of familiars, Sutors and Servantes, some frends and some Foes. Then is he offended with fallinge downe of plate, breakinge of Tables, or some other part of his furniture: or haply disturbed by cryinge out of some drunkard. For the tables of Rich men are ever used to this inconvenience, that amonge many geastes some have not their fill and others eate till they be sicke: because fewe doe feede temperately. In the meane tyme the Hall smelleth unsavorly, and everie rome loathsome to beholde. In one place is wine spilte, in another Fishe caste, or bones lefte. So may the dyninge place be most truely called a slaughter house, then a Hall of civill metinge. The Compaine thus filled with aboundance of meate, and Drinke, or loathed with sight or sente of a fowle Howse, they departe to their Chambers, bearing about them a surcharged Stomacke, and perhapps a troubled conscience also.

Far otherwise is yt with the solitarie Man who beinge a companion more meete for Angells then riotouse Men, appeareth with a sweete breath and good complexion. His diet is moderate, his conversation sober, his table untroubled, never loaden with superfluitie, never prepared for Gluttonie, nor at any tyme uncleane. There is all waies modest mirth, and beastialitie banished. There Temperance is Ladie and Misteris, there the bedde be sweete and chaste.

But the busied Man riseth from dinner, eyther drunke or surcharged with eatinge, his geastes also become sicke or in distemper. But the solitarie Man sitteth secure, never exceedinge the measure of frugallitie. The riotous Man is ever angrie, or seldome in perfecte patience. But the Solitarie Man escheweth all the distempers and liveth securely to himselfe. The busied Man consumeth his tyme in sensualitie, sleepe and idle cogitacions. But the Solitarie Man singeth prayses unto God and entertayneth himself with liberall studdie: eyther inventinge some what newe or callinge to minde what he had before seene or read. Content he is with his owne, and more doth not desire. *Contentus rebus suis, certissime divitiae.*

CA. 6.

The Sonn assended to the highest, and the daie become warme, the busied man falleth to preatinge, and finding faulte at everie thing. He is all waies fearefull and full of doubte least somewhat is lefte undon. For this propertie is common to Men that desire earnestly, that they are ever impatient. Whatsoever such a Man wisheth, maie not be deferred a momente. Which is the cause that he whoe desireth to be riche quickly is ever angrie: for noe vice can suffer restraint, because temeritie is joyned to precipitacion. Contrariwise the Solitarie Man doth all thinges with deliberacion, never forgettinge such circumstances as appertaine to everie accion, and cheifely he liveth prepared for Death: ever hopeing from the fountaine of Gods inexhausted mercie, to be comforted. *Deo servire, libertas est.*

CA. 7.

The day spent and eveninge come, the busied Man is forced againe to walke the Streetes and search out those Men with whome he hath converse. Then the night neare at hand, hee retorneth homewarde, musinge what proffitt he hath made that day, and what somes of money he is to receive: forgettynge what good fame he hath lost, and how greatly he hath charged his conscience. But certen yt is, that in exchange of gould he hath gayned dishonest reputacion, and parcase some burden of conscience also. Duringe these doinges the Solitarie Man beholdeth the highe Mountaines, the shaddowed Rivers, or Sea-Shoare, rejoysinge to have spent the daie without Sinne or Shame. Then as one securely armed againste the perill of night, and assaultes of the Divell, he taketh in hande the Targett of Fayth, and with all humblenes of hart recommendeth himselfe to God: and so retorneth to his owne howse, assured that daie to have made no dishonest proffitt, nor coveted any. But as the busied Man doth daiely endevor to spoyle the livinge, so the

Solitarie Man prayeth for the quicke, and prayseth God for the Dead. The one maketh Martiers, the other doth ymitate the Saintes. The one honerith good Men, the other doth torment them. The one excludeth evill compaine, the other doth embrace them. *Facilius est excludere peruitiosa quam regere.*

CA. 8.

When night is come the busied man beinge in authoritie, retorneth home in pompe: accompanied with a greate trayne as yt were to the funerall of a quicke corpes. When he draweth nere the Howse, Trompetts, Sagbotts, Cornetes, and other winde Instruments doe sounde. After this solemne Musicke, he dismounteth from Horse, richly attyred and sweetely perfumed. Beinge entered the Howse he is fourthwith buried in costly guyshinges and there sitteth downe, for the most parte, sittinge. Then he calleth for a solemne supper which being added unto an undisgested dinner, causeth a certen loathsome satietie. But contrariwise, the Solitarie Man persuadeth himselfe ofte tyme to have supped without eatinge, or governeth his appetite accordinge to the diet which *Plato* used. For saide hee, I will in nowise fill my belly twise a daie. Howsoever he eateth, noe doubte his meale is moderate, but the busied Man tasteth of everie dishe thoughe his stomack abhorr them all. *Fastidientis stomachi est, multa degustare.*

CA. 9.

With all temperance, the Solitarie Man commaundeth his appetite: but the busied Man farr otherwise disposed, goeth to bedd full of cares, full of meates, full of wyne, full of feares, full of anger: swelled and offended with himselfe: disquiet in minde, besett with Servantes, Companions, and followers: saluted with letters, and called upon by Messengers, his Fame in question, his person terefied, and his minde perplexed, abused by lyes, tyred with peticions, and tempted with Divells. His mynde thus occupied, he findeth himselfe combersome to Neighbours, formedable to inferiors, uncomefortable to frendes, of all Men suspected, of noe Man assured. So after some slomberinge he revesteth his bodie with costly clothinge. Then as one having made proofe of all pleasures, and loathed with his owne familiers, he desireth to entertaine others: yet at laste overwearied with watchinge, is surprised with sleepe: but his inward cares doe ever watch, his troubled mynde doth seldome reste, and that which is the greatest tormente, he burnynge fyer and ever livinge worme of conscience, doth never cease to eate. Besides these secrete molestacions, he is troubled with remembrance of Suitors whome he abused, of poore Men whom he oppressed, of Tenants whose Fermes he hath taken from them, of Virgins whome he deflowred, of young Men whom hee cozoned, of Wyddowes whom hee ruyned, of Innocentes whome he sterved. All which furies and revengers of impietie his conscience continewally feeleth. But the Solitarie Man liveth full of joye, full of hope, never in furie as *Nisus,* but like unto Peter the Apostle full of conscience, full of integritie, full of securitie, and feare of God. He is not troubled with surfetinge, but liveth alone, silent and peaceable. He is terrible to noe Man, but loved of all Men. Noe bodie entereth his Chamber ympudently or sodenly breaketh his sleape. His rest is sweete, his quiet never interrupted. His dreames not troubled with offensive visions, but entertayned with sweete thoughtes and pleasing cogitacions. For certen yt is, that as the vertues of mynde (cheifly temperance) doth much conserve bodylie health, so intemperate diet greatly hindereth the good Estate hereof. *Temperantia possessio bonorum.*

CA. 10.

Hetherto we have described, as well the busie as the Solitarie Man: behold them seriously and by consideringe their contrarie qualities you may conceive how all Men live. This onely I add, that as the labor of the one is more then I can expresse, so the quiet of the other exceedeth all happines: the one hath travell without ende, the other enjoyeth rest and securitie. But most infortunate be they that are employed in business of other Men, for they are governed as others directe, and what they must doe, is to be looked for in an other Mans eyes. They dwell in other Mens Howses, they sleepe not when they woulde, but when they maye and eate when others doe. Yea that which most is, they sigh or smyle as others shall please to commaunde. They negotiate other Mens affayres and neglecte their owne: they live for others not for themselves. Which the Saterike Poet seemeth to note, writing to a friende in Courte thus

> Si te propositi nondum pudet atque eadem mens est,
> ut bona summa putes aliena vivere quadra.

Certenly I finde this onely difference betwene those that live servantes to meane Masters, and others attendinge great Princes. Which is no more, but that the one is tyed in fetters of Iron, the other in gyves of goulde. The one weareth a simple coate, the other a riche Liverie, but theire bondage is like, and he is most to be blamed, whoe doth that by election, which others are constrayned unto. Therefore in myne opinion those busied Men are most in miserie, that live at others commaunde, and their owne coste, not unlike the poore Plowman that soweth corne whereof not he, but his landlorde eateth the breade. The Apostle sayeth whoe planteth a Vine and hopeth not to gather the grapes? Yet some comforte it is to plant for posteritie. For albeit the Planter aspecteth noe profitt himselfe, yet willingly he doth what he ought. Cicero sayeth the Husbandman asked for whome he sowed Corne, answered, for the Gods ymmortall. Howe miserable then are they that sowe corne and hope of noe better cropp then labor. But theise Men cannot ympute their calamitie to any other but themselves because wittingly and willingly they give theire libertie to others reserving to themselves onely base bondage. Neyther doe they labor for God, but offende him, to please Men. Yea they endevor to inriche those by whome ofte tymes they are oppressed. In which case, the best comeforte is to suffer patiently. *Lenimentum omnium malorum, est pati.*

Ca. 11.

By that hath bine formerly saide yt appeareth, that all Men busied, are generally unhappie; and cheifely they that have in hande the affayres of other Men. Because those Men beare the burden of theire owne miserie and other Mens also, and thereby reape noe commoditie at all. Yet have there bine (and parcase some are) exceedingly well occupied. For by theire endevor, themselves and other also have taken profitt. And what can be more pleasinge to God then to healpe other Men. Which whoe so refuseth to doe beinge able, semeth to omitt the office of humanitie and incurr the infamie of unnaturall. Cicero sayeth yt is a life accordinge to nature to healpe and preserve, yf it be possible, all Men livinge. By imitacion of Hercules, whoe for the fame of his admirable labors was admitted into Heavenly Counsell, suche busines noe doubt, ought bee preferred before Solitarie life. Notwithstandinge I suppose a few examples of Men so well deservinge shall not cansell the commendacion dewe to Solytude. For many take in hande affayres vulgarly reputed profitable, and some professe devote Solytude: but whoe doth fully performe soe much as he promiseth? Some saye a fewe, some say divers, but shewe me one. Well I knowe that Clerkes exclayme against Vice and extoll vertue: yet I feare that not one of them can clerely escape the Satires tooth. But you say that learned Men speake that whereof others take profitt. I doe also so thinke, but Phisition himselfe is not ever cured by that medecyne he ministreth to others. I mislike not reasons wittily framed. Of every Artificer I commende a skillfull peece of worke. But this we have in hande is not a schoole of art or eloquence, but a rule and order of life. Neyther doe we affecte commendacion of well speakinge, but endevor the perfeccion of a quiet mynde. I forget not the counsell of Seneca, saying lay aside all lettes and labor to gett a good mynde, where unto noe Man doth attaine that is bound to busines. Neyther can solitude enforce to felicitie, though I suppose that thereby yt is conserved, as the same Author semeth to affirme, sayinge place helpeth lytle to make the mynde quiet, yet doth it offerr furtherance. In one other place also he writeth thus: we ought both for health of bodie and manners to chuse a holesome habitacion. Hee likewise sayth flee from Courte and nere abidinge thereunto. For as the thicke ayre offereth indisposition to sounde bodies, so is it unholesome for corruptible myndes. If then such is the difference, how can it so be, if no cause thereof proceeded from the place? Somewhat therefore I certenly thinke is in the place and with Seneca his patience, be it saide verie muche, yet not all. For the cheife cause as himselfe sayth is in the mynde. *Animus est, qui sibi commendat omnia.*

CA. 12.

As before we said of place, so in the minde somewhat there is which causeth quietnes. Yet neyther in the one, nor in the other consisteth all; but onely soe muche as by the one opertunitie is offered, and the other yieldeth reason. Quiet of mynde is a devine guifte, proceedinge from God. This guifte of grace is most tymes bestowed on those that live solytarie, as hath bine shewed and by examples shall be hereafter proved. For everie Man capable of truth, will confesse that whoe so converseth with the Worlde is pleased with applause and loveth to be admired: but Man's soule intendeth cheifely one thinge, and neglecteth manie. Hereof it cometh that eloquent Men are in accion slowe, and such as be but blunt in speeche, performe the greatest accions. Likewise Men of modestie do flee from pleasures, and they that affecte pleasure, contemne modeste manners. Men carefull of private thrifte, are careles of publike affayres: and others musinge muche of matters publike, forgett their private busines. One winde serveth not to sayle contrarie wayes. Then marvell not thoughe in this worldly navigation you finde the like effecte. He that loveth busines delighteth in bable, but contemplacion is cupled with silence. Therefore as the busie Man shooneth solitude, so they that live retired mislike muche speakinge. Hee that converseth with fewe Men, neede not be troubled with great busines. *Vivi tibi, tecumq[ue]: habita nec grandia tentes.*

CA. 13.

Each man with himselfe should determine what course of life to take. For ympossible it is that all men should ayme at one ende. Everie one therefore is to consider what squareth most fitly with his nature, and what manner of man he desireth to be. For as we commende the solitarie life, so others doe hold it discomfortable and wourse then death itselfe: which conceite doth sonest possesse the unlearned. For everie Man ignorant of letters and wantinge a companion to conferr with, knoweth not what to saie unto himselfe. But the learned Man, at all tymes, and in all places, can intertayne himselfe with readinge, or rumynatinge upon somewhat he had formerly founde in bookes. Therefore Solitude without learning is to those men not lesse displeasinge then exile, imprisonment and torture. But to him that is learned, everie place is as his owne countrie, libertie and delight. Cicero sayth *Quid dulcior, otio literato?* and *Seneca* writeth, *Otium sine litteris mors est, et vivi hominis sepultura.* Nowe albeit theise noble Philosophers so highly have commended solitude, yet some lovers of learninge did nevertheless delight to live in accion and converse among the multitude. Theise were they that yielded themselves prisoners unto pleasure, or such as followed affayres for gayne, or ells those men that ambitiously desired the acquaintance and love of people, thereby to aspire unto honor and office: of which persons in everie Kingdome and Commonweale is noe small number. Amonge those Men learninge is used, not as a light and comfort of life, but as a crafte or skill to compasse wealth and worldly promotion. For in experience wee finde, that parentes so mynded, do use to inforce their sonnes to learne cheifely for profitt, whereby yt appeareth that they are sente not to a schoole of knowledge, but be instructed how to make profitt. And no Man neede to doubte, that learninge thus gotten is ever covetously and corruptly used: because the intention of him that is learned was to sell, and paye his paynes with excessive profitt. I exhort not such Men to live solitarie, nor yf they woulde should be permitted. For as Fishes out of water, so those Men from Citties and Compaine knowe not how to live: because they are not delighted with honest ease, nor desirous of quiet, whereby they are combersome to themselves. But the best is, that beinge wearie in Solitude or intised with Townishe pleasure, they sone retourne to the Cittie. Neyther will I persuade any frende (where is suche disproportion of mynde and diversitie of delightes) to doe as myselfe doth. For as is before saide, Solitarie life is onely fitt for men learned, or lovers of vertue. *Otium sine litteris mors est.*

CA. 14.

Whoeso resolveth to alter the order of life, or desireth to retire, must therein proceed accordinge to nature, and not followe his owne vayne fancie. Neyther ought he to take that waie which sodenly semeth best, but that which squareth most fittly with naturall inclinacion. It therefore behooveth a man to be a severe sensor of himselfe. For some have I sene so desirous to ymitate an other, as they forgott themselves, and were laughed to scorne. This onely and specially I have taken from Philosophers, that everie Man eyther in private or publike conversation, must grace himselfe with that is properly and naturally his owne. For my parte I finde my disposition farr differinge from the people. I affecte learninge not to boast thereof, but delight myselfe as becometh a lover of Solitarie life. I use not bablinge nor delighte in drowsines. All myne endevor is to studie privately, without ostentacion, without hope of rewarde or expectacion of profitt. I flee from Banquetts, Suppers, playes, and other Cittie pleasures: and this have I done not by perswation of other men, but the instigacion of nature inciting me to solitarie life: because I thinke yt good and secure. Let other men finde theire owne humours, myne owne I knowe. Tumultuous companie and busines by all endevor I shoone: yet so, as if necessitie doe drawe me to the Cittie, I have learned to be solitarie amides the multitude: and in the grestest tempest, I knowe howe to save my selfe in the haven of Solitude. Such is my resolucion grounded upon experience, and supported with authoritie of Auntient Authors: whose opinion is that silence and solitude do make the minde free. I neede fewe thinges and desire not muche. *Parvo contentus non eget mendicitate.*

CA. 15.

Everie Man in his grenest yeares ought to make choice of that life which fitteth best with his natural disposition and judgment, and not depart from that path unlesse by urgent reason he be enforced. Such a resolucion was made by Hercules, as Xenophon sayth. But because we take not that waie, but followe the untrue steppes of other Men, we wander as blinde Men do without a gyde and knowe not where we are or would be. Therefore yf fortune or false election hath caused us to err in youth, I woulde wishe (even in ould age) like a Traveller out of his waie, we should retorne into the right waie, and close up our lives accordinge to Judgment, Temperance and Pietie. This resolucion is profitable, and possible. And lett noe man thinke that late, whicħ he knoweth good. Of which minde were many learned Philosophers and Princes. *Augustus Caesar* was wont to saie, *Sat cito fit, quicquid fiat satis bene,* and *Plato* writeth, *Beatum cui etiam in senectute contigerit ut sapientiam verasque opiniones assequi posset.*

CA. 16.

Albeit I have heretofore commended Solitude, yet will I add that the Solitarie Man in his Howse exerciseth himselfe daily in prayer and godly contemplation, wherewith he useth the studie of Philosophie, both devine and humane. Also for recreacion, he is ofte pleased with Musicke and conversinge with frendes, contemneth not to entertayne theire companie at playe: theise are his domesticall exercises. In Fieldes and Woodes he is never wourse imploied then in Hawkinge, Huntinge, Fishinge, and Fowlinge: in which places and actions noe man needeth to attire his person in silke or perfume his Garmentes with sweete savors. There are noe princes whome he neede to please: there is no body to abuse him, there may he speake truely without disgizinge, there is he subjecte to noe commaundement, but his, whose sighte perceth the darkest desert. There, is noe Poyson of the bodie, nor corruptinge of the minde. There is he not forced to flater the people, nor admire the magestrates. There needeth he not bowe his knee to betters, nor adore any but God above: for it is written, *Si simplex fuero hoc ipsum ignorabit anima mea.* Thus ever well occupied, he shooneth the snares of Satan, and assisted with Gods ayde, repulceth all his assualtes. So livinge securely, he inhabiteth a Castle inexpugnable. Percase everie Man is not apt to like of such a life, and thoughe reason do drawe many, yet noe Man is forced. Thought is free, which libertie I assume to myselfe and may not denie yt to others. When all is done, mans life is but labor and vanitie. *Omnis vita supplitium.*

CA. 17.

Plotinus, a philosopher, and follower of *Plato,* distinguished the vertues into foure degrees, amonge which the vertues politicall doe houlde the lowest place, as most fitt for Men of action, whose endevor is the health and hapines of a weale publike. The next are the vertues contemplative which be cheifely in Men that live solitarie and retyred. For as the former doe temper the passions, so theise Men will not be moved. In the third degree, are the vertues of a perfitt and pure minde, the propertie whereof is to contemne those perturbacions which the vertues politicall had qualified and the vertues purgatorie hath utterly extirped. These are onely in persons of perfeccion: but where they are I knowe not. Yet certen yt is, that yf anie suche have bine, they were lovers of private and solitarie life. The fourth and most excellent vertues are onely in men exemplarie, because theire lives are lefte as a rule to all posteritie, or as *Plato* sayth, such vertues are ideas imprinted in the memorie of Man, by God. For they neede noe other lawe because they live (as it were) faultlesse. *Perfecta virtus lege non eget.*

CA. 18.

What joye and contente yt is to possesse present pleasure, and live in hope of better: and in exchange of shorte solitude, to live ever in companie of Angells, beholdinge the face of God, whoe can expresse. For that is the ende of our desires and wishing. In exchange of mourninge there is rejoysinge. Instead of temporall fastinge, there is celestial feastinge. In supplie of povertie there is true riches. For rurall silence there is heavenly musicke. Then shall we see what is lost and what we have founde: there shall we enjoye comeforte not comprehensible, and be acquite of worldly woes and all miserie. There are devine cogitacions, spirituall companie, blessed visions, and Christ himselfe: for he is ever presente, that is in all places ever: as the scripture sayth, *si ascendero in caelum, tu illic es, si discendero ad infernum ades.* Hee seeth us in darknes and heareth us before wee speake. He is that celestiall spirite, which saide unto Moses, why doste thou cry out unto me, thy prayers and love hath comm unto me. He knoweth from farr our thoughtes, that is before they are. He heareth our prayers before they be pronounced. Hee seeth our necessities before they come. He foureknoweth our end, before we be borne. He loveth us, allthoughe we are unworthie, and taketh pittie of us: yf our obstinacie doe not refuse his commisseracion. *Pietas in caelum via.*

CA. 19.

Whoesoever is persuaded that God beholdeth all, and beareth witnes what he doth, needeth not any other testimonie of his doinges. *Epicurus,* albeit for some opinions evell reported, writinge to a frend, saide, do ever so as yf Epicurus did see thee. *Marcus Cicero* likewise, in an Epistle which he writeth to his Sonne, amonge many excellent perswations to vertue, concludinge sayth, easily shall thou doe well, so longe as thou thinkest upon me, whome thou endevors to please. Imagine then, I am alwaies with thee, and at all tymes present. Certenly a wise companion doth muche profitt a generous mynde, and remembereth him contynewally to meditate upon vertue. In like sorte, *Seneca* exhorteth *Lucilius* his dearest frende, ever to presuppose the presence of some reverende person, sayinge, *Prodest sine dubio custodem sibi imposuisse, et habere quem respitias, quem inter-*

esse tuis cogitationibus judices. Addinge that what so he did, to do yt so, as yf other men were presente: and committ thyselfe to be governed by some grave personage, as Cato, Scipio, or Lelius: in whose sight he would be ashamed to doe evill. Touchinge a witnes imaginarie, lett this suffise. But a Christian needeth none of theise witnesses: knowinge himselfe looked upon by God and his Angells. *St. Augustin* sayth, yt is the propertie of a noble mynde, to separate the Soule from the Sences, and devide the cogitacions from custome. Let us then with all endevor captivate our sensuall appetites and (custome vanquished) be holly governed by the Soule. Let us open our inward eyes, for so shall wee see the glorious presence of God. *Marcus Cato* refused to beholde a Man to die. Howe muche more ought a Christian to be ashamed (in Gods presence) to see a Man live evill, or committ any dishonest action before so greate a witnes as cannot be deceaved, and is ever livinge. Hee is all waies and everie where present: he heareth everie thinge and seeth whatsoever is don. Hee is present in all places, and noe where more easilye founde and spoken unto, then in solitude. For there is noe clamor, nor intisinge sightes to divert the mynde from celestiall cogitacions: God and a good conscience beholdeth all. *Conscientia mille testes.*

CA. 20.

But omittinge to saye more of that matter, albeit we are by thee (o God) created, to the ende we should rest in thee, otherwise unfortunately borne: yet howe muche are we also to esteme those thinges which be as it were common: I meane to wander where we will, to enjoye the pleasure of gardens and Fieldes, to repose in the shadowe, to warme us at the fiere, to eate when we are hungrie, drinke when we are thirstie, and (that which exceedeth all) to live as we liste: and in all Seasons and places to be our owne: farr from troubles, and tumultuous companie, never compelled, never enforced, nor commaunded: never convited to feastes, never provoked to speake, desiringe to be silent, never combered with companie nor bound to converse with the people. For whoe woulde be gazed on as a Monster? Whoe would be marked with what grace he goeth? Whoe woulde be noted with what countenance he enterteyneth? Whoe woulde be observed in all his jestures? Whoe woulde be tyred with busines? or growe olde in the multitude? Whoe woulde busie his braine with infinite matters? Whoe woulde sweate in Winter, or be bounde to sitt at home in Sommer? Whoe woulde be tyred with busines, or made wearie of those Men we love? Hate our selves and be so imployed in other mens affaires, as to neglecte our owne? The Apostle sayth to the Romaynes, there is none of us that liveth to himselfe, and noe man dieth to himselfe. Yf we live, we ought to live to the Lorde, or yf we die we ought to die to the Lorde. So livinge or dyinge to ourselves, is to live and dye in the Lorde. In the meane tyme as from a Watchtower we may behoulde the troubles of Men and treade them under foote. Let us observe what other Men doe, and chiefelie our selves: so as, old age at hande, we may be prepared: and in the meane, take order that our bodies be sounde, and our myndes quiet: ever restinge resolved this life is a shaddowe, an Ostry for Passengers, and noe place of aboade; a common travelled waie, noe countrie of habitacion: no Chamber to rest in, but a lodge to looke whoe passeth: we ought therefore never to desire any thinge present, nor wishe for any thinge to come: patiently sufferinge whatsoever hapeneth, and never forget we are mortall: yet destyned to immortalitie. Then let us remember how all ages have passed, let us also reade what notable men hath heretofore bine, forgevynge and forgettinge all offenders: then elevatinge oure mindes to heaven, let us meditate what is there don, and kindle a desire to assend thether: which is the ende and excellencie of Solitarie life. After these good and godly cogitacions, we shall best know to emploie our tyme in readinge holie scripture, and sometymes solace ourselves with consideringe what was done in former ages, by our forefathers as we finde them recorded: revivinge (so muche as wee can) the memorie of that is lost: never ceasinge to reade and observe the workes of excellent writers. *Lectio certa prodest, varia delectat.*

CA. 21.

We reade that Apollo for his admirable skill in Musicke was reputed a God. Aesculapius likewise for his excellencie in Phisicke, Saturnus and Ceres for Agriculture, Vulcanus for Iron workes, Osiris in Athens and Minerva in Egypt were also honored as Gods, the one for inventinge lynnyng cloath, the other for finding the use of Oyle. If any man aske by what meanes and where those men attayned to so singular knowledge, certen it is they lived in contynewall studdy and Solytude. For what places can be so fitt for contemplation and the Muses, as those which are ever voyde of compaine. In experience we finde that the minde of Man is there provoked to studdie, and the place offereth tyme and laysor. Whereof Artistotle and Plato semeth to allow, saying that for suche purpose, in Egypt the Priestes did dwell divided from other people: to the ende their oportunitie for studie might be the more, and theire chastitie in lesse perill of polution. Of these men Cheremon the Stoicke sayth that settinge aside all affaires they remayned contynewally in the Temple to meditate upon the nature of Planetts and Starrs. They conversed with noe Women, they kepte noe companie with theire Kinsfolke, Frendes, or Children, nor ever did see them, after they had entered into Religion. Also from fleshe and Wyne they refrayned. Wherunto he addeth, that everie thirde daie they fasted, thereby to depresse the motions of lust, which by rest and want of exercise did growe upon them. *Veneris voluptas, pecudum propria.*

CA. 22.

Some Enemies of solitarie life produce for theire assistance *Aenius Seneca,* sayinge *Omnia nobis mala solitudinem persuadent,* and in one other place he writeth, that in solitude evell Counsells are contrived, wicked projectes are moved, audatious resolucions are determined, and all lewde cogitacions are begon: which so beinge, we ought to oppose our selves to *Seneca,* or utterly abandon the defence of Solitude. True it is that Seneca so said, but he applieth his speech to Fooles, or such folke as are oppressed with muche passion: which by his owne wordes after, most playnely appeareth. For said he, we must take heede that men in sorrowe, or feare, be not left alone. If then any man be forbidden solytude, be sure that such passions are causes thereof: so are those sayinges of *Seneca* reconsiled and his counsell in eyther of them, good. But for certen proofe that *Seneca* loved Solitude, yt appeareth in his advise to his dearest frende *Lucilius,* sayinge, flee from the multitude, flee from a fewe, flee from one; which is a counsell of exceedinge bitternes. For albeit I flee from the multytude willingly, and can also flee from a fewer nomber, yet to flee from everie one is the most extreame condition of solitude, because to noe further strait, can I be enjoyned, unlesse I also flee from myselfe: and then I knowe not with whome to converse. For yf I have cause to conferr with you, or any other frende, what were then to be done? And yf I shutt my selfe from all accesse, the most severe lovers of Solitude will call me a stone, or at the least, a man voide of all humanitie. Yea *Seneca* himselfe moved Lucillius to be accompanied with some frende, and I also doe recommende solytarie life, cheifely to wise and learned Men, not to fooles, or others of unsettled mynde. I love the companie of a fewe and flee the concourse of many. *Cum paucis pax laeta manet, turba omnis abesto.*

CA. 23.

Albeit I have muche praysed Solitarie life, yet did I not perswade that for love thereof the bonde of amitie should be broken. I said the concourse of men, not accesse of frendes shoulde be shunned. Yet I will add this caution, that he whoe useth to be frequented with flockes of frendes, shall be sure by some of them to be deceaved. Moreover, as in other thinges, so in frendshipp, some one man is more pleasinge then a nother. Neyther did I perswade the retyred Man to receive all frendes together, but intertayne them some and some, rather then in great troopes: thereby to have solace and comforte, not be pestered or molested. For as frendly familiaritie is sweete, so exceese of complementes is combersome. From which meane whoe so departeth shall seme to have learned noe curtesie in the Cittie, but is come to the Countrie a Beare or a Lyon: the meane course therefore is to be kepte. For some men are not contente unlesse they live amides the multytude, whoe are to be pittied. One other sayeth flee from all Men, and live alone. To such a one I wott not what to saye, for as hee pleadeth the authoritie of *Seneca,* so the other is contrarie to Mans nature. *Cicero* discoursing the nature of frendshipp, sayth that amytie is of all thinges most pleasant: and proveth that neyther man of sower disposition, nor they that flee the compaine of others (as scarce one such can be founde) but he will seeke some bodie, though no frende, to whome he may utter the abondance of his bitternes. To this purpose also tendeth the sayinge of Archita the Tarentyne, for (quoth he) there is nobodie in so great aboundance or blisse, nor so much favored of the heavens, but desireth to be accompanied: at the least with some one, to whome he maye impart his minde. So appeareth yt that nature loveth not to be alone. Therefore concludinge we saye that such a solytude as we commende, is neyther to mingle with the multytude, nor be so retyred as to deserve the name of inhumayne. *Seneca* said flee from the thronge, but he said not flee from such companions of whom thou may learne or be instructed. For whoe so excludeth all companie, shall finde solitude extreamely sower and irksome. My solitude therefore shall not be troubled with the companie of frendes but rather comforted. Fynally, yf needes I must forgoe all companie, then had I rather forsake solytude, then be left all alone. My resolucion therefore is, that noe Man should be so solytarie, as to abandon the companie of Frendes. *Seneca* sayth, *Nullius boni sine sotio jucunda possessio.* I therefore admitt frendes and exclude all evell companie. I also hate the odious solytude of *Tiberius,* whoe in the Isle of Caprea kepte continewally a shopp of creweltie and lust, beinge (himself) an olde man beastially desposed. Likewise the solitarie life of Servilius Vatia is ridiculous, for he (all his life) lurked, and became olde nere unto the hills of Cumea in the kingdom of Naples. He was famous onely for his unprofitable laysor, never removeinge from his owne house. *Gloriari otio, mea ambitio.*

Ca. 24.

For so muche as action and affayres are accompanied as well with adverse as good fortune, whoso retyreth himselfe to solytude may here recounte in silence, what toyle and tribulacion he hath formerly endured, and herein take joie: sayinge with Vergill, *haec olim meminisse juvabit.* Sweete is yt to remember passed perrills. For noe prosperitie is so perfecte, but sometymes doth perticipate of misadventure. Everie gayne is accompanied with losse, yea the ende of worldly pleasure is for the most part displeasinge and excessive prosperitie is ofte close upp with greate disgrace. Which moved the lamentinge father to saye, *Quam metui ne quid Libiae tibi regna nocerent?* Whereunto he addeth, in howe great pleasure and securitie are they that live a private life. So semeth yt that the solitarie Man is provedent, and ever prepared for all fortunes. *Vivit presentibus laetus, futuris securus.*

Ca. 25.

But passinge more perticulerly to other troubles, do you not thinke yt a pleasure to be acquit of so many other molestacions which almost everie Cittie dweller is forced to endure? Not onely such as one man offereth to an other, but also by those discordant thoughts which eyche Man findeth in his owne mynde. For whoe so observeth the troopes of people, metinge them in the streetes, shall heare them use the Grammarians complainte, which is, I am wearie, I am troubled, I repent: or as *Terence* said, I knowe not what to doe, I beleve everie thinge, and cheifely that which is newest. But if theise men did knowe what they did, all complayninge should cease. For whereof are they wearie, but onelie of their owne follie, and ignorance? *Seneca* sayth *Omnis stultitia laborat fastidio sui.* Such Men mislike theire owne lives, and not with out reason, because they cannot resolve, nor perciste in any one mynde, nor live pleased with any thinge that is their owne: as the same author sayth, *Nisi sapienti sua non placent.* They knowe not what to doe, and are ignorant what should be done. Of necessitie there fore they wot not to what end they live. How is it possible they should love their owne lives, not knowinge to what purpose they live. Some men we see to live as though onely for eating they had bine borne, which undoubtedly shall appeare yf you aske, whether yf a Man were by nature so made as he should never neede to eate, never drinke, never sleepe, never gett children, whether he could like better of such a life, or that we now have, beinge ever subjecte to many necessities? Surely as ofte as I have heard the question propounded, rarely did I see that any man would preferr a life so happie before this present miserie. Whereunto they ever answered (as boastinge of theire owne madnes) what should we doe yf meate, drinke and sleepe be taken from us? And what a life shall we leade, the actions of livinge beinge gone? Whereby is most impudently confessed, that men live to no other ende, then that which is common to all livinge creatures. Thus is appeareth, they thinke that tyme not employed in eatinge, drinkinge, sleape, and sensuall pleasure, is utterly lost. As though honest accion, contemplacion, exercise of vertue, and studdie of letters, were tyme not well spent. But certen it is that men so beastially minded are ever inwardly afflicted. *Sceleris in scelere supplitium est.*

Ca. 26.

Some Men wee see from theire youth so delighted with lascivious pleasure, as no maturitie of age can drawe them to deciste from such follies. And albeit they take no delight therein, and indeede disprise it, yet by some foule and filthie endevor they contynewe theire long accustomed vices. Not unlike to infortunate travellors almost tyred, doe notwithstandinge love the waye, and desire still to travell. So theise Men longe used to incontynencie, are content sometymes to confesse theire faulte. Yet is that done with such difficultie, as rather by shame then judgment, they yield to reason. Of which men St. Augustine in his booke of true religion writeth thus. They regarde not their health, and had rather eate then be satisfied: they had rather use incontinencie then indure provocation. They had rather sleepe then wake: they had rather be thirstie to drinke, then modestly to take so much as may content nature. The same author addeth, whoe woulde be drie, or whoe woulde be hungrie? But onely he that pleaseth his pallett, and would be provoked to appetite, ever forgettinge the paines that follow such sensuall pleasure. For no man is so farr from wishinge his owne health, as can patiently abide payne: yet sayth he, theise Men cease not to desire such pleasures as are the beginninge of paine and sicknes. It is therefore certen, that as everie effecte followeth the cause, so in lovinge sensuall pleasure, the effecte of paine is conteyned: and concludinge terribly (he sayth) that suche Men do ende their delightes with weepinge and gnashinge of teeth. Thus it appeareth that from the cause the effecte cometh: and because they loved to satisfie provocacion, they gayned greefe. Besides these reasons the godly man produceth often admonitions against the love of sensuall pleasure, but popular error doth not let them to be beleved: whereby the greatest nomber of Men, eyther willingly or constrayned by common custome, (like unto brute beastes) do subjecte themselves to the appetites of the bodie, or neglectinge the minde, doe live contrarie to rule of reason. Hereof it cometh that a man hateth his owne life, from hence proceedeth his wearines, from hence arise his disquiet thoughtes then which noe mortall man, in this life can induce more torment. Noe marvell then that the manners of such men are sensuall, and theire counsell inconsiderate. What they bigone, before the ende, doth displease. They wot not what they woulde, nor stand firme without staggeringe. But as no signe of wisdome is so certen, as certenly and ever to affecte one thinge, so inconstancie and wishinge is a most apparant proofe of folly. Hereof Seneca sayth, that yf a Man of such mynde do aske in what haven he should arive, he may be answered, there is noe winde fitt for his purpose: because which waie soever his course is shaped, before he arive, he repenteth and is wearie. Those Men are now merrie now sadd, now humble now proude, now grave now light, now pleasant now sower, and everie hower as changeable as Children: which humor *Horace* thinketh to be also in some ould Men, whose instabilitie is worst of all: because they have libertie, and are protected with authoritie. So by theire example they infecte others: everie age hath his perticuler vice, yet ymitation addeth aptnes to followe other mens evill manners. For whoe did ever err that never ymitated any man, but himselfe? But we desire to excell and exceede others. We covet to goe before those whom we followed, which was (to saye truely) the precept of *Quintilian* the Orator, whoe counselled that everie one should imitate some other man of excellencie in that he desired to learne, and not onely to become equall, but also (yf it were possible) excell him. For, said he, noe man can precisely treade the steppes of another man, but of necessitie shall goe with more speede, or slower. Yet here is to be remembered that Quintilian geveth this reason to Schollers onely, not to all Men generally. For as ymitation of vertue is commendable, so to follow others in vice is reprovable. *In vitia alter alterum trudimus.*

Ca. 27.

If any Man aske from whence wanton and as it were ridiculous variacion in garments and new founde facions doe come, sometymes so longe as hide the heele, and rayse duste from the grounde, and sometymes so shorte as scarsly cover the elbowes or wast: also from whence the alteracion of speech, newe found phrases and affected wordes doe proceede? it may be answered, they were brought hether, by Men not contente with theire ould customes and auntient facyons. For how is it possible that any order of livinge should contynewe amonge men, that yeelde not to be governed by the rule of vertue, discretion and counsell, but are everie day transported with emulacion of other mens inconstancie, whoe scorninge the custome of theire owne countrie imbrace the use and faccion of strange places when any thinge they see that pleaseth theire variable fancie. This is the cause that causeth noe ende of ymitacion. For to suche persons all other Mens are pleasinge, and whatsoever is theire owne they mislike. They wish rather to be any thinge, then that they are. *Seneca* laughed to scorne the affectacion of one *Aruntius,* who endevored in all thinges to ymitate *Salustus,* which semed in those daies, strange. But now everie streete hath his Aruntius and everie place is full of Apes that countrefaite other Men, in speech, garmentes and behavior: soe is noe man determined to be himselfe: and consequently the cause that everie man is most unlike to himselfe. It semeth therefore that is come to passe which many yeares since was written, *Omne in praecipiti vitium stetit.* But noe longer without the exersion of good order can the custome of ymitacion and variacion be endured. Private and solitarie life is free from such follies. Let us therefore exclayming saye, whether will you goe? What madnes maketh you so inclyned to change? Why treade you not the steppes of youre Forefathers? Why doe you ymitate the manners of your enemies, whom heretofore you subdued by armes, and nowe are conquered by theire vices? Retorne to the customes of your Auncestors, and laye aside those of strangers. Endevor to live honestly and contented with comelines. So shall you affecte one thinge and doe ever according to discretion and reason. *Ratio dux fida sophorum.*

Ca. 28.

Next unto affectacion and vayne ymitation in Towne dwellers, yt is a matter markable to see how comebersome, superfluous, and costly a custome yt is amonge them, to visite and feast one another. For whoeso observeth shall finde, that visitacions (eyther for reverence or courtesie) for the most parte, do worke a contrarie effecte and are the cause eyther of unkinde conceite or quarrel. For he that is visited, beinge eyther occupied in more earnest affayres, or not esteminge the person of him that visiteth, geveth so sower a welcome, as ofte tymes the visiter retourneth home evill satisfied: and he that is visited, eyther not pleased with the matter whereof they conferred, or manner of the man, suffereth him to depart with contempt, or at the least lyttle thanked for his labor. Thus theise externall demonstracions of kindnes, hapely well intended, causeth an unkinde evente. The like fortune doth accompany convitacion and Feastes. For rarely or never are all the geastes well pleased, or the Ost that did convite them, well satisfied: the one because they like not their cheare, companie, or places and the other feareth to receive no hartie thankes. For one thinketh he was faintly wellcomed, an other he was placed beneath his inferior. One sayth the Oast never saluted him, an other he never druncke to him, an other he sate not at ease, and other he liked not the meate, an other disprayseth the Coockerie, an other findes faulte with the Wyne, some had not theire fill, some were sicke of over muche eatinge, and finally neyther the Oste honored as he aspected, not the guestes well pleased. Suche is the sequell of banquetes, and feastinge. But the Solitarie Man seeketh no bodie, and shooneth occasion to be sought, unlesse urgent occasion do so require. For idle visitacions are true markes of flatterie, and often visitation discovereth a secret intention to deceive: whereof the Florentine proverbe arose, saying, *Chi te carezza piu che non suole, o ingannato ti ha, o ingannaiti vuole.* As for feastes the solitarie man frequenteth none, but is content with his owne table, and seeketh noe companions superior to himselfe, or baser then are fitt for his qualitie, whereby he is not combered with complementes, nor reputed of abjecte mynde. He desireth nothinge, nor needeth any bodie. *Contentus suo, nihil sperat nec timet.*

Ca. 29.

For so muche as heretofore we have shewed a right waie to others, let us take heede that the blinde do not leade the blinde, for ofte by unknowne waies we are conducted, and by other Mens examples ledd hether and thether, not knowinge what we woulde. For (as is beforesaid) ignorance of the ende is that which troubleth us. A Man unadvised knoweth not what to doe.

Whatsoever he taketh in hande, fourth with he is wearie: because he standeth in doubte and consequently perplexed. Hereof arise inwarde crossinge discourses, continewall discordinge thoughtes, and before any thinge finished, the begynninge repented; so is nothinge fully don. Then he asketh howe the daie may be spente, and (as thoughe the Sonn were slowe) desireth nyghte. How common is that sayinge, let us doe some what, that in the meane space, the daie may passe. But indeed the daie ought be stayed, not driven a waie. To suche Men daie semeth longe, and the nyght longer. For everie life is longe, that is displeasinge. In Winter we wishe for Somer, in Somer we desire Winter: in the Morninge we praye for Nyght, at Nyght we looke for Morninge, and both the one and the other come, we still live discontented. It is written, like as the hart desireth shaddowe, and the Marchant wisheth an ende of his affayres, so have I had idle monethes and nombered by displeasant Nyghtes. Yea, sleepinge I said to myselfe, when shall I rise? And agayne it is saide, Shall I looke for the eveninge or shall I be full of greefe, till yt be darke. Thus spoake Job. The same also do wise Men saye: for they are full of sorrowe, livinge in expectacion and strivinge with nature, finde faulte with tyme. But tyme hath more neede of a bridle, then a spurr. These Men do fare as though Death (which above all thinges they feare) were at hande, and life, which they most wishe for, were past. So loathinge life, they are enforced to desire death. *Mors omnium dolorum finis.*

CA. 30.

But happily you aske to what purpose we neede be troubled? Seeinge the sweetnes of solytarie life, doth preserve us from all molestacions. For the Solytarie Man passeth the tyme present, pleasantly, and expecteth time to come, patiently: never wishinge for the next daye, nor deferringe any thinge till the third daye, which he may do this day. This course he keepeth continewally, for well he knoweth it is a great folly to desire or hope of any thinge that is not in his owne power, and in the meane space neglecte a thinge which is certen. Whoesoever hopeth to have any thinge to morrow, shall never leave hopinge: because the last of all daies wanteth a next daie, and onely the first daie of all dayes, wanted a daie preceadinge. What greater evill can be, then by ever hopeinge, never to rest contented. Not unlike to a hungrie Dogg whoe followinge an Hart (all most at everie stepp) snarleth in vayne, still hopinge to take her in his teeth. Such is a mans estate, that hopeth: for the next daie comm, is noe more the next daie, but a newe next daie appeareth, and so proceedinge everie daie when yt cometh, hath an next daie. Then do we follow that daie, and so everie daie, one precedinge another, the nearnesse doth deceive us: for when any daie is come, it soddenly passeth. In the meane space tyme goeth on, yet so nere, as we are incited to follow that, which this daie might have bine dispatched. But the Solytarie Man resolved to thinke of no perticuler tyme, but his hole life, thinketh no daie or nyght longe, but percase shorter then he woulde. For, being well ymployed, before nyght cometh, his work is don: yet useth hee to add the nyght unto the daye and the daie unto the nyght, yf cause so requier, and make them both as one. Yea he so handleth the matter, as althoughe the tyme passe, yet he useth neyther spurr nor bridle to make more hast or longer tarienge; for his whole endevor is no more, but to live free from hope, free from feare, and free from discontentment. Thus he liveth to daye and (life lastinge) so shall live to morrowe. In the meane tyme the busied man followeth his affayres, doinge as he was woont, hope of what he woulde, deceave and practise. He promiseth himselfe muche, hopeinge to circumvent others to his owne profitt. He knoweth the simplicitie of Men, is such, as they embrace, as well hope, as effecte. But the Solytarie Man seketh to abuse no man, nor disguise himselfe. He observeth all circumstances, what garmentes, what speech and what manners in all ages do best become, and accordingly frameth his facion and behavior. Hee useth no mutacion nor ymitacion, but such as age and discretion do enforme. Hee seeth no bodie whom he will counterfaite, but looketh backe unto Nature, and her he followeth. Of which mynde was Cicero, sayinge, a man that liveth in Solytude, contenteth himselfe with rurall foode, and domesticall delightes and thoughe he want many thinges fitt to ornefie a happie life, yet it is no small comforte that untroubled with concourse of Men, peceably and pleasantly he passeth the whole yeare as one daye. But the busied Man eyther of duetie or curtesie must endevor to please: and the Cittizen leadinge his life in plentie and pleasure, becometh rather wearie of aboundance, then contente with suffitiencie. *Ad saturitatem, non est opus fortuna.*

CA. 31.

It was the opinion of Cato, that a man of generouse mynde, ought not onely to attende honest affayres but also afford himselfe laysor. The same advise Seneca giveth unto all Wisemen perswadinge them to retyre from tumultuouse companie and harbor themselves in the haven of quiet and rest there; to meditate on matters devine. Who so is troubled with any earnest action, compleyneth that tyme stealeth a waie, and Death, unawares, doth over take him. *Aristotle* thought that rest and quiet did make the mynde of Man to become wise. *Plutarch* said that quiet did best become a discreete man: as perswaded, that for exercise of art and studdie, silence and Solytude was necessarie. *Socrates* was of opinion that everie man ought so to governe his life, as of himselfe, not of others, he might take pleasure. *Euripides* was wont to saye the Man that is busied in many thinges, committeth most errors, meaninge cheifely men ambitious and coveteous Persons. *St. Augustin* in his book *de Civitate Dei* writeth thus, *Nemo bonus negotium quaerit, nemo improbus in otioso fructuoso conquiescit,* which is no good Man seeketh busines, nor any evill Man taketh rest in honest laysor. A good mynde (sayd he) seeketh an holy quiet; and Charitie admitteth onely honest busines, otherwise, better to do nothinge.

St. Gregory said the life contemplative is no more, then to love God above all, and thy Neighbour as thyselfe. Which don to rest from earthly action. For as a great faulte yt is to be evell amonge good Men, so is it a great prayse to be good amonge evill Men. Whoso is myndfull of Worldly busines, is forgetfull of Heavenly cares.

Isidorus *de summo bono* sayth, the more affayres a Man hath in hand, the more is he oppressed with vices. Lovers of the World are unwise, not onely in that they covet base thinges in lieu of the best, but also because they enjoye them with sinne. No man sayth Augustin can be ignorant of so muche as apperteyneth to laudable laysor. Evell Men are by lawes forbidden to abuse laysor, and

Barnard sayth, *Otium est vacare Deo, imo negotium negotionum.* It is good laysor to serve God, and the best busines to obaye his commaundements: which ought to be the cheife of all affayres.

Seneca writeth, *Plus agunt, qui nihil agere videntur.* They do most, that are sene to do least.

Volteranus telleth of many excellent Men that for love of honest laysor abandoned worldly dignitie. The same Author writeth of many that were induced to forsake busines and became lovers of Solytude, being resolved with Cicero, *Nullus beatus nisi quietus.*

Ca. 32.

Thus havinge towched the qualitie as well of the Solytarie as busied life, thereunto addinge what is in everie of them to be observed, I saye that who so loveth quiet, accompained with libertie and learninge, shall best do to remove himselfe from tumultuous Townes, Citties, and all other places where people popularly resort. For the more commodious doinge thereof yt behoveth to ymitate great Kinges, Princes and Commaunders, whoe at theire first entrie, do proclayme and prosecute justice, soe severely as thereby to banishe from Courte and Camp all sortes of evell People and mutenouse Souldiers: likewise to drive from them all other persons of lewde life and dishonest profession, as *Scipio* did at Numantia, whoe at his comeinge, sent awaye twoe thousand Strumpetts that followed his Armie.

And with those ministers of Misrule, he banished all Bawdes, Jesters, Juglers, Mynstrells, Stage players, Typlers and other unprofitable persons. By ymitacion of which proceding, albeit we take not upon us to prescibe Lawes or Ordinances for Kingdomes, Citties, and Armies, yet do we endevor a peceable commonweale of mans mynde: and so governe the same, as the preturbacions thereof, may be made obedient to reason, wherein shall appeare how great a Warr and difficultie yet is for Man to governe himselfe. The some therefore that we have in hande is no more but to take charge of our owne Soules, and defend them from sinfull affeccions whereby they perish. For what torment can be greater, then to live distracted in mynde and in the end, to perish everlastingly. Therefore yt behoveth to chase away all unruly affections and lewde libertie, so Horace adviseth, sayinge

Scelerum si bene paenitet.
[eradenda cupidinis]
pravi sunt elementa et tenerae nimis
mentes asperioribus
formandae studiis.

Some endevor to governe a Cittie, others have charge of Souldiers, but our care is to suppresse civill and secret discention in the minde. For do you thinke any Cittie is oftner assaulted then Mans Soule? Or do you thinke that Scipio mett with more terible enemies at Numantia? He fought against one Cittie and one people, but we make warr with the whole worlde, the fleshe and the Divell. Are not theise enimies united and valient, as any whome Scipio incountered? Scipio undertooke the rule and reformacion of an Armie composed of cowardly Captaines and ignorant Souldiers: we have in hande a multytude of corrupte myndes, amonge whome I finde my owne. He labored to establishe a mortall Government, but wee endevor ymmortall honor and presente peace of mynde. If then we preferre the more to a lesse, or our owne, before other mens quiet, with how great care ought we reciste the ympeachments of our tranquilitie? But saye you how may this be done? Marry by banishinge vice, which neyther Kinges nor Lawes could yet do. So are we forced by some other art to remove mischeves of muche difficultie: which is to take awaye insolencie from rich Men, thefte from Servantes, lamentinge from poore Men, envie from inferiors, pride from fortunate folke, corruption from Tribunalls, Wantonnes from Courte, fraude from Advocates, decevinge from Marchantes, perjurie from Jurors, coozeninge from artificers, and discorde from the multitude. All which I wishe, thoughe hope thereof I can no more, then to draw out all the Sulphuire in Eathna and all moisture from marrishe groundes. For so great flames of wickednes and so full a store howse of Sinne remayneth in everie Cittie, as ympossible yt is to quench the one or clense the other. Everie wiseman therefore shall best do to remove himselfe from thence. What is then more to be don? For sooth this is my Counsell, flee from those vitious persons, that will not be reformed, and rest assured that the onely haven and harborowe of tranquilitie, is a private solitarie life: whereof I have discoursed. *In freto vivimus, in portu moriemur.*

Ca. 33.

But why have I labored so longe to commende the retyred and solytarie life, when more easily we might have proved that noe life at all is desiderable and all that this world promiseth is meere deceipte and troomperie: for what falce promises doth this Worlde make daylie? To one yt promiseth longe life, health and happines, and cutteth him of in the midest of his dayes: another is put in hope of Riches and honor, yet after longe service and endevor, casteth him into contempte and beggerie. Goe you over the whole worlde and behoulde the Pallaces of Princes, looke into Citties and Townes, harken at the dores and windowes of private Howses and you shall heare of nothinge so muche, as of lamentinge and complainte, one for that he hath lost, another, for that he hath woon, a third, for that he is not well rewarded and many thousands for that they were deceived. Now can there be any greater deceipte then to promise glorie, honor and fame, as the Worlde doeth to her followers and not withstandinge suffer them to be forgotten, so soone as they be dead? Whoe doth nowe speake of many notable and excellent Kinges, Captaynes, Counsellors and other worthie personages, whome the Worlde hath heretofore knowne and admired? Noe Man (alas!) doth now speake of them. Did not Job tell truely that theire rememberance should be as ashes trodden under foote, and David said, that they shall be as duste blowne abroade with the winde. Infinite are the deceiptes and dissimulacions of this Worlde which semeth in shewe gorgious and good, but beinge come to handlinge, yt proveth of no more weight then a feather, and being earnestly looked unto, yt is nothing ells but a shaddowe, when yt cometh to weight, yt is no better then smoke. O myserable and most deceiptfull Worlde, said St. Augustine, whose tribulacion is true and delight false, whose sorrowes are certen and pleasures uncerten, whose paynes are parmanent, and repose transitorie, whose toyles are intollerable, and rewardes most contemptible. To theise misseries we may adde the brevitie and incertentie of worldly prosperitie, for the fortunate Man desireth nothinge so muche as to have his prosperitie constant and parpetuall, as we reade in Ecclesiastes. O Death howe bitter is thy remembrance unto a Man that hath peace in his Riches. How many Men have we sene advanced to great Offices and not contynewed twice ten daies in their prosperitie. How many cupples have we knowne married together with much joye, and theire accorde have not endured thrise three monathes? How many of these and like examples have wee sene and readd shewinge the inconstancie of Fortune, and this deceivinge Worlde. How great a greefe was it to Kinge Alexander, when havinge conquered many Kingdomes in twelve yeares, and then, could noe longer live to enjoye them: when life was to him most sweete and glorious. How dolfull a daye thinke you is it when rich Men are taken from theire goulde, theire landes, theire greate Howses, theire fayre Wives, theire sweete Children, theire kinde Kinsfolke, frendes and flatarers? Of these miseries there is no ende. For as the poore post horses that all the daie were ridden by great Lordes or as wretched Moyles, that caried a Princes treasure, beinge come to the ende of theire jorney, as torned out of theire rich trappinges and with gauled backes sent unto a poore Stable: so the glorious inhabitors of this worlde, and owners of all landes, goulde and all sortes of worldly possessions, are at length taken from them, and their owne persons turned into the Earth, or haply cast into Hell. Besides theise, remember what discontentments doe accompany prosperitie, and every perticuler delight of this life. Consider what sauce everie pleasure hath. Aske of everie one in prosperitie whether they rest contented. The possession of Riches if followed with such feares as are aforesaide. Honor is subjecte to Servitude. Pleasure of the flesh, though it be honest, yet is yt (as St. Paul sayth) accompanied with trouble of the flesh. Bodies are apte to receive many diseases, many infirmities, and are also subjecte to misadventures and perrilles. Our myndes are afflicted with passions, as sorrowe, joye, envie and many other. What can recounte the adversities we suffer for our goodes, or nomber the offences we endure by our neighbors. One calleth us into lawe, an other seeketh our lives, an other laboreth to make us infamous. One hateth us, an other doth envie us, an other deceiveth us, an other by oppen armes assaulteth us. Finally there are not so many dayes in mans life, as the misseries which we are subjecte unto: and yf wee had all the happines of this worlde, one defecte onely, as a soare arme, a soare eye, or a foote infected with the goute, all the pleasures wee knowe could not make us merrie. And to close up these worldly calamities, we dailie see the innocent condemned, the guiltie acquitted, the wicked advanced, the vertuouse oppressed, justice soulde, truth wrested, no Shame, no equitie, nor playne dealinge. Everie Man is discontented, or at the least complayninge. One is sorrie for his want of Children, an other compleyneth they prove not to his expectacion. One is lame, one is blinde, one is sicke, one lacketh libertie, one is in debte, one hopeth, an other feareth. One is troubled with ambition, an other forced to daylie labor. One heateth his braine to become rich, an other doth feare to loose what he hath gotten. To conclude, all those things wherewith mans mynde is falsely delighted, as money, honor, and authoritie, which wee so much desire and wishe, with labor they are gotten, with envie they are looked on, and for the most parte are causes of ruyn to those that possess them. Lett us then with Seneca saye, *Omnis vita supplitium.*

PART II

. . . as unhappie and exiled. Alone, he [Adam] lived in rest and joye, but accompained in labor and sorrowe. Beinge single, he was immortal, but havinge a fellowe, became mortall: and therein appeared, what his posteritie should hope of by Womans compaine.

Abraham likewise, the father of manye nations, lived not in Palaces or proude Citties where daylie delightes and solempne Feastes are used, but in tentes and open fieldes: and there founde so muche grace as to speake with God and be ever accompanied with celestiall Angells. His Feastes were not in stately howses adorned with princely hanginges, nor beautified with guilded postes. He used to eat in the shaddowe of an Oke tree and the fruite thereof his most delicate dishe. So greate was the obaydience of that good Man, as he refused not to sacrifice his Sonne unto God, addinge other testimonie, of pietie and praysing the Almightie. All which thinges were don in Solitude.

The like life, retyred from concourse of Men, his sonne Izacke lived, whose dwellinge was in a poore and unpleasante hoate region. He used to walke alone for noe idle pleasure, but to praye and meditate. For the life of Man doth differ from other creatures, to the ende he should ever thinke of his salvacion. Cicero therefore seemed to saye well, *"Docto viro, vivere est cogitare."* For this purpose he haunted no Cittie nor Theater, but poured fourth his prayers in the fieldes, farr from accesse of people, as a place most meete for contemplacion. In Solytude also was his sonne Jacob, that great Patriarke, when he behelde the ladder where uppon the Angeles assended to Heaven.

Moyses in like manner lived in Solytude and became so acceptable to God, as he published the Lawe, and obtayned a most memorable victorie. In those daies he dwelled not in any Cittie of Siria or Egipt, but in woodes and the topp of highe Mountaines: where he wrought many Miracles, over longe to be rehearsed. To these mighte wee add the Solytarie lives of *Elias, Hieremias, St. Augustine, St. Jerome, St. Barnard* and others.

CA. 3.

Many wisemen, and chiefely they that for excellencie were called Philosophers, to the ende they might attaine unto perfeccion of Wisdome and Learninge, retyred into Solytude. I meane not those philosophers whose wordes persuaded men to vertue, and theire workes shewed the contrarie but those that in puritie in life performed the vertuous preceptes they preched, of which condicion are fewe, if any at all: for that is indeede the true and absolute wisedome. Theise I saye are those men of whome I speake, and everie of them lovers of Solytude. Of which nomber was Plato, whome the Academy of Athens so highly praysed. With him we may joyne Plautinus, a second Prince in Philosophie: whoe to attende the studdie of Wisedome, abandoned the worlde, and confined himselfe within the boundes of Campagna, where albeit his ende was misserable, yet his election glorious. Aske howe Pithagoras was disposed and you shall heare that to informe himselfe in the nature of all thinges, he did not onely looke uppon pleasant regions and fayre champion Countries, but also clymed highe Mountaynes and entered the most darke deserts. By which examples his Schollers and followers, being before that tyme frequentors of company and pleasure, retyred to Solytude and deserte places, callinge themselves Pithagorians. Whoe hath not heard that Democrites put out both his eyes, purposely never to see the vanitie of Men, as enemies to true Wisdome. Parmenides and Athlanta also lived amonge the Mountaynes, whose names be there extante. Prometheus likewise (as in fables we finde) with marvelous attencion studdieng the secret causes of thinges upon Mounte Caucasus, was there bound and eaten by Ravens. Certen yt is that ofte tymes place provokith the mynde to studdie, and therefore learned men retyred themselves to eschew the ympression of innumerable vayne sightes daylie sene amides the people, which sightes may deverte or take a way good cogitacions. For that reason also some Philosophers (as St. Jerome writeth) did not onely abandon compaine and concourse of people in Citties as the seate of disquiet, but also thought good never to behold gardens and Orchardes, least suche places of pleasure and nerenesse to the Cittie, might estrange the mynde from more serious cogitacion. The same (as I thinke) may be sed of Socrates and Aristotle: but the Majestie of theire Disciples and the Empire, together with commaundement and necessitie, might happely with holde them from so solytarie a life.

CA. 4.

What should I now saye of HOMER the Father of all Poetes, and with him Orpheus and Musitians, whoe by a certen simpathy of humors delighted to live so retyred, as scarcely theire names are to us knowne. This noble Poet, beinge (as Cicero sayth) blynde, discribed so well the solitarie places of Graetia and Italy, as the same may be thought to have bine by him perfitly observed and sene. Somewhat must I also saye of Vergill, whoe fled from Rome and for admeracion of his witt florished all that Kinges raigne, but notwithstanding all favor, with great and earnest suite, he desired a solytarie libertie: but untymely death prevented him and acquitted him of that care. Yet was he fully perswaded, that without the ayde of Solytude, his devine works coulde not be finished. Horatius Flaccus openly confessed he liked not so well of Rome (the Quene of all Citties) as of emptie Tibur and peceable Tarentum. Which wordes do importe his love was more to Solitude then the Cittie: havinge had experience of eyther, as in divers his Poems may appeare. *Scriptorum chorus omnis amat nemus et fugit urbem.* To the same purpose Francis Petrarcha sayth, *Silva placet musis, urbs est inimica poetis.* Horace also commendeth Solytude, preferring quiet before great riches. And one feilde [t]here is somewhat remote from the Cittie, where he used to walke, and notwithstandinge the possession of many other owners, it yet called, Campus Horatii. Whereof he wrote thus, *Otia divitiis Arabum, liberrima muto.*

CA. 5.

Seneca that great Sage, born at Corduba in Spayne, became a Cittizen and Senator of Rome: from whence he was banished and confyned to the Isle of Corsica: where findinge rest and laysor, he preferred that sweete ease and obscure solytude, before the busie and troublesome honor wherein before he lived. Reade that Tragedie wherein he discourseth of exchange of habitacion, and by conference of the one to the other, yourselfe may judge in whether fortune he was most happie. His opinion also of this matter appeareth by that counsell which he gave to Lucillus, for thereof may be conceived that as a retyred life is perfecte libertie and freedome, so is yt most fitt for the studdie of Philosophie. For (said hee) the life of Man is ever in the Cittie subjecte to mens Crewelty: by which wordes he semeth to pronosticate his owne lamentable ruyne.

CA. 6.

Amonge other learned Men, Cicero semeth to like leaste of Solytarie life: not so muche for the matter, as the cause which moved him. For beinge as well an Orator as a Philosopher, he coulde not have gained so great glorie in Solytude, as in speakinge before the people and multytude, which moved him to be sorrie, when pleadinge privately before Julius Caesar, he might not speake publikely for Kinge Diodatus his Clyent, in presence of the Senate and People of Rome. It is also a qualitie singuler and proper to Orators to be sene in Citties, thereby to make shewe of their eloquence: and consequently to hate silence and Solytude. Therefore as other Orators of lesse reputacion commended the places of theire dwellinge, so Cicero highly extolled the Cittie of Rome, his native Countrie. Howsoever he did or semed to take like of compaine, certen yt is that of an excellent Orator, he became a great Philosopher. How muche he excelled in Lattine eloquence everie man knoweth, and that knowledge could not be attayned unto, but in studious Solytude. Also in one of his workes he writeth thus, beinge by Publike Affayres and forrayne Warre empeached, I desire rest, and so leavinge the Cittie I went to the Countrie, and lived alone. By which complainte he semeth sometymes to comforte himselfe: addinge, that in shorte tyme, when the Common Weale was disturbed, I wrote more then in many yeares I had when yt florished. And truely therein he semeth to have said well. For who can sufficiently commende the noble laysor and glorious Solytude of this Man? For by his travell and labor, the lawes were made at Arpina, Cumana, Firmo, and Tusculan, where also erected an Universitie. Moreover he wrote a booke of Rethoricke, a booke of Offices, a booke of the nature of Gods: therein also he removed the causes of many errors. There he f[r]amed discourses concerninge the endes of good and evell. There he compiled a most noble exhortacion and commendacion of Philosophie, to be a guide of good life: which St. Augustin much alloweth. Fynally, lest by sayinge muche, and by over great affeccion I err, sommarily I saye he teacheth contempt of Death, and by patience to overcome sorrowe, by reason to remove sadnes, to extirpate the causes of all sicknes, and to speake in breefe, he doth honor to all Philosophers, enforminge that by ayde of his reasons, a Man may live well and contented, contrarie to the doctrine of other worthie writers. So as that which others had simply saide, he with mightie and many great reasons hath proved: mixing profitt with delight, addinge hereunto also wordes full of majestie and dignitie. Thus yt appeareth, that solytude though yt was to him accidentall and contrarie to his will, yet did yt greatly invite him to studdie. Howe muche more had the same bin to purpose, yf his Solytude had been voluntarie. But what sorte of life soever he best liked, yt playnly appeareth in his Offices that for studdie of Philosophie he thinketh Solitude to be most meete: sayinge many Men have so earnestly desired quiet, that layinge aside all affayres they affected nothinge so muche as Solytude and Private life. Amonge those were many Philosphers and great Personages, with other grave Men of severe Wisedome, whoe not enduringe the manners eyther of princes or people, retyred themselves to the Countrie, entertayninge the tyme with theire owne private affayres. The one and the other of them did ymitate Kinges, which is not to neede any thinge, but live at libertie and subject to noe Man. Thus yt appeareth, that althoughe Cicero called the life active most profitable for a Weale publike, which we also confesse, yet must we affirme that private life is more pleasant and secure, where unto maye be added, yt is also to others lesse offensive. Whereof maye be inferred, upon just cause suche a life is to be liked, cheifely in those Men that are of excellent Wit and learninge, thoughe Cicero lived otherwise. But afterwardes oppressed with many sorrowes, and cheifely the death of his deare Daughter, he wished to live privately, as appeared by that he wrote to *Atticus,* sayinge, Nowe I loathe all thinges and like nothinge so muche as Solytude. And he sayth moreover, that a retyred life was to him as a Native Countrie, and for many reasons he fled from the Cittie. In one other place likewise he writeth thus, to me nothinge is so pleasante as Solytude, where I may be without compaine and alone. Everie morninge I walke into the thicke wood, and there remayne untill the eveninge. By all which appeareth he greatly loved Solytude, as a place most apte for contemplacion.

CA. 7.

I suppose that Demostines was in disposition like unto Cicero, though percase sometymes he altered his mynde, which I have not readd. They were both of one profession, and sometymes pleased with Womans daliance. This is that Demostines whoe shewed himselfe in Citties so excellent an Orator, whereunto he attayned in Solytude. Quintilianus sayth that Demostines was so great a lover of private places, as he used to meditate at the Sea-side, when the waves did roare most lowde, the terror of which noyse, did not amuse him. In private places farr from compaine he used to speake a loude, what he intended to pronounce in publike. He used to saye that wearie he was of pleadinge for profitt, neyther did he desire any thinge whereof he myght repent. Hee would never boast of worldly wealth, but labor to doe all in hope of eternitie. Also it is to be remembered that many excellent Men both in armes and letters, eyther by eleccion or constrainte lived in Solytude, as Ulisses, Aristides, Thucidides, Themistocles, Alcibiades, Codrus, Theseus, Eumolpus, Aristotle, Camillus, Corolianus, with others.

Ca. 8.

No doubte there is, but the manners of Philosophers differed from Orators, and the endes whereat eyther of them aymed, was also divers. The one desired applause of people, the other endevored to drawe the mindes of Men to vertuose knowledge and contempte of vayne glorie. For what a one thinke we was Anaxagoras? Howe greate was his constancie, and howe admirable was the abstinence of *Xenocrates* that most severe Philosopher? How notable was *Xeno,* the father of Stoickes, and how paynefull was *Carneades,* whoe by extreame studdie, ofte tymes lost his memorie. Do you not thinke that after Nyntie yeares of his age, he should have don better to live in Solytude, then converse so contynewally with the multytude? And hardly am I perswaded that eyther Ericippus had an howse, or Diogines a tubb, in any Cittie, where Men might ever see or salute them: and the presence of a great Kinge to controule them. Yet so said St. Jerome. Solon likewise, one of the Sages of Grecia, whoe made the lawes of his Countrie, maye be nombered amonge men solytarie, for when he composed lawes and ordinances, ledd on with desire of more knowledge, he travelled into unknowne landes, as one delighted with the peregrination of Egipt and other strange Regions.

Ca. 9.

Whoe will wounder that solytarie life shoulde be pleasinge to Men studious, when Emperors, Kinges and great Captaynes were therewith delighted? Julius Caesar, thoughe at that tyme yonge, havinge passed some stormes and trouble, determined to retyre to the Isle of Rhodes, and there to imploye his tyme in studdie: but he was sone called from thence, by incurtion of pirates, by Civill Warr, and at last by forraine assaults. Yet therein appeareth his intente to live retyred. Augustus Caesar also, being as yt were in the topp of humaynge happines and mortall blisse, used muche to inhabitt the Countrie, and there ofte tymes walked in the woodes to recreate his Spirit, after long cogitacion on waightie affayres. Whereof may be conceived he was one of those that delighted in Solytarie life. For continewally he wished to enjoye suche a rest: what soever he thought or said, in the ende hee desired quiet as that which is the comforte of present wearines, the rewarde of passed travell, and hope of time to come. Moreover this most fortunate Prince, preferred honest ease before honor, riches and Empire. Fynally as wearied and loathinge aboundance of treasure and humayne glorie, he desired onely quiet: which by his owne writinges (perhaps yet extant) appeareth. So deepely did the eyes of his understandinge peirce, as to preferr a retyred life before all worldly felicitie. For albeit he had all thinges, yet did he want, and wishe for quiet. And being above all Men, for wante of laysor he was inferior to many.

CA. 10.

That which Augustus wished Dioclesianus enjoyed. This was the first Emperor that woulde be adored as God. This is he that ware on his garmentes Margarites and many sortes of pretious stones and used to apparrell his Person with exceedinge pompe. This was he that triumphed over the Persians and Parthians, causinge theire Ensigne, Prisoners and Spoyles to be caried before him: yet, sodenly changinge his mynde, wished himselfe poore, and private. So castinge a waie the care of ymperiall affayres, he fled unto the haven of a most humble life: not unlike a sillie saylor, that to save himselfe from sinkinge swimmeth naked unto shore. Now looke what Dioclesianus did after he was Emperor, the same Antoninus Pius had done before he was Emperor, as Julius Capitolinus the historian sayth, for indeede he lived retyred, yet was he famous, in all places.

Ca. 11.

Omyttinge to speake of the Quintii, Catoni, Fabientii, and many other noble Captaynes of Rome whoe lyved almost privately in the Countrie, let us somewhat saye of Numa the seconde Kinge of Rome and first founder of Pietie and Justice. He of a stranger and pilgrime, was elected Kinge, and so beinge, endevored to plant in Rome, pietie conjoyned with pollicie. For before that tyme the people lived lawles and barbarously. This Kinge used to studdie in a certen solitarie and deserte place, aboute fiftene myles from the Cittie, which myne eyes have sene. In that place, at the foote of an hill called Aricino, is a certen stone, large and great, which geveth a shaddowe, and out of yt cometh a fine water. Also aboute that grounde groweth a thicke woode, within which is no waye or path for people to travell, but all is solitarie and silent. Even there, as is said, this learned Kinge wrote his lawes, and sett fourth ceremonies for the service of the Gods, where when he had longe studied, at the last, as yt were in a deepe meditacion, he came fourth alone, bearinge in his handes the lawes written. By those ordinances and religious ceremonies, the feirce people were reduced to order. Therein as is said, he ymitated Minos Kinge of Candia, whoe by his craftie eloquence perswaded the people, that in the nyght tyme certen Gods used to resorte unto him, and by their Counsell the lawes were made, and longe tyme after put in practise, yet in the ende, by commaundement of the Pretor and Senate (next to the Kinges Tombe) were burned. Thus appeareth yt that Solytude was the fountaine from whence the firste Romayne lawes and many other good thinges, had there beginninge.

Ca. 12.

Romulus the first Kinge of Rome, founder of that Cittie, and predecessor to Numa, frequented Solytarie places, Woodes and poore Cottages, ever cogitatinge upon good lawes and ordinances, how his mightie Empire mighte be governed. We reade likewise that *Hercules* when he had longe mused in Solytude and excersiced armes, whereby he became terrible to the Citties of Asia and Grece, at length leavinge the path of pleasure, entered the waie which leadeth to vertue and honest life, and in that course contynewed so longe as he attayned not onely humane glorie, but also the name of a God. So yt appeareth the branches of his renowne did springe from Solytarie life.

Ca. 13.

Now to say some what of twoe most excellent Captaynes called Cipioni, who were as Virgill called them, the thoonder of Warr. The first had no souner attayned unto Mans estate, as Livius writeth, but he daylie used in his howse to be alone, before he went unto the Capitol to consult of matters publike, which custome he contynewed all his life, so as in the ende he was highly honored, not onely by the superstitious fables of the Gretians, but also in authentike histories of the Romaynes, whereby appeareth it was for his grate vertue reputed to discende from the race of Gods. This mightie Commaunder framed the foundacion of his government upon Religion, the true marke whereof is solytude.

The seconde Scipio, as he resembled the former in vertue, so was he also well knowne a lover of Solytude. For after everie of his services millitarie and victories, he all waies retyred himselfe to Liternum, Caieta, or some such solitarie place, accompained onely with a fewe of his dearest frendes. O most noble spectacle and worthie prayse, exceedinge the pompe of all princes, to see a most noble Captayne defendor of his Countrie and all Italy, after he had conquered Nations and prosperously acquite the people from bondage, to leave his Souldiers in the Cittie, and laye downe the triumphall robes with all other ensignes of dignitie, and that don, all alone to walke a monge the hills, and on the sea shore, some tymes to take upp prettie shells, and strange stones of rare proportion. Fynally a matter worthie observacion it is as Cicero modestly and with reverence noteth, to see howe this and other great Captaynes rejoyced to take pleasure in the fieldes, when theire attendance and busines was ended in the Cittie. Yet true it is, that theire Solytude was not occupied otherwise, then in some excellent cogitacions, or some noble exployte to be performed. Cato his emulation, was wount to saye of himselfe, he lived never lesse at laysor, then at such tymes as he had most laysor: nor lesse alone, then when he was without compaine. The glorie of which prayse, *Ambrose* semeth to take unto himselfe, sayinge that while the Civill Warrs of Rome held, and other men therein occupied, he was ever fightinge with his bookes. The memorie of these noble Captaynes doth also occasion me to thinke of divers great princes, whoe lothed with worldly delightes, and tyred in affayres of this life, retyred to Solytude: as Ramirus Kinge of Aragon, Verecundus Kinge of Spayne, Ludovicus, Kinge of Naples, Guglielmus Kinge of Pictes, Carolus magnus the sonne of Carolus Martellus, Lotharius and Lodovicus Kinges of Fraunce, Batilda a Quene of France, Amurat Kinge of Turkye, with many other Princes and great Personages of whome writers have at large discoursed.

CA. 14.

It semeth that Scipio Affricanus allowed best of such a solytarie life, as is not altogether a lone, but accompanied with some fewe frendes, and they well chosen: likewise that laysor and quiet he thought commendable which was well and profitably imployed. For those Men that are contynewally alone, and idle, stretching and turninge theire lasie bodies, are ever sad and malancoly, for they are neyther occupied in honest busines, nor interteyne theire myndes in any honest studdie. The soome therefore of my meaninge is to allowe of laysor, yet with some exersice of affayres: the ende whereof is no toyle, no gayne, noe base profit: but delectacion, vertue, and honor. Let the bodie sometymes rest and keepe holy daye, but the mynde must ever be busied in true laysor, which is ymployment in good cogitacions, thereby to become better. For as the Earth is sometymes to be tilled, and sometymes to lye fallowe, so the mynde requireth intermission: as necessarie to make yt the more fertill.

I commende generouse busines and good companie, not onely in Solytude, but in the Cittie also: neyther is any thinge more pleasinge or contentinge. Yea, without yt, both in Cittie and Solytude the life of Man is misserable. I will likewise that Men lyvinge retyred, should be accompanied with bookes of divers kindes, to be studied privately, or caried about as comfortable companions: beinge ever apte to speake or be silent. They are likewise readie to rest at home, or accompanie us in the woodes, in travell and in the field. Fit they are for confabulacion, solace and admonishment. By them we maye also be enformed the nature of all thinges. They can also tell of actions don, and what order of life ought be observed. Of them likewise maye be learned, contempte of death, temperance in prosperitie, fortytude in adversitie, and constancie in all accions. They are pleasant, affable and learned companions, without irksomnes, without comber, without wranglinge, without mourmuringe, without envie or crafte. Amonge which qualities, they neede noe meate nor drincke, and maye be harbored in everie poore Howse. Yet are they, even to enemies, great treasure. Into our Solytude I also admitt frendes, Kinsfolke, and all vertuose Men: without whome, I accompte no life comefortable nor well furnished. And because twoe persons (haveinge betwene them a certen simpathy of mynde and manners) are as one: love hath vertue to make one of twoe, otherwise Pithagoras commaundeth a thinge impossible: which is, that divers should be made one: and so beinge, everie place is capable of twoe. Concluding therefore I saye, that noe place is so solytarie, noe house so small, nor noe Cabbinet so close, but may receive a frende.

CA. 15.

To serve God is true libertie, and to meditate on matter Celestiall no place is so fitt as Solytude. Also he that endevoreth the knowledge of good artes, or write any thinge to be lefte unto Posteritie, yt behoveth him to retyre and studdie privately, lest laboringe to save other Men from Shippwracke in the waves of humayne affayres, he be himselfe by the burden of busines, drowned. Moreover whatsoever we commende, let the same be done accordinge to judgment. For a common infirmitie it is to reprehende others of that faulte which wee our selves committ, because our wordes and workes do not accorde.

CA. 16.

Cicero writinge to his frende, sayth, you have ofte heretofore, and now also perswaded me to aspire unto honor, and gladly would I so do: but when shall I live? Certenly this answere is shorte and subtill. For so everie perswation to such purpose maye be answered. That you move me to advance myselfe, willinge I am yf it be possible: but I saye agayne, when shall we begine to live? For in takeinge suche a course as you commende, I cannot presently live: because an ambitious life, contynewally dependinge upon hope, is not life, but a certen meditation thereof, which percase shall never be, and is ever in the meane space, doubtfull. Amonge other thinges a certen Poet writeth thus, *crede mihi non est sapientis discere vivam.* In myne opinion therefore the counsell of Alcibiades extendeth farr, and maye many waies be applied. For whoso laboreth to aspire, is forced to meete with many perturbacions of mynde and daylie incounters of fortune. It behovith him to hazard in the warr, and please in peace, never forgettinge the advice which Plato did give unto Aeschines, *aut place, aut tace,* when he went to serve Kinge Alexander. For when all is don, we deylie see both in Courte and Campe, that more Men are advanced by fortune, then by due desertes. Shee is like unto the Sonn that shineth upon the good and the evell, and favoreth fooles and wisemen all alike. Notwithstandinge which indiscretion of Fortune, the vertuouse Man endevoreth to assend by the due degrees of vertue, and not prevaylinge, magnanimously contemneth honor, riches, and all other graces the blinde Goddesse can bestowe. For he is content with necessarie riches and such honor as is for vertue due: though percase he never receive any. For it is all one to a vertuous Man to have honor, or not to desire yt. Which moved Aristotle to saye, *Beata vita nihil desiderat sed seipsa contenta est,* and maye be most fitly don in private and solytarie life.

CA. 17.

Who so considereth from whence the ympeachmentes of quiet and securitie do proceede shall finde theise; (viz.) hope, envie, hatred, feare and contempte. Now are we to knowe howe such molestacions may be eschewed. Hope inciteth evell Men to covet suche honors, wealth or other ornamentes of life as wee possesse. To be acquite from that trouble, the best meane is not to have any thinge excellent or muche desirable. Envie may be avoyded by livinge retyred and seldome sene: also, by concealinge from sighte of other Men those goodes which wee possesse. Hate doth rearely arise where no offence is, or where conversation is modest. Feare proceedeth eyther of our owne insolencie or molestinge other Men and therefore must aspecte the like: or ells of other Mens avarize whoe endevor to take from us. The one may be avoyded by beinge content with our owne, the other by manfull defence thereof. Everie Man hath power to offende, and he that is feared, doth also feare. Contempte cometh by bacenesse of mynde, for no man is contemned unlesse he disesteme himselfe, and consequently cause of his owne disestimation. But no Man that is wise, juste, valient, or otherwise vertouse, was ever contemned. Neyther is any Man learned or otherwise skillfull in any honest art. This inconvenience is also avoyded by beinge favored of princes, or great Personages. It is likewise a waye to eschewe contempte yf wee live Solytarie and intermedle litle with other Men.

CA. 18.

Haveinge seriously considered the reasons and examples before saide, lett us take leave of Citties and all other places of concourse, where the moste parte of Men live in trafficke and daylie affayres. We must not so muche as thinke of those matters nor looke back, but determyne never to retorne unto that ungratefull monster with many heades, I meane the people. Let us ymitate the good Lentulus, who desiringe true life and perfeccion, made choyce of everlastinge exile: whereto albeit no love of quiet, yet hate to the troublesome multytude, ought to perswade us. To these examples may others be added. But lett us clearely extirpate the causes of busines, and breake the cheane which houldeth us bounde to worldly affayres. That don, cast downe the bridge behinde, to the ende noe hope of fleinge or retorne shall remayne. Arise then and with speede and abandon concourse of Men and Citties. Lett them be inhabited by Marchantes, Advocates, Usurers, Phisitions, Appoticaries, Drapers, Cookes, Bakers, Brewers, Painters, Diers, Smythes, Weavers, Carpenters, Carvers, Minstrells, Juglers, Conngerers, Pickpurses, Paresites, Inkeepers, Taverners, with innumerable others occupied in ignoble and base busines. Let us leave wise men in Townes, to tell money and use theire Arithmeticke: we will accompte our treasure without studdie or art. No reason I see of envie, nor admire those men more, then beinge Children we woundered at whirligiggs. Take awaie trapinges and other furniture from horses, then are they, for the most part, but slowly soulde. For as no wise man will take to Wife an evell favored woman, because she is pompously apparelled, even so take a waie from fortunate folke theire externall ornaments, then will the misery of theire deformities appeare. Let everie one labor to have true riches, and intertayne himselfe with vertuous qualities: I meane those that are eternall: for so shall worldly riches, honor, and earthly pompe, be lightly regarded: yea, those delightes we now so dearely imbrace, will forsake us. For all those thinges which vulgar people admire, do vanishe in a moment. Under the Empire of fortune they are, and yf shee do not, yet death will take them awaye. He that possesseth the most pretious riches, shall ere longe accompte them of noe prise. And those ill gotten goodes, which with great labor were gayned, a thanklesse heire. . . .

NOTES

THE LETTERS

Letter 1.

Printed from the original in the British Museum, Lansdowne MS. 13, No. 38. Although this letter, written by Harington when he was a ten-year-old Etonian, may be only an exercise in formal and ceremonious letter-writing, it was sent, as the endorsement indicates, to a Mistress Penn, probably a member of Lord Burghley's household. Cf. Epigram 94. The manuscript was once in the possession of Sir Michael Hicks, Burghley's secretary.

Letter 2.

This letter is printed from a transcript, Tanner MS. 169, f. 62. The manuscript containing this letter is a commonplace book kept by Sir Stephen Powle. The letter is headed "1580 A Letter of Master Harringtons now Sir John Harr: written by him to his Fathers deare Freind Edward Dier for reconciliation. Given me by Lord Arundell at Parris." In 1580 Harington was still in residence at Cambridge. Sir Edward Dyer, courtier and poet, was, like Harington, a Somersetshire man. Harington speaks of him as "a man ever of great wit and worth," and twice quotes passages from his poetry. (Notes following Books VIII and XVI of his translation of *Orlando Furioso,* 1591; ed. 1634, pp. 63, 126.)

My Tutors Lettres. The tutor was Dr. Samuel Fleming, whom Harington, in the preface to his translation of *Orlando Furioso,* mentions as "a grave and learned man, and one of a very austere life." A marginal note adds, "Samuel Flemming of King's Colledge in Cambridge." (*Orlando Furioso,* ed. 1634, Sig. ¶, 8v.)

Student at the Inns of the Courte. After taking the M.A. degree at Cambridge in 1581, Harington was admitted to Lincoln's Inn, November 27, 1781. (Venn, *Alumni Cantabrigienses.*) After his father's death in 1582, he married Mary Rogers, of Cannington, Somersetshire, September 6, 1583. (*Miscellanea Genealogica et Heraldica,* IV, 1884, 195; *Somerset Parish Registers,* ed. W. P. W. Phillimore, VI, 1905, 94.)

Sir John Byrons sonne and heire. Anthony Byron, son of Sir John Byron, of Newstead, Nottinghamshire, and Clayton, Lancashire, matriculated from Queen's College in 1573, and was married at Trinity Church, Cambridge, in February, 1576. (Venn, *Alumni Cantabrigienses;* for the circumstances of his irregular marriage, see Searle, *History of Queen's College,* 345.)

Letter 3.

Printed from the original, State Papers, Domestic, Elizabeth, Vol. 102, 325.

Letter 4.

Reprinted from *Nugae Antiquae,* 1804, I, 183.

Master Bellot. A confidential servant of Lord Burghley. "He [Lord Burghley] made Over-seers of his Will, Gabriel Goodman, Deane of Westminster, a most upright man; and Tho. Bellot, Steward of his house: to which Thomas he left a great sum of mony, to be bestowed in religious uses: which he most faithfully performed." (Camden, *Annales,* 1635, 496.) Because of his benefactions to the Church of SS. Peter and Paul, Bath, mentioned in Letter 51, Harington in Letter

53 refers to him as "saynt Billet." He is mentioned also in Fenton's letter to Harington, May 23, 1597 (*infra,* p. 382) and in Bowles's Diary (Francis Peck, *Desiderata Curiosa*).

At the Bathe. At the town of Bath, three miles from Harington's great house at Kelston.

Blacke Sauntus. These verses are printed in *Nugae Antiquae,* 1804, I, 14, and with the music in Harington's *Metamorphosis of Ajax,* 1596, 1814, 1927.

Maister Tallis. Thomas Tallis (? 1510–1585).

Bishop Gardener. Bishop Stephen Gardiner, as Queen Mary's Lord Chancellor, had caused Harington's parents to be imprisoned for nearly a year because of their loyalty to the Princess Elizabeth.

Signature. Harington almost invariably signed his name "John Haryngton." Henry Harington, the first editor of *Nugae Antiquae,* always spelled the name "Harington." In this volume, the letters reprinted from *Nugae Antiquae,* in the absence of any other source, retain the spelling of the original edition of the letters.

LETTER 5.

Printed from the original in the British Museum, Lansdowne MS. 82, No. 88.

Lady Russell. Elizabeth, daughter of Sir Anthony Cooke, was the sister-in-law of Lord Burghley and Sir Nicholas Bacon, and the aunt of Sir Robert Cecil and Sir Francis Bacon. In 1558 she married Sir Thomas Hoby (1530–1566), the translator of Castiglione's *Il Cortegiano,* and in 1574 John, Lord Russell, heir of Francis Russell, second Earl of Bedford. Lord Russell died before his father, upon whose death the title passed to his nephew, Edward Russell, who in 1594 married Lucy Harington, daughter of the first Lord Harington of Exton, cousin of Sir John Harington of Kelston.

This fantasticall treatise. The Metamorphosis of Ajax (1596).

The first two leaves of yt. The Black Sanctus mentioned in Letter 4.

The devyce yt self. The sanitary device that Harington invented and, in *The Metamorphosis of Ajax,* discussed.

Tiballs. Theobalds was the great house of the Cecils that Sir Robert Cecil surrendered to King James, May 22, 1607.

LETTER 6.

Printed from the original in the Library of Gonville and Caius College, MS. 606, p. 62. The letter is written to Sir William Dethick, Garter king-at-arms. "Master Clarencieux" is William Camden, the historian.

The grant was confirmed and testified by Camden and Dethick, November 20, 1597. "John Harrington of Kelston, Somerset, s. of John and Isabel, his wife, dau. of Sir John Markham, with a label gu. of three points or quartering arg., a cross patonce az.; crest differenced with the label as in the arms." (*Grants of Arms named in Docquets and Patents to the End of the Seventeenth Century,* ed. W. H. Rylands. Harleian Society, Vol. 66, London, 1915, p. 115.)

LETTER 7.

Reprinted from *Nugae Antiquae,* 1804, I, 236.

Sir Hugh Portman. The son of Sir Henry Portman, of Orchard Portman, near Taunton. He was M.P., 1597, and Sheriff, 1590, 1600. He died in 1603. (Collinson, *History of Somersetshire,* I, xxxii ff.; F. W. Weaver, *Visitations of the County of Somerset,* 63.) Sir Hugh, writes Harington, was a "rich man, a wise man, a builder, and especially a bachelor." (*An Apology,* printed with *The Metamorphosis of Ajax,* 1814, 37.) Harington addressed four epigrams to him. (Epigrams 32, 193, 257, 351.)

Lord Treasurer. Lord Burghley died August 4, 1598.

My cosen Sir John Harington, of Exton. He later became first Lord Harington of Exton, guardian and tutor of the Princess Elizabeth, daughter of King James. He died in 1613.

My Lady Arundel. Margaret Willoughby, one of Queen Elizabeth's maids of honor, who became the wife of Sir Matthew Arundell of Wardour, and the mother of Sir Thomas Arundell.

LETTER 8.

Reprinted from *Nugae Antiquae,* 1804, I, 264.

Date. "Sunday last" was August 5, 1599, when the English were defeated in the Curlew Mountains in the northern part of Connaught. (Letter 9; *Calendar State Papers, Ireland, 1599–1600,* 113; Birch, *Memoirs of the Reign of Queen Elizabeth,* II, 425–426.) After the engagement the English forces retired to Athlone. This letter was written between Tuesday, August 7 and Sunday, August 12, 1599. Harington's journal, covering the campaign from May 10 to July 3, 1599, appears in *Nugae Antiquae,* I, 268–293.

Sir Anthony Standen. A somewhat mysterious person, formerly employed by Sir Francis Walsingham as a spy, and at this time in the service of the Earl of Essex. (Edmund Lodge, *Illustrations of British History,* 1838, III, 12, note; Birch, *Memoirs of the Reign of Queen Elizabeth,* II, 502.)

The governor. Sir Conyers Clifford, Governor of Connaught.

Captain Lister led the forlorn hope. The phrase *forlorn hope* means literally *lost troop.* "In early use, a picked body of men, detached to the front to begin the attack; a body of skirmishers." (*NED.,* s. v. forlorn hope.)

Captain Jephson. Captain John Jephson commanded a troop of one hundred horsemen. (Birch, *op. cit.,* II, 425.)

Sir Griffith Markham. Sir Griffin Markham (? 1564–? 1644), Harington's first cousin. Cf. Letter 9.

My cozen Sir H. Harington. Cf. Letter 10. Sir John has told the same story in the notes following Book XII of his translation of *Orlando Furioso* (1591).

LETTER 9.

Reprinted from *Nugae Antiquae,* 1804, I, 253–263.

Date. The dates in the first paragraph are obviously incorrect. Later in the letter Harington states that Essex spent the preceding day at Arbrachan [Ardbraccan], which is on the Blackwater about five miles from the Boyne River. There Essex spent two days, August 30 and 31, and did not later return. (Birch, *Memoirs of the Reign of Queen Elizabeth,* II, 427; *Calendar State Papers, Ireland, 1599–1600,* 137, 140–141.) Essex, on September 24, 1599, left Ireland, and on September 28 arrived at Nonesuch (E. P. Cheyney, *A History of England from the Defeat of the Armada to the Death of Elizabeth,* II, 503). This letter, then, should be dated August 31 or September 1. It is possible, of course, that Harington was ignorant of Essex's whereabouts, or that, for some inexplicable reason, he was intentionally inaccurate.

Master Combe. Thomas Combe, Harington's confidential servant.

Sir Griffin Markhams sake, and three Markhams more. Sir Griffin Markham was the eldest son of Thomas Markham, of Ollerton, a brother of Harington's mother. The "three Markhams more" were Robert, Francis, and Gervase, sons of Robert Markham, of Cottam, a nephew of Harington's mother. (*D. N. B.*)

Gave mee and some others the honour of knighthood in the field. Harington was knighted July 30, 1599. (Venn, *Alumni Cantabrigienses.*)

Sir Henry Davers. His name is often written "Danvers." "The cowardice of the English foot soldiers, so constantly complained of in these Irish campaigns, was due to the circumstances of their levy, their forced service and difficult surroundings." (Cheyney, *A History of England from the Defeat of the Armada to the Death of Elizabeth,* II, 482–483.)

The book you so prays'd, and other books of Sir Griffin Markham's. In the *Dictionary of National Biography* and in the *Catalogue of Printed Books in the British Museum* there are attributed to Gervase Markham three books to which Harington may here allude: (1) *The Souldier's Accidence, or an Introduction into Military Discipline . . . [By] G M[arkham];* (2) *The Souldier's Grammar: containing the high, necessarie and most curious rules of the art militarie . . .* By *G[ervase] M[arkham], Gent.;* (3) *The Souldier's Exercise, in three books.* Harington's comment leads one to suppose that these books were written by Sir Griffin Markham, who had served under Sir Francis Vere in the Netherlands and under the Earl of Essex before Rouen, rather than by Sir Griffin's less soldierly young kinsman, Gervase.

As Olympia was forsaken by the ungrateful Byreno. The story is told in *Orlando Furioso,* Books IX–XI.

Apparel for an officer in winter. Further details may be found in Lodge, *Illustrations,* 1838, II, 540.

LETTER 10.

Reprinted from *Nugae Antiquae,* 1804, I, 247–252. Henry Harington, who first printed this letter, gives no date except the year 1599. (*Nugae Antiquae,* 1779, II, 1.) Thomas Park dates the letter April, 1599 (*Nugae Antiquae,* 1804, I, 247.) The letter was written after October 18, 1599, when the conference with Tyrone ended, and before October 29, 1599, when Sir John Harington left Dublin for London, taking with him a letter from the Lords Justices Loftus and Carey to the Privy Council. (*Calendar State Papers, Ireland, 1599–1600,* 207.) Park's error has led to confusion in the accounts of Essex's relations with Tyrone. (Cf. L. H. Cadwallader, *The Career of the Earl of Essex,* 35–36.)

Justice Carey. Essex, upon his departure from Ireland, September 24, 1599, appointed two lords justices to serve as heads of the civil government in his absence. The men named were Adam Loftus and Sir George Carew.

The arch-rebel. Hugh O'Neill, third Baron of Dungannon and second Earl of Tyrone (? 1540–1616). As a young man he spent several years in England, probably attached to the household of the Earl of Leicester. He again visited England in 1590. From 1574 to 1593 he was acknowledged by the English government as one of the intermediary chieftains relied upon to secure the obedience of the still unconquered tribes. For a time he was in command of native troops paid by the English government. In 1593, however, he allied himself with the hostile tribes of Ulster and later with the Spanish, whereby English supremacy in Ireland was endangered. The rebellion reached its height in 1598. (E. P. Cheyney, *A History of England from the Defeat of the Armada to the Death of Elizabeth,* II, 455–502.)

Sir William Warren. He had previously served as an intermediary between Tyrone and the English. (*Calendar Carew Manuscripts, 1589–1600,* 337.) Essex and Tyrone had agreed upon an armistice, September 7, 1599. There was to be a cessation of hostilities for six weeks, and the truce was to be renewed every six weeks until May 1, 1600, unless either party should give two weeks' notice of its termination. The truce was kept by both sides for the first six weeks, but in October it was reported that the Earl of Ormonde, an Irish ally of the English, had attacked the natives. Warren was at once sent to conciliate Tyrone.

Warren's official report of the interview confirms and supplements Harington's account. It is dated October 20, 1599.

"The Declaration of Sir William Warren, Knight, touching my second journey to Tyrone, since the departure of the Lord Lieutenant, according his Lordship's former commission.

"On Tuesday, the 16th inst., I met with Tyrone three miles below Dundalk, but through the great rain the waters were grown so high as we could not come so near as to speak or hear one the other.

"On the 17th I met him again, and, the waters being fallen, we came together. He was unwilling to agree to any further cessation, because O'Donnell was not yet come, and he had been advertised that the Earl of Ormond had slain seven or eight score of his men. In the end he consented to a fortnight's cessation, and would not conclude upon any further time until O'Donnell came to him.

"On the 18th we spent some time in conference. He was still unwilling to yield to any further time, alleging 'that it was now winter time and our army weak, and therefore he being stronger than we, and able to keep the field, now was the time of his harvest, in which he made no doubt but to get the whole spoil of the country; alleging farther that he knew very well the Lord Lieutenant's tarrying in England was but to procure a great army to come upon him on all sides the next spring.'

"During this cessation a messenger came to us from O'Donnell with a letter or message to Tyrone, that he should proceed himself in this negotiation, and that though O'Donnell could not then come, he would stand to whatever Tyrone should conclude. Hereupon Tyrone, with a show of great unwillingness, agreed to a month more, making six weeks from the expiration of the first cessation agreed upon with the Lord Lieutenant.

"I perceived an intention in him to go within a short time to the river of Shenon to confer with the supposed Earl of Desmond and others of his confederates, and, if they were desirous of peace, to learn what conditions they would stand upon." (*Calendar Carew Manuscripts, 1589–1600,* 341.)

The earl's coming. The coming of the Earl of Tyrone.

At my lord of Ormond's. The Earl of Ormonde, the head of the Norman Irish family of the Butlers, was in command of the military forces in Ireland before the arrival of Essex. In 1586 Harington had spent some months in Ireland (MS. Rawlinson, B. 162, f. 3; *Orlando Furioso,* ed. 1634, 80; *Cambridge Modern History,* III, 599).

My English translation of "Ariosto." Orlando Furioso, 1591.

The beginning of the 45th canto.

> Looke how much higher Fortune doth erect
> The climing wight, on her unstable wheel,
> So much the nigher may a man expect,
> To see his head, where late he saw his heele:
> *Polycrates* hath prov'd it in effect,
> And *Dionysius* that too true did feel:
> Who long were lul'd on high in Fortune's lap,
> And fell down sodainly to great mishap.

My Lord Lieutenant. The Earl of Essex.

Sir Henry Harington. A kinsman of Sir John. A detachment of troops under his command had been defeated at Arkloo [Arklow], near Wicklow, May 29, 1599. (*Calendar State Papers, Ireland, 1599–1600,* pp. 58–59.) Essex dealt severely with the defeated soldiers.

From Dublin, July 11, 1599, he wrote to the lords of the council in England: "On Monday last [July 9] I called a martial court upon the captains and officers, who were under sir *Henry Harrington,* when our troops having advantage of number, and no disadvantage of ground, were put to the rout, and many cut in pieces without striking a blow. In this court *Pierce Walsh,* lieutenant to capt. *Adam Loftus,* for giving the first example of cowardice and dismaying to the troops, was condemned to die, and afterwards accordingly executed. The other captains and officers, tho' they forsook not their places assigned them, but were forsaken by their soldiers; yet because in such an extremity and distress they did not something very extraordinary, both by their example to encourage the soldiers, and to acquit themselves, were all cashiered, and are still kept in prison. The soldiers being before condemned all to die, were by me most of them pardoned, and, for example sake, only every tenth man executed. Sir *Henry Harrington,* because he is a privy counsellor in this kingdom, I forbear to bring to trial, till I know her majesty's pleasure." (Birch, *Memoirs of the Reign of Queen Elizabeth,* II, 420–421.)

LETTER 11.

Reprinted from *Nugae Antiquae,* 1804, I, 309.

Sir Anthony Standen. Cf. Letter 8.

I came to court. Harington, bearing a letter from the Lords Justices Loftus and Carey to the Privy Council, left Dublin, October 29, 1599, and reached Richmond, November 6, 1599. (*Calendar State Papers, Ireland, 1599–1600,* 207, 235–236.)

Going to see Tyrone. Cf. Letter 10.

My Lord Keeper is a widdower. Thomas Egerton, to whom a few months later Harington addressed an epigram upon the occasion of his marriage to Lady Alice Stanley, widow of Ferdinand Stanley, fifth Earl of Derby. (Epigram 248.)

Doctor Eaton hath eaten the bishoprick of Ely. Dr. Martin Eaton was consecrated as Bishop of Ely, February 3, 1599/1600. (Francis Godwin, *A Catalogue of the Bishops of England,* ed. 1615, 283.)

Master Edmondes. Thomas Edmondes (1563?–1639) was employed on various diplomatic missions. He was knighted by King James I, May 20, 1603.

You wonder I write nothing of one. The Earl of Essex was still a prisoner at York House.

Till these great businesses be concluded. Suspicion and intrigue were everywhere. Harington probably means the negotiations with James, King of Scotland.

LETTER 12.

Printed from the original preserved at Hatfield House, Hatfield MSS., 80, 62.

Sir Robert Cecil. The most powerful political rival of Essex. It must be remembered that Essex had made an unsatisfactory truce with the Earl of Tyrone, and had returned to England without the Queen's consent. When, on September 29, 1599, the day after his arrival at court, he was called before the privy council, Cecil presented, in the name of the Queen, a number of complaints against him. "The earl answered with the utmost temper, gravity, and discretion the matters laid to his charge, his contemptuous disobedience of her majesty's letters and will, in returning; his presumptuous letters written from time to time; his proceedings in Ireland, contrary to the points resolved upon before he went; his rash manner of coming away from Ireland; his making of so many knights; and his overbold going the day before to her majesty in her bed-chamber." (Birch, *Memoirs of the Reign of Queen Elizabeth,* 1754, II, 434.)

In October, 1599, while Essex was a prisoner at York House, a proclamation was drawn stating that he had disregarded instructions given him before leaving England by bestowing the dignity of knighthood "beyond all moderation," and that after Queen Elizabeth had sent him a letter commanding him "not to knight any man more, but to leave that reward to her," he had made a great number of knights in the months of August and September. The proclamation named the thirty-eight persons knighted after the date of her letter, and declared their titles null and void. (*Calendar State Papers, Ireland, 1599–1600,* 218.) The proclamation was not issued. The question was again raised at the trial of Essex, June 5, 1600. Chamberlain wrote, July 1, 1600, "The Quene was very vehement the last weeke to disgrade some of my Lord of Essex Irish knights, specially such as were made after a certain letter she wrote, that he shold make no more." (*Letters of John Chamberlain,* 86.) Cecil, however, "by his interest stopped the warrant signed for this proclamation," for fear it would bring discredit upon action taken under the great seal. (Birch, *Memoirs of the Reign of Queen Elizabeth,* II, 455–456; *Sydney Papers,* II, 204.)

Harington, in Letter 12, suggests what was perhaps the real objection to issuing this proclamation. Among the "many more seriows consyderacions" was the likelihood that the popularity of Essex, the widespread sympathy that his misfortunes had evoked, and the growing hostility to the Cecil faction among the disaffected, would be increased by taking the action proposed. Few of the Essex faction were "so good philosophers as to neglect honor, and embrace paciens."

Since Harington had been knighted July 30, 1599, his rank would not have been affected by the proclamation.

The moste noble Lord Admyrall. Charles Howard, Earl of Nottingham.

Letter 13.

Printed from the original preserved at Hatfield House, Hatfield MSS., 251, 121.

The Erls of Northumberland and Rutland. Henry Percy, ninth Earl of Northumberland, and Roger Manners, fifth Earl of Rutland. The latter supported Essex in his rebellion in the following February.

The letter I wrote to yowr honor in that busynesse. Presumably Letter 12.

Letter 14.

Printed from a transcript in the possession of John E. M. Harington, Esq., a descendant of Sir John Harington of Kelston. (Vol. IX, ff. 88–89.)

Harington wrote Letters 14, 15, 16, and 17 when he was seeking to recover lands escheated by the attainder of Sir James Harington, Dean of York. In 1465 Sir James Harington of Brierley was granted certain lands for having taken prisoner King Henry VI. In the first year of the reign of King Henry VII an attainder was passed against Sir James Harington, afterwards Dean of York, because his father, Sir Robert Harington of Badsworth, and his uncle, Sir James of Brierley, had remained loyal to King Richard III at Bosworth Field. Their eldest brother, John Harington of Hornby Castle, who had died in 1460, was survived by two daughters. The elder became the wife of Sir Edward Stanley, Lord Mounteagle, to whom in 1489 the forfeited estates were granted, subject to reversion to the Crown in default of male issue. Accordingly, the estates continued with the Stanleys. In 1522, however, Sir James Harington of Wolphege, Clerk of the Bakehouse or Kitchen, received a grant of the Crown's reversionary interest in these lands, subject to reversion to the Crown in case of failure of male representatives of Sir James's line. Sir James of Wolphege had three sons, two of whom died without issue. Stephen, the surviving son, lived until 1598. In 1570 the Crown's reversionary interest was granted to John Harington of Stepney and to his heirs male, of whom John, afterwards Sir John of Kelston, was the eldest. In 1580 the heirs male of the Lords Mounteagle failed, and in 1598 Stephen

Harington, representing the rights under the contingent grant of Henry VIII, died. Then John Harington began to assert his title. (*Miscellanea Genealogica et Heraldica,* III, 1880, 269–270; Manuscripts of John E. M. Harington, Esq., IX, ff. 75, 88–89.)

Harington sought the help of his most influential friends. In a memorandum he preserved the names of those who in August and September 1600 wrote letters to aid him in his suit. Queen Elizabeth wrote "Master Justyce Walmsley, Master Robert Heskyth, hyghe Shreeve of Lancashyre, Master —— Swyft, hyghe Shreeve of Yorkshire." Sir Robert Cecil wrote "Master Thomas Heskith, Attorney of the Wardes" and Sir Richard Mollineux. Egerton, the Lord Keeper, wrote three letters, Sir Thomas Gerard two, and the Earl of Cumberland one. (F. J. Poynton, *Memoranda, Historical and Genealogical, relating to the Parish of Kelston, in the County of Somerset,* 1885, Part III, 36.)

Sir John's attempts to recover these lands were unsuccessful. The claims were revived by his son, John Harington of Kelston. For surrendering to King Charles I his interest in the lands of Sir James Harington, attainted, he received from the King, on June 21, 1635, the grant of one-fifth of all profits from the lands so surrendered, the remaining four-fifths being assigned to the St. Paul's Cathedral. (*Calendar State Papers, Domestic, 1635,* 137.)

Judge Walmsley. Thomas Walmsley was constituted a judge of the Common Pleas in 1589. On King James's accession he was reappointed and knighted. It appears that Justice Walmsley went the Western Circuit with Justice Fenner for five consecutive years, from 1596 to 1601. (Edmund Foss, *A Biographical Dictionary of the Justices of England,* 1870, 698.)

LETTER 15.

Printed from a transcript in the possession of John E. M. Harington, Esq. (Vol. IX, f. 90.)

Sir John Stanhope. He was Vice-Chamberlain and Treasurer of the Chamber. He was created Baron Stanhope of Harrington, Northamptonshire, May 4, 1605. (*Calendar State Papers, Domestic, 1603–1610,* 214.)

Surveyor . . . of the Cowrt of Wardes. A minor official of the Court of Wards and Liveries.

LETTER 16.

Printed from a transcript in the possession of John E. M. Harington, Esq. (Vol. IX, f. 91.)

LETTER 17.

Printed from a transcript in the possession of John E. M. Harington, Esq. (Vol. IX, f. 92.)

The last sentence of this letter, with a few verbal changes, is included in *Nugae Antiquae* (1779), II, 230, but with no indication of date or authorship. Thomas Park, in his edition, ascribes it to John Harington of Stepney, the father of Sir John Harington of Kelston. (*Nugae Antiquae,* 1804, I, 118–119.) Although, as Park points out, John of Stepney presented to Queen Elizabeth several costly gifts, among them in 1572 a "prety Jewel" (Nichols, *Progresses of Queen Elizabeth,* 1823, I, 295; II, 2, 77), there can be little doubt that the letter is Sir John's and the year of its composition 1600.

A Tedyous and Dangerous and Chargeable Jorney. Harington had visited, apparently late in 1600, the lands for which he had been suing. Sir Robert Sidney, brother of Sir Philip Sidney and of Mary Herbert, Countess of Pembroke, mentions the journey in a letter to Harington, written sometime during the year 1600. (*Nugae Antiquae,* 1804, I, 312–316):

"Worthy Knight,

"Your presente to the Queen was well accepted of; she did much commend your verse, nor did she less praise your prose. Your Irysh business is less talked of at her Highness's palace, for all agree that you did go and do as you were bidden; and, if the great commanders went not where they ought, how shoud the captains do better withouten order?—But, mum, my worthy knight; I crave all pardon for touching your galled back.

"The Queen hath tasted your dainties, and saith you have marvellous skill in cooking of good fruits. If I can serve you in your northern suit, you may commande me: I hear you have been to those parts, and taken possession of Harrington Parke. Our Lawyers say your title is well grounded, in conscience, but that strict law doth not countenance your recoveringe those landes of your ancestors, as the Queen's ryghte is somewhat extinguished by your cosins Stephen and James, who left issue; and hereby it comyth not straight to the Queen, whose good will towarde you is ever apparent. I have seen ancient recordes, wherein it appeareth, that Sir James Harington, slain in Bosworth field, did give by wyll all these landes to his brother, Sir Robert, who was attainded by Hen. VIIth, for siding with the Yorkists. Our Queen's Father did grant them by reversion to your father; and so far I learn from Master Sherwood, a cunning lawyer: what I can do herein I will to serve you. Visit your friendes often, and please the Queen by all you can, for all the great lawyers do much fear her displeasure. I know not how matters may prosper with your noble commander, the Lord Essex; but must say no more at this time of writing. My sister [Mary Herbert, Countess of Pembroke] beareth this in privacy, and therefore so safe; but I will not trust to ill fortune which crosseth good purpose, and leadeth oft to danger. My malady is much abated. My wife hath been my doctor, my nurse, my friend, and my sovereign cure. I supp broth from the Queen's kitchen, and eat of her Majesties sweet cakes, which do nourish my poor blood, and cherish good humours. I do read 'Ariosto,' and commenced the translator to all friends, which you mark as the best good will I can shew you.

"Now you have left the sword in Ireland, and taken to the plough in England; let me have proofs of your employ, and send me verses when you can. I do see the Queen often; she doth wax weak since the late troubles, and Burleigh's death doth often draw tears from her goodly cheeks; she walketh out but little, meditates much alone, and sometimes writes in private to her best friends. The Scottish matters do cause much discourse, but we know not the true grounds of state business, nor venture farther on such ticklish points. Her Highness hath done honour to my poor house by visiting me, and seemed much pleased at what we did to please her. My son made her a fair speech, to which she did give most gracious reply. The women did dance before her, whilst the cornets did salute from the gallery: and she did vouchsafe to eat two morsels of rich comfit cake, and drank a small cordial from a gold cup. She had a marvelous suit of velvet borne by four of her first women attendants in rich apparel; two ushers did go before, and at going up stairs she called for a staff, and was much wearied in walking about the house, and said she wished to come another day. Six drums and six trumpets waited in the court, and sounded at her approach and departure. My wife did bear herself in wondrous good liking, and was attired in a purple kyrtle, fringed with gold; and myself, in a rich band and collar of needlework, and did wear a goodly stuff of the bravest cut and fashion, with an underbody of silver and loops. The Queen was much in commendation of our appearances, and smiled at the ladies, who in their dances often came up to the stepp on which the seat was fixed to make their obeysance, and so fell back into their order again. The younger Markham did several gallant feats on a horse before the gate, leaping down and kissing his sword, then mounting swiftly on the saddle, and passed a lance with much skill. The day well nigh spent, the Queen went and tasted a small beverage that was set out in divers rooms where she might pass; and then in much order was attended to her palace, the cornets and trumpets sounding through the streets. One knyght (I dare not name) did say, the Queen had done me more honour than some that had served her better; but envious tongues have venomd shafts: and so I reste in peace with what hath happened, and God speed us all; my worthie Knight.

"I wish you in health and good cheer, and when fortune doth favour, I hope to see you this way and taste wit, and you shall taste our wine. Thus I will lay down my quill, which seldom wearys in a friendly tale; but achs, and pains, and sleep, and haste, do all conspire against further matter of writing. Ever remaining, in kind remembrance,

Your Friend,

Rob. Sydney."

LETTER 18.

Printed from the original in the Cambridge University Library, Add. MS. 337, f. 1.

Lady Jane Rogers, of Cannington, Somersetshire, widow of Sir George Rogers, who died in 1582. (*The Visitation of the County of Somerset in the Year 1623,* ed. F. T. Colby, Harleian Society, XI, 1876, p. 99; *Miscellanea Genealogica et Heraldica,* III, 1880, 219.)

My long promisd Orlando. His translation of *Orlando Furioso* (1591), to which he has added this letter and fifty-two epigrams.

LETTER 19.

Printed from a transcript in the Library of the Inner Temple, Petyt MS. 538, vol. 43, f. 303 b.

Lucy, Countess of Bedford, was the daughter of Sir John's kinsman, Sir John Harington, first Lord Harington of Exton, whose mother was Lucy Sidney, daughter of Sir William Sidney.

Trulie devine translation of three of Davids psalmes. The psalms are numbers 51, 104, and 137. (Petyt MS. 538, 43, f. 284.) Among various memoranda Harington, in a list of "things sent to London the 29th of Jan: 1609" [1609–1610], includes the "Countess of Pembr: psalms: 2 copies." (British Museum Addit. MSS. 27632, f. 30.) The translation was not printed until 1823, when it appeared as *The Psalms of David translated into divers and sundry kinds of Verse. Begun by the noble and learned gent. Sir Philip Sidney, Knt., and finished by the right honorable the Countess of Pembroke his sister. Now first printed from a copy of the Original Manuscript Transcribed by John Davies of Hereford in the reign of James the first, 1823.*

That Excellent Countesse. Mary Herbert, Countess of Pembroke, "Sidney's sister, Pembroke's mother." She and Lord Harington of Exton were first cousins.

Som shallowe meditations of myne owne. Harington sends ten of his epigrams (Petyt MS. 538, 43, ff. 289 b, 290, 290 b), numbered 188, 272, 31, 81, 337, 66, 90, 267, 338, 122. It does not appear that the Countess of Bedford either accepted or praised them, or that Harington was "embouldned to present more of them, and to entytle some of them" to her.

LETTER 20.

Printed from the original preserved at Hatfield House, Hatfield MSS., 76, 29.

Sir John Stanhop. Stanhope. Cf. Letter 15.

Dr. James. John James was appointed physician to Queen Elizabeth's household in 1595. He died about January 26, 1601. (Venn, *Alumni Cantabrigienses.*) On February 3, 1601, John Chamberlain wrote, "Michael Heneage died at Christmas, and the keeping of the records in the Tower was promised to Dr. James of the Court, but he is dead also." (*Calendar State Papers, Domestic, 1598–1601,* 544.)

I went to the North. Cf. Letter 17.

Master Attorney of the Wards. Thomas Heskith was then Master of the Court of Wards and Liveries, having been appointed in 1589. (Venn, *Alumni Cantabrigienses.*) Sir Robet Cecil, who was Master of the same court, had written Heskith in behalf of Harington during the preceding August or September. Cf. Letter 14 and notes.

LETTER 21.

Printed from the original, Hatfield MSS., 88, 28.

Master Arthur Hoptons place. Sir Arthur Hopton, K. B. (1603), of Witham, Somersetshire, son of Sir Owen Hopton, Lieutenant of the Tower. (*The Visitation of the County of Somerset in the Year 1623,* Harleian Society, 1876, pp. 56–57.)

The Lord Levetenant. The Earl of Hertford had recently succeeded the Earl of Pembroke as Lord Lieutenant of Somersetshire. (*Acts of the Privy Council, 1599–1600,* 551–552; *Acts of the Privy Council, 1600–1601,* 304.) The appointment of a "Coronell" was made by the Privy Council. "The Lord lieutenant was . . . as bound . . . to perform the instructions sent down to him by the council as were the justices of the peace and the sheriff." (E. P. Cheyney, *A History of England from the Defeat of the Armada to the Death of Elizabeth,* II, 364.)

Pure speryted fellows. One of Harington's contemptuous terms for Puritans.

In the yeer 88. my Cowntry can witnesse my forwardnes, and the last 8th of february yowr honor was an ey witnesse of my redynesse. No evidence is at hand to show what service Harington rendered in the defence against the expected Spanish invasion in 1588 or in putting down the rebellion of Essex, February 8, 1601.

LETTER 22.

Reprinted from *Nugae Antiquae,* 1804, I, 317.

Sir Hugh Portman. Cf. Letter 7.

My Lord Buckhurst. He succeeded Lord Burghley as lord treasurer.

The city business. The Essex rebellion, February 8, 1601.

Our sweete Lady Arundel. Margaret Willoughby, wife of Sir Matthew Arundell of Wardour, and mother of Sir Thomas Arundell. She was one of Queen Elizabeth's oldest friends, and had been, with Harington's mother, in attendance upon Elizabeth before her accession. Cf. Letter 7.

LETTER 23.

Printed from the original preserved at Hatfield House, Hatfield MSS., 93, 117.

I retorned by Grantam, whear I herd the tragicomedy of the Maypole and the minister in which women wear soch agents as the men wear at last forced to be pacient. Though Harington may allude to a drama, it is more likely that he is writing of some little event that had taken place at court, some matter of precedence or of social rivalry.

Capten Lovell that drayneth the fenns thear. July 13, 1597, there was made a "grant to Capt. Thos. Lovell, for 21 years, of the sole privilege in England of draining marshes and overflowed grounds, scouring and cleansing ports and havens, making turf called Boggeringe, drifts to take fowl, called Veugle coyes, and fen barns, called Barghues, provided his experiments have been first invented beyond seas, and he meddle with no ports nor marshes without the owners' licence." (*Calendar State Papers, Domestic, 1595–1597,* 458.)

Yowr moste worthy fathers tombe. William Cecil, Lord Burghley, who died August 4, 1598, was buried in Stamford Church.

Pallace of Burleghe. Not Burghley House, at Westminster, but the ancestral estate at Burghley, Northamptonshire, at this time the property of Thomas Cecil, Sir Robert Cecil's half-brother.

The paradyce of Theballs. Theobalds, in Hertfordshire, one of the most splendid country houses of Elizabethan England, was owned by Sir Robert Cecil.

Cambridge, the Nursery of all my good breedinge. Harington matriculated as a fellow-commoner from King's College; he received the B.A. degree in 1577–1578, and the M.A. in 1581. (*Venn, Alumni Cantabrigienses.*)

So worthy a chawncellor. Sir Robert Cecil served as Chancellor of the University of Cambridge from 1601 to 1612.

Yowr sweet sonne. William Cecil matriculated as fellow-commoner from St. John's College, 1602. (Venn, *Alumni Cantabrigienses.*)

"But which was straung whear earst I left a wood
A wondrous stately pallace now thear stood."

Harington's translation of Ariosto's *Orlando Furioso* (1591), Book 43, stanza 124.

"And unto this a lardg and lyghtsom stayr
Without the which no roome ys truly fayr."

Orlando Furioso, Book 42, stanza 69.

Myne own poor howse. At Kelston, Somersetshire.

My eldest sonne. John Harington (1589–1654).

His godfather. The Kelston Registers record that Robert Harington was baptized June 29, 1602, and buried February 2, 1605. The following letter (Hatfield MSS., 94, 13), from John Wynter to Sir Robert Cecil, indicates that Cecil consented to act as godfather.

"Right honorable. According to youer directions to my exceding joye that you wold imploie me as a deputi for youer honor I have Cristinid Sir John Haringtons childe and named hym Robert.

"I was accompanied with Sir Morris Barkely mistris Cooper deputie for my Ladie Hastings. I presented a Riche bowle and cover of doble guilt plate with youer honorable good wishes to the childe wich the parents toke veri joifullie. I allso bestowed youer farther liberalliti upon the midwife and nurses.

"And so with my most humble thankis for youer honorable regarde and respect of me, I rest what I am able in all ocasions at youer Honors comaundement redie to do you faithfull service. The Almighti god kepe you allwaies happy. And me in youer good faver. July 8 Ano 1602.

youer Honors humblie at Comaunde,
John Wynter."

Sir Morris Barkely. Sir Maurice Berkeley of Bruton in Somersetshire.

Ladie Hastings. Sarah Harington, sister of John, first Lord Harington of

Exton, and widow of Francis Lord Hastings, son of George Hastings, fourth Earl of Huntingdon. Francis died before his father, but in the same year, 1595.

LETTER 24.

Printed from the original preserved at Hatfield House, Hatfield MSS., 93, 150.

A homely present. The sanitary device that Harington discussed in his "ydle discowrse on this subject." (*The Metamorphosis of Ajax,* 1596.)

Theballs. Theobalds, Sir Robert Cecil's country house in Hertfordshire. Cf. Letter 23.

Yowr howse in the Strand. Sir Robert was then building Cecil House in the Strand on the site now occupied by the Hotel Cecil. (Algernon Cecil, *A Life of Robert Cecil,* 1915, 165.)

My retowrn out of the cowntry. The letter was written seven days before his son's baptism, for which he visited Kelston, Somersetshire.

LETTER 25.

Reprinted from Edmund Lodge's *Illustrations of British History, Biography, and Manners* (1838), II, 552–554, where it is attributed to Sir John Harington, later second Lord Harington of Exton, who was at this time only ten years old. The original is in the library of the College of Arms, Talbot MSS., Vol. M, f. 61. Since the College of Arms will not permit the copying of the Talbot MSS., this letter and Letter 36 are here reprinted from previously published versions. The editor is indebted to the College of Arms for permission to examine this letter and others by Harington and to take notes for use in this volume.

The first paragraph deals with the subject discussed in Letter 24.

Master Secretary. Sir Robert Cecil.

Biron. Marshall Biron, who had been French ambassador to England, and whose tragic career so closely resembled that of the Earl of Essex, was tried for treason July 28, 1602, convicted, and beheaded. (Cheyney, *A History of England from the Defeat of the Armada to the Death of Elizabeth,* II, 553–555.)

Sir Edward Conway, of the Brill. Then Governor of the Brill.

Sir Oliver Sentjohn. St. John later became President of Munster and eventually Lord Deputy of Ireland.

The progress holds still, where it was, and as it was. Queen Elizabeth planned a long "progress" for the summer of 1602. John Chamberlain, July 8, 1602, wrote, "We speak of a Progress to begin toward the end of this month; first to Sir John Fortescue's, in Buckinghamshire; then to the Earl of Hertford's and the Chief Justice [Popham] . . . and so to Bath and Bristol." (Nichols, *Progresses of Queen Elizabeth,* 1823, III, 578.) "On or about the last day of July" she was the guest of Lord Keeper Egerton at Harefield Place, Middlesex, where unusual storms kept her much indoors. (Nichols, *op cit.,* III, 582; Lodge, *Illustrations,* II, 560–561.) Increasing weakness and unpleasant weather led the Queen to change her plans, and she did not visit the Earl of Hertford at Elvetham in Hampshire, where she had been a guest in 1591. On August 3, 1602, Thomas Edmonds wrote the Earl of Shrewsbury, "Her Majesty hath had compassion, notwithstanding her earnest affection to go her progress, yet to forbear the same in favour to her people, in regard of the unseasonableness of the weather; and for that purpose doth appoint to return by the end of this week." Chamberlain wrote, October 2, "The Queen's Progress went not far—first, to Chiswick to Sir William Russell's, then to Ambrose Copinger's; . . . then to Harvil [Harefield] to the Lord Keeper's, and then to Sir William Clarke's by Burnham." (Lodge, *op. cit.*, 562; Nichols, *op. cit.*, III, 578.) When Harington wrote this letter, the Queen was probably at Harefield.

My Lord Admiral. Charles Howard, Earl of Nottingham.

Letter 26.

Printed from the draft retained by Harington, British Museum Add. MS. 12049, p. 194.

My sonne. John Harington (1589–1654). At the age of fifteen, he matriculated from Trinity College, Oxford, December 7, 1604. He migrated to Cambridge and was incorporated there in 1607. (Venn, *Alumni Cantabrigienses.*)

Exercyses to the queen and some of my Lords. These "exercyses" in Latin verse, with the English translation, follow this letter. (British Museum Add. MS. 12049, pp. 195–201.) All are in Harington's autograph.

Letter 27.

Reprinted from *Nugae Antiquae,* 1804, I, 320–324.

I finde some lesse mindfull of whate they are soone to lose, than of what they may perchance hereafter get. This sentence is perhaps dictated by the uneasy conscience of the courtier who only nine days before had completed his tract advocating the succession of James, and who had sent the King of Scotland as a Christmas present laudatory verses and an elaborate lantern, with the motto, "Lord, remember me when thou comest in thic kingdom." (Harington, *A Tract on the Succession to the Crown,* ed. Clements R. Markham, 1880, 123; *Nugae Antiquae,* 1804, I, 325–335; Nichols, *The Progresses of King James I,* 1828, I, 48–49.)

Her affectione to my mother who waited in privie chamber. Isabella Markham, daughter of Sir John Markham, of Cotham, was of the queen's privy chamber from the Hatfield days until her death in 1579. (Harington, *A Tract on the Succession to the Crown,* pp. 40–41.)

She gave me a message to the Lord Deputie. Charles Blount, Lord Mountjoy, was Lord Deputy. The rebellion of Tyrone had been put down, and the rebel had offered to accept the queen's terms. It appears that she selected Harington to take a letter to Mountjoy, who was carrying on negotiations with Tyrone in Dublin.

My manne Combe. Thomas Combe, Harington's confidential servant. Cf. Letter 19.

Letter 28.

Reprinted from *Nugae Antiquae,* 1804, I, 336–339.

Lord Thomas Howard. Second son of Thomas Howard, fourth Duke of Norfolk, attainted. Born in 1561, he was restored in blood as Lord Thomas Howard, December, 1584. In January, 1603, a few months before the date of this letter, Howard had been host to Queen Elizabeth at the Charterhouse. (*Calendar State Papers, Domestic, 1600–1603,* 285; Nichols, *Progresses of Queen Elizabeth,* 1823, III, 602.) King James made Howard a privy councillor, May 4, 1603, and Earl of Suffolk, July 21, 1603.

Oure new Kynges cominge. James, after a leisurely journey from Edinburgh, reached London, May 7, 1603.

I maye call Sir Roberts no ill borden to Edenborrow. Sir Robert Carey, in defiance of the wishes of the Privy Council, anticipated the official messengers in carrying to King James of Scotland the news of Queen Elizabeth's death. He was appointed one of the Gentlemen of the Bedchamber, but on the King's coming to England he was discharged from that post and disappointed in the promises made to him. Carey's conduct was branded by the Privy Council as "contrary to such commandments as we had power to lay upon him, and to all decency, good manners, and respect."

LETTER 29.

Printed from the original, Hatfield MSS., 100, 28.

My very good Lord. King James had raised Sir Robert Cecil to the peerage under the title of Lord Cecil of Essingdon, May 14, 1603. Harington's letter to Cecil, dated May 21, 1603, had apparently not reached Cecil before the composition of the following letter to Sir John (*Nugae Antiquae,* 1804, I, 344–346):

"My Noble Knyght,

"My thankes come wythe your papers and wholesome statutes for your fathers householde. I shall, as far as in me lieth, patterne the same, and geve good heed for due observaunce thereof in my own state. Your father did muche affect suche prudence; nor dothe his sonne lesse followe his faire sample, of worke, learninge, and honor. I shall not faile to keep your grace and favor quick and lively in the Kinges breaste, as far as good discretion guideth me; so as not to hazard my own reputation for humble suing, rather than bold and forward entreaties. You know all my former steppes: good knyght, reste content, and give heed to one that hathe sorrowde in the bright lustre of a courte, and gone heavily even to the beste seeminge faire grounde. 'Tis a great taske to prove ones honestye, and yet not spoil ones fortune. You have tasted a little hereof in our blessed Queenes tyme, who was more than a man, and (in troth) sometyme less than a woman. I wishe I waited now in her presence-chamber, with ease at my foode, and reste in my bedde. I am pushed from the shore of comforte, and I know not where the wyndes and waves of a court will bear me; I know it bringeth little comforte on earthe; and he is, I reckon, no wise man that looketh this waye to heaven. We have muche stirre aboute councels, and more about honors. Many knyghts were made at Theobalds, duringe the kynges staye at myne house [May 3–7, 1603], and more to be made in the cittie. My father had muche wisdom in directing the state; and I wish I could bear my part so discretely as he did. Farewel, good knyght; but never come neare London till I call you. Too much crowdinge doth not well for a cripple, and the Kynge dothe finde scante roome to sit himself, he hath so many *friends,* as they choose to be called, and Heaven prove they lye not in the end. In trouble, hurrying, feigning, suing, and such-like matters, I nowe reste

Your true friende,

R. Cecil.

29 May, 1603."

John Skinner. Cf. Letter 48 and notes, especially Harington's deposition in 1609. John Chamberlain, October 23, 1602, wrote to Dudley Carleton, "Alderman Skinners eldest sonne, having spent the most that he had, and bought a place in Barwicke, hath ben tampering with somwhat that he is called in question for, and clapt up close prisoner in the Gatehouse." (*Letters Written by John Chamberlain,* Camden Society, 1861, 170–171.)

Old Markham. Thomas Markham, of Ollerton, brother of Isabella Markham, Harington's mother, and father of Sir Griffin Markham.

LETTER 30.

Printed from the original, Hatfield MSS., 187, 66.

My uncle. Thomas Markham, of Ollerton.

My unaccustomed Lodging. Harington was lodged in the Gate-House Prison, Westminster. Cf. Letter 42.

LETTER 31.

Printed from the original, Hatfield MSS., 187, 69.

Sir Roger Ashton. Sir Roger Aston or Ashton was an Englishman in the service of King James before his accession to the English throne. He was a Gentleman of the Bedchamber and Master of the Wardrobe. (Lodge, *Illustrations,* III, 31.)

LETTER 32.

Printed from the original, Hatfield MSS., 101, 99.

Master Georg Brookes servant. George Brooke (1568–1603) was a brother of Henry Brooke, eighth Lord Cobham. After receiving the M.A. degree at Cambridge in 1586, he obtained a prebend in the church of York. Queen Elizabeth promised him the mastership of the hospital of St. Cross, near Winchester, but she died before the vacancy was filled, and King James gave it to another. Brooke, disappointed and angry, became a conspirator in the Bye Plot to seize the government. He was apprehended in July, 1603, and was executed December 5, 1603, despite the fact that he was Cecil's brother-in-law. (*Dictionary of National Biography.*)

Timothee Elks. Possibly the man mentioned by Cecil in a letter to Sir Ralph Winwood, July 25, 1611, as "one Elkes a Servant to the Earle [of Northumberland]. (*Winwood Memorials,* III, 287–288.)

Sir Griphin Markham. Cf. Letter 9. Sir Griffin Markham, like Brooke, was involved in the Bye Plot. He was arrested in July, 1603, at the same time as Raleigh, Lords Grey and Cobham, George Brooke, and others. He was convicted of high treason, reprieved on the scaffold, and banished from England. He went to the Low Countries, where he lived in poverty until his death about forty years later. (*Dictionary of National Biography;* Birch, *Memoirs of the Reign of Queen Elizabeth,* I, 158.)

Lady Markham. The wife of Sir Griffin Markham was Anne, daughter of Peter Roos of Laxton.

Sir Thomas Erskin. Sir Thomas Erskine (1560–1639) had been educated and reared with King James, and enjoyed his favor until the King's death. In August, 1600, when the sons of the first Earl of Gowry attempted to assassinate James, Erskine and others prevented and killed them. His conduct on that occasion Harington praised in an epigram (Epigram 247; British Museum Add. MS. 12049, pp. 172–173.) Among the manuscripts of John E. M. Harington, Esq. (IX, 126) there is, in Harington's autograph a copy of a letter from Erskine to Harington, written early in 1603:

"*To the honorable knyght my trustie freind Sir John Harington by Bathe.*

"Honorable Sir. I resaived your Letter sent by this gentillman, who delivered to his Majesty that vas committed to him. All yow sent to Master Hunter your assured and constant freind is sa weill accepted of his Majestie that I do not dout but in the anon tyme ye vill fynde more in effect, nor I can express by pepier. And althoughe for the present I doe not advertise particulerly yet must I intreat your favourable censure as one that shall ever love you, and do his best for the accomplishement of your desair. In short time I hope to see qz and qu

I am not certaine, but then shall yow know more of our maisters Love to your selfe, and my devotion to doe yow service, qu shall constantly remayne

Your assured freind

T. Areskyne."

In 1603 Erskine was appointed captain of the yeomen of the guard, and later was created first Earl of Kellie.

To the releefe of my distresse by the Markhams, hee hath sayd in his princely word I shall have theyr forfeyture. At about this time Harington wrote Gilbert Talbot, seventh Earl of Shrewsbury, an undated letter, endorsed 1603. (College of Arms, Talbot MSS., Vol. M, f. 84.) He thanks Shrewsbury for some great favor, and hopes to perform more than he promises if God give him health in "this contagious time." He has moved King James for the benefit of Sir Griffin Markham's forfeiture, and he asks Shrewsbury's favor to advance his suit, especially with the Lord Treasurer of Scotland, Sir George Hume. The Lord of Mar and the Lord of Kinlisshe have promised to further it. Sir Thomas Lake would do much if Shrewsbury will "animate" him in it.

Almost a year later, June 28, 1604, Harington was granted all the lands escheated by attainder of Sir Griffin Markham. (*Calendar State Papers, Domestic, 1603–1610,* 125.)

Letter 33.

Printed from the original, Hatfield MSS., 97, 54, 55. Undated, but endorsed 1603.

Dobbinson. Ralph Dobbinson, Bailiff of Westminster. (*Calendar State Papers, Domestic, 1603–1610,* 302, 608.)

Okey. William Okey or Oky, Keeper of the Gate-House Prison, Westminster. (*Acts of the Privy Council, 1601–1604,* 234, 458.)

Sir William Wade. Sir William Wade or Waad was a clerk of the council in 1600; he was made Lieutenant of the Tower, September 22, 1605. (*Acts of the Privy Council, 1600–1601,* 52; *Calendar State Papers, Domestic, 1603–1610,* 234.)

The Fryer eskaped last day. A Jesuit, "brave in his apparel and wearing a great black feather in his hat," had arrived at Dover in 1603, and had been lodged in the Gate-House Prison. (Hatfield MSS., 100, 52, 57, 73.)

Sir Walter Cope. He was one of Cecil's most intimate friends.

To Letter 33 and to other letters that have apparently not been preserved, Cecil wrote a sharp reply, a rough draft of which, dated October 26, 1603, he retained. (Hatfield MSS., 187, 120.)

"Although I have not so good leasure, as you have, to write; nor have so well studied other mens humours, as you; yet I conceave I have that knowledg, which is most necessary, which is, to know God and myself; and therefore, although I love counsaill, and have ben taught pacience by undergoeing the sharp censures of busye braynes, yet your advise at this tyme to me, to bannish all passion, but compassion, was as superfluous as many other labors of yours, which I coud never conn without booke, and therefore cannot so particularly remember you of them, as you can doe me of the faults of my lettre: I will therefore onely answer you now in truth and playnness, with what minde I wrote my lettre; first I assure you I had both compassion of your Imprisonment and your escape; for in the first I knew you had suffered misery, or rather affiction (for so you prescribe me to call it) which I alwaie pitied, when it falls upon gentlemen that have any good partes in them. Secondly I was greeved in your behalf, because the reasons sayd to be used by you for your escape, especially concerning my self, proclaimed you to the world to have neither honesty nor conscience, both which should alwaies be founde in those whome I respect, as I have done you. You picked passion owt of my lettre. I confesse I was not without grief (nay passion if you will have it) to see you were part of the occasion of my infortunity to be exclamed on in the world, for being privy to such a shyft (whereof my soule was innocent) and whereby other men should be undone: of whome both in common Justice, and by the accident of their places, I had cause to take compassion: Thus have you the motyve of my lettre and my passions, which yf it hath wrought any other effects then it deserves in your minde to one of my place, or shall become your penn (which men say is alwaies so full of inke as in many of your writings many blotts droppe upon the paper) I shalbe sensible of it, howsoever other men have swallowed your censorious writings. And therefore looke over my first lettre to your wyf, and yf you finde, that being informed of naughty reports raysed of me by you, I writt respectively to my Lady and with suspense of beleef, tyll I heard your answer, which course could geve you no cause to be so picquant with me, then mend your error, or I wille appeale to him that knowes both you and me, and can best judge what appartayneth to us. for your offer to acquaint Sir William Waade, and Sir Walter Cope with the course you intend, I lyke it well, and have written to them, to heare it. for the reports of Dobbinson and Okey, his speaches may be truly sett doune for oght I know, onely this I say, where you informe that they reporte that I have had lent me money in that they belye me, as I will make them both confesse, yf you can make good that they have said it; tyll which tyme, because it becomes not one of my place to be credulous, I must say that I am apter to beleeve you in some other matter. Lastly for your information now that Sir Griffin Markhams mother hath used long spite and scorn to me and myne, it can no way moove me (yf I dyd beleeue it) to pursue Sir Griffin the rather, for that matter howsoever your hope of his land may moove you the rather to accuse them; and therefore Sir John Harrington trust no more thereby to make me your solicitor then to purchase grace of the tyme present the sooner by rayling (as you are accused to doe) of the later Queen of famous memory at your dynners, for if you knew my soveraine lorde as I do you wold quickly find that such woorks are to him unacceptable sacrifices. Thus have you from me the answer which your lettre deserveth and shall in all things else have just measure, expecting from you satisfaction in the last point and an excuse for your fiery and captious lettre, which if you doe I will say this Errantis sit medecina confessio and will remaine as I have ben

Your loving frend"

LETTER 34.

Reprinted from *Nugae Antiquae,* 1804, I, 340–343.

I have lived to see that damnable rebel Tir-Owen broughte to Englande, curteouslie favourede, honourede, and well likede. In February, 1603, Elizabeth authorized Mountjoy, the Lord Deputy, to promise the Earl of Tyrone life, liberty, and pardon on certain conditions to which he readily agreed. He came to England, and was graciously received by King James, June 4, 1603. In August he returned to Ireland. (Cheyney, *A History of England from the Defeat of the Armada to the Death of Elizabeth,* II, 501; *Dictionary of National Biography.*)

I . . . did returne wyth the Lorde Leiutenante. Harington returned to England some five weeks after Essex. He left Dublin, October 29, 1599, and reached Richmond, November 6. (*Calendar State Papers, Ireland, 1599–1600,* 207, 235–236.) Essex reached Nonesuch, September 28.

I muche feare for my good Lord Grey and Raleigh. The conspiracy of Raleigh, Cobham, Lord Grey of Wilton, and others to place Arabella Stuart on the throne was discovered in July, 1603.

Carewe. Sir George Carew, President of Munster, and later Ambassador to France.

I onlie swym nowe in oure bathes. Harington apparently wrote this letter from Bath, or from his country-house at Kelston, three miles from Bath.

LETTER 35.

Reprinted from *Nugae Antiquae,* 1804, I, 366–371.

My Sovereigne Prince. King James I.

Whome he had so late honourede and made a barone. Sir John Harington of Exton was created Lord Harington of Exton at the coronation of King James, July 21, 1603. Thomas Park incorrectly dated this letter January, 1607. (*Nugae Antiquae,* 1804, I, 366.) Henry Harington, who first published the letter, dated it 1604. (*Nugae Antiquae,* 1779, II, 116.)

The Queene his mother was not forgotten, nor Davison neither. Mary Queen of Scots and her Secretary of State.

The new weede tobacco. In 1604 King James published *A Counterblaste to Tobacco.*

LETTER 36.

Reprinted from *Nugae Antiquae,* 1804, I, 346–348. The original is in the library of the College of Arms, Talbot MSS., Vol. M, f. 285. Cf. Letter 25.

Lenton. In Nottinghamshire. Cf. Letter 38.

Sir John Skinner. Cf. Letters 29, 48.

My Lord Tresorer. Lord Buckhurst.

My Lord of Northampton. Henry Howard, Earl of Northampton.

My Lord Cecill. Robert Cecil.

My Lord Chawncellor. Thomas Egerton.

On March 11 and 12, 1604, Harington wrote Gilbert Talbot, seventh Earl of Shrewsbury. These letters are preserved in the library of the College of Arms, Talbot MSS., Vol. M, ff. 204, 210.

In his letter of March 11 he acknowledges many favors done him by the Earl since his "dismall distresse." He has some comfort from King James in that he is now empowered to sell his land in Nottinghamshire in fee farm, and in that King James have given charge that he shall have satisfaction of his debt from Sir Griffin Markham before the latter has his pardon. He is sorry to think how hard it will be for the latter unless Sir John Skinner is compelled to pay his debt. Since the Earl has so nobly procured favor for Charles and Thomas Markham, who were seduced by their brother, and has forgotten the unkindness of their parents, he now begs his support in their and the writer's complaints against Sir John Skinner, who has been the ruin of their estates and "the shaking of mine." He hopes that his complaint against Sir John Skinner will be heard before the Lords, and that the Lord Chancellor will grant a *habeas corpus* for him (Harington) to come to the Council Chamber on Tuesday.

Harington, in his letter of March 12, sends Shrewsbury a note of the demesnes of Lenton, as one Don, who is his tenant for thirteen years to come, pays him. He has been informed that there is coal in his grounds, and last year he was offered £100 a year for twenty-one years. Now his imprisonment, sickness, and other causes force him to sell it before he can search it. His land extends to within forty yards of the land of Sir Percival Willoughby, where Sir Francis

Willoughby made £1000 a year out of coal. He has been offered sixteen years' purchase for it on behalf of some one who, they say, can go by sea to it from his house. His eagerness for liberty makes him sell in haste.

LETTER 37.

Printed from the original, Hatfield MSS., 188, 110. A brief similar to that which accompanies this letter is preserved in the College of Arms, Talbot MSS., Vol. M, f. 249.

LETTER 38.

Printed from the original, Hatfield MSS., 188, 126. On June 23, 1604, Harington received the grant of the King's reversion to the site and demesnes of the Priory of Lenton, Nottinghamshire. The same grant was made, June 28, to Michael Hicks, and on the same day, apparently to compensate Harington for the exchange, the King granted him the manors of Gamston and Claworth in Nottinghamshire, Camps in Essex and Cambridge, and all other lands escheated by attainder of Sir Griffin Markham. (*Calendar State Papers, Domestic, 1603–1610,* 124, 125.)

From the baylyvs howse. Presumably the house of Ralph Dobbinson, Bailiff of Westminster. (*Calendar State Papers, Domestic, 1603–1610,* 302, 608; Letter 37.)

LETTER 39.

Printed from the original, Hatfield MSS., 188, 129.

Sir Thomas Lake. Latin Secretary to King James, and after March 9, 1604, Keeper of the Records at Whitehall.

I am defendant against my wives onely and naturall (yet to unnaturall) brother. Cf. Letter 37.

LETTER 40.

Printed from the original, Hatfield MSS., 188, 12.

The Cawse in the starchamber. Cf. Letter 37.

My Lord of Shrewsbury. Gilbert Talbot, seventh Earl of Shrewsbury.

Lord Knolls. William Knollys, son of Sir Francis Knollys, was created Baron Knollys of Rotherfield Greys in 1603.

Lord Wotton. Edward Wotton was created Baron Wotton of Marley in 1603. He had been one of Queen Elizabeth's privy councillors.

Justyce Fenner. Justyce Yelverton. Edward Fenner and Christopher Yelverton were at this time judges of the Court of King's Bench.

Sir Thomas Lake. Cf. Letter 39.

Master Michael Hix. Michael Hicks, who had been one of Lord Burghley's two chief secretaries, served Sir Robert Cecil in a somewhat similar position, and became one of his closest friends. He was knighted August 6, 1604. Cf. Letter 38.

LETTER 41.

Printed from the original, Hatfield MSS., 188, 137.

Your Lordships officer. Presumably Ralph Dobbinson, Bailiff of Westminster. Cf. Letter 33.

LETTER 42.

Printed from the original, Hatfield MSS., 189, 38.

Viscount Cranborne. Robert Cecil had been created Viscount Cranborne, August 20, 1604.

The gatehouse. The Gate-House Prison, Westminster.

Master Okey. William Okey or Oky, Keeper of the Gate-House Prison. (*Acts of the Privy Council, 1601–1604,* 234, 458.)

In that contagious tyme. During the summer of 1603 the plague was unusually deadly. In a letter to the Earl of Shrewsbury, July, 1603, Harington mentions the perils of "this contagious time." (Talbot MSS., Vol. M, f. 84.) One John Hercy, in a letter to Shrewsbury, September 13, 1603, comments upon the difficulty of avoiding contagion: "There died, as report goeth, of the sickness in and about the suburbs of London, above 3000 this last week; and in the other week before, 3385. I beseech your Lordship to be pleased to direct your letters according to your last, for I cannot get any lodging, otherwise than in inns, within ten miles of London. In Inns at Highgate, and other places within four or five miles of London, I may have choice of lodgings, but they are so dangerous, by reason of the general infection, that I dare not to adventure in any of them." (Lodge, *Illustrations,* III, 24–25.) The virulence of the plague in 1603 caused the city to attempt to enforce laws closing the theatres whenever the death-rate rose to thirty or forty deaths a week above the normal rate. (F. E. Schelling, *Elizabethan Drama,* I, 148.)

Master Dobbinson. Ralph Dobbinson, Bailiff of Westminster. (*Calendar State Papers, Domestic, 1603–1610,* 302, 608.)

Sir Hugh Beeston. Sir Walter Cope, Sir Michael Hicks, and Sir Hugh Beeston were close friends of Cecil. (Algernon Cecil, *A Life of Robert Cecil,* 335.)

Letter 43.

Printed from the original, Hatfield MSS., 110, 97.

This short relation (for yt ys to long for a lettre) contayning my humble and zelows offer for his Majesties sarvyce in Ierland. The "relation," addressed to Cecil and Charles Blount, Earl of Devonshire, contains a discussion of Irish problems, a statement of his qualifications as a public servant, and the request that Cecil and Blount urge King James to appoint him to the vacant offices of Archbishop of Dublin and Lord Chancellor of Ireland. He was not appointed. (MS. Rawlinson, B. 162; *View of the State of Ireland in 1605,* ed. W. D. Macray, Oxford, 1879.)

Letter 44.

Reprinted from *Nugae Antiquae,* 1804, I, 348–354.

Place. Thomas Park named London as the place from which this letter was written. (*Nugae Antiquae,* 1804, I, 348.) Internal evidence shows that it was written at Theobalds, Cecil's country house in Hertfordshire, where King James and his brother-in-law, Christian IV, King of Denmark, were entertained from July 24 until July 29.

I came here a day or two before the Danish King came, and from the day he did come untill this hour, I have been well nigh overwhelmed with carousal and sports of all kinds. It appears that Harington arrived at Theobalds July 22 or 23, and wrote this account July 29 or 30. Cecil's record of expenditures serves to corroborate Harington's statements, the five days' visit costing £1180. (Hatfield MSS., 119, 162–163.)

Solomon his Temple and the coming of the Queen of Sheba. This masque is mentioned nowhere else. (M. S. Steele, *Plays and Masques at Court,* Yale University Press, 1926, 150.)

I was sometime an humble presenter and assistant. Harington is not mentioned, even as "an humble presenter and assistant," in Nichols' *Progresses of Queen Elizabeth* or in Robert Withington's *English Pageantry.*

The gunpowder fright is got out of all our heads. The Gunpowder Plot had been discovered in December, 1605.

The Lord of the mansion. Robert Cecil, Earl of Salisbury.

The uniting of the kingdoms is now at hand . . . Bacon is to manage all the affair. The efforts of James I to unite England and Scotland failed; political union was not to come for ninety-nine years.

My cosin, Lord Harington of Exton, doth much fatigue himself with the royal charge of the princess Elizabeth. By privy seal order, dated October 19, 1603, Lord Harington received the charge of the Princess Elizabeth, daughter of King James, and later Queen of Bohemia. He established her with his wife and family at Combe Abbey. His own daughter, Lucy, Countess of Bedford, was a favorite of Queen Anne. The attempt of the conspirators of the Gunpowder Plot to abduct Elizabeth and proclaim her queen is told in his letter to his kinsman, Sir John Harington of Kelston (*Nugae Antiquae,* 1804, I, 371–375):

"*Much respected Cosin,*

"Our great care and honourable charge, entrusted to us by the Kings Majesty, hath been matter of so much concern, that it almost effaced the attention to kyn or friend. With Gods assistance we hope to do our Lady Elizabeth such service as is due to her princely endowments and natural abilities; both which appear the sweet dawning of future comfort to her royal father. The late divilish conspiracy did much disturb this part. The King hath got at much truth from the mouths of the crew themselves; for guilt hath no peace, nor can there be guilt like theirs. One hath confessed that he had many meetings at Bathe about this hellish design; you will do his Majesty unspeakable kindness, to watch in your neighbourhood, and give such intelligence as may furnish inquiry. We know of some evil-minded catholics in the west, whom the prince of darkness hath in alliance; God ward them from such evil, or seeking it to others. Ancient history doth shew the heart of man in divers forms: we read of states overthrown by craft and subtilty; of Princes slain in field and closet; of strange machinations devised by the natural bent of evil hearts; but no page can tell such a horrid tale as this. Well doth the wise man say, that "the wicked imagineth mischeif in secret." What, dear cosin, coud be more secret or more wicked? A wise King and wise council of a nation at one blow destroyed in such wise as was now intended, is not matchable. It shameth Caligula, Erostratus, Nero, and Domitian, who were but each of them fly-killers to these wretches. Can it be said that religion did suggest these designs; did the spirit of truth work in these mens hearts? How much is their guilt encreased by such protesting! I cannot but mark the just appointment of Heaven in the punishing of these desperate men, who fled to our neighbourhood; you hear they suffered themselves by the very means they had contrived for others. A barrel of gunpowder was set on fire during the time that the house was besieged, and killed two or three on the spot; so just is the vengeance of God! I have seen some of the chief, and think they bear an evil mark in their foreheads, for more terrible countenances never were looked upon. His Majesty did sometime desire to see these men, but said he felt himself sorely appall'd at the thought, and so forbare. I am not yet recoverd from the fever occasioned by these disturbances. I went with Sir Fulk Grevile to alarm the neighbourhood, and surprize the villains, who came to Holbach; was out five days in peril of death, in fear for the great charge I left at home. Wynter hath confessed their design to surprize the Princess at my house, if their wickedness had taken place at London. Some of them say, she woud have been proclaimed Queen. Her Highness doth often say, "what a Queen shoud I have been by this means? I had rather have been with my royal father in the Parliament-house, than wear his crown on such condition." This poor lady hath not yet recoverd the surprize, and is very ill and troubled.

"I hear by the messenger from his Majesty, that these designs were not formed by a few: the whole legion of catholics were consulted; the priests were to pacify their consciences, and the pope confirm a general absolution for this glorious deed, so honourable to God and his holy religion. His Majesty doth much medidate on this marvellous escape, and blesses God for delivering his family, and saving his kingdom, from the tryumphs of Satan and the rage of Babylon. My being created Baron of Exton did give much offence to some of the catholics; and his Majestie's honouring my wife and self with the care of the Lady Elizabeth, stirred up much discontent on every side. I only pray God to assist our poor endeavours, and accept our good will to do right herein, maugre all malice and envious calumny. If I can do you any service with the King, you may command my friendship in this and every other matter I can. He hath no little affection for your poetry and good learning, of which he himself is so great a judge and master. My Lady Sydney desires her remembrance to you, as do all friends from Warwickshire. I hope your disorder is much better; may you feel as much benefit from the Baths as I did aforetime.

"Thus, dear cosin, I have given my thoughts in large of our sad affright, as you desired by your son's letter, which is notably worded for his age. My son is now with Prince Henry, from whom I hope he will gain great advantage, from such towardly genius as he hath even at these years. May Heaven guard this realm from all such future designs, and keep us in peace and safety. My hearty love waits on Lady Mary [Harington], and every one belonging to her houshold. Pray remember what I desire as to noticing evil-minded men in your parts, as it is for the King's sake and all our own sakes.

Adieu, dear cosin,
Harington.

From Comb. Abbey,
Jan. 6."

LETTER 45.

Reprinted from *Nugae Antiquae,* 1804, I, 354–363.

Master Robert Markham. Harington's cousin. Cf. Letters 6 and 8.

My Journale wyth our Historie, duringe our marche against the Irishe rebells. (*Nugae Antiquae,* 1804, I, 268–293.)

Ladie M. Howarde was possessede of a rich border. If Harington is correct in stating that this incident occurred when he was a boy, the owner of the "rich border" can hardly have been the same person whose undutiful conduct displeased Queen Elizabeth in 1597. The following letter (*Nugae Antiquae,* 1804, I, 232–235), from William Fenton to Harington, May 23, 1597, throws more light upon the Queen's difficulty with Lady Mary Howard:

"Most respectede Friende,

"It seemethe marvellous that our gracious Queene hathe so muche annoyance from her most bounden servaunts; I verily think her Highnesse cannot demande what is not due from any of her subjects. Her owne love hathe so wrote [wrought] on us all, that the hearte muste be evil that dothe pay her its small dutie so grudgingly as some have done of late. I have not seene her Highnesse, save twice, since Easter last, bothe of which times she spake vehementlye and with great wrathe of her servante, the Ladie Marie Howarde, forasmuche as she had refused to bear her mantle at the hour her Highnesse is wontede to air in the garden, and on small rebuke did vent suche unseemlie answer as did breede much choler in her mistresse. Again, on other occasion, she was not ready to carry the cup of grace during the dinner in the privie-chamber, nor was she attending at the hour of her Majesties going to prayer. All whiche dothe now so disquiet her Highnesse, that she swore she would no more shew her any countenance, but out with all such ungracious flouting wenches; because, forsoothe, she hathe much favour and marks of love from the younge earl, which is not so pleasing to the Queene, who dothe still muche exhort all her women to remaine in virgin state as muche as may be. I adventured to say, as far as discretion did go, in defence of our friende; and did urge muche in behalfe of youthe and enticinge love, which did often abate of righte measures in faire ladies; and moreover related whatever might appease the Queene, touchinge the confession of her great kindness to her sister Jane before her marriage; all which did nothinge soothe her Highnesse anger, saying, "I have made her my servante, and she will now make herself my mistresse; but in good faith, William, she shall not, and so tell her." In short, pitie doth move me to save this ladie, and woud beg such suit to the Queene from you and your friendes, as may winn her favour to spare her on future amendmente. If you coud speak to Master Bellot to urge the Lord Treasurer on this matter, it might be to goode purpose, when a better time dothe offer to move the Queene than I had; for wordes then were to no availe, tho as discreetlie brought as I was able. It might not be amisse to talke to this poor younge ladie to be more dutiful, and not absent at meals or prayers; to bear her Highnesse mantle and other furniture, even more than all the reste of the servantes; to make ample amends by future diligence; and always to go first in the morninge to her Highnesse chamber, forasmuche as suche kindnesse will muche prevail to turne awaie all former displeasure. She must not entertaine my lorde the earle, in any conversation, but shunne his companye; but moreover be less carefull in attiringe her own person, for this seemethe as done more to win the earl, than her mistresse good will.

"Suche, and other advice, as you and other friendes are more able to give on these matters, may prevent all other extreme proceedinge, especiallye if it be urged by my Lord Treasurer, in assurance of her good behaviour. If we consider the favours shewed her familie, there is ground for ill humour in the Queen, who dothe not now beare with such composed spirit as she was wont; but, since the Irish affairs, seemethe more froward than commonlie she used to bear herself toward her women, nor dothe she holde them in discourse with such familiar matter, but often chides for small neglects; in such wise, as to make these fair maids often cry and bewail in piteous sort, as I am tolde by my sister Elizabeth.

"Pray observe secresy in discovering my good will, when you speake to Master Bellot, or write to the Lorde Treasurer; as it is not safe to bee too meddling in such matters. Commende me to your Ladye Mall, not forgetting her brothers and childerne. And now in all love I hie to mine office and dutie, remaining

Your Servante,

W. Fenton.

May 23, 1597."

LETTER 46.

Printed from the draft retained by Harington. (British Museum Add. MS. 12049, page e.)

Right Gracious and inestimably deere Prince. Harington is addressing either King James or his son Henry, Prince of Wales. Harington prepared a manuscript volume of epigrams for presentation to King James before his accession to the English throne. For this presentation manuscript Harington wrote the epigram headed "To James the VI king of Scotland. The dedicacion of the copy sent by Cap. Hunter." (Epigram 347.) It is certain that Harington presented to Prince Henry, before 1608 and probably after 1603, a manuscript volume of his epigrams. (*Nugae Antiquae,* 1804, II, 44; Royal MSS., 17 B. xxii, f. 324 b.) Letter 46, in the opinion of the editor, is addressed to Prince Henry in 1607 or a year or two earlier.

This collection or rather confusion of all my ydle Epigrams. The manuscript in which this epistle dedicatory appears contains 414 epigrams in Harington's autograph. In his *Supplie to the Catalogue of Bishops* (1608) Harington wrote, "Your Highnes knows I have written otherwise in a booke of mine I gave you, *Lib.* 3, num. 80," and quoted four lines of verse, which are from an epigram numbered III, 80 in Add. MS. 12049. (*Nugae Antiquae,* 1804, II, 44; Royal MSS. 17 B. xxii. f. 324 b.) It appears, therefore, that Add. MS. 12049 may be the source of Prince Henry's presentation manuscript.

Those yowng years and the barbatula or french Pe[cke] Devaunt. Harington apparently sent a picture of himself as a young man with a short beard trimmed to a point, or "pickedevant," a fashion affected by young men. He uses the word elsewhere: "Seldom goeth devotion with youth, be it spoken without offence of our Peckedevanted Ministers." (*Orlando Furioso,* notes following Book XLI, ed. 1634, p. 349.)

Letter 47.

Reprinted from *Nugae Antiquae,* 1804, I, 363–365.

I here sende by my servant such matter as your Highness did covet to see, in regard to Bishop Gardener of Winchester, which I shall sometime more largely treat of, and lay at your feet. In 1608 Harington presented to Prince Henry a copy of Francis Godwin's *A Catalogue of the Bishops of England* (1601). This volume is preserved in the British Museum (Royal MSS. 17 B. xxii). In manuscript, beginning at page 314 is "A Supplie, or Addicion to the Catalogue of Bishops, to the yeare 1608," written by Harington, and dated February 18, 1608 (f. 402 b). Harington's "Supplie, or Addicion" was first printed by Chetwind as *A Briefe View of the State of the Church of England* (1653). It was included by Henry Harington in *Nugae Antiquae* (1779) and by Thomas Park in his edition (1804).

A saucy sonnet. These verses are included in Harington's account of Bishop Gardiner in "A Supplie, or Addicion" (*Nugae Antiquae,* 1804, II, 70–71).

No ill written letter. This letter is printed in *Nugae Antiquae,* 1804, I, 63–66.

Letter 48.

Reprinted from James Peller Malcolm, *Londinium Redivivum,* 1803, I, 397. Malcolm ascribes this letter and later letters to Lord Harington of Exton.

Master Sutton. Thomas Sutton, founder of Charterhouse. He was one of the wealthiest Englishmen of his day.

Sir John Skinner. Cf. Letter 29.

Camps. Castle Camps, in Essex and Cambridgeshire, was one of the manors escheated by attainder of Sir Griffin Markham, and granted to Harington, June 28, 1604. (*Calendar State Papers, Domestic, 1603–1610,* 125.) Sir John Skinner later acquired title to Camps, and in 1607 conveyed the manor and advowson to Sutton for £10,800. (Malcolm, *op. cit.,* I, 397.) Immediately thereafter Skinner was imprisoned for debt. From the Fleet Prison he wrote Lord Chancellor Ellesmere, explaining that he had sold Thomas Sutton lands for £10,800, of which he owed Sir John Harington £3000, and William Smith £3100. The remainder he was to have received. The deeds upon the agreement were sealed, containing an acquittance for the whole sum, of which Sutton paid but a small part, and left London. Skinner therefore prayed for satisfaction.

Ellesmere then wrote Sutton a severe letter informing him that the case has been laid before the King, and that his Majesty has referred it to him, Lord Bruce, and others, commanding them to satisfy the creditors, to have Skinner freed from imprisonment, and to provide for his wife and children. Ellesmere concludes: "I must therefore let you know, yf you persist in this dealing towarde him, I must (in regard of the speciall care and charge layed upon us by his Majestie in the said reference) acquaint his highness with the matter, who, I am persuaded, will not take it well; and therefore wishing you forthwith to give the gentleman that reasonable satisfaccion that he may have no just cause further to prosecute his complaint, (which, no doubt, will moove some straighter course to be taken against you then I would wish, or your self will well like of,) I bid you hartily farewell. At York, 17 Aug. 1607."

To this letter Sutton replied in no great haste:

"Right honorable,

"Understandinge that your lordship had referredd the matter in question touchinge the extent uppon the mannor of Camps, extended by Wilbrahan's recognizance to the use of Master Wynne, and expectinge daylye some goode order therin, for the freinge of the said extent; I have forborne as yett to deliver all the money out of my hands to sir John Skinner; and hopinge that some good course may yet be verie shortly taken herin by those Doctors whom your lordship hath assigned to examine that busines, that beinge the greatest present matter of trouble and incumbrance to me and to the land. And that beinge discharged . . ., and some reasonable and indifferent course taken with sir John, for the quallifying of the rest of the momentarye business and wherewith the land is chargable, I will most willingly pay unto him all the money yet behinde. And lookinge daylye for some speedye end herin to be procured by sir John Skinner, I am perfectly at your lordships commandment.

"I have stayed at London untill I was in great danger of the plague, and hazarded my health, which I knowe not when I shall recover, for the want wherof is the lett that I cannot attend your lordship at this present as my dutye is. I most humbly beseech your good lordship on my knees that you would vouchsafe to spare my farther answere at this tyme, and not to procure the King's Majestie to be my heavy lord upon this occasion. And soe I wish unto you all honnor and happyness. This third of September, 1607.

Your lordships pore humble sycke servant,
Thomas Sutton."

The following deposition, made by Harington in 1609, will, in the absence of complete information, serve to explain in part the complicated and somewhat irregular transactions in which Harington, Thomas Markham, Sir Griffin Markham, Sir John Skinner, and Thomas Sutton were concerned:

"The trewe report concerning a statute of 10,000 l. acknowledged to Master Sebastian Harvie, now shereif of London, by sir John Skinner.

"Uppon the 29th of April 1600, being the 43d of queen Eliz. Thomas Markham tooke up, upon his bond and mine, of sir Edward Brabson 1000 l. which money he lent to sir John Skinner, to buy the chamberlainshippe of Barwicke of sir

John Cary, now Lord Hunsdon. Upon the loan herof sir John Skinner promist to enter into a statute to Master Markham himselfe of 10,000 l. for conveying over Camps to him for his securitie. Master Markham, being then in danger of outlawries, was persuaded by sir Griffin Markham to take the statute from sir John Harvie in the name of Master Sebastian Harvie, which was done without maister Harvie's privitie (but the trust whollie entended for Master Thomas Markham, as myselfe and Master Anthonie Nevile can testifie, and ready to depose); neither was there ever any act done to transfer the right therof to sir Griffin. When sir John Skinner was arrested upon this statute, he sought to abate the writt by answer, because he was called therein Skinner, esquyer, not Skinner, knight; and soone after he pleaded performance of the extended defeasance, but alwayes denyed it to be for payment of money, or in trust for sir Griffin Markham. The act of parliament provided against all the incombrances of Skinner and Markham, of which this was one of the chiefe, the act penned and drawn by Master Moore of the Temple specially to that purpose. My lord Cooke being to buy the land, and examining everie thing verie strictlie, hearing this statute was cancelld and vacated, and seeing the act of parliament, was very well satisfied therof, and never made further question. Upon which, Master Sutton, by my perswasion, bought the mannor *bona fide* most justlie and honestlie, and gave in present monie more by 500 l. than my lord Cooke should have given, to the great reliefe of sir John Skinner and all his, who is much to blame to shew himself so unthankfull for yt.
23d November 1609.

By me John Haryngton.

(Malcolm, *op. cit.*, I, 397–401.)

LETTER 49.

Reprinted from James Peller Malcolm, *Londinium Redivivum,* I, 399.

I recommended two commendable matters unto you, devotion and honor. The "two long lettres" are missing. Harington urged Sutton to contribute money to the Church of SS. Peter and Paul, Bath, and to make Charles, Duke of York, his heir, in the hope of being made a baron, and perhaps with the definite promise of that honor. Cf. Letters 50 and 51.

LETTER 50.

Printed from the original, Hatfield MSS., 191, 68.

Earl of Salisbury. Cecil was created Earl of Salisbury, May 4, 1605.

Castle Camps. Cf. Letter 48 and Notes.

Soon after the date of this letter (November 9, 1607), Sutton wrote the following letter to Thomas Egerton, Lord Chancellor Ellesmere, and to Robert Cecil, Earl of Salisbury and Lord Treasurer:

"May it please your Lordships,

"I understand that his Majesty is possessed by Sir *John Harrington,* or by some other by his means, that I intend to make His Highness's Son, the Duke of *Yorke,* my Heire; whereupon, as it is reported, His Highness proposeth to bestowe the Honour of a Baron on me, whereof as I am most unworthy, so I vowe to God, and your Lordships, I never harboured the least thought, or proude desire of any such Matter. My Mynde in my younger Times hath been ever free from Ambition, and now I am going to my Grave, to gape for such a Thing, were mere dotage in me, so unworthie allso, as I confess unto your Lordships; that this Knight hath been often tampering with me to that purpose, to enterteyne Honour, and to make the Noble Duke my Heire is true, to whom I made that Answer, as had he either Witte, or Honestie, (with Reverence to your Lordships be it Spoken) he never would have engaged himself in this Business so egregiously to delude his Majesty, and wrong me. My humble Suite unto your Lordships is, that, considering this Occasion hath brought me into Question, and in Hazard of His Highness's Displeasure, having never given Sir *John Harrington,* nor any Man lyvinge, either promise, or semblance to do any such Act, but upon his motions grew into utter dislike with him for such idle Speeche, Your Lordships will vouchsafe me this Favour to inform His Highness aright, howe things have proceeded directly without my Privitie; and, withall, that my Trust is in His Gracious Disposition, not to conceit the worste of me for other Men's follies; but that I may have free Liberty with his Princely Leave, wherein I rest most assured, to dispose of myne owne, as other his Majesties Loyal Subjects. And so most humbly recommending my Dutie, and Service to your Lordships, for the increase of whose Honours, and Happiness I shall ever pray.

I rest
Your Lordships
poor Beadsman
Thomas Sutton"

(Philip Bearcroft, *Thomas Sutton,* London, 1737, 20–22.)

LETTER 51.

Reprinted from Philip Bearcroft, *Thomas Sutton,* London, 1737, 23.

Bath church. Three miles from Harington's country house of Kelston.

Master Billett. Cf. Letter 4 and Notes.

Our bountifull bishop, Dr. Montague. James Montague was consecrated Bishop of Bath and Wells, April 17, 1608. "Hee gave one thousand pounds towards the reparation of the Abbey church at Bathe: and moreover built a faire Pulpit of free stone in the same." (Francis Godwin, *A Catalogue of the Bishops of England,* edition 1615, 386.) Henry Harington included in *Nugae Antiquae* a probably apocryphal account of Sir John's successful attempt to obtain the help of Bishop Montague. "The brilliancy of genius did not obliterate the virtues of the heart. A laudable spirit of promoting good works was manifested on many occasions; one instance deserves our relating, and respects the repairing the church of Bath, to which our Author was most zealously inclined, and which he most diligently effected: One day as he was conversing with Bishop Montague, near the church, it happened to rain, which afforded the opportunity of asking the Bishop to shelter himself in the church: Special care was taken to convey the prelate into that isle which had been spoiled of its lead, and was near roofless. As this situation was far from securing his Lordship from the weather, he often remonstrated to his merry companion that it rained; doth it so, my Lord? Then let me sue your bounty towards covering our poor church; for if it keep not us safe from the waters above, how shall it ever save others from the fire beneath? Hereat the Bishop was so well pleased, that he became a most liberal benefactor both of timber and lead; and to this instance of public spirit was owing the complete roofing of the north isle of the Abbey Church, after it had lain in ruins for many years." (Edition 1779, III, p. vi. Another account follows in the same volume, p. xii–xxi.)

Master Robert Hopton. Probably Robert Hopton, of Witham, Somersetshire, the son of Sir Arthur Hopton. (*The Visitation of the County of Somerset, 1623,* ed. F. T. Colby, London, 1876, 57.)

LETTER 52.

Reprinted from *Nugae Antiquae,* 1804, I, 380–384.

My rare dogge. His name was Bungey, and his picture is to be found on the title-page of Harington's translation of *Orlando Furioso* (1591, 1607, 1634). The poet's "printed dog," according to one contemporary writer, was well known. Sir John Davies, author of *Orchestra* and *Nosce Teipsum,* wrote:

"Peace, idle Muse, have done! for it is time,
Since lousie Ponticus envies my fame,
And sweares the better sort are much to blame
To make me so well nowne for my ill rime:
Yet Bankes, his horse, is better known than he.
So are the Cammels and the westerne hogge,
And so is Lepidus his printed Dog."

(Grosart, *The Works of Sir John Davies,* Epigram 48.)
Harington alludes to this epigram in Epigram 51, "*Against* Momus, *in praise of his dogge* Bungey." Twice in *Orlando Furioso* Harington writes of Bungey: "I fancie the spaniell . . . whose picture is in the device [on the title-page], and if any make merry at it (as I doubt not but some will) I shall not be sorrie for it: for one end of my travel in this worke, is to make my friends merrie, and besides I can alledge many examples of wise men, and some verie great men, that have not onely taken pictures, but built cities in remembrance of serviceable beasts." Later he mentions "my servant Bungy (whose picture you may see in the first page of the booke, and is knowne to the best Ladies of England)." (*Orlando Furioso,* 1634, notes following Books XLI and XLIII, pp. 349, 373.)

I have an excellente picture, curiously limned, to remaine in my posterity. John E. M. Harington, Esq., has a painting of Bungey. The dog was a large water spaniel, liver-colored and white.

LETTER 53.

Reprinted from James Peller Malcolm, *Londinium Redivivum,* I, 399.

Your mortmayn. Cf. Letters 56 and 57.

Yeer fraues. German women. Malcolm points out that Harington alludes to the marriage portion of the Princess Elizabeth, who was to marry the Elector of Hanover.

Saynt Billet. Cf. Letter 4 and Notes.

LETTER 54.

Reprinted from *Nugae Antiquae,* 1804, I, 384–389.

Thus saith a poet:

Treason dothe never prosper;—What's the reason?
Why;—if it prosper, none dare call it Treason.

Harington himself is the author of this distich. (Epigram 259.)

The eagle's force subdues. . . . Thomas Park points out that these six lines of verse are to be found in the thirteenth stanza of Thomas Churchyard's *Legend of Jane Shore.* He adds, charitably, that Churchyard may have borrowed King Henry's "special verse." (*Nugae Antiquae,* 1804, I, 388, note.)

LETTER 55.

Printed from the original, State Papers, Domestic, James I, Vol. 49, 33.

It appears that attention was given to Harington's request, for on January 29,

1612, and again on July 9, 1612, John Chamberlain informed Dudley Carleton that Viscount Rochester and Sir John Harington had the reversion to Sir John Roper's office. (*Calendar State Papers, Domestic, 1611–1618,* 115, 137.)

LETTER 56.

Reprinted from James Peller Malcolm, *Londinium Redivivum,* I, 400.

My lady Arbella. Lady Arabella Stuart.

LETTER 57.

Printed from a rough draft in Harington's autograph, British Museum Addit. MS. 27632, f. 31. A note follows the letter: "The awnswer was thankes that I was more myndful of him then he was of himself." J. P. Malcolm (*Londinium Redivivum,* I, 401) prints the first paragraph as the complete letter.

The man that above all others . . . did seke your disturbance and defamation. The context indicates that the man is Sir John Skinner. Of his representation upon the stage and of the circumstances of his death information is lacking.

LETTER 58.

Printed from a rough draft in Harington's autograph, British Museum Addit MS. 27632, f. 31 v. Although it is undated, it is preceded by a letter dated February 4, 1609 [1610] and it is followed by a memorandum dated February 5 "anno Jacobi septimo" [1609/1610].

LETTER 59.

Printed from a rough draft in Harington's autograph, British Museum Addit. MS. 27632, f. 42.

Lord Compton. William Lord Compton, who was created Earl of Northampton in 1630.

Date. The letter was written after the death of Lord Compton's father-in-law, Sir John Spencer, March 3, 1610. Lady Compton inherited so great a fortune that for a time her husband lost his sanity. It is probably of that illness that Harington writes.

That same honest stratagem of myne for Duke Charles. Cf. Letter 50 and Notes. What Lord Compton said or did is not known.

The cheifest and most famous clothing place of England. During the middle ages Bath was a centre of the cloth-trade. Chaucer's Wife of Bath surpassed "them of Ypres and of Gaunt." Compton's father-in-law, Sir John Spencer, a member of the Clothmakers' Company, had been wealthy and parsimonious.

My Lord Byshop. James Montague. Cf. Letter 51 and Notes.

LETTER 60.

Printed from a rough draft in Harington's autograph, British Museum Addit. MS. 27632, f. 42 v.

Cosen Sheldon. This man remains unidentified.

Cutler. Unidentified.

absurdly: illogically.

Lady Candish. Lady Cavendish.

Lady Markham. The mother of Sir Griffin Markham.

Sir M. Hicks. Sir Michael Hicks. Cf. Letter 40.

Sir griph. Sir Griffin Markham.

Kerby. Unidentified.

Stannope. Probably Sir John Stanhope. Cf. Letter 15.

Skinner. Sir John Skinner. Cf. Letter 48 and Notes.

Evn reck[*oning*] *makes long frends. Evn:* even, "having no balance or debt on either side" (*NED., s. v.* even, 10). Cf. Harington, *Metamorphosis of Ajax* (1814), p. 14, "For a man to make even his reckonings."

LETTER 61.

Printed from a rough draft in Harington's autograph, British Museum Addit. MS. 27632, f. 37.

The selected psalms. Several of them are included in *Nugae Antiquae,* 1804, II, 403–406.

LETTER 62.

Printed from a rough draft in Harington's autograph, British Museum Addit. MS. 27632, f. 45.

My Lord Bishop of Elie. Launcelot Andrews was translated from Chichester to Ely in 1609. Harington wrote of him with the utmost respect and admiration. ("A Supplie or Addicion to the Catalogue of Bishops," *Nugae Antiquae,* 1804, II, 189–195.)

THE EPIGRAMS

The following MS. sigla are used: A indicates British Museum Additional MS. 12049; B indicates Cambridge University Library Additional MS. 337.

1. *Snites:* snipes. A. p. 2.

2. *Meere:* absolute, downright. A. p. 2.

3. A. p. 3.

4. A. pp. 3–4.

5. *Touch:* touchstone, a hard black marble used as a test for gold. Try, prove. Harington's eldest son, John, was born 1589. *Miscellanea Genealogica et Heraldica,* ed. J. J. Howard, IV (1884), 191. See also Venn, *Alumni Cantabrigienses.* A. p. 4; B. p. 2.

6. The source is Martial, IX, 81. Jonson's *Epicoene,* 1609, contains the lines:

> "Our wishes, like to those make public feasts,
> Are not to please the cookes tastes, but the guests."

Prologue, 7–8. A. p. 5.

7. A. p. 6.

8. *Conueiance:* cunning management. A. p. 6; B. pp. 2–3.

9. The word *occupy* had an obscene meaning. Cf. Jonson, *Epigrams.* No. 117, and Shakespeare, *2 Henry IV,* II. iv. 150–153. "These villains will make the word captain as odious as the word occupy, which was an excellent good word before it was ill sorted." *Chawcers iest.* Cf. *Five Hundred Years of Chaucer Criticism and Allusion,* ed. Spurgeon, 1925, III, Index, p. 18. A. p. 7.

10. The source is Martial, III, 61. A. pp. 7–8.

11. A. p. 8.

12. Source is Martial, V, 18. A. p. 8.

13. This visit of Queen Elizabeth occurred in 1592. Harington's brother, Francis, "was sometime student to this Doctor Reynolds." (*Tract on the Succession,* 113; similar statement in "A Supply" in *Nugae Antiquae,* 1779, I, 180.) Doctor Reynolds became President of Corpus Christi College in 1598. For Harington's entertaining account of the Queen's visit, see *Nugae Antiquae,* 1779, I, 156–158; 173. Reynolds is called *"Bellarmines correcter"* because he wrote *Responsio ad apologiam Cardinalis Bellarmini* [Cardinal Robert Bellarmine].

14. A. p. 10.

15. A. p. 10.

16. *Casaneus.* Bartholomaeus Cassanaeus, *Catalogus Gloriae Mundi.*

17. *Cuckolds hauen.* "Cuckolds' Haven or Cuckolds' Point was a spot on the Surrey side of the Thames a little below Rotherhithe Church and near to the present Thames Railway Tunnel. The place was formerly distinguished by a tall pole with a pair of horns at the top. It was under this title that *Eastward Hoe* was revived [by Nahum Tate] and acted in 1685." F. E. Schelling, *"Eastward Hoe" and "The Alchemist"* (Belle Lettres Series), 1909, 154. A. p. 13.

18. Reprinted with slight changes in *A Thousand Outlandish Proverbs* (1640; edition of 1817, p. 186), and in *Wit Restored* (1655; 1658; edition of 1817, pp. 230–231). Harington was a bitter enemy of the Puritans. A. pp. 13–14.

19. A. p. 15.

20. A. p. 16.

21. A Latin version of this epigram is included in Sir John Stradling's *Epigrammatum Libri Quatuor,* 1607, p. 32, where the English original is attributed to Harington. *He bought a Bible of the new translation.* The date precludes the possibility of supposing that Harington is referring to the Authorized Version. Since the epigram is a gibe directed at a Puritan tailor, the reference may be to the Geneva translation. *Venetians downe below the garters.* Venetians or galligaskins were a kind of hose or breeches reaching below the knee. The fashion was brought to England from Venice. A. pp. 17–18.

22. Cf. Martial, II, 32. A. p. 18.

23. *Totquots:* general dispensations. A. p. 19.

24. The source is Martial, X, 31. A. p. 20.

25. A. p. 20.

26. A. p. 21; B. pp. 3–4.

27. A. p. 21.

28. *Whish:* hushed, silent. A. p. 22; B. p. 4.

29. A. pp. 22–23; also in 1615, Sig. D4.

30. A. p. 24.

31. A. p. 25.

32. The source is Martial, XI, 35. Sir Hugh Portman was M.P., 1597, and Sheriff, 1590 and 1600. (Collinson, *History of Somersetshire,* I, xxxii ff.) He was the son of Sir Henry Portman, of Orchard Portman, near Taunton. He died in 1603. (F. W. Weaver, *Visitations of the County of Somerset,* 63.) Sir Hugh, writes Harington, was a "rich man, a wise man, a builder, and especially a bachelor." (*An Apology,* 1814, p. 37.) A. p. 26.

33. A. pp. 5–6.

34. In Marlowe's *Edward II* Mortimer sends the ambiguous message *Edwardum occidere nolite timere bonum est* (V. iv. 8). Marlowe found the line in Holinshed. *Edward II* was entered in the *Stationers' Register* under the date July 6, 1593. There is no specific evidence of the year of its composition, but it is commonly assigned to 1590–1591. A. p. 27.

35. A. p. 27.

36. A. pp. 27–28.

37. A. p. 28.

38. A. p. 29.

39. A. pp. 33–34; B. p. 5.

40. Suggested by Martial, II, 20. A. pp. 34–35.

41. A. p. 35.

42. A. p. 35.

43. Turberville was living in 1594. Harington praises him in *Orlando Furioso* (1591), ed. 1634, 39. A. pp. 35–36.

44. *The Metamorphosis of Ajax* appeared in 1596. A. p. 36.

45. A. p. 36.

46. A. p. 37.

47. A. p. 37.

48. A translation of a Latin epigram by Sir Thomas More. In *Ajax* (p. 38), Harington prints More's epigram and his own translation. A. pp. 37–38; B. p. 6.

49. This epigram is printed with a picture in *Ajax* (pp. 33–34). Harington adds: "I remember in my rhyming days, I wrote a short elegy upon a homely emblem; which, both verse and emblem, they have set up in Cloacina's chapel, at my house, very solemnly. And I am the willinger to impart it to my friends, because I protest to you truly, a sober gentleman protested to me seriously, that

the conceit of the picture and the verse was an occasion to put honest and good thoughts into his mind." A. p. 38.

50. The source is Martial, II, 12. A. p. 38.

51. A. p. 38.

52. A. p. 39.

53. A. p. 39.

54. A. p. 39.

55. A. p. 40.

56. *Picke a thanke.* A pickthank is a flatterer. A. pp. 40–41.

57. A. p. 46.

58. A. pp. 46–47.

59. A. p. 47.

60. In B, it is entitled *"To a great Lady."* The source is Martial, VIII, 76. A. p. 47; B. p. 29.

61. A. pp. 49–50.

62. A. p. 50.

63. Harington adds a marginal note, A. p. 51: "this ep. may begin heere [i. e. 17] thus, Two squyers of Wales arrived at a towne." It is so printed in the edition of 1615, Sig. F2v.

64. Cf. Ep. 58. A. pp. 52–53.

65. The source is Martial, II, 3. A. p. 53.

66. A. p. 3.

67. A. p. 5.

68. A. p. 7.

69. *Stellified:* made into a star, glorified. The first eight lines of this epigram are to be found in A. p. 10; p. 11 is blank.

70. Harington included this in his "Supply" (1608) with the comment, "I wrote [it] ten yeeres since to Dr. Eedes," Dean of Worchester. *Nugae Antiquae,* 1779, I, 232. A. p. 14.

71. Fans of feathers were common.

"When a plum'd fanne may shade the chalked face." (Joseph Hall, *Virgidemiarum,* IV, 4.) See also Steevens' *Shakespeare,* I, 273. A. p. 15.

72. A. p. 16; B. p. 3.

73. A. pp. 18–19; also 1615, Sig. D2v.

74. *Not passe a rush.* Green rushes were strewn on the floors. A rush was "a symbol of something of no value or importance, esp. in negative phrases." (*NED.*) Cf. Epigram 154: *neuer to care a rush.* A. p. 21.

75. A. p. 22.

76. *Carknets:* collars or necklaces of gold or set with jewels. *NED.* s. v., carcanet. The source is Martial, XI, 27. Harington had five daughters. Frances was married in 1606, Jane in 1613, Ellina or Helena in 1620, Elizabeth in 1634. Mary, the fifth daughter, was baptized in 1600, and buried in 1605. Helena was baptized in 1591. Wood, *Athenae Oxonienses,* II, 641–642; *Miscellanea Genealogica et Heraldica,* III (1880), 316. A. p. 22.

77. Harington seldom uses the sonnet form. A. p. 23.

78. A. pp. 24–25; B. pp. 4–5.

79. A. p. 25.

80. *Slurre.* "To slip or slide (a die) out of the box so that it does not turn." (*NED.,* s. v. slur, V2.) *Sincts:* fives. A. pp. 28–29.

81. Cf. Epigram 302. A. p. 29; B. p. 25; ed. 1615, Sig. E3.

82. A. p. 30.

83. A. pp. 30–31.

84. A. p. 31.

85. A. p. 32; B. p. 5.

86. The source is Martial, II, 44. A. pp. 32–33.

87. *Promoter:* a professional accuser, a common informer. The source is Martial, *On the Public Shows,* 4. This epigram is included in the notes following Book XVII of *Orlando Furioso.* A. p. 33.

88. The source is Martial, XII, 34. Part of this epigram is printed in "A Supply" in *Nugae Antiquae* (1779), I, 204. A. p. 33.

89. A. p. 34.

90. A. p. 34; also in edition of 1615. Sig. E3.

91. A. p. 40; B. pp. 6–7.

92. A. p. 42; also in edition of 1615, Sig. Cv.

93. *Cammington* is usually written Cannington. A marginal note in Harington's handwriting in the copy of *The Metamorphosis of Ajax* (1596) that he sent to Thomas Markham reads, "The Lady Rogers: called, in her young days, the fair nun of Cannington." (*Ajax,* 1814, 21.) The last two lines of this epigram are a proverbial formula. Harington, in *Orlando Furioso,* Book XLIII, stanza 136, writes:

> "Yet will I do to thee no further wrong,
> But pardon thee, and thou shalt me forgive,
> And quite each other, all old debts and driblets,
> And set the hares head against the goose gyblets."

In a marginal note he adds, "Driblets used for petty recknings. A Proverbe used in English." The same expression occurs in *A Trick to Catch the Old One* (*Middleton's Works,* ed. Dyce, II, 78) and in Dekker's *Shoemaker's Holiday* (*Representative English Comedies,* ed. Gayley, III, 37). A. pp. 43–45; B. pp. 7–9.

94. *Duke Humfrey.* "The phrase of dining with Duke Humphrey . . . originated in the following manner: Humphrey, duke of Gloucester, though really buried at St. Alban's, was supposed to have a monument in old St. Paul's from which one part of the church was termed *Duke Humphrey's* walk. In this, as the church was then a place of the most public resort, they who had no means of procuring a dinner, frequently loitered about, probably in hopes of meeting with an invitation, but under pretense of looking at the monuments." (*Nares' Glossary,* ed. Halliwell and Wright, London, 1905.) The middle aisle of St. Paul's is called the Duke's gallery in Dekker's *Gull's Hornebook.* See also Hall's *Virgidemiarum,* Book III, Satire 7, and Haughton's *Englishmen for My Money,* ed. A. C. Baugh, Philadelphia, 1917, line 883. A. p. 45.

95. A. p. 50.

96. The source is Martial, I, 73. A. p. 53.

97. A. p. 55; B. pp. 10–11.

98. Gervase Babington, of whom Harington wrote in "A Supply" in *Nugae Antiquae* (1779), I, 150, was translated from Landoff to Exeter in 1594, and to Worcester in 1597. A. p. 53.

99. Suggested by Martial, II, 15. A. p. 54.

100. The source is Martial, I, 74. A. p. 54.

101. The source is Martial, IV, 69. A. p. 54.

102. A. pp. 54–55.

103. A. p. 53.

104. A. pp. 55–56.

105. *Dizzard:* stupid. The source is Martial, VIII, 17. A. p. 56.

106. The source is Martial, I, 81.

"A servo scis te genitum blandeque fateris,
cum dicis dominum, Sosibiane, patrem."

"Dominus" was employed not only as a title of respect, but as a term for a master of slaves. A. p. 58. This epigram is included in *Orlando Furioso,* 1634, 382.

107. A. p. 58.

108. A. p. 58.

109. A. pp. 58–59.

110. The source is Martial, IV, 21. This epigram is included in *Orlando Furioso,* 1634, 277. A. p. 59.

111. The source is Martial, XII, 90. A. p. 59.

112. A. p. 60.

113. A. p. 60.

114. A. pp. 60–61.

115. Cf. Martial, II, 91. A. p. 61; B. p. 11. It is impossible to date this epigram, for the Kelston Registers do not record the baptisms of all of his eleven children.

116. A. p. 61.

117. A. p. 62.

118. A. p. 62.

119. A. pp. 62–63; B. p. 11.

120. A. p. 63; B. p. 12.

121. A. pp. 63–64.

122. Cf. Epigram 329. A. pp. 64–65.

123. The source is Martial, III, 87. A. p. 65.

124. The source is Martial, V, 76. A. p. 66.

125. The source is Martial, III, 15. A. p. 66; also in edition of 1615, Sig. C2.

126. A. pp. 66–67.

127. A. p. 67.

128. A. p. 68.

129. *Paracelsian:* alchemist. A. pp. 69–70.

130. A. p. 70.

131. A. pp. 70–71; B. p. 26.

132. Gabriel Harvey's controversy with Thomas Nashe was begun in 1592 and was continued for five years, with scurrilous attacks on both sides. Harington writes in his *Ajax:* "The old proverb, as well as emblem . . . doth admonish us not to contend with base and ignominious persons:

'Hoc scio pro certo, quod si cum stercore certo
Vinco ceu vincor, sempor ego maculor.' "

Edition of 1814, 35. A. p. 72.

133. In *Ajax,* Harington writes, "For the shrewd wife read the book of Taming a Shrew, which . . . made a number of us so perfect, that now every one can tame a shrew in our country, save he that hath her." (Ed. of 1814, 95.) *The Taming of a Shrew* is one of 129 plays that Harington included in his library. British Museum Addit. MS. 27632, f. 43; printed by Furnivall in 7 *Notes and Queries* (1890), IX, 382. A. p. 72.

134. A. pp. 72–73.

135. A. pp. 73–74.

136. The source is Martial, V, 75. A. p. 74; also in ed. of 1615, Sig. C3v.

137. A. p. 75.

138. A. p. 75.

139. *Bodging:* botching, bungling. A. pp. 75–76.

140. A. p. 76; B. pp. 13–14; in ed. of 1615, Sig. C–Cv.

141. A. pp. 76–78.

142. A. p. 78; ed. of 1615, Sig. Vv.

143. The source is Martial, VII, 65. A. p. 78.

144. The source is Martial, VI, 41. A. p. 79.

145. A. p. 79.

146. *Poore-Iohn:* a kind of fish, salted and dried; it was cheap and coarse. The source is Martial, I, 99. A. p. 79.

147. The source is Martial, IX, 48. A. pp. 79–80; B. p. 14.

148. A. p. 80.

149. A. pp. 80–81.

150. *Alborne:* a sixteenth-century spelling of auburn, nearly white; whitish. *NED.* s. v., auburn. *Alborne Coney* means prostitute. A. p. 81.

151. A. p. 82.

152. A. p. 82.

153. A. pp. 82–83.

154. A. p. 83.

155. A. p. 83.

156. *Brauery:* elaborate dress. Cf. 364. A. p. 84; ed. 1615, Sig. F3.

157. A. p. 84.

158. A. p. 85.

159. A. pp. 85–86.

160. Thomas Bastard, *Chrestoleras; Seven bookes of Epigrammes,* 1598. He was chaplain to Charles Blount, Earl of Devonshire. A. pp. 87–88.

161. A. p. 88; ed. 1615 F3v.

162. The source is Martial, VI, 12. It is included in *Orlando Furioso,* 1591, 265. Wearing periwigs became the fashion about the middle of the sixteenth century. In Elizabeth's time many were sandy-colored out of compliment to her. The satirists inveighed against the custom, and Shakespeare mentions it. *Much Ado,* II. iii. 36; *Two Gentlemen of Verona,* IV. iv. 194. A. pp. 88–89.

163. Cf. 219, 388. *Orchestra* by Sir John Davies, the author of *Nosce Teipsum. Orchestra* was entered *S. R.,* June 25, 1594, but it was not published until 1596. A. p. 89.

164. The source is Martial, II, 55. A. p. 89.

165. The source is Martial, I, 27. A. p. 90.

166. A. pp. 90–91.

167. The source is Martial, IV, 15. A. p. 91.

168. The date of Harington's marriage is September 6, 1583. *Somerset Parish Registers,* ed. W. P. W. Phillimore, VI, 94. A. p. 93; B. pp. 14–15.

169. The source is Martial, IX, 9. A. p. 94.

170. A. pp. 94–95.

171. The source is Martial, VI, 66. A. p. 95; ed. 1615, Sig. F3.

172. *No forse:* it is of no consequence or importance. (*NED.,* s. v. force, 20.) A. p. 95.

173. A. pp. 95–96.

174. A. p. 96; ed. 1615, Sig. E2v.

175. Cf. Harington's *The Englishmans Doctor, or The Schoole of Salerne,* 1607.

"Canary and Modera, both are like
To make one lean indeede (but wot you what)
Who say they make one leane wold make one laffe
They meane, they make one leane upon a staffe."

A. pp. 96–97.

176. Cf. *A C. Mery Talys,* No. 56; *Much Ado,* IV. i. 278–285. Included in John Cotgrave's *Wits Interpreter, the English Parnassus,* 1662, 286. A. p. 97; ed. 1615, Sig. D3v.

177. A. p. 97; B. p. 15.

178. The source is Martial, IX, 10. A. p. 98.

179. A. p. 98; ed. 1615, Sig. D.

180. Cf. 160. A. p. 99.

181. *Norrys.* Sir John Norris. A. pp. 99–101.

182. A. pp. 101–102; B. p. 26.

183. Harington left with Essex, 1599. A. p. 103; B. p. 16.

184. Cf. *An Apologie of Poetrie, Orlando Furioso,* Sig. ¶4. A. p. 102.

185. To meet the expense incurred in repulsing the Spanish Armada, Queen Elizabeth borrowed from 2416 of her subjects a total of about £75,000. In 1589 the loan was called for by circular letters addressed to the wealthiest of her subjects, under sanction of the Privy Seal. The amount demanded was not always paid readily or punctually, and in some cases not at all. Harington was one of the thirteen residents of Somersetshire who were assessed £50 each; three residents of the county were assessed for £100 each. *The Names of those Persons who subscribed toward the Defence of this Country at the time of the Spanish Armada, 1588, and the amounts each contributed,* ed. T. C. Noble, London, 1886. *Notes and Queries for Somerset,* I, 37. For an account of loans on privy seal, see Cheyney's *A History of England from the Defeat of the Armada to the Death of Elizabeth,* II, 218–225. A. pp. 102–103.

186. A. pp. 103–104; B. p. 27.

187. *Malum,* etc. is an old proverb. A. p. 104.

188. A. p. 109; B. pp. 24–25.

189. A. pp. 109–110.

190. The source is Martial, I, 85. A. pp. 111–112.

191. For Harington's quarrels with his brother-in-law, Edward Rogers, see Introduction. A. p. 112; B. p. 17.

192. Cf. 183. A. pp. 112–113; B. pp. 17–18.

193. Cf. 32. The term "iron age" is derived from Juvenal XIII, 28 ff. R. M. Alden, *The Rise of Formal Satire in England.* Harington in 1591 thought a distich from Ovid appropriate:

"Aurea nunc vere sunt secula, plurimus auro
Venit honos, auro concilatur amor:

In English thus,
This may indeed, be call'd the age of gold,
For honour, love and all, for it is sold."

Orlando Furioso, 167. A. p. 114.

194. A. pp. 114–115.

195. Cf. *Merry Wives of Windsor,* IV. v. 104; *Henry VIII,* V. i. 7. "Each player had four cards dealt to him, one by one; the seven was the highest card in point of number that he could avail himself of, which counted for 21; the six counted for 18; the five for 15; the ace for the same; but the two, three, and four for their respective points only. The knave of diamonds was commonly

fixed upon for the *quinola,* which the player might make what card or suit he thought proper; if the cards were of different suits, the highest number was the *primero* (or prime); but if they were all of one colour, he that held them won the flush." (Nares' *Glossary.*) A. pp. 115–116.

196. *Censure:* judgment. A. p. 115.

197. A. pp. 116–117.

198. Jasper and Ellis Heywood, the sons of John Heywood, "were for a time very wild to the great grief of their father." Wood, *Athenae Oxonienses,* 1813, V, 663. A. p. 117.

199. Jasper Heywood was a zealous Jesuit, and in 1584 was imprisoned in the Tower. A. p. 118.

200. A. pp. 125–126.

201. The source is Martial, II, 21. A. p. 130; ed. 1615, Sig. B3.

202. "I wrote of a certaine Poetaster some yeeres past, who left me out of the bead-roul of some riming-paper blotters that he called Poets." *Nugae Antiquae,* 1779, I, 196. A. p. 130; ed. 1615, Sig. Ev.

203. A. p. 131.

204. A. p. 132.

205. A. p. 136.

206. A. pp. 136–137.

207. A. p. 117.

208. A. p. 118.

209. A. pp. 118–120.

210. A. p. 121.

211. A. p. 121.

212. *Petty-fogger:* "a legal practitioner of inferior status, who gets up or conducts petty cases; *esp.* in an opprobrious sense, one who employs mean, sharp, cavilling practices; a rascally attorney." (*NED.,* s.v., pettifogger.) *Cogger,* cheater. A. f. 121.

213. A. p. 122.

214. This epigram is supposed by Collier to date from 1592. Collier's Dodsley, VIII, 243–245; cited by Tucker Brooke, *P.M.L.A.,* XXXVII (1922), 385. *Smith.* Henry Smith (1550?–1591), a Puritan preacher. A. p. 122.
A. p. 122.

215. A. pp. 122–123.

216. *Cotsold Lyons.* "A sheep was jocularly called a *Cotsold* or *Cotswold lion,* from the extensive pastures in that part." (*Nares' Glossary,* ed. Halliwell and Wright, 1905, s.v. Cotsale.) A. pp. 124–125; ed. 1615, Sig. Fv.

217. A. p. 126; ed. 1615. Sig. C4v.

218. A. p. 126.

219. Cf. 163, 388. *A Witty Writer,* Sir John Davies, author of *Nosce Teipsum,* wrote this epigram:

> "Peace, idle Muse, have done! for it is time,
> Since lousie Ponticus enuies my fame,
> And sweares the better sort are much to blame
> To make me so well nowne for my ill rime:
> Yet Bankes, his horse, is better knowne than he.
> So are the Cammels and the westerne hogge,
> And so is Lepidus his printed Dog."

Grosart, *Works of Sir John Davies,* 347–348. Davies' epigrams were written before 1596. They are quoted in *Ajax,* 1596, ed. 1814, 42, and in Bastard's *Chrestoleros,* 1598, II, 15. They were in print in 1599. Tucker Brooke, *P.M.L.A.,* XXXVII (1922), 398. The "printed Dog" is to be seen on the elaborate title-page of Harington's *Orlando Furioso,* 1591, 1607, 1634. Harington writes of this dog in the notes on *Orlando,* 349, 373, and in an interesting letter to Prince Henry (1608) he tells many stories of this remarkable animal. (Letter 52.) A. pp. 126–127.

220. A. p. 127.

221. A. pp. 127–128.

222. A. p. 128; B. p. 19.

223. In Harington's *Supply* (1608), written for Prince Henry, he writes of Richard Fletcher, Bishop of London: "What shall I say for him? *Non erat hoc Hominis vitium sed temporis?* I cannot say so, for your Highness knowes I have written otherwise in a Book of mine I gave you Libri 3. numero 80." *Nugae Antiquae,* 1779, I, 29. The reference is to A. p. 129.

224. This epigram follows the "Address to the Reader" before *The Commonwealth and Government of Venice.* It was translated by Sir Lewis Lewkenor, from the Italian of Cardinal Gasper Contareno. Cf. Spenser's sonnet prefixed to the same book. *Works of Spenser,* Globe Edition, 608. "That noble Dame" is the Lady Anne, Countess of Warwick, to whom Lewkenor's translation is dedicated. A. p. 129.

tion is dedicated. A. p. 129.

225. A. p. 130.

226. A. p. 131.

227. A. p. 131.

228. A. p. 134.

229. A. p. 134.

230. A. p. 135; ed. 1615, Sig. D3.

231. *Gleekes:* gibes, jests. (*NED.,* s.v. gleek.) A. pp. 139–140.

232. A. p. 140.

233. *Gregorian:* "a variety of wig worn in the sixteenth and seventeenth centuries, said by Blount in 1670 to be named after the inventor, Gregory, a Strand barber." (*NED.*) A. p. 140.

234. *Ringoes.* Eryngo is "the candied root of the Sea Holly (Eryngium maritimum), formerly used as a sweetmeat, and regarded as an aphrodisiac." (*NED.*) A. pp. 140–141.

235. A. p. 141; B. p. 20.

236. A. pp. 141–142; ed. 1615, Sig. D.

237. A. pp. 145–146.

238. The heading in A is as follows: "The Hermaphrodite translated out of Latten done formerly by one Kendall: & after in *Albions England* lib. 2: cap: 10:" A. p. 153. It is the first epigram in Timothe Kendall's *Flowers of Epigrammes,* 1577. Spenser Society Publ., 1874, 17. Kendall attributes it to "Pvlix an auncient Poet." It is also in ed. 1615, Sig. E2.

239. A. pp. 154–156; ed. 1615. Sig. C2.

240. A. p. 158.

241. A. p. 174; ed. 1615. Sig. C.

242. A. p. 190.

243. A. p. 164.

244. A. pp. 146–147.

245. A. p. 168.

246. A. p. 173.

247. In 1582, William Ruthven, first Earl of Gowrie, with other nobles seized James. For this act of treason, the first Earl of Gowrie was executed in 1584. (*Cambridge Modern History,* III, 550.) Gowrie's sons, in 1600, attempted to

assassinate James, but John Ramsey and Thomas Erskine prevented and killed them. (Camden, *Annals of Elizabeth,* 1635, 529.) A. pp. 172–173.

248. Alice, widow of Ferdinando Stanley, fifth Earl of Derby, married, in 1600, Thomas Egerton, Lord Ellesmere, who in 1596 became Lord Keeper, and in 1603 Lord Chancellor. She was a daughter of Sir John Spenser, of Althorp, Northamptonshire, whom Harington addressed in *The Metamorphosis of Ajax* as follows: "You have a learned writer of your name, make much of him, for it is not the least honour of your honourable family." (*An Apology,* ed. 1814, 30.) Spenser had in 1591 dedicated to her *The Teares of the Muses,* and Milton wrote *Arcades* (*ca.* 1635) for her. *Comus* was written for the inauguration of her son-in-law, the Earl of Bridgewater, as President of Wales. A. p. 173.

249. A. p. 166.

250. A. p. 174.

251. A. p. 174.

252. Reprinted in *A Thousand Outlandish Proverbs.* 1640; ed. 1817, 186. A. pp. 176–177.

253. Reprinted with slight changes, in *A Thousand,* etc., 146. A. p. 174.

254. *ne're the neere:* never the nearer. *Near* is the comparative of nigh (A.–S. *neah*). Cf. Abbott, §478. A. p. 168.

255. The source is Martial, I, 38. Reprinted in *A Thousand Outlandish Proverbs,* 1640; ed. 1817, 198. A. p. 61; ed. 1615, Sig. A4.

256. The source is Martial, I, 40. A. p. 74; ed. 1615, Sig. A4.

257. The source is Martial, IX, 14. A. p. 3; ed. 1615, Sig. A4.

258. Harington was married September 6, 1583. *Somerset Parish Registers,* VI, 94. The date of this epigram is 1597. A. p. 143; B. pp. 20–21; ed. 1615, Sig. A4.

259. A. p. 110; ed. 1615, Sig. A4v.

260. *Sparuers.* A sparver is the canopy or wooden frame at the top of a bed. *Bonny Clabo:* sour buttermilk. Cf. Jonson, *New Inn,* I. i. 70. "Bonnyclabber in Ireland means thick milk. Irish bainne [pronounce, *bonny*] milk, and *clabair,* anything thick or half-liquid." Skeat and Mayhew, s. v. bonnyclabber. Harington was in Ireland with the Essex expedition in 1599. A. pp. 107–108; B. pp. 16–17; ed. 1615, Sig. A4v.

261. A somewhat similar epigram Grosart attributes to Sir John Davies. (*Complete Works of Sir John Davies,* 1869, 352.) Harington's epigram, in abbreviated form, appears in *A Thousand Outlandish Proverbs,* 1640, ed. 1817, 163. A. p. 4; ed. 1615, Sig. B.

262. A. pp. 41–42; B. p. 7; ed. 1615, Sig. B.

263. Reprinted anonymously in *Wit Restor'd,* 1658, 189. A. pp. 152–153; ed. 1615, Sig. Bv.

264. A. p. 166; ed. 1615, Sig. Bv.

265. Thomas Deloney's *The Gentle Craft,* 1597, from which Thomas Dekker borrowed the plot of his *Shoemakers' Holiday.* Deloney was not a shoe-maker, as Harington supposed, but a silk-weaver. (Cf. *The Works of Thomas Deloney,* ed. F. O. Mann, Oxford, 1912, pp. vii–xiv.) *Dudgeon haft:* the hilt of a dagger made of dudgeon, "a kind of wood used by turners, esp. for handles of knives, daggers, etc." (*NED.*) A dagger with a handle of this material was cheap and often was regarded as an inferior, unreliable weapon. *Roues a shaft:* shoots an arrow without fixed aim; hence, utters at random. Cf. *Apology* (*Ajax,* 1814, 39), "After they had roved three or four idle words to praise a man, straight they marr all at the buts." *Nugae Antiquae* (1804, II, 47), "Manie bowlts were roved after him, and some spitefullie feather'd." A. p. 92; ed. 1615, Sig. C3v.

266. A discussion of these games is to be found in K. L. Bates' edition of Heywood's *A Woman Killed with Kindness* (Belle Lettres Series), 1917, 130–134. Cf. Epigram 195. A. pp. 187–188; ed. 1615, Sig. B2.

267. This epigram is included, with the following comment, in Harington's "Breefe Notes and Remembraunces," *Nugae Antiquae,* 1779, II, 209–229. The entry is undated. "My Lorde of Essex is . . . my friende, and that not in bad sorte. He bides me lay goode holde on her Majesties bountie, and aske freely; I will attende tomorrowe, and leave this little poesie behinde her cushion at my departinge from her presence." Epigram 267 follows, signed "From your Highnesse saucy Godson." II, 216–217. A. p. 181; ed. 1615, Sig. B2.

268. A. p. 108; ed. 1615, Sig. B2v.

269. These two witticisms are included in his "Supply or Addition," *Nugae Antiquae,* 1779, I, 19. Bonner was Bishop of London from 1540 to 1549, and from 1553 to 1559. A. p. 24; ed. 1615, Sig. B2v.

270. The source is Martial, I, 75. A. pp. 151–152; ed. 1615, Sig. B2v.

271. Dr. John Still was Bishop of Bath and Wells from 1592 to 1607. Cf. Letter 34. A. pp. 29–30; ed. 1615, Sig. B2v.

272. A. p. 5; ed. 1615, Sig. B3.

273. A. p. 64; ed. 1615, Sig. B3.

274. A. p. 106; ed. 1615, Sig. D2v.

275. Reprinted in *A Thousand Outlandish Proverbs,* 1640, ed. 1817, 116. A. p. 20; ed. 1615, Sig. B3v.

276. A. p. 176; ed. 1615, Sig. B3v.

277. Reprinted in *A Thousand Outlandish Proverbs,* 1640, ed. 1817, 28. A. pp. 192–193; ed. 1615, Sig. B3v.

278. A. p. 176; ed. 1615, Sig. B4.

279. Not in A. Ed. 1615, Sig. B4.

280. A. p. 68; ed. 1615, Sig. B4.

281. A "piller" is one who "pills" or robs. A somewhat similar epigram appears in *A Thousand Outlandish Proverbs,* 1640, ed. 1817, 164. John Weever has an epigram playing on the word "pillar." *Epigrammes in the Oldest Cut and Newest Fashion,* 1599; ed. 1911, 70. A. p. 74; ed. 1615, Sig. B4.

282. A. p. 66; ed. 1615, Sig. B4v.

283. The source is Martial, XII, 93. A. p. 15; ed. 1615, Sig. B4v.

284. Not in A. Ed. 1615, Sig. B4v.

285. A. p. 16; ed. 1615, Sig. B4v.

286. A. p. 162; ed. 1615, Sig. F3v.

287. Included in his "Treatise on Playe," written before 1603; *Nugae Antiquae,* 1779, II, 188. "These olde verses," he writes, are "patched by me togeather owt of I know not what olde wryters." Chapman's translation of Virgil's "Epigram of Play" contains the line "At play put passions down, as moneys are." *The Poems, and Minor Translations of George Chapman,* 1875, 152. A. p. 26; ed. 1615, Sig. C.

288. *Of Trinidade, in cane, in leafe, or ball:* tobacco prepared in three ways. Cf. Induction to Ben Jonson's *Cynthia's Revels,* "I have my three sorts of tobacco in my pocket." A. pp. 59–60; ed. 1615, Sig. C.

289. The source is Martial, VI, 79. B. p. 3; ed. 1615, Sig. C.

290. Cf. Ep. 281. A. pp. 120–121; ed. 1615, Sig. Cv.

291. The source is Martial, I, 64. A. pp. 81–82; B. p. 14; ed. 1615, Sig. C2.

292. A. p. 178; ed. 1615, Sig. C2v.

293. A. p. 188; ed. 1615, Sig. C2v.

294. A. p. 188; ed. 1615, Sig. C3.

295. A. p. 113; ed. 1615, Sig. E4v.

296. A. p. 156; ed. 1615, Sig. C4v.

297. A. pp. 189–190; ed. 1615, Sig. C3v.

298. A. p. 69; ed. 1615, Sig. C4.

299. A. pp. 177–178; B. p. 24; ed. 1615, Sig. C4.

300. A. p. 147; ed. 1615, Sig. C4v.

301. Cf. Henry Hutton, *Satyricall Epigrams,* 1619, Ep. 8. Percy Society, 1842. Not in A. Ed. 1615, Sig. C4v.

302. A. p. 29; B. p. 25; ed. 1615, Sig. E3. Cf. Epigram 81.

303. A. p. 184; ed. 1615, Sig. E4v.

304. The source is Martial, I, 54. A. p. 84; B. p. 27; ed. 1615, Sig. Dv.

305. The source is Martial, *Suppos.* 5. A. p. 23; ed. 1615, Sig. Dv.

306. The source is Martial, I, 19. Not in A. Ed. 1615, Sig. Dv.

307. A. p. 170; ed. 1615, Sig. D2.

308. Not in A. Ed. 1615, Sig. D2.

309. Not in A. Ed. 1615, Sig. D2v.

310. The source is Martial, XII, 10. Not in A. Ed. 1615, Sig. D2v.

311. *Androes.* Lancelot Andrewes (1555–1626). In 1589 he obtained the living of St. Giles', Cripplegate, and was made chaplain ordinary to the queen. He became Bishop of Chichester in 1605, of Ely in 1609, and of Winchester in 1618. Harington elsewhere praises him. *Nugae Antiquae,* 1804, II, 189–195. Cf. Ep. 345. A. pp. 135–136; ed. 1615, Sig. D2v.

312. Suggested by Martial, I, 109. Not in A. Ed. 1615, Sig. D3.

313. A. p. 52; ed. 1615, Sig. D3.

314. A. pp. 67–68; ed. 1615, Sig. D3.

315. Not in A. Ed. 1615, Sig. D3v.

316. The source is Martial, II, 38. A. p. 49; ed. 1615, Sig. D3v.

317. Cf. a Martin Marprelate pamphlet, *Pap with a Hatchet,* 1589, attributed to John Lyly. F. E. Schelling, *English Literature during the Lifetime of Shakespeare,* New York, 1910, 114. Queen Elizabeth was excommunicated in 1570. A. p. 6 contains a Latin epigram signed by Sir John's brother, Francis. Epigram 317 is an almost literal translation. A. p. 113; B. pp. 29–30; ed. 1615, Sig. D3v.

318. A. p. 161; ed. 1615, Sig. D4.

319. A. pp. 181–182; ed. 1615, Sig. D4.

320. A. p. 15; ed. 1615, Sig. D4v.

321. Not in A. Ed. 1615, Sig. D4v.

322. Not in A. Ed. 1615, Sig. D4v.

323. A. p. 159; B. p. 22; ed. 1615, Sig. E.

324. A. p. 165; ed. 1615, Sig. E.

325. A. p. 139; ed. 1615, Sig. E.

326. A. p. 43; ed. 1615, Sig. E.

327. Not in A. Ed. 1615, Sig. F4.

328. The source is Martial, IV, 72. A. p. 26; ed. 1615, Sig. Ev.

329. A. pp. 64–65; ed. 1615, Sig. Ev.

330. A similar epigram appears in Kendall, *Flowers of Epigrammes,* 1577, Spenser Society, 1874, 95. Kendall translated it from Bruno. In an altered form it is reprinted in *A Thousand Outlandish Proverbs,* 1640, ed. 1817, 51. A. pp. 163–164; ed. 1615, Sig. E2.

331. A. pp. 160–161; ed. 1615, Sig. E3v.

332. A. p. 123; B. pp. 18–19; ed. 1615, Sig. E2v.

333. A. p. 157; ed. 1615, Sig. E3.

334. A. pp. 47–48; ed. 1615, Sig. E3v.

335. The source is Martial, V, 61. A. p. 14; ed. 1615, Sig. E4.

336. In his *Tract on the Succession* he includes this epigram with a further expression of his pity for Mary, Queen of Scots, and his indignation at the injustice of her trial. He urges his readers to "transferre all that good conceit you had of or towardes her to her more noble son, to whome by all lawes of nature and nations it is due by inheritance." *Tract on the Succession,* 119–120. This epigram was written before December 19, 1600, for it is included among the epigrams that he sent Lady Jane Rogers at that time. Cambridge University Library, Add. MSS. 337, p. 29. A. pp. 110–111; B. p. 29; ed. 1615, Sig. E4.

337. A. pp. 113–114; B. p. 18; ed. 1615, Sig. E4v.

338. A. pp. 48–49; B. pp. 9–10; ed. 1615, Sig. F.

339. A. pp. 171–172; ed. 1615, Sig. Fv.

340. Cf. Daniel's version of this epigram. The question was put to Daniel by Edward Seymour, Earl of Hertford. (*The Complete Works of Samuel Daniel,* 4 vols., ed. Grosart, I, 273–276.) A. pp. 185–186; ed. 1615, Sig. F2.

341. *At the steere:* at the helm or rudder. (*NED.,* s.v. steer, sb.^{2}.) A. p. 186; ed. 1615, Sig. F2.

342. Not in A. Ed. 1615, Sig. F3.

343. Not in A. Ed. 1615, Sig. F3.

344. A. p. 106; ed. 1615, Sig. F3.

345. Addressed to "Lady Killdare," A. p. 178. Frances Howard, the daughter of the Lord Admiral and the widow of Henry Fitzgerald, twelfth Earl of Kildare, became, in May, 1601, the wife of Cobham. *Androes,* cf. Ep. 311. *Tuch,* black marble. A. pp. 178–181; ed. 1615, Sig. F4.

346. Not in A. Reprinted in *A Thousand Outlandish Proverbs,* 1640, ed. 1817, 132.

347. *Amused:* distracted, bewildered. Harington sent James some verses and an elaborate lantern as a New Year's gift, 1603. James' acknowledgment, dated April 3, 1603, appears in *Nugae Antiquae,* 1779, II, 231. A. p. 1.

348. *Prepostrous:* inverting the natural order of things. Lady Jane Rogers died in January, 1601. A. p. a.

349. A. p. a.

350. A. p. 26.

351. Cf. Ep. 32 and note. A. pp. 56–67.

352. A. p. 57.

353. A. pp. 65–66.

354. A. pp. 68–69.

355. *Vtter:* put on sale. Cf. *Romeo and Juliet,* V. i. 67. A. pp. 71–72; B. pp. 12–13.

356. *Magnificats corrector:* presumptuous faultfinder. *NED* (s. v., Magnificat) cites Elyot (1533): "Accomptyng to be in me no lyttell presumption, that I wylle in notynge other mens vices correct Magnificat." No later use of the expression is there recorded. It is used in the same sense by Harington elsewhere, and by Gabriel Harvey. See G. Gregory Smith, *Elizabethan Critical Essays,* I, 117; II, 29, and note. A. pp. 83–84.

357. A. pp. 84–85.

358. Cf. Ep. 160. A. pp. 92–93.

359. A. pp. 97–98.

360. In 1597 a skirmish took place in Blackwater between the Irish rebels and the English troops. Among the slain were "two foster brothers of the Earle of Kildare, whose death hee tooke so heavily, that hee dyed of griefe within a few

days after." The English sustained heavy losses there in 1598. Camden, *Annales of Elizabeth,* 1635, 483, 501. A. p. 99.

361. A. pp. 104–105; B. p. 28.

362. Cf. Sir Thomas Browne, "Of the Picture of Moses with Horns," *Pseudodoxia Epidemica,* Book V, chapter 9. A. p. 105; B. p. 28.

363. A. pp. 106–107.

364. Cf. 156. A. p. 108.

365. A. p. 111.

366. A. p. 120.

367. A. pp. 123–124.

368. A. p. 125.

369. A. p. 132; B. pp. 19–20.

370. A. pp. 132–133.

371. A. p. 133.

372. A. p. 134.

373. Essex was executed February 21, 1601. A. p. 135.

374. *Family of love:* a religious association founded in Holland about 1550. The sect was attacked by Middleton in his comedy, *The Family of Love.* A. pp. 137–138.

375. This appears, slightly altered and not in Harington's autograph, in MS. Ashmole 781, p. 134. It is printed at the end of his *Tract on the Succession to the Crown,* p. 123, where it is dated December 18, 1602. A. p. 139.

376. A. p. 143.

377. A. pp. 143–145.

378. A. p. 145.

379. A. p. 146.

380. A. p. 146.

381. A. p. 147.

382. A. pp. 147–148. B. p. 21.

383. A. p. 148.

384. A. p. 148.

385. A. p. 149.

386. A. p. 149.

387. *Tutch.* "Often used for any costly marble; properly the *basanites* of the Greek, a very hard black granite. It obtained the name *touch* from being used as test for gold. It was often written *tutch* or *tuch.*" (Skeat and Mayhew, s. v. touch.) *Allablaster.* "The spelling in 16–17th c. is almost always *alablaster;* app. due to a confusion with *arblaster,* a cross-bowman, also written *alablaster.*" (*NED.,* s. v. alabaster.) A. pp. 149–150.

388. Cf. 126, 163, 219, and notes. Davies, the author of *Orchestra, Nosce Teipsum,* and many epigrams, was knighted in 1603. The following epigram appears in *The Complete Poems of Sir John Davies,* Fuller Worthies' Library, p. 333:

> "Haywood, that did in Epigrams excell,
> Is now put down since my light Muse arose,
> As buckets are put downe into a well,
> Or as a schoole-boy putteth downe his hose."

An allusion to this epigram occurs in *Ajax,* 1596, 41. "This Haywood, for his proverbs and epigrams, is not yet put down by any of our country, though one [Marginal note, M[aster] Davies] doth indeed come near him, that graces him the more in saying he puts him down." Thomas Bastard, in *Chrestoleros,* 1598, Book II, Epigram 15, writes:

"*Heywood* goes downe saith *Dauie,* sikerly,
And downe he goes, I can it not deny.
But were I happy, did not fortune frowne
Were I in heart, I would sing *Dauy* downe."

A. pp. 150–151.

389. A. p. 152; B. pp. 21–22.

390. A. p. 152; B. p. 22.

391. *Poore Iohn.* "A kind of fish, salted and dried. It was cheap and coarse." (Halliwell, s. v. poor-John.) A. p. 153.

392. A. p. 156.

393. Charles Fitzgeffrey, *Affaniae,* 1601. *Flower de Luses.* Coins bearing the cross and the *flower-de luce,* the heraldic lily, the armorial emblem of France. A. pp. 156–157.

394. A. pp. 158–159.

395. A. pp. 158–159.

396. A. p. 160; B. p. 30.

397. A. p. 160.

398. Mary Sidney, Countess of Pembroke, translated the Psalms. A. p. 161.

399. A. p. 162.

400. A. pp. 162–163.

401. A. p. 163.

402. A. p. 164; B. p. 23.

403. A. p. 165.

404. Included in *Wit Restor'd in Several Select Poems not formerly publish'd,* 1658; ed. 1817, 182. A. pp. 165–166.

405. A. pp. 166–167.

406. A. p. 167.

407. A. pp. 168–169.

408. A. pp. 169–170; B. p. 23.

409. *Fortune:* happen. So used by Shakespeare only once. *Two Gentlemen of Verona,* V. iv. 169. A. p. 170.

410. A. pp. 170–171.

411. A. p. 171.

412. *Riggs:* wantons. Halliwell, *s. v.* rig. A. p. 171.

413. A. pp. 174–175.

414. *Farr fett:* lit. far-fetched, cunningly devised. A. p. 177.

415. *Reames:* realms. *Realm* was pronounced like *ream* (of paper), and quibbled upon. A. p. 182.

416. Cf. 345. A. pp. 182–183.

417. A. p. 183.

418. A. p. 183.

419. Cf. Horace, *Odes,* IV, 12, 27. *D. Dale.* Dr. Valentine Dale, Dean of Wells, and a Master of the Requests. He died in 1588 or 1589. A. pp. 183–184.

420. A. p. 184.

421. *His right vertuos cosen the Lady Hastings* was Sarah Harington, sister of Sir John Harington, first Lord Harington of Exton. This epigram celebrates the second of her four marriages: (1) to Francis, Lord Hastings, eldest son of the fourth Earl of Huntingdon; (2) Sir William Kingsmill; (3) Edward la Zouche,

eleventh Lord Zouche of Harringworth; (4) Sir Thomas Edmondes. A. pp. 184–185.

422. *Turne:* spinning wheel. A. pp. 190–191.

423. A. pp. 193–194.

424. A. p. 205.

425. A. p. 216.

426. A. pp. 216–217.

427. A Latin version with the English title is included in A. pp. 217–218. The English version here printed is taken from Park's edition of *Nugae Antiquae,* 1804, 333–334. Park's copy was made from the original, which was sent to King James, and which in 1802 was in the University Library, Edinburgh.

428. One of some sixty mock-encomiastic poems prefixed to Thomas Coryate's *Crudities,* 1611; ed. 1776, I, Sig. D7v–D8. Coryate was born at Odcombe in Somersetshire.

THE PRAYSE OF PRIVATE LIFE

Proheame. Harington's Proem is derived from Petrarch's *De Vita Solitaria,* Book I, Tractate i, Chapter 1. Harington disregards Petrarch's Foreword addressed to Philip, Bishop of Cavaillon, and abridges his discussion in Chapter 1.

Capitulum 1. Condensed from *De Vita Solitaria,* I, i, 3.

Capitulum 2. Paraphrase, with omissions, of *De Vita Solitaria,* I, ii, 1.

Capitulum 3. Paraphrase of *De Vita Solitaria,* I, ii, 2.

Mens Sana, in Corpore Sano. Juvenal, *Satires,* X, 356.

Capitulum 4. Paraphrase of *De Vita Solitaria,* I, ii, 3.

I[ce]land Doggs perfumed. Iceland dog "a shaggy, sharp-eared white dog, formerly in favour as a lap-dog in England." (*NED.*)

Brasting their Gorges. Brast: "northern form of burst." (*NED.*) Gorge: "the contents of the stomach." (*NED.* s. v. gorge, I, 5.) Harington in many places does violence to Petrarch's Latin. Petrarch, in this passage, describes merely the elaborate and exotic dishes served.

Frigida pugnabunt . . . Ovid, *Metamorphoses,* I, 19–20.

Ornefieth: adorneth.

At the beginning of this chapter Harington's free paraphrasing is exemplified in his rendering of the following passage with which Petrarch's chapter opens:

"Venit prandii tempus, ille sub ingenti et ruinam minitantem aula componit, pulvinaribus obrutus sepultusque, resonant variis tecta clamoribus, circumstant canes aulici muresque domestici, certatim adulatorum circumfusa acies obsequitur, et corrosorum turba familiarum, confuso strepitu mensam instruit verritur putre solum, et foedo pulvere re cuncta completur: volat atriis argentum auro infectum, et pocula cavis gemmis expressa, scamnum serico vestit, ostro paries, terra tapetibus, dum servorum nuda interim cohors tremit."

Capitulum 5. Paraphrase of *De Vita Solitaria,* I, ii, 4, with many changes.

Capitulum 6. Condensed paraphrase of *De Vita Solitaria,* I, ii, 5.

Preatinge: prating.

Deo servire, libertas est. Harington's use of this phrase is one of many indications of his familiarity with *The Book of Common Prayer.* He has, however, borrowed neither the phraseology of Cranmer, "whose service is perfect freedom," nor that of the Sarum Breviary, "cui servire regnare est."

Capitulum 7. Derived from *De Vita Solitaria,* I, ii, 6.

Capitulum 8. Paraphrase of *De Vita Solitaria,* I, ii, 7, with a few omissions and additions. To illustrate further Harington's practice in paraphrasing, Petrarch's chapter is subjoined:

"Ecce redit nox, ille redit ad crapulam, pompa ingens, ante retroque longum agmen: vivi hominis funus putes, precedunt funeralia et tibiae, ne quid desit exequiis, et sumptuosissimum cadaver, perfusum caris odoribus, rursus inter pulvinaria sepelitur adhuc tepidum, adhuc spirans, inde gravem coenam indigesto superaddens prandio, venturae luci nauseam parat, et alteri prandio praecludet iter. Iste vel se coenasse persuadet sibi, vel ita coenat ut Platonicum illud ipsa reprobet: nullo modo mihi placet, inquit, bis in die saturum fieri."

Fastidientis est stomachi multa degustare. Seneca, *Epistle* 2.

Capitulum 9. Paraphrase of *De Vita Solitaria,* I, ii, 8.

Capitulum 10. Derived, with many changes, from *De Vita Solitaria,* I, iii, 1.

Si te propositi . . . Juvenal, *Satires,* V, 1–2.

The Apostle sayeth whoe planteth a Vine and hopeth not to gather the grapes? I Corinthians, IX, 7.

Aspecteth: expecteth.

Cicero sayeth the Husbandman asked for whome he sowed Corne, answered, for the Gods ymmortall. De Senectute, Chapter 7.

Capitulum 11. Paraphrase, with many omissions, of *De Vita Solitaria,* I, iii, 2.

Cicero sayeth yt is a life accordinge to nature to healpe and preserve, yf it be possible, all Men livinge. De Officiis, Book III, Chapter 5.

I forget not the counsell of Seneca, saying lay aside all lettes and labor to get a good mynde, where unto noe Man doth attaine that is bound to busines. Epistles, 53.

The same Author semeth to affirme . . . *Ibid.,* 55.

In one other place also he writeth . . . *Ibid.,* 51.

Hee likewise sayth flee from Courte and nere abidinge thereunto. Ibid., 28.

Somewhat therefore I certenly thinke is in the place and with Seneca his patience. Ibid., 55.

Capitulum 12. Derived from *De Vita Solitaria,* I, iii, 3.

Capitulum 13. An abridgment of *De Vita Solitaria,* I, iv, 1.

Cicero sayth, Quid dulcior, otio literatio? Tusculans, Book V, Chapter 36.

Seneca writeth, Otium sine litteris mors est, et vivi hominis sepultura. Epistles, 82.

Capitulum 14. An abridgment of *De Vita Solitaria,* I, iv, 3.

Capitulum 15. A paraphrase, with many omissions, of *De Vita Solitaria,* I, iv, 2.

Augustus Caesar was wont to saie, Sat cito fit, quicquid fiat satis bene. Suetonius, Book II, Chapter 25. Petrarch wrote, "Sat celeriter fieri quicquid fiat satis bene."

Plato writeth, Beatum . . . *posset.* Laws, 653 A. Petrarch quotes from Cicero, *De Finibus,* Book V.

Capitulum 16. Derived, with many changes, from *De Vita Solitaria,* I, iv, 4.

Si simplex fuero hoc ipsum ignorabit anima mea. Job, IX: 21 (Vulgate).

Capitulum 17. Abridgment, with many changes, of *De Vita Solitaria,* I, iv, 5.

Plotinus . . . *distinguished the vertues into foure degrees. First Ennead,* Book II.

Capitulum 18. Paraphrase of *De Vita Solitaria,* I, iv, 7.

Si ascendero in caelum . . . *Psalms,* cxxxix, 8.

He is that celestiall spirite, which saide unto Moses, why doste thou cry out unto me. Exodus, xiv, 15.

Capitulum 19. Abridgment of *De Vita Solitaria,* I, iv, 8.

Marcus Cicero . . . *sayth, easily shall thou doe well, so long as thou thinkest upon me, whome thou endevors to please. Epistles,* ad Quinctum, F. I, 46.

Prodest sine dubio . . . Seneca, *Epistles,* 25.

St. Augustin sayth, yt is the propertie of a noble mynde, to separate the Soule from the Sences and devide the cogitacions from custome. Petrarch mentions St. Augustine, but he is here quoting Cicero, *Tusculans,* Book I, Chapter 16.

Marcus Cato refused to beholde a Man to die. Harington has changed Petrarch's meaning. Petrarch wrote, "Et si de Marco Catone scriptum est, qui puduit gementem, illo teste, mori, quanto magis pudebit Christo. . . ."

Capitulum 20. Abridgment of *De Vita Solitaria,* I, iv, 9.

The Apostle sayth to the Romaynes. . . . Romans, xiv, 8.

Capitulum 21. Derived from *De Vita Solitaria,* I, iv, 10. There are many omissions.

Capitulum 22. Abridgment of *De Vita Solitaria,* I, v, 3.

Omnia nobis mala solitudinem persuadent. Seneca, *Epistles,* 25.

In one other place he writeth, that in solitude evell Counsells are contrived. Ibid., 10.

We must take heede that men in sorrowe, or feare, be not left alone. Ibid., 10.

Flee from the multitude, flee from a fewe, flee from one. Ibid., 10.

Capitulum 23. Abridgment, with many omissions, of *De Vita Solitaria,* I, v, 4.

Cicero . . . sayth that amytie is of all thinges most pleasant. . . . De Amicitia, Chapter 23.

To this purpose also tendeth the sayinge of Archita the Tarentyne. . . . Petrarch quotes Cicero, *De Amicitia,* Chapter 25.

Nullius boni sine sotio jucunda possessio. Seneca, *Epistles,* 6.

Capitulum 24. Abridgment of *De Vita Solitaria,* I, v, 5.

Haec olim meminisse juvabit. Virgil, *Aeneid,* I, 203.

Quam metui ne quid Libiae tibi regna nocerent? Aeneid, VI, 694.

Capitulum 25. Paraphrase of *De Vita Solitaria,* I, vi, 1.

The Grammarians complainte, which is, I am wearie, I am troubled, I repent. Harington translates "piget, taedet, poenitet."

As Terence said, I knowe not what to doe, I beleve everie thinge, and cheifely that which is newest. Eunuchus, I, i, 28.

Omnis stultitia laborat fastidio sui. Seneca, *Epistles,* 9.

Nisi sapienti sua non placent. Ibid., 9.

Capitulum 26. Abridgment of *De Vita Solitaria,* I, vi, 2.

St. Augustine in his booke of true religion writeth thus. . . . De Vera Religione, Chapter 53.

The same author addeth. . . . Ibid., Chapter 54.

Seneca sayth, that yf a Man. . . . Epistles, 71.

Which humor Horace thinketh also in some ould Men, whose instabilitie. . . . Epistles, II, i, 99.

The precept of Quintilian the Orator. Institutes, Book X, Chapter 2, 9–10.

Capitulum 27. Abridgment of *De Vita Solitaria,* I, vi, 3.

Seneca laughed to scorne the affectacion of one Aruntius. Epistles, 114.

Omne in praecipiti vitium stetit. Juvenal, I, i, 149.

Capitulum 28. This chapter Harington interpolated; there is no corresponding discussion in Petrarch. Cf. Epigrams 116, 137.

Aspected: expected.

Capitulum 29. Paraphrase of *De Vita Solitaria,* I, vi, 4.

Thus spoke Job. Job, VII, 2–4.

Capitulum 30. Abridgment of *De Vita Solitaria,* I, vi, 5.

Of which mynde was Cicero. . . . De Senectute, Chapter 2.

Ornefie: adorn.

Capitulum 31. Derived in part from *De Vita Solitaria,* II, iii, 5, 8, 14.

Capitulum 32. Abridgment, with many changes, of *De Vita Solitaria,* I, vi, 6.

Scelerum si bene. . . . Horace, *Odes,* III, 24, 50–54.

Capitulum 33. There is in *De Vita Solitaria* no chapter or section corresponding to this chapter.

Moyles: mules.

Part I of Harington's *The Prayse of Private Life* ends with Chapter 33. Part

II lacks Chapter 1 and the beginning of Chapter 2. Throughout Part I Harington's plan follows closely that of Petrarch. In Part II, however, Harington omits several of the early chapters of Book II of *De Vita Solitaria,* and from others borrows only an idea or a sentence or two.

Capitulum 2 is derived largely from *De Vita Solitaria,* Book II, Tractate ii, Chapters 2–8; Tractate iii, Chapters 5, 6, 14.

Docto viro, vivere est cogitare. Cicero, *Tusculans,* xxiv, 62.

Capitulum 3. Abridgment of *De Vita Solitaria,* II, vii, 1.

Capitulum 4. Abridgment of *De Vita Solitaria,* II, vii, 2.

Scriptorum chorus omnis amat nemus et fugit urbem. Horace, *Epistles,* II, 2, 77.

Silva placet musis, urbs est inimica poetis. Petrarch, *Poetic Epistles,* Book II, Epistle 3.

Otia divitiis Arabum, liberrima muto. Horace, *Epistles,* I, 7, 36.

Capitulum 5. Paraphrase of *De Vita Solitaria,* II, viii, 1.

Capitulum 6. Abridgment of *De Vita Solitaria,* II, viii, 2.

In shorte tyme, when the common Weale was disturbed, I wrote more then in many yeares I had when yt florished. Cicero, *De Officiis,* Book III, Chapter 1.

Nowe I loathe all thinges and like nothinge so muche as Solytude. Cicero, *Ad Atticum,* xii, 18.

And he sayth moreover, that a retyred life was to him as a Native Countrie. Ibid., xii, 26.

To me nothinge is so pleasante as Solytude. . . . Ibid., xii, 15.

Capitulum 7. Abridgment of *De Vita Solitaria,* II, viii, 3.

Quintilianus sayth. . . . Quintilian, *Institutes,* Book x, Chapter 4.

Did not amuse him: did not bewilder him.

Harington's treatment of his source for this chapter is illustrative of his practice throughout this section of his discourse:

"Qua in re unanimem cum Cicerone Demosthenem fuisse auguror, et nisi forte aliquam quoque consilii ratio incesserit, quod non legi, idem sensisse illum, semper quod hic noster aliquando senserit. Nam et professio eadem amborum, et est ille leviculus, quod Cicero idem ait, qui delectaretur illo muliercularum susurro, ut fit a tergo insibilantium. Hic est ille Demosthenes: et si constet eum Oratorium illam vim, quam in urbibus tam potenter exercuit, maxime in solitudine dedicisse. De quo Quintilianus inde idem inquit. Ille tantus amator secreti Demosthenes, in littore, in quo se maximo cum sono fluctus illideret meditans consuescebat concionum fremitus non expavescere, nec te moveat quod supra dictum est, hunc ipsum Demosthenem locum tacitum atque undique abditum eligere solitum, hic undisonum patentemque, ibi enim ingenium acuebat, hic vocem exercebat, utrumque tamen in solitudine faciebat. Disserebant soli quod in populis venderent, meditabantur in silvis, quod in urbibus ostentarent, excusabatque professio, quibus intentio una esset, vel loquendo vel tacendo rem augere, quod de Cicerone non memini, Demosthenem constat, quod in noctibus Atticis scriptum est, pretium quoque silentii pepigisse, nobis quibus venale nihil penitus, nihil ostentui esse debet, sed omnia ad salutem vitaeque legem temporalis et aeternae spem, in solitudine discendum est, quod restat in solitudine exercendum, in solitudine vivendum, in solitudine moriendum. Quod cupio quidem valde, et si Deus pie nos aspicit spero etiam."

Capitulum 8. Paraphrase of *De Vita Solitaria,* II, viii, 4.

Capitulum 9. Abridgment of *De Vita Solitaria,* II, ix, 1.

Capitulum 10. Abridgment of *De Vita Solitaria,* II, ix, 2.
Capitulum 11. Abridgment of *De Vita Solitaria,* II, ix, 3.
Capitulum 12. Abridgment of *De Vita Solitaria,* II, ix, 4.
Capitulum 13. Abridgment of *De Vita Solitaria,* II, ix, 5.
Harington adds details not in Petrarch.
Capitulum 14. Abridgment of *De Vita Solitaria,* II, ix, 6.
Confabulacion: conversation. It had no humorous connotation.
Capitulum 15. Paraphrase of *De Vita Solitaria,* II, x, 3:

"Sive itaque Deo servire volumus, quae una libertas est atque una felicitas, sive artibus bonis ingenium excolere, qui proximus egregius labor est, sive aliquid meditando et scribendo nostri memoriam posteris relinquere, atque ita dierum fugam sistere, et hoc brevissimum quidem vitae tempus extendere, sive simulhaec omnia praestare propositum est nobis, fugiamus oro, jam tandem, et id quantulumcunque quod superest in solitudine transigamus, omni studio caventes, ne dum opem ferre naufragis videmur, ipsi rerum humanarum fluctibus obruamur, rerum humanarum scopulis allidamur. Denique quod probamus id agamus, ne qui morbus est publicus, quodque in aliis saepe reprehendimus, committamus, et juditia sermonesque nostri ab actionibus discrepent."

Capitulum 16. Abridgment of *De Vita Solitaria,* II, x, 5.
Harington adds details not in Petrarch.
Cicero writinge to his frend, sayth. . . . Cicero, *Ad Quintum, Fr.,* III, i, 12.
Crede mihi non est sapientis discere vivam. Martial, *Epigrams,* I, 15, 11.
Capitulum 17. A few ideas are borrowed from *De Vita Solitaria,* II, x, 7.
Capitulum 18. Abridgment of *De Vita Solitaria,* II, x, 8.

INDEX